History of
The XIII. Hussars

DEATH OF COLONEL JAMES GARDINER AT PRESTONPANS.

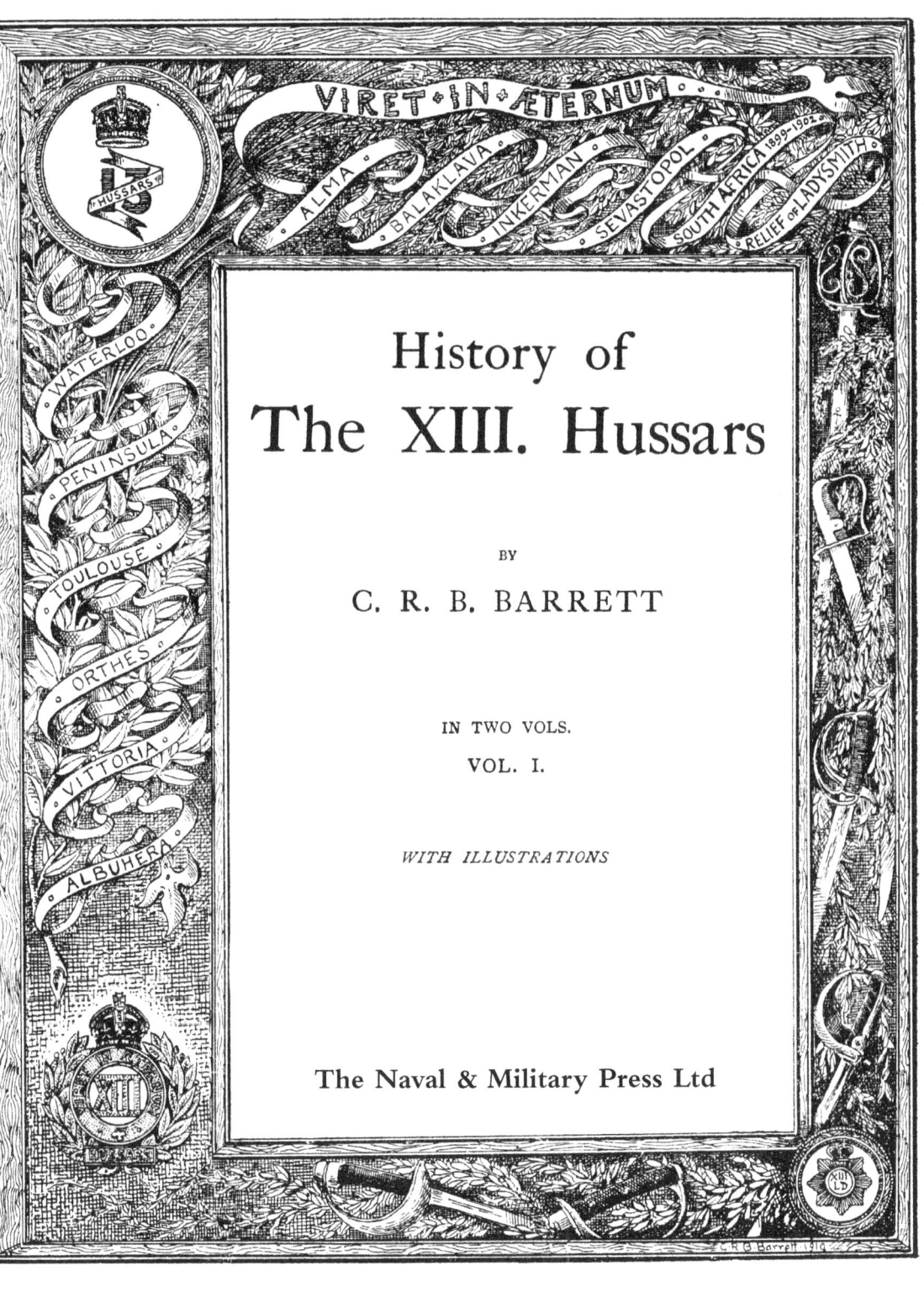

History of
The XIII. Hussars

BY

C. R. B. BARRETT

IN TWO VOLS.
VOL. I.

WITH ILLUSTRATIONS

The Naval & Military Press Ltd

Published by

The Naval & Military Press Ltd
Unit 10 Ridgewood Industrial Park,
Uckfield, East Sussex,
TN22 5QE England

Tel: +44 (0) 1825 749494
Fax: +44 (0) 1825 765701

www.naval-military-press.com
www.nmarchive.com

In reprinting in facsimile from the original, any imperfections are inevitably reproduced and the quality may fall short of modern type and cartographic standards.

PREFACE.

In the following pages I have endeavoured to write the history of the regiment now designated the 13th Hussars.

I trace the services of the regiment, whether in times of peace or war, whether at home or abroad, from the date of its raising in 1715 as Munden's Dragoons, down to the 31st of December 1909.

The following campaigns are included in my survey. First, the Jacobite Rebellion of 1715, then that of 1745. Next, the Maroon War of 1796-98, when that terrible scourge, yellow fever, all but destroyed the regiment.

Succeeding to these come the campaigns in Portugal, Spain, and France, when from 1810 to 1814 the regiment, then designated the 13th Light Dragoons, gained laurels of which it is justly proud. The year 1815 saw the 13th Light Dragoons at Waterloo, where more distinctions were worthily earned, and the high reputation of the regiment was not only sustained, but increased.

Some years later the 13th Light Dragoons, who served in India from 1819 to 1840, saw service in the East, at Kurnool and Zorapore. Fourteen years elapsed, till in 1854 the regiment experienced the perils of war and sickness in the arduous Eastern campaign usually known as the Crimean War. In this service more honours were gained. A brief and bloodless service in Southern Afghanistan in 1880 - 81 was followed by a short spell in South Africa; after which the regiment, now for some years designated the 13th Hussars, was again actively employed in the South African campaign of 1899-1902. Here again honours accrued to the regiment.

At the present time the 13th Hussars are serving their third term in India.

The honours of the regiment are mentioned as they were bestowed in the course of the Military History; a complete list of them appears on the title-page.

And here it may be well to state that the history of a regiment does not imply a history of the British Army as a whole, nor can it be expected that the course of every division concerned in a campaign can even be touched upon. A book of this kind treats only of the story of the regiment itself—that is to say, where it went, what it did, and with what other units of the British Army and its allies it was nearly and personally concerned while upon active service.

The reasons why Regimental Histories have their value is this. Military Histories are concerned with the performances of regiments practically as a whole. Here and there special mention may be made of detachments and individuals, but the detail of the life of a regiment is not for such publications.

Most regiments, however, possess Manuscript Records, and should these ever be lost or destroyed, it would be absolutely impossible to compile any account which had the slightest approach to accuracy.

The Manuscripts of the regiment, which were deposited in the care of Lieut.-Colonel Leetham, the Secretary of the Royal United Service Institution, for the purposes of this book, are contained in seven folio volumes, of which three are historical and four the "Records of Officers."

Of the earliest officers there is, however, no regular record until about 1790. But beyond these there is a highly interesting private historical record compiled by Colonel Sir Patrick Doherty, C.B., K.C.H. This is more ample than the Regimental Record, though following it mainly in important matters. It contains also many despatches, &c., referring to the Peninsular and Waterloo campaigns.

In its pages are also included a number of water-colour drawings signed by Colonel Doherty, "P. D.," of which use has been made in the illustrations.

A private diary, unfortunately embracing but a short period of the Peninsular campaign, and written by Captain James Gubbins who fell at Waterloo, has also been largely laid under contribution.

The book and the letters of Colonel Anstruther-Thomson were

lent, and proved of much assistance in the period just before and during the Crimean War. For the rest, many printed books have been consulted in the Royal United Service Institution; the Public Record Office, the Reading, Newspaper, and Manuscript Rooms at the British Museum have been searched; and from the Library of the India Office much valuable information was obtained on one period of the history of the regiment. Every care has been taken to ensure accuracy, and the writer trusts that he has therein succeeded.

Volume I. takes the regiment down to the conclusion of the Crimean campaign.

Volume II. completes the military history and then continues with chapters on uniforms, arms, guidons and drum banners and regimental medals, the regimental motto, the band, regimental plate and trophies, and regimental soubriquets. The section on sport includes hunting, flat racing, steeplechasing, and polo.

Lastly, an Appendix is given which contains a list, with commission dates, services, honours and distinctions of all the officers, as far as it has been possible to discover them, who have ever served in the regiment. In some cases biographical details are given in this list, in others in the Military History. The proofs, while the book was in the press, were submitted to Lieut.-Colonel Leetham (late 13th Hussars), and to Major Symons who still is serving in the regiment, and from both the writer received valuable suggestions for which he desires to offer his thanks. The selection of the illustrations was committed to the care of Colonel Leetham, and the author trusts that they will be found as full, complete, and interesting as the subject requires. That many will greatly adorn the pages of the book he expresses a confident hope. To the artists of the six coloured plates — Lieut.-General Sir R. Baden-Powell, K.C.V.O., K.C.B., Mrs Battine, Mr Harry Payne, and Major Wymer, the author offers his grateful thanks. In this connection he may be permitted to observe that in lieu of single uniform subjects, the coloured plates consist of incidents selected from the history of the regiment. The thanks of the writer to others for the loan of pictures, letters, books, and papers, will be separately given.

The book itself was written partly in the Royal United Service Institution, where the author received the utmost kindness and consideration from Colonel Leetham, and also from the Librarian, Major Wylly (late South Staffordshire Regiment), and Mr Harper, the clerk (late 5th Dragoon Guards). The remaining portion was written in the Library of the War Office, where the valuable and generous assistance given to him by A. D. Cary, Esq., the Parliamentary librarian, cannot be too highly estimated. Without the aid of this gentleman, it would have been morally impossible for the writer to have obtained a large amount of important details, notably on uniforms, early warrants, submissions, orders, documents, and many other points. It should perhaps be noted that records of social functions, dinners, and other regimental hospitalities are omitted. A chronicle of menus has no place, or should have no place, in volumes of this kind.

The smaller illustrations have all but one been selected from the valuable collections in the Museum of the Royal United Service Institution,—an exhibition which is in this country unique, and of whose educational and artistic value it is impossible to speak too highly.

Perhaps the author may be permitted to express regret that the relics of the regiment figured are so few. Every possible effort was made to obtain them. Extensive advertisement was resorted to, but the response was disappointing. Drawings of the sword and helmet of Colonel Chamorin, and the sword given in exchange by Captain Maclean to Captain Doherty, among others, would have been most welcome, and sketches of the regimental medals should have appeared. Here and there in the country there must be many more objects, drawings of which ought to have found a place in these pages, but it was not to be.

Finally, in presenting these volumes to the 13th Hussars whose history it relates, and to the general public whom I trust they may interest, with a full knowledge of my own shortcomings, I lay down my pen.

C. R. B. BARRETT.

BRENTWOOD, *May* 16, 1911.

The author desires to express his most sincere thanks to the following ladies and gentlemen who have so kindly permitted him to use for the purpose of this book miniatures, pictures, photographs, prints, diaries, letters, &c., and also for the verbal or written information upon many points with which they have been so good as to furnish him :—

The BARONESS DE PALLANDT.
Miss MANNING.
EARL BEAUCHAMP.
LORD HARLECH.
Major-General Sir STANLEY DE ASTEL CALVERT CLARKE, G.C.V.O., C.M.G., &c., &c.
Colonel Sir FITZROY DONALD MACLEAN, Bart., K.C.B.
Sir RICHMOND THACKERAY RITCHIE, K.C.B., Permanent Under Secretary of State for India.
Colonel LONSDALE HALE.
Major WILLIAM ANSTRUTHER-GRAY, M.P.
Lieut.-Colonel COVENTRY WILLIAMS.
Lieut.-Colonel ARTHUR LEETHAM.
Lieut.-Colonel E. A. H. WEBB.
Major R. R. GUBBINS, D.S.O.
Captain L. R. J. S. BATTYE.
Lieut.-General Sir ROBERT STEPHENSON SMYTH BADEN-POWELL, K.C.V.O., K.C.B.
Captain JOHN TYSON WIGAN.
Major A. SYMONS.
Captain C. W. SCOTT, R.A.
Captain H. J. J. STERN.
Lieut. W. C. A. VANNECK.
Lieut. J. N. LUMLEY.
Lieut. T. KNOWLES JACKSON.
Bandmaster LARTER.
J. A. E. MALONE, Esq.
THOMAS U. SADLEIR, Esq.
Messrs HAWKES.
Messrs COX & Co.
Messrs WILKINSON Ltd.

Also to the 'Cavalry Journal,' and to the Royal United Service Institution for permission to avail himself of their publications, library, and the collection contained in the museum.

CONTENTS OF VOLUME I.

CHAPTER I.

THE RAISING OF THE REGIMENT. Richard Munden, Family and Arms—Notices of the Earliest Officers—March to Preston . . . 1

CHAPTER II.

PRESTON, 1715. SERVICE IN ENGLAND, 1715-1718. Capture of Preston—Losses in the Engagement 18

CHAPTER III.

IRELAND, 1718-1742. Regiment placed on Irish Establishment—Enlistment of Irishmen forbidden—Evasion of this Order—Death of Brigadier-General Munden—Slackness of Officers—Bad Arms and Equipment—Regulations to enforce Discipline and the due Presence of Officers—Subsistence of Dragoons—Lord Harrington vacates Colonelcy—New Colonels and Lieutenant-Colonels 23

CHAPTER IV.

PRESTONPANS, 1745. Jacobite Rebellion expected—Precautions of the Government—State of Troops in Scotland—Movements of Cope—Lack of Artillery—Landing of Prince Charles—March of Cope—Lack of Bread—Movements of Prince Charles—Garrisons of Forts strengthened—Cope's March deflected to Inverness—Cope's March thence to Aberdeen—Embarkation for Leith—Fleet makes for Dunbar—Non-arrival of Reinforcements—Brigadier Fowke joins General Cope at Dunbar—Bad State of Horses and Men at Edinburgh—Colonel Gardiner's Statements thereon—Retirement towards Leith—Orders on the Occasion—Illness of Gardiner—Proceedings of Cope—Arrival at Prestonpans—Various Dispositions of Cope's Army there—Lack of Artillerymen—The Battle of Prestonpans—List of Officers of 13th Dragoons present—Story of Mrs Sadleir—Unusual Method of Rebel Attack 34

CHAPTER V.

FALKIRK MUIR, JANUARY 17, 1746. Francis Ligonier gazetted Colonel—Movements of Jacobites—Strength of Jacobite Forces—Hawley's Disposition of the Royal Army—Death of Whitney—Battle—Fate of Ligonier—Philip Naizon appointed Colonel 52

CHAPTER VI.

IRELAND, 1748-1768. Officers of Regiment and Quarters of Troops—Death of Colonel Naizon—Major-General Sir Charles Armand Powlett appointed Colonel—Hon. Henry Seymour Conway appointed Colonel—John Mostyn appointed Colonel—Scarcity of Recruits—Light Dragoons, a Memorial on—Height of Recruits lowered—Horse Sickness in Dublin—Establishment of Irish Dragoon Regiments—Hearts of Oak Riots—Regiment almost entirely composed of Irishmen—Excise Duty heavy on the Men—Discharge of Long-Service Men—Trumpets introduced instead of Hautboys . . . 55

CHAPTER VII.

IRELAND, 1769-1778. Unfavourable Reports on Regiment—Fraudulent Enlistment of Apprentices—Evolutions at Inspection—Captain-Lieutenants—Pay of Private Dragoons in Ireland—Barracks in Ireland—Barracks, Cost of Maintenance—Orderly Books badly kept—Bad Arms—Height of Men and Horses—Protestant Recruits—Orders against recruiting Catholics—Curious Promise of a Roman Catholic Chaplain made by a Recruiting Officer—Strength of the Regiment—"A Regiment in its Infancy"—Conversion of 12th Dragoons to Light Dragoons in progress, no Review in consequence—Date of Conversion of 13th Dragoons discussed—A Pair of Pistols stolen or captured by Mob—Novelties in Evolutions 63

CHAPTER VIII.

IRELAND, 1779-1795. Disturbances in North—Military Riot in Cork—Brutal Treatment of Soldiers in Kilkenny—Mr Fitzgerald and Castlebar—Expedition to capture him—Barracks and Billets—Absentee Lieutenant-Colonel, he being an M.P.—Major-General O'Hara's curious Comment on a Regiment—Equipment of Cavalry and Dragoons—"Proprietary" Colonels—Irish Currency and English, Differences between—White Boys, Right Boys, and Peep-o'-Day Boys—Crowded Jails—Cutting from Dublin Newspaper—Warrant Men, Changes—Off-reckonings—Horseless Quartermasters—Faulty Arms—"No music, 6 Trumpeters"—Militia Act—Troubles in Roscommon and Sligo—Sir Edward Crofton's Experience—Draft for Colonel the Hon. George Walpole 73

CONTENTS.

CHAPTER IX.

THE WEST INDIES, 1796-1798. Formation of the 20th Dragoons or Jamaica Regiment—Two Troops of 13th ordered on Foreign Service—Arrival at Winchester of two Troops—Remainder of Regiment ordered on Foreign Service—Route—Embarkation at Southampton—Expedition sails to Cove—The Voyage to West Indies interrupted by Storms—Serious Fire on board the *Concord*—State of Affairs in Jamaica—Account of the Maroons — Arrival of Regiment in Barbadoes—American Horses received — Expedition reaches St Domingo—The Brigands of Bombard—Port Wine—Yellow Fever—Arrival at Jamaica—Account of Maroon War—Colonel Walpole—Breach of Faith by Jamaica Parliament—Drafts to 20th Dragoons—Return to England—Casualties during the Campaign 86

CHAPTER X.

ENGLAND, 1798-1809. Recruiting—Threat of French Invasion—Brigaded with 12th Light Dragoons—Riot at Taunton 100

CHAPTER XI.

THE PENINSULAR WAR, 1810. Ordered on Foreign Service—Embarkation—Arrival at Lisbon—Bad Accommodation—Two Troops sent to Cadiz — Regiment proceeds to the Front—The first Bivouac—Corn scarce—Captain White's Exploits—Major Charles Vigoureux—Sickness of Troops at Escalos de Cima—Long Marches—Busaco—Cadiz Squadron rejoins — Bad Guides — Accident to Lieut.-Colonel Doherty's Horse—Pay issued in Dollars—A Merchant of Thomar—Sufferings of the Inhabitants — Portuguese Hospitality — Wreck of Alhandra—A Ruined Home—Horrible Scenes—Passage of the Tagus 106

CHAPTER XII.

THE PENINSULAR WAR, 1811. Field Days—Starving Inhabitants—Relief Measures—A Ruined Portuguese Gentleman—Campo Mayor, March 25, 1811—Conflict as to Facts—Marshal Beresford—Controversy—Casualties—Death of Colonel Count Chamorin—Corporal Logan—The Surprise near Olivenza—The Ruins of Albuera—Enemy sighted near Los Santos 124

CHAPTER XIII.

THE AFFAIR AT LOS SANTOS Lieut.-Colonel Doherty Invalided—Siege of Badajos in progress—Battle of Albuera—Extracts from the Diary of Captain James Gubbins—His Visit to Badajos—Douny and his Legion — Arroyo del Molino — Capture of Guns by the 13th—Losses of the Enemy—Losses of the Allies—Captain Gubbins's Account of Battle — He visits Campo Mayor — French Officer's Account of Arroyo del Molino — The Murder of Lieutenant King—La Nava—Mismanagement 146

CHAPTER XIV.

1812. Retirement into Portugal—Discrepancy in Accounts of March—The 13th cross the Guadiana, charge and pursue the Enemy—Siege of Badajos—Heavy Outpost Duty—Brigands—Destruction of the Bridge of Almaraz and the Forts there—Severe Grass Fire—Affairs near Villalva and Bienvenida—Retreat of French—Enemy decline Battle near Bolanja—Affair near Robeira—Gallantry of Lieutenant Smith—Affair near Villa Tobas—The Great Stampede—Madrid—Retreat—Occupation of Alba de Tormes 166

CHAPTER XV.

ALBA DE TORMES, 1812. Famished Troops—The Bullock Stampede—Wet Camping-grounds—Captain Gubbins and the Prince of Orange—Rearguard Action—Horses Starving—Winter Quarters at Crato . 192

CHAPTER XVI.

VITTORIA, 1813. Health of Colonel Head—Staff Corps formed—New Pattern Clothing—A Series of Marches—Alba de Tormes again—French driven thence—The Battle of Vittoria, June 21—Position of French Army—Capture of Royal Carriages—Capture of War Material—Advance towards Frontier—Roncesvalles—March past Pampeluna . 200

CHAPTER XVII.

PYRENEES. 1ST BATTLE, JULY 28, 1813. Cavalry not actively employed—Sufferings of British Wounded—Pyrenees, 2nd Battle, July 30, 1813—Pampeluna surrenders—Bar-iron found at Roncesvalles—Army enters France—Soult's Position—Loss of Baggage—Captain Doherty at Espinelle—The Passage of the Nive forced—Hasparen—The British Custom of paying for Supplies 213

CHAPTER XVIII.

BAYONNE, DECEMBER 13, 1813. The 13th Light Dragoons and the 50th, 71st, and 92nd Regiments—Gallantry of Private James Armstrong—Urguit—French Conscripts—Bastide—Severe Outpost Duty—Bad Weather—Soldierly Behaviour of Lieutenant Phillips during Retirement near Briscous—British Attack succeeds—Pounded Furze for Forage—St Pé—Garis—The Allied Attack succeeds—Gallantry of Private Owen Shreeman 223

CONTENTS.

CHAPTER XIX.

AFFAIR NEAR SAUVETERRE, FEBRUARY 17, 1814. Death of Lieutenant Geale — Casualties — Passage of the Gave de Oleron — Lieutenant Nesbit's Exploit—Brion 232

CHAPTER XX.

ORTHES, FEBRUARY 27, 1814. The Dohertys charge three abreast at the Head of the Regiment—Death of Trumpeter Sincock—Ayre, March 2, 1814—Anecdote by a Staff Surgeon—Sergeant Grey and his Patrol—Soldierly Conduct of Lieutenant Mill—Lieutenant Maclean wounded and taken Prisoner—Robbed of his Watch by Marshal Soult's A.D.C.—Sevignac, Captain Doherty's Caution—Lieut.-Colonel Doherty commands the Light Brigade 236

CHAPTER XXI.

TARBES AND ST GAUDENS, &C., MARCH 20, 1814. Charge through the Town—Fight on the Road beyond—Treacherous Attempt on Colonel Doherty—Lieutenant Doherty's Prisoner—Losses of the French—Toulouse reached—Forage scarce—Temperance of Troops . . 248

CHAPTER XXII.

TOULOUSE, APRIL 10, 1814. British Attack—Position of 13th—Last Draft and Remounts join during Battle—Entry into Toulouse—Napoleon's Statue smashed to Pieces—Abdication of Napoleon—Hostilities still continue—War concluded—Ragged Condition of Men of 13th and 14th Light Dragoons—Supplies obtained—Sad Plight of Horses—Route March to Boulogne—Arrival at Ramsgate—Statistics of Marches, Battles, Affairs, Casualties, &c.—David Westall, a Veteran . . 256

CHAPTER XXIII.

ENGLAND AND IRELAND, 1814. Movements of the Regiment—Promotions, Honours, and Rewards 266

CHAPTER XXIV.

THE WATERLOO CAMPAIGN, 1815. Ordered on Foreign Service—Embark at Cork for Ramsgate and sail thence to Ostend—Strength of Regiment—Officers' Lists—Reviews near Scendelbeck—Regiment arrives at Nivelles—Sent on to Quatre Bras—Serious Illness of Colonel Doherty—Covering the Retreat on June 17—June 18, 1815—Waterloo—Lieutenant Turner's Letter—Captain Moray—Officers present at Battle—Casualties—Death of Captain James Gubbins—Honours and Rewards—The Pursuit—Advance on Paris—Stationed at Abbeville—Movements of the Regiment—Ordered Home—Arrival at Dover—Marches, Casualties to Men and Horses 269

CHAPTER XXV.

ENGLAND, 1816-1818. Reduction of Establishment — Regiment leaves Romford for York—Assistance to Civil Authorities—Bad State of the Country—Brighton—Manchester—Ordered to India—Embarkation at Tilbury 285

CHAPTER XXVI.

INDIA, 1819-1840. Arrival at Madras—Arcot—Movements of Regiment—The Mutiny at Bangalore—Massacre of Regiment intended—Sentence on Native Conspirators—The Affairs at Kurnool and Zorapoor—The Nawab's Military Stores—Extraordinary Guns—Heroic Death of five Rohillas—Capture of Nawab—Casualties—Strength of British Force—Officers present—Cholera 292

CHAPTER XXVII.

HOME SERVICE, 1840-1854. Arrival in England—Losses from Cholera—Establishment, six weak Troops — Mess Table presented by 14th Light Dragoons — Colonel Anstruther-Thomson's Reminiscences — A Riot at Lynn—Manœuvres in Germany—Regiment leaves Norwich for Hampton Court—Exeter—Dublin—Major Wathen—Escorting Meal-carts for Relief of Poor—The Affray at Dolly's Brae near Castlewellan — Savagery of Orangemen — Regiment goes to Edinburgh, Glasgow, and Hamilton—Hounslow and Kensington—The Camp at Chobham — Birmingham — Ordered on Foreign Service — Regiment marches to Portsmouth and embarks—Strength of Regiment . 307

CHAPTER XXVIII.

THE EASTERN CAMPAIGN, JUNE 1854 TO OCTOBER 24, 1854. Arrived in the Bosphorus—Disembarkation at Coolalie—Two Troops sent to Varna—Arrival of Remainder of Regiment at Varna—Experiences on the Voyage — Description of Landing — Syrian Ponies — The Dobrudscha Patrol — Lieutenant Percy Smith's Adventure with the Bashi Bazouks — Regiment again United — A lost path — Ponies' Packs lost — Omar Pacha's Opinion of British Cavalry — Forage scarce—Cholera—Yeni Bazar—Varna—Trumpeters forbidden to ride Grey Horses—Deaths from Cholera—Funeral Music forbidden—Food Supply—Issue of Rum—Illicit Liquor Traffic—Violence offered by an Offender—Voyage to the Crimea—Landing at Eupatoria—Bulganak, September 19, 1854—Casualties—The Alma, September 20, 1854—Losses of Russians at Bulganak—Spectacle of the Battle of the Alma—Position of 13th Light Dragoons—Description of Battle—Death of Lieutenant and Adjutant Irwin—"An Extraordinary Errand"—Katche River — Vedette Duty — Capture of Russian Stores — The "Flank March"— Mackenzie's Farm — Flight of Russians to Sebastopol—Capture of Balaclava—The Adventures of a Reconnoitring Party—Outlying Pickets—Construction of Redoubts—Concentration of Russian Force in the Rear—Capture of a Sergeant 323

CONTENTS.

CHAPTER XXIX.

BALACLAVA, OCTOBER 25, 1854. Phases of the Battle—Description of Ground—Story of the Battle—Charge of the Heavy Cavalry—Lord Raglan's Orders—State of Regiment on October 25—Officers present—Captain Nolan and Lord Lucan—Lord Lucan and Lord Cardigan—Charge of the Light Brigade—Death of Nolan—Attack on Russian Battery by D'Allonville and the 4th Chasseurs D'Afrique—Lord Lucan does not support by attacking the Causeway Heights — Sergeant Mitchell's Adventures—Lieutenant Percy Smith—Casualties—Captain Oldham's Death — Lieutenant Chamberlayne — Letter of Captain Jenyns—Tribute to Lieutenant Percy Smith—Sergeant Malone wins the V.C.—His subsequent Career—Casualties—Sergeant Mitchell on the Charge—Account from the Regimental MS.—The Lucan-Cardigan-Nolan Controversy — Notice of Captain Nolan's Life — Opinions of Officers 349

CHAPTER XXX.

THE EASTERN CAMPAIGN — *continued*. After the Battle—Sufferings for Want of Clothing—Burial of the Dead—Stampede of Russian Horses—Sickness—The Windmill Camp—Inkerman, November 5, 1854—Description of Battle—Losses—The Chasseurs D'Afrique—Captain Jenyns on Inkerman and After—A Terrific Storm—Sergeant Mitchell's Account thereof—Sufferings of the Horses—French Care for its Cavalry—Lord Raglan's unjust Estimate — The Effective Strength of the Regiment five Mounted Men—With Sir Colin Campbell—Death of Lord Raglan—Arrival of Drafts from England—Tchernaya—Description of the Battle—Russell's unjustifiable Statement — Casualties—Evacuation of Sebastopol—Sebastopol on Fire—Conclusion of the Eastern Campaign — Regiment ordered to Eupatoria — On an Expedition commanded by D'Allonville—Skirmishes with the Enemy—Sent to Scutari—Drafts from England—The Fire at the Haidar Pasha Palace—Captain Percy Smith's Account of it—The Death of Troop Sergeant-Major Linkon, May 31, 1910, also of Private John Brooks, March 1911, both Survivors of the Balaclava Charge — Regiment ordered Home—Arrived at Gosport—Reviewed by Queen Victoria — Casualties during the entire Campaign — Rewards, Promotions, Honours, &c. 375

ILLUSTRATIONS TO VOLUME I.

COLOURED PLATES.

DEATH OF COLONEL JAMES GARDINER AT PRESTONPANS	*Frontispiece*
DEATH OF LIEUTENANT S. D. KING OUTSIDE BADAJOS .	*To face page* 163
CAPTURE OF KING JOSEPH BONAPARTE'S BAGGAGE AT VITTORIA	,, 208
LORD HILL AND THE 13TH LIGHT DRAGOONS AT WATERLOO—"DRIVE THEM BACK 13TH!"	,, 278
BALACLAVA—SERGEANT JOSEPH MALONE GAINS THE V.C.	*To face half-tone plate, Captain Joseph Malone, V.C.*

HALF-TONE PLATES.

CLEMENT NEVILL — FIRST LIEUTENANT-COLONEL OF THE REGIMENT	*To face page* 11
13TH DRAGOONS (1742)	,, 34
PLAN OF THE BATTLE OF PRESTONPANS	,, 45
JAMES GARDINER, COLONEL 13TH DRAGOONS, 1743 TO 1745—SLAIN AT THE BATTLE OF PRESTONPANS, SEPTEMBER 21ST 1745	,, 47
CAPTAIN LAWRENCE DUNDAS . From a Portrait lent by Colonel H. J. BLAGROVE, C.B.	,, 86
LISBON POLICE CAVALRY	,, 108
LISBON POLICE GUARD. ARMED PEASANT OF ALGARVA	,, 109
PEASANT OF THE CORREGIMIENTO OF SALAMANCA	,, 110

ILLUSTRATIONS.

A PEASANT BOY OF NISA	*To face page*	111
OFFICER, 13TH LIGHT DRAGOONS (1800)	,,	115
A PORTUGUESE GENTLEMAN	,,	120
PEASANT OF TORRES VEDRAS	,,	121
PRIVATE OF FRENCH INFANTRY	,,	126
A FRENCH DRAGOON	,,	127
POPE PIUS VI. BLESSING OFFICERS OF THE 12TH LIGHT DRAGOONS, VATICAN, 1794	,,	128
CORPORAL LOGAN, 13TH DRAGOONS, SLAYING COLONEL COUNT CHAMORIN AT CAMPO MAYOR	,,	139
A PRIVATE OF 13TH LIGHT DRAGOONS Drawn by Colonel PATRICK DOHERTY.	,,	148
SPANISH MILITARY COSTUME (LIGHT INFANTRY AND ARTILLERY) SPANISH GRENADIERS SPANISH HEAVY HORSE SPANISH INFANTRY		158, 159
ARMED PEASANT OF THE CIUDAD MILITIA	*To face page*	172
PORTUGUESE OFFICERS (ENGINEERS AND INFANTRY)	,,	173
A PRIVATE OF THE 13TH LIGHT DRAGOONS Drawn by Colonel PATRICK DOHERTY.	,,	201
CAPTAIN JAMES GUBBINS—KILLED AT WATERLOO From a Miniature lent by Major R. R. GUBBINS, D.S.O.	,,	275
OFFICER, 13TH LIGHT DRAGOONS (1832)—SCARLET TUNIC	,,	295
13TH LIGHT DRAGOONS (1845)	,,	309
CAVALRY CAMP, CRIMEA (1854) From SIMPSON's 'Seat of War in the East,' 1855-56.	,,	336
THE CHARGE OF THE LIGHT BRIGADE, BALACLAVA From SIMPSON's 'Seat of War in the East,' 1855-56.	,,	360
THE BALACLAVA GROUP From a Photograph taken the day after the battle.	,,	363
CAPTAIN J. A. OLDHAM—KILLED AT BALACLAVA From a Picture lent by Colonel SIR FITZROY MACLEAN, Bart., K.C.B.	,,	364
CAPTAIN JOSEPH MALONE, V.C.	,,	367
EVELYN WOOD, 13TH LIGHT DRAGOONS, 1855	,,	388

ILLUSTRATIONS.

LINE DRAWINGS.

THE ARMS OF MUNDEN	*Page* 3
"PRESTON IN 1715"	,, 19
From an old Map "Drawn on the Spott by P. M., Esq. H. Halfbergh, Sculp."	
MONUMENT TO COLONEL JAMES GARDINER ERECTED ON THE SPOT UPON WHICH HE RECEIVED HIS MORTAL WOUND	,, 47
ONE OF THE SIX GUNS NOW AT SOUTHWOLD-ON-SEA, SUFFOLK	,, 54
Captured by the rebels at Prestonpans, recaptured at Culloden, and presented to the town by the Duke of Cumberland.	
KEY TO BALACLAVA GROUP	,, 363
SHAKO PLATE (AFTER CRIMEAN CAMPAIGN)	,, 393

MAPS.

SKETCH MAP SHOWING THE PRINCIPAL PLACES TO WHICH THE REGIMENT WENT DURING 1810, FROM 2ND APRIL TO 31ST DECEMBER	*To face page* 122
CAMPO MAYOR, MARCH 25TH 1811	,, 131
CAMPO MAYOR, MARCH 25TH 1811 (ANOTHER SKETCH MAP)	,, 135
SKETCH MAP OF THE COUNTRY ROUND ABOUT CAMPO MAYOR, FROM THE OFFICIAL PORTUGUESE MAP	,, 137
SKETCH MAP SHOWING MOST OF THE PLACES TO WHICH THE REGIMENT WENT DURING 1811	,, 164
SKETCH MAP SHOWING THE CHIEF PLACES AT WHICH THE REGIMENT HALTED DURING 1812	,, 198
SKETCH MAP SHOWING THE CHIEF PLACES TO WHICH THE REGIMENT WENT DURING 1813, FROM JANUARY 1ST TO NOVEMBER 10TH, ON WHICH DATE THE FRENCH FRONTIER WAS CROSSED	,, 218
SKETCH MAP SHOWING THE CHIEF PLACES AT WHICH THE REGIMENT WAS FROM NOVEMBER 10TH 1813, UNTIL APRIL 13TH 1814, WHEN PEACE WAS DECLARED	,, 258
SKETCH MAP SHOWING APPROXIMATELY THE GROUND COVERED BY THE REGIMENT DURING THE PENINSULAR CAMPAIGN	,, 262

HISTORY OF THE 13TH HUSSARS.

CHAPTER I.

The Raising of the Regiment.

By the wholesale disbandment and reduction of regiments which immediately preceded the signing of the Treaty of Utrecht, April 11, 1713, the strength of the British Army had already been dangerously weakened.

Further proceedings of a similar nature followed, and before the summer of 1715 the lack of troops available for service became a source of grave peril to the safety of the kingdom.

The political factors which produced this state of affairs were somewhat diverse,—an alleged desire for economy, a rooted objection to a standing army, and Jacobite intrigue.

Of the last, every engine that could be brought to bear on the Government was employed without scruple. Nor was a reason far to seek, since on the military weakness of Great Britain rested the main hope of the opponents of the House of Hanover.

True, Queen Anne had died in August 1714, and the succession of George I. had been accomplished without breach of the peace. Yet the Jacobite party were buoyed up by hopes for a restoration of the exiled Stuart House, and by the summer of 1715 the less clear-headed of that party deemed the time propitious for a recourse to arms. How they fared is written in the pages of history.

And here it may be well briefly to explain the custom with regard to the disbandment and reduction of regiments and the position of the officers and men whose services were thus dispensed with.

Hitherto it had been the policy of Government in time of need to raise such additional regiments as might be held needful, and when the trouble was over to disband them.

Regiments thus raised were termed "young," in distinction to the older established troops.

But in 1712 and the following years all the regiments disbanded were not those that had been newly raised.

Successful Jacobite intrigue caused the breaking of regiments especially known to be Hanoverian and Protestant in their sympathies.

The year 1712 witnessed the disbandment of no less than thirteen regiments of dragoons, and twenty-two of foot, before the end of the year.

The next year saw the suppression of many companies of "Invalids"—companies of old soldiers enlisted to do garrison duty at home during the absence of the regular army on service abroad.

The total number of troops disbanded amounted to about 30,000, and of the troops not disbanded 8000 were employed on garrison duty in Flanders.

In 1714 the total of the British establishment (exclusive of Ireland) was only a meagre force of 30,000 men.

And what was the position of those whose services had been dispensed with?

To the private soldier a small bounty was paid, and inducements were held out to persuade him to enlist in the colonial forces. As a disbanded soldier his position among his fellow-countrymen was most uncomfortable. Soldiers were unpopular, whether still serving with the colours or disbanded. Rightly or wrongly, they were, as a class, the objects of hatred, suspicion, and contempt. Nor was the position of the officer on half-pay by any means to be envied. He had frequently spent the best years of his life in the service, and, what is more, had often expended his private means in the raising of a troop or troops of horse, or a company or companies of foot. Half-pay was his portion—and more often than not, oblivion,—and his half-pay a mere pittance, his prospects for the future a bare— a very bare—chance of future military employment. Of the regiments disbanded at this period those of known Hanoverian sympathies were the special objects of Jacobite intrigue. On officers of foreign extrac-

THE RAISING OF THE REGIMENT.

tion—descendants of refugees mainly on grounds of religious persecution and pronounced Protestant tendencies—the blow fell very heavily. A glance through the names in various MS. records tells its tale. Of officers of British nationality who suffered professional eclipse there were even more.

Among those so placed on half-pay in 1712 was Richard Munden, and to him, in 1715, was given the honour of raising the Regiment now known as the 13th Hussars. Here, in connection with the treatment of half-pay officers, an important letter from Marlborough should be mentioned. In it he desires that all commissions vacant should be filled by half-pay officers. That no person through favour, interest, or other practices should get a commission in prejudice of a senior officer. That regard should be had to seniority, always provided that character, merit, zeal, and fidelity be assured. Lastly, that half-pay officers should always have their old rank in a new regiment. This letter is dated July 30, 1715.

Richard Munden was the posthumous child and only son of Sir Richard Munden, Kt., R.N., and nephew of Rear-Admiral Sir John Munden, Kt. According to the printed pedigree his grandfather was Richard Munden, "the ferryman of Chelsey." In those days the right to levy tolls at the horse-ferry at Chelsea was a most valuable property, bridges and horse-ferries over the Thames being alike few. After her husband's death the mother of Munden obtained a grant of arms, "to her children and her husband's brother Sir John Munden, Kt., Rear-Admiral of the King's Fleet," and the form of this grant is in this respect peculiar. These arms were: Per pale gu. and sa. on a cross engrailed ar. five lozenges az. on a chief or, three eagles legs erased à-la-quise of the second, on a canton ermine an anchor or. Crest—on a rostral crown or, a leopard's head sa. bezantée. To quote this grant

The Arms of Munden.

of arms at length may at first appear hardly germane to the subject in hand, yet it is so, and for this reason. In 1715 and until the first order forbidding the practice in 1743 it was almost the invariable custom to incorporate in the Standards or Guidons of Cavalry and in the Colours of Infantry parts, or the whole, of the armorial bearings of the colonel of the regiment for the time being. Of the Guidons of the 13th Hussars the earliest recorded date from 1751. It is in the hope—a faint one, it is true—that further information on this point may be obtained by means of the particulars here inserted, that special attention has been drawn to this grant of arms.

In the MS. book labelled "Persons recommended to be officers in the newly raised Regiments" is a notice referring to Munden.

> Lt.-Col. Munden. Has spent a good part of his Estate in the Service, and had the honour to command the Battalion of Guards at Schellenberg. He says he has some sort of promise from your Grace [Marlborough] last year at Harwich. The Earl of Orkney recommends him as having very good friends to assist him to raise a Regiment.

The "Letter of Service" which authorised the raising of the regiment does not exist.

In the War Office Miscellany Books now at the Public Record Office is the letter (a copy) sent to Brigadier Bowles, and dated 23rd July 1715. As will be seen from the list at the end of the document, it records that a similar "Letter of Service" had been sent to Munden.

GEORGE R.

Order for Raising a Reg^{t.} of Dragoons under the Command of Brig^{r.} Bowles.

Whereas We have thought fitt that a Regiment of Dragoons be forthwith Raised under your Command for Our Service which is to consist of six Troops, of One Serjeant, Two Corporals, One Drummer, One Hautbois, and Thirty private Dragoons including the Widdows Men in Each Troop, These are to Authorize You by beat of Drumm or otherwise to raise So many Voluntiers as shall be Wanting to Compleat the Said Regim^{t.} to the above Numbers. And when you shall have Listed fifteen Men fitt for service in any of the said Troops, You are to give Notice to Two of Our Justices of the Peace of the Town or County wherein the same are who are hereby Authorized and Required to View the said Men and Certify the Day of their so doing, from which Day the said fifteen Men and the Commission and Non-Commission Officers of such Troops are to enter into Our Pay. And You are to Cause the said Voluntiers to be raised and Levy'd as aforesaid to March under the

THE RAISING OF THE REGIMENT.

Command of Such Commission Officers as you shall Direct to Reading In Berkshire. Appointed for the Rendezvous of the said Regiment and all Magistrates, Justices of the Peace, Constables and Other Our Officers whom it may Concern, are hereby required to be Assisting unto You in providing Quarters, Impressing Carriages and otherwise, as there shall be Occasion. Given at Our Court at St James's this 23rd Day of July 1715 In the first Year of Our Reign.

By His Maj$^{tys.}$ Command.
WM. PULTENEY.

To Our Trusty & Wel belov'd Phineas Bowles, Esq$^{r.}$ Brigad$^{r.}$ Gen$^{l.}$ of Our Forces and Colonel of One of Our Reg$^{ts.}$ of Dragoons, or to the Officer or Officers appointed by him to raise Voluntiers for that Reg$^{t.}$

A like order of the same date for raising a regiment of dragoons under the command of—

> Brigadier Gore.
> Maj.-Gen$^{l.}$ Pepper.
> Colonel Wm. Stanhope.
> Brigad$^{r.}$ Richard Munden.
> Col. Richard Molesworth.
> Maj.-Gen$^{l.}$ Wynn.
> Sir Robert Rich.
> Brigad$^{r.}$ Dormer.
> Col. Cha. Churchill.
> Col. Newton.
> Brigad$^{r.}$ Honywood.

On the same date another circular was issued from Whitehall, July 23, 1715.

SIR,—I am commanded to desire that you will transmit to me a list of the names of such officers as you shall think fit to recommend to His Majesty to serve in the Regiments under your command, and also to return to my Office the name of the place you desire your Regiment to rendezvous in. Of which you are not to fail to acquaint me by eight o'clock to-morrow night.—I am, Sir, etc.

WM. PULTENEY.

To Maj.-Gen. Wynne.   Col. Newton.
„   „   Pepper.   „   Churchill.
Brigadier Gore.   „   Tyrell.
„   Honywood.   „   Molesworth.   }Dragoons.
„   Bowles.   „   Wm. Stanhope.
„   Munden.   Sir Robert Rich.
„   Dormer.
and to eight colonels of Regiments of Foot.

6 HISTORY OF THE 13TH HUSSARS.

In the face of these two documents it is curious to find that the commissions of all the officers of Munden's Dragoons were signed July 22, 1715. The list is here appended, and it differs somewhat from that which is given by Cannon.

In the "Commission Book," against every man's name is the troop to which he is appointed, and that of the officer commanding that troop.

CAPTAINS OF TROOPS.	LIEUTENANTS.	CORNETS.
Richard Munden, Col.	Henry de Grangues, Capt.-Lieut.	{ Wm. Freeman. { Wm. Williamson.
Clement Nevill, Lt.-Col.	Frances Hull.	John Watson.
Samuel Freeman, Maj.	Thomas Mason.	[Blank.]
Francis Howard, Capt.	Philip Bridgeman.	Martin O'Brian.
Lutton Lister, Capt.	John Molyneux.	Charles Greenwood.
Wm. Heblethwaite, Capt.	Henry Dawson.	Gerrett [Gerald] Fitzgerald.

Chaplain—Samuel Dunster [or Dunstor], D.D.
Surgeon—Richard Hansard.
Adjutant—John Houghton.

All these commissions are dated July 22, 1715. The next document is curious from the fact that in transcription by the War Office clerk its date is given as June 25th instead of July 25th.

GEORGE R.

REGIMENTS.

Horse.
- Royal Regim^t· of Guards.
- Gen. Lumley's R^t·
- Lord Windsor's.

Dragoons.
- Royal Regim^t· commanded by the Lord Cobham.
- Col. Kerr's Reg^t·
- Lt.-G^l· Carpenter's.

Aug. 18th, 1715.
- Maj.-G^l· Wynn.
- Maj.-G^l· Pepper.
- Brig^r· Gore.
- Brig. Honywood.
- Brig. Munden.
- Brig. Dormer.
- Col. Newton.
- Col. Churchill.
- Col. Tyrrell.
- S^r· Robt· Rich.
- Col. Molesworth.
- Col. Stanhope.

Whereas we have thought fitt that Our Severall Regim^{ts}· of horse and Dragoons in South Britain named in the Margin be forthwith compleated according to Our Establishments and put into the best condition of Service that may be with respect to their horses, arms, Cloaths, and accoutrements, We do hereby in the most earnest manner Recommend to You the care and Inspection of the Performance thereof, and to give immediate Notice of this Our Pleasure to the Respective Colonels or Commanding Officers of those Reg^{ts}· who are hereby requird to give you from time to time an Exact Account of the Condition of their Respective Reg^{ts}· and you are to see that their Arms and Clothing be kept in good order and condition. And Our Further pleasure is, That as soon as and as often as conveniently may be You make a strict Review of the said Regim^{ts}· and thereupon Report to Us or to Our Captain Genl· the condition you shall find them in as well with reference to their Numbers as to their Arms, Cloaths, and

THE RAISING OF THE REGIMENT.

Accoutrements and likewise the Disipline and goodness of men and horses and to make such further observations relating to their Officers or otherwise as You shall judge may be most conducing to Our Service for Our further Orders where it may be necessary. Given at Our Court at St James's this 25th Day of June 1715 In the ffirst Year of Our Reign.

By his Maj$^{tys.}$ Command.
WM. PULTENEY.

To Our Trusty and Welbeloved Henry Lumley, Esq$^{r.,}$ Gen$^{l.}$ of Our horse and Colonel of Our Own Regim$^{t.}$ of horse.

Obviously it would be contrary to common-sense to order a regiment to be completed and reviewed before it had been ordered to be raised.

It will be noticed that no cornet has been assigned to Major Freeman's troop. This, too, may be an error. Still, the book definitely gives for Cornet Williamson: "William Williamson Gent to be Cornet to that Troop whereof the Col. himself is Cap$^{t.}$ in Do. Reg$^{t.}$"

Orders for patterns of clothing to be laid before the Board of General Officers with all possible expedition are dated July 23, 1715.

Orders for arming the regiment are dated July 26, 1715.

Patterns of clothing are commanded to be exhibited before the Board of General Officers for inspecting and regulating the clothing of the Army, either on the 2nd, 4th, or 6th of August before 10 A.M.

On August 5, quartermasters were appointed to each troop.

To the Colonel's Troop	Jonathan Cockran.
,, Nevill's	Richard Henson.
,, Freeman's	Richard Parry.
,, Howard's	William Ellis.
,, Lister's	John Price.
,, Heblethwaite's	Claudius Lambert.

On October 28 Richard Henson, the quartermaster of Nevill's Troop, was gazetted cornet " of the Troop of which he had been Q.M." It would not appear that Brigadier Munden had any difficulty in filling the ranks of his regiment. Men—and men too who had served—

were plentiful, possibly also some of them had belonged to their Colonel's old regiment—Munden's (late Lovelace's) Foot.

At any rate, bearing date 25th October 1715, the following document was issued:—

GEORGE R.

Order for augment^s. Sir Robt. Rich's Reg^t. of Drag^s.

These are to authorize you by Beat of Drum or otherwise in any County or Part of this Our Kingdom of Great Britain to Raise so many Voluntiers with horses fitt for Service as shall be wanting to Recruit and fill up the respective Troops of Our Reg^t. of Dragoons under your Command from thirty to forty men in each, Widdows Men included, and as you shall raise of the said additional Men You are to give notice to Our Commissary or Deputy Commissary Genl. that they may be mustered according to Our Directions in that behalf And all Magistrates, etc.: Given at Our Court at St James's this 25th day of Octr. 1715 In ye Second year of Our Reign.

By etc.

W^M. PULTENEY.

To Our Trusty and Welbelovd
Sir Robt. Rich, Barr^t. etc.

Like orders of the same date for augmenting the following Regiments, viz.:—

Roy^l. Reg^t. Drag^s.	E. of Stair's.	Brig. Honywood's.
Col. Churchill's.	Col. Kerr's.	Maj.-Gen. Wynn's.
Col. Molesworthy's.	Maj.-G. Pepper's.	Brig. Munden's.
Brig. Gore's.	Brig. Dormer's.	Col. Tyrrell's.
E. Portmore's.	Col. Stanhope's.	Col. Newton's.
Lt.-Genl. Carpenter's.	Brig^r. Bowles's.	

Also for

Royal Reg^t. of Horse.
Col. Lumley's Horse of 9 troops.
Lord Windsor's Horse.
Col. Pitt's Horse of 6 troops.

At what precise date horses were received to mount the men does not appear. It was, however, prior to October 19, 1715, as by that time the regiment, which had been raised, it is stated, in the Midlands, had made a rendezvous at Northampton. This we learn from the following order:—

THE RAISING OF THE REGIMENT.

GEORGE R.

Order for the march of Brig^{r.} Munden's Reg^{t.} of Drag^{s.} to Leeds and Halifax.

Our Will and Pleasure is That You Cause the severall Troops of Our Reg^{t.} of Drag^{s.} under your Command, to march immediately from Northampton (according to the Route annexed) and be dispos'd of as follows. Viz. Three Troops at Leeds, and Three Troops at Halifax where they are to remain until further Order. And the Officers etc. Given at Our Court at St James's this 19th of Oct. 1715 In the Second Year of Our Reign.

By His Maj^{tys.} Comm^{d.}
WM. PULTENEY.

To Brig^{r.} Munden, etc.

Route for Brig^{r.} Munden's Reg^{t.} of Dragoons from Northampton to Leeds and Halifax.

    Harborough,
    Leicester,
    Nottingham,
    Bolsover,
    Rotherham,
    Wakefield,
    Leeds, where Three Troops are to remain and the other Three Troops to march to
    Halifax, there to remain.

The next document signifies to sundry colonels—Brigadier Munden among them—that their regiments have been placed under the supreme command of Major-General Wills.

WHITEHALL, *Oct.* 31, 1715.

SIR,

His Maj^{ty.} having thought fit to order Maj.-Gen. Wills to command several of his forces on an expedition, hath commanded me to signify to you his pleasure that you do with the Regiment of Dragoons under your command follow such orders as you shall receive from him without waiting for further instructions from hence.—I am, etc.   WM. PULTENEY.

To Maj.-Gen. Wynne.   Col. Newton.
    Brig^{r.} Dormer.   ,, Fane.
    ,, Honywood.   ,, Pitt.
    ,, Munden.   Maj.-Gen. Sabine.
    ,, Preston.

Numbers:—One Reg^{t.} of Dragoons to consist of Six Troops with one serjeant, two corporals, one drummer, one Hautbois, and twenty-eight effective Private Dragoons.

The strength of the regiment thus appears to have been 198 "non-commission" (to use the old form) officers and "private" dragoons, six quartermasters, a chaplain, surgeon, and adjutant, and nineteen "commission" officers.

Mention has been made in one of the documents quoted of "Widdows Men," and the meaning of this term needs explanation.

In a regiment, at this period, what were known as "Widdows Men" existed only on paper. They appeared to be borne on the strength of the regiment, but were so only as regards the receipt of their pay. This pay formed a fund for the purposes of supplying pensions to the widows of deceased officers. There were a certain number of "widdows men" to each troop. A warrant of George I. on this subject is dated 26th April 1717. The adjutant of a regiment in 1715 held quite a different position from that of an adjutant later. His duties more nearly approached those of a regimental sergeant-major in these days. A commission as adjutant, however, was signed by the king, and in it he would be styled "Gentleman."

The commissions or warrants of quartermasters, however, were not signed by the king, but by the colonel; and in them a quartermaster is also styled "Gentleman." It would appear that to be a quartermaster was often a stepping-stone to a commission as cornet or ensign, and at times those holding the rank of quartermaster had in a previous regiment held superior rank. The cost in pay and allowances of Munden's Dragoons for the first year of its existence was £12,849, 13s. The regiment consisted of six troops of forty-nine men each, officers included, and "widdows men."

In tracing the military careers of the first list of officers in Munden's Dragoons, it is interesting to note that several of them had served with their colonel in a regiment known as Lovelace's Foot. To the colonelcy of this regiment Munden succeeded in 1708. From this fact it may be deduced that the Whitehall Circular of July 23, 1715, desiring the names of officers, which has already been quoted, was either post-dated or was a second circular of the same tenour.

Brief notices of the military careers of Munden and his officers may well be here inserted.

Cannon, in his History of the 13th Dragoons, states that Munden served under King William III. in the Netherlands. Though there

CLEMENT NEVILL.

FIRST LIEUTENANT-COLONEL OF THE REGIMENT.

THE RAISING OF THE REGIMENT.

is no documentary evidence to support this statement, its truth is very probable. William died March 8th, 1702. Munden's first commission in the British Army is dated April 22, 1702. There he appears as Captain and Lieutenant-Colonel in the 1st Foot Guards, now the Grenadier Guards. This points to previous and good service elsewhere. Munden fought at Schellenberg (Donauwerth), July 2nd 1704, when he led eighty men of his regiment into battle, and returned with twenty only. This, it will be remembered, was Marlborough's first big battle. One account states that Munden then commanded a brigade of the Guards, another that he led the Forlorn Hope. He appears to have received a bounty of £49, 10s. In the "Blenheim Roll," Dalton, in a note, mentions that Munden served at Ramillies. This is open to question, for he had retired from the Guards before the date of the battle, and was appointed Lieutenant-Colonel of Lord Lovelace's newly raised Regiment of Foot on April 12, 1706. In this regiment he remained for some years, becoming Colonel in 1708. He was promoted Brigadier-General 12th February 17$\frac{10}{11}$. Up to this time his regiment had been stationed in Ireland; but in 1711 it embarked for Spain. Here the regiment suffered disaster, being a part of the force under General Stanhope which was surrounded at Brighuega and taken prisoners.[1] In 1712 the regiment was disbanded in England, and the officers placed on half-pay. In 1715 Brigadier Munden was ordered to raise the Regiment of Dragoons now known as the 13th Hussars. This regiment he continued to command until 1722, when he was transferred to the colonelcy of the 8th Dragoons. He was now a Major-General, and died in command of this regiment September 20, 1725. It is interesting to read that General Munden was one of the eight generals who, with Marlborough's old Quartermaster-General, attended the funeral of the Great Duke. This body of veteran officers walked in the procession immediately after the troops and bands.

Clement Nevill was appointed an Ensign of Foot, December 31, 1688; Lieutenant in Sir John Hanmer's Regiment of Foot, 1st February 1691; Captain, 9th April 1703; Lieutenant-Colonel in Lovelace's

---

[1] The surrender at Brighuega came about in the following manner. Stanhope omitted to place either pickets, outposts, or advance guards on any of the neighbouring heights, and relied for information on bribed peasants. Don Joseph Villejo, on the contrary, though he had only 1200 irregular horse with him, utterly prevented any information filtering through to Stanhope. Hence the result. As an example of good and bad cavalry work it is very noteworthy.

Regiment of Foot, August 31, 1706 (his supplementary commission as Major bears the same date); at Brighuega he was taken prisoner; Brevet-Colonel, November 15, 1711; Lieutenant-Colonel in Munden's Dragoons, July 22, 1715; Colonel of the 14th Dragoons, April 9, 1720; Colonel of the 8th Dragoons, to which he was transferred in 1737; in 1739 promoted Major-General; 1740, Colonel of the 6th Horse, now the 5th Dragoon Guards; 1743, Lieutenant-General. Clement Nevill died in Dublin on August 3, 1744, "Lieutenant-General in rank, Major-General on the Irish establishment, and Colonel of Horse and eldest commissioned officer in the service."

Samuel Freeman first appears as an Ensign of Foot, 15th January 1685. He became Lieutenant, November 30, 1688; Captain-Lieutenant in Sir Robert Peyton's Regiment of Foot (Lancashire Fusiliers), February 28, 1689; Captain, 6th September 1690; exchanged into Colonel Samuel Venner's Regiment of Foot, 17th November 1691. His commission was renewed in 1702, at which time he had exchanged into the Earl of Marlborough's (24th) Foot. On August 25, 1704, he was still a captain in that regiment,—the regiment being then known as Colonel Tatton's Foot. On September 1, 1706, he became Major, and on 1st April 1707, Lieutenant-Colonel. It was, however, with the rank of Major that he joined Brigadier Munden's Dragoons, July 22, 1715. Major Freeman did not succeed to the lieutenant-colonelcy of his regiment, and appears to have left the service prior to 1720.

Francis Howard obtained his commission as Ensign in the 1st Foot Guards, April 5, 1704. He was Captain in Lovelace's Regiment, April 12, 1706. Apparently he had served with Munden in the Guards, and went with him to his new regiment. On December 29, 1711, he is found acting as Lieutenant to Captain Alexander Horne in Slane's Regiment at Barcelona. This regiment was sent to Spain in that year, and was disbanded in 1712. Howard became Captain in Munden's Dragoons, 1715, and went on half-pay in 1722. He was alive and still on half-pay in 1740.

Lutton Lister. Of this officer the details are scanty. The date of his commission as Ensign cannot be ascertained. On March 22, $170\frac{8}{9}$, he was a Captain in Lovelace's Foot. Placed on half-pay in 1712, he became Captain in Munden's Regiment of Dragoons, 22nd July 1715, and was serving in 1717.

William Heblethwaite was appointed Captain in the regiment of foot commanded by the Marquis de Montandre, December 23, 1709. The regiment was disbanded in 1713. This regiment, it may be remarked, surrendered *en masse* at Alicante in 1707. The circumstances of the surrender were the reverse of creditable. It is due, however, to the Marquis de Montandre to state that he was at this time absent, being in Staff employ elsewhere.

Henry de Grangues. In an MS. at the War Office this officer is stated to be "descended of an English family in Somersetshire." This is an error. Henry de Grangues was, in fact, a French marquis, and belonged to a family long established in Normandy. He obtained his first commission as a Cornet of Horse, June 4, 1695. Later he obtained a Captain's commission in Flanders in the regiment of Baron Waleffe "*vice* Ramburis decd." This commission was signed at the camp at Meldert, July 22, 1707, by Marlborough. It is registered in the W. O. Commission Book for 1712. On July 14, 1712, de Grangues became Major of Baron de Borle's Dragoons, his commission being signed by the Duke of Ormond at Chateau Cambresis. He was placed on half-pay in 1713.

In the Journals of the House of Commons, 1715, on a question arising out of pensions and half-pay, the case of the Protestant officers of Baron de Borle's late Regiment of Dragoons, among them being Henry de Grangues, is ordered to be referred to the consideration of a committee. De Grangues became Captain-Lieutenant of Munden's Dragoons on July 22, 1715, and in virtue of this rank he acted as Lieutenant in the troop of which the Colonel was Captain. He was Major in Sir Robert Rich's Dragoons (late Munden's), with seniority in the army from 14th July 1712, before 1727. On July 1, 1737, he was Lieutenant-Colonel of the Royal Dragoons; January 21, 1741, Colonel of a newly raised regiment of foot. This regiment was numbered the 60th, but was afterwards disbanded. On October 24, 1742, de Grangues was transferred to the Colonelcy of the 30th Foot; removed to the 9th Dragoons, 1st April 1743; Brigadier-General, June 10, 1745; Major-General, 24th September 1747; Colonel of the 7th Dragoon Guards, November 1, 1749. He died in June 1754.

Francis Hull served in a company added to the Artillery Train in Spain during the years 1708-10 as Gentleman of the Ordnance. He was present at the battles of Almenara, Saragossa, and Villa Viciosa. In the last-named battle the guns were lost and several officers killed. Hull had then reached the rank of Lieutenant. Placed on half-pay in 1714, he obtained a Lieutenancy in Munden's Dragoons, July 22, 1715.

Philip Bridgeman was 1st Lieutenant in Lovelace's Foot on April 12, 1706. Of his going on half-pay, or his services until 1715, there is no record.

John Molyneux was appointed Lieutenant to Captain Charlton in Colonel Roger Townshend's Regiment of Foot on March 22, 1711. The regiment was disbanded in 1712 and he was placed on half-pay. This was a regiment which suffered severely at the siege of Douay in 1710, and lost many men in the Canadian Expedition of 1711.

Henry Dawson obtained his commission as Ensign in Lord Paston's Regiment of Foot on March 24, 1709. A part of this regiment served at the battle of the Caya in that year. It was disbanded in 1712.

Samuel Dunster, the first Chaplain of Munden's Dragoons, was a rather distinguished man.

He was born in 1675, and educated at Merchant Taylors School and Trinity College, Cambridge (B.A. 1693, M.A. 1700, D.D. 1713).

Dunster was ordained in 1700. In 1704 he was curate of St James's, Westminster. Before 1708 he was Chaplain to Charles, Earl of Maynard. He filled a similar post in the household of Charles, Earl of Shrewsbury, in 1712, and some years later was Chaplain to the Duke of Marlborough.

His connection with the army began on May 7, 1708, when he was appointed to the Chaplaincy of Lieut.-General Thomas Erle's Regiment of Foot (19th Regiment). He served at Malplaquet, but was out of the regiment in 1713.

Dunster held the following clerical appointments: Rector of Chinnor, Oxon, 1716 (Patron, Queen Anne); Prebend of Netherbury, in Salisbury Cathedral, 1717. This post he exchanged in 1720 for Grimston Yatminster, in the same cathedral, which stall he held till 1748, when he resigned it to his son Charles.

Samuel Dunster was for years the absentee Chaplain of the regiment — in fact, till he was succeeded by his son Charles in 1740. In 1720 he was collated to the stall of Forendon in Lincoln Cathedral. In 1722 he succeeded to the Vicarage of Rochdale.

He died July 1754. Dunster was "a dignified clergyman and a useful magistrate," but a "poor and verbose preacher." Lady Cowper mentions him as preaching "an intolerably dull sermon at Court." He had in later life High Church and Nonjuring leanings, and associated with the active Jacobite party in Manchester.

Dunster wrote sundry poetical works: 'Lacrymae Cantabrigienses in obitum seren. Reginae Mariae,' 1694-5. He is credited with the authorship of 'Anglia Rediviva,' 1699; 'Wisdom and Understanding the Glory and Excellence of Human Nature,' 1708; 'The Conditions of Drexelius in Eleusis,' a poem in defence of popular education (three editions), 1710; 'Satyrs and Epistles of Horace,' done into English, in 1710, and a second edition with the 'Ars Poetica' in 1717, published with the translator's portrait.

This was a very dull book, and was satirised by Dr T. Francklin thus—

> "O'er Tibur's Swan the Muses wept in vain
> And mourned the Bard by Cruel Dunster Slain."

Dunster also translated from the Latin of Baron de Danckleman, in 1716, 'A Panegerick on his Majesty King George.'

Thomas Mason. Ensign of Foot, 22nd April 1709; Lieutenant of Foot, 2nd July 1710.

John Watson. Ensign of Foot, 23rd December 1710; Cornet of Munden's Dragoons, 22nd July 1715; Lieutenant, 28th October 1715.

There is no record to inform us which lieutenant retired on this date, but it is clear that Watson was succeeded by Richard Henson, the Quartermaster.

William Freeman. Ensign, 1st December 1709; Cornet, 22nd July 1715.

William Williamson. Ensign, 28th August 1711; Cornet, 22nd July 1715.

Martin O'Brian. Ensign, 12th April 1712; Cornet, 22nd July 1715.

Charles Greenwood. Ensign, 23rd November 1710; Cornet, 22nd July 1715.

Gerald Fitzgerald. Ensign, 25th October 1710; Cornet, 22nd July 1715.

John Houghton. Ensign, 17th February 1707; Adjutant, Munden's Dragoons, 22nd July 1715.

Of the other quartermasters and the surgeon there do not appear to be any records.

With regard to the regiment the position of affairs was now this. By October 19, 1715, it had been considered to be sufficiently complete to march from its rendezvous at Northampton to Leeds and Halifax, where three troops were left at each place.

On October 31, Brigadier Munden is notified that his regiment with others forms the force under the command of General Wills.

At the time General Wills was at Chester, and on November 5th, having received advices that the rebels from the Borders were marching towards Lancaster, despatched orders for nine regiments of dragoons and foot which were in and about that part, and which formed his command, to draw together to Warrington. Thither General Wills went to place himself at their head "with resolve," says 'The London Gazette,' "to march against the Rebels without giving them any Respite."

From a letter to General Carpenter from William Pulteney (afterwards Earl of Bath, Secretary at War) we gather the following information. The letter is dated November 3, 1715. In it General Carpenter is informed—

1. That Major-General Wills is at Chester with "the same powers and jurisdictions as you had."
2. That he is to have "the Regiments that lye thereabouts," Wynne's, Munden's, Honywood's, Newton's, and Dormer's Dragoons; Pitt's Horse, and Sabine's, Preston's, and Fane's Regiments of Foot, should he need them.
3. He is to march through Lancashire "or wherever the Rebels are drove by you, or there is any jurisdictions against the Government."
4. Carpenter is directed to keep in correspondence with Wills, "or at least, on any extraordinary occasion, send him by Express an account of your motions, and those of the Rebells."

Cannon in his History states that the 13th Dragoons had been in Chester, but this is an error. At the time that Wills left that city they were at Leeds (three troops) and Halifax (three troops).

THE RAISING OF THE REGIMENT.

General Wills ordered his troops to assemble at Manchester, and to march thence to Wigan. At Manchester he detached Colonel Newton's Regiment of Dragoons to overawe the populace, as the town was in a most disaffected state.

He reached Wigan on November 11, and was joined there by Stanhope's Dragoons and Houghton's Militia troops, which had retired from Preston when that town was occupied by the rebels.

At Wigan, intelligence reached Wills that Carpenter, who had been in Durham, was advancing on Preston to attack the rebels in flank, having left that city on November 7. At dawn on November 12, marching due north, Wills left Wigan.

His army marched in the following order:—

An advance guard of fifty musketeers and fifty dismounted dragoons.

Preston's Regiment of Foot.

Three Brigades of Cavalry: Wynne's and Honywood's, commanded by Brigadier Honywood; Munden's and Stanhope's, commanded by Brigadier Munden; Pitt's and Dormer's, commanded by Brigadier Dormer.

The baggage was in the rear, under a guard of fifty of Stanhope's Dragoons detached for that purpose.

The exact position of Sabine's and Fane's Regiments of Foot, or of Houghton's Militia, during the march is not recorded.

By noon on November 12 Wills reached the bridge over the Ribble at Preston.

The events which took place at Preston will be more conveniently treated in the next chapter.

The regiment was now raised. It was officially declared to be a disciplined force belonging to the regular army on October 31, 1715.

Twelve days later it was on active service, and, what is more, wa within musket-shot of the enemy.

CHAPTER II.

Preston, 1715. Service in England, 1715-1718.

THE town of Preston, in those days a comparatively small place—its population eighty-five years later being under 12,000,—was bounded on its south side by the river Ribble, which runs roughly in the form of half a hexagon south-west, east, and north-east. Near the north-easterly bend was the Warmington Bridge, the only bridge over the river.

From the bridge end on the town side the road from Wigan and Manchester bent round in a north-westerly direction till it joined the main street of the town.

This road, some 900 yards in length, ran through low ground for the most part, having steep banks on either side.

Obviously it would have been only a common precaution for the rebels to have been prepared to dispute the passage of the bridge. Equally it would have been wise to have secured the hollow road above-named. For this last there was a precedent, for had not the Royalists on that spot in 1648 (August 17), under Langdale, made a desperate defence against Cromwell.

But to "General" Forster no such precautions appeared needful.

True, there had been some discussion as to placing a guard on the bridge, and 100 Highlanders had been told off for that purpose, but these were withdrawn on the approach of the royal army.

Forster seems to have made some sort of attempt at reconnaissance by crossing the bridge at the head of some horse.

He, however, returned to the town, leaving the bridge unguarded and the hollow road void of defence.

It seems hardly credible that, situated as the rebels were, and having had warning eighteen hours previously that Wills at any

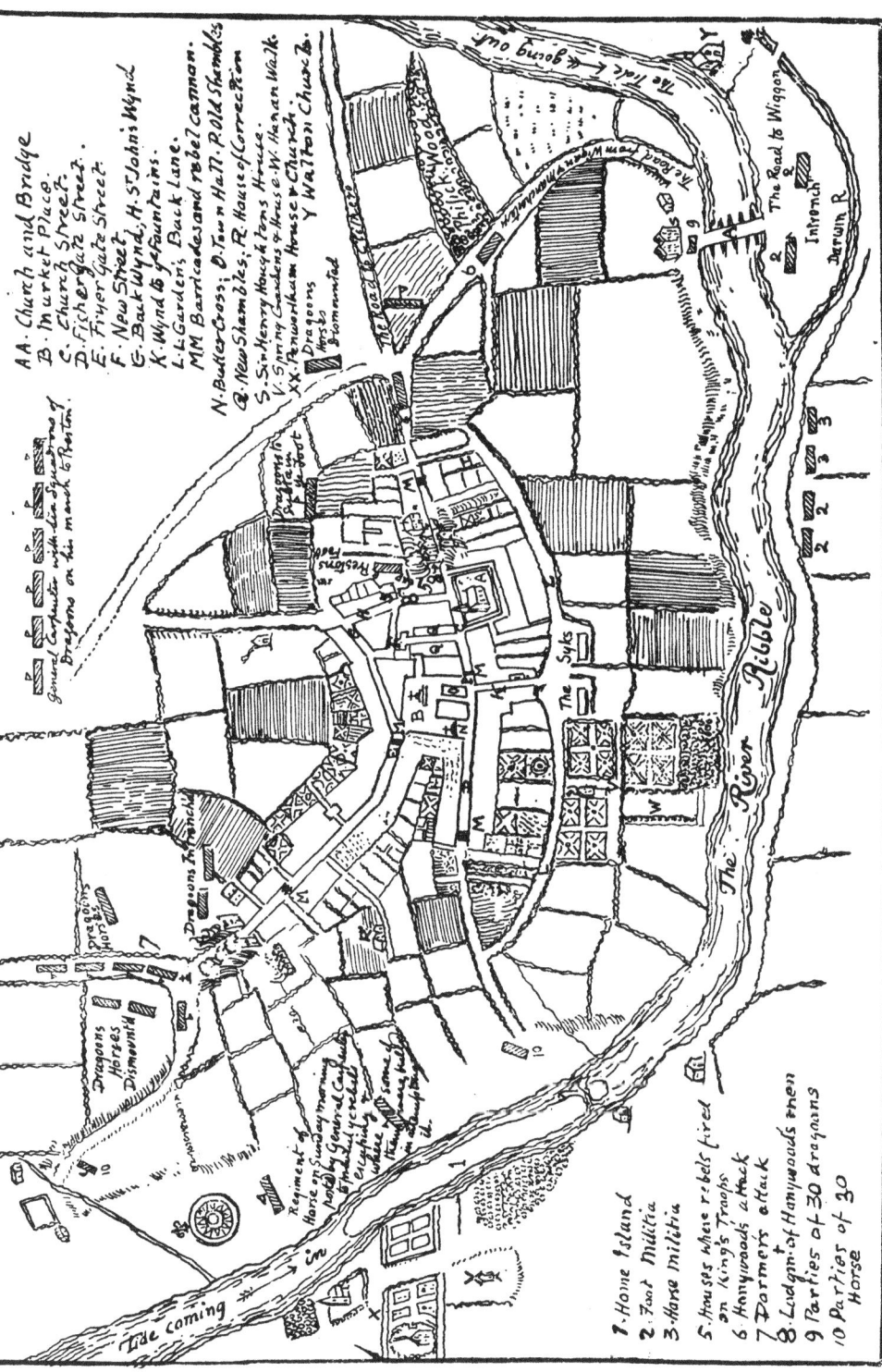

"PRESTON IN 1715."

From an old map "Drawn on the Spott by P. M., Esq. H. Halfbergh, Sculp."

rate was on the march thither and meant fighting, the rebels should have relied for their defence merely on a few barricades. To Lord Kenmure the rebels were indebted for such scanty preparations as were made.

On arrival at the Ribble bridge, General Wills, finding it unoccupied, made a reconnaissance. He crossed the unoccupied bridge, rode along the hollow road as far as its junction with the Clithero Road, which farther on made the main street. Here a barricade was sighted, and the party was fired on, two men being killed.

How General Wills learnt that there were only four barricades is not to be ascertained. All that is known is that he found himself with not more than sufficient troops to attack two, and that such attack should at once be made were his immediate orders. His position was this. In numbers he was very much inferior to the rebels. In cannon he was entirely lacking, while his opponents had two pieces of cannon at each barricade. The two barricades which Wills elected to attack were those on the roads to Wigan and to Lancaster. General Wills's force was thus disposed: against Wigan barricade he sent Preston's Regiment, commanded by Lord Forrester; a captain and 50 dragoons of each regiment, with a colonel, lieutenant-colonel, and major to command them, were dismounted to support the infantry, and the regiment of Brigadier Honywood mounted in support. Of this force the command was given to Honywood.

Against the Lancaster Road barricade, which was on the opposite side of the town, the regiments of Wynne and Dormer and one squadron of Stanhope's Dragoons were dismounted, and acted under the command of Dormer. Brigadier Munden, with his own regiment and that of Pitt and the remaining squadron of Stanhope's Dragoons mounted, acted as a support to Dormer.

Honywood's attack was first to develop. Here the enemy had two barriers, one some distance behind the other. At the first there was but little resistance, the rebels retiring on the second, which was much stronger, "both by Nature and Art, and on which they had two pieces of cannon." To take this inner defence by assault Honywood considered would entail a great loss, and therefore he seized two large houses within about fifty yards of it. By this means he secured his men from the enemy's fire and was able to annoy his opponents from the windows. Here he remained until nightfall, having set fire to the houses which intervened between his men and the second barricade. This operation was not carried out, however, without loss.

At night Brigadier Honywood caused breastworks to be thrown up by his men to secure his force should sallies be attempted by the rebels; and by a series of posts which he established at that part of the town it was impossible for the enemy to escape.

Brigadier Dormer having worked round the town arrived at the opposite side. At the barricade he was met by a most severe fire from the enemy, who had occupied the houses on either side of the road. Many men fell. A part of the barrier was carried, but later was retaken by the rebels. A second attack was made, only to meet with a second repulse and a heavy loss. The houses on either side of the barricade were, however, fired, and were burnt right up to that defence. So matters rested till nearly dawn, when General Wills rode round the posts and directed that "a Communication betwixt the two attacks" should be made "in order to sustain each other in case they were pushed."

On Sunday November 13 General Carpenter reached Preston with three regiments of dragoons, those of Cobham, Churchill, and Molesworth. He arrived at noon. Two hours later negotiations for surrender were entered upon by the rebels. An armistice was agreed upon. Hostages were given on the rebel side. At daybreak on November 14 the rebels surrendered. Brigadier Honywood was shot in the shoulder, Major Bland in the arm, and his horse through the neck. In Honywood's attack 2 captains, 1 ensign, and 28 soldiers were killed; Lord Forrester, Major Lawson, 2 captains, 1 lieutenant, 4 ensigns, and 50 private men wounded. Total casualties, 82 men.

Brigadier Dormer lost 9 men killed, and was himself wounded, together with 1 captain, 1 lieutenant, 1 cornet, and 39 men. Total killed and wounded, 48.

Thus the loss in both attacks amounted to 130.

From 'The London Gazette' of November 19, 1715, we gather that "All the Troops expressed great Zeal and Resolution on this Occasion, and the new Regiments appeared in perfect good Order."

There seems to have been some ill blood between Major-General Wills and Lieut.-General Carpenter on the subject of the taking of Preston.

Undoubtedly the fighting was done by the troops under Wills's command, though it is perfectly clear that the advent of General Carpenter with his three regiments of dragoons hastened the surrender of the rebels.

Both claimed the credit, apparently, and an open rupture occurred. General Carpenter, within a few weeks, challenged Wills to a duel. By the interposition of the Duke of Marlborough, however, the difference was composed and the duel averted.

Of Munden's Dragoons it is recorded that four men and twelve horses were wounded. Brigadier Munden, who at one period of the fight led a storming-party, is stated to have been thanked for his gallant conduct on the occasion.

Of the fate of the prisoners and the vengeance meted out to them by the Government there is no occasion to write here.

After the surrender, Munden's Dragoons were employed in the unpleasant duty of escorting rebel prisoners to jail, and possibly, also, in pursuit of those in hiding. Details of this time are lacking, but it is an established fact that the regiment was placed in cantonments in Lancashire, and remained stationed there till April 1716. Where the regiment was stationed exactly is not apparently to be discovered. It was, however, at Manchester in April 1716, and was there inspected, prior to marching into Wiltshire, where it was scattered in various towns.

In the month of April 1717 a move was made into Berkshire and Hampshire till the winter, when the regiment was posted at Worcester and Bromsgrove. In the following spring the regiment marched to Gloucester and Tewkesbury.

CHAPTER III.

Ireland, 1718-1742.

IN the year 1718 a reduction of the army took place. Several regiments—viz., two of dragoons and six of foot—were disbanded in Ireland.

To replace one of these regiments of dragoons Munden's was ordered to Ireland.

The following document in the Record Office refers to this reduction, and is as follows:—

1718, 8th Nov.

By the Lords Justices General & Genl Gov^{rs} of Ireland.
Witt^d Dublin, Wm Conolly.

Dragoons.
Brig^r Bowles's.
Brig. Munden's.

Foot.
Col. Handasyde's.
Maj.-Genl Sabine's.
Brig^r Preston's.
Lord Shannon's.
Lord Hinchinbroke's.
Col. Egerton's.

In pursuance of His Maj^{ts} Letters unto Us bearing Date the 15th of October 1718 (a Copy whereof herewith sent). These are to Direct and Require you to Place upon His Maj^{ts} Establishment of this Kingdom Two Regiments of Dragoons and Six Regiments of Foot whose names are Respectively mentioned in the margin hereof, from the 11th Day of November instant inclusive, which are to be paid from thenceforth out of the Revenue of this His Maj^{ts} Kingdom in like manner as the other Regiments of Dragoons and Foot are subsisted and paid, and for so doing, this shall be Your Warr^t

Given at His Maj^{ts} Castle of Dublin the 8th Day of Novr 1718.

By their Ex^{cies} Command.

CHARLES MADDOCKES.

To the Must^r Mas.-Genl of this Kingdom, or his Deputy.

The letter mentioned contains the order to disband

Dragoons.—Col. Newton's.	Foot.—Col. Armstrong's.
Brig^{r.} Croft's.	Brig^{r.} Ferrer's.
	Col. Nassau's.
	Col. Dubourgay's.
	Col. Pocock's.
	Col. Haas's.

It is dated from Hampton Court, 15th October 1718.

The barrack accommodation in Ireland at this time was very scanty indeed.

For dragoons there were only sufficient to house twelve troops. A list gives the following details :—

- 12 barracks for foot, to accommodate 22 companies.
- 6 for dragoons, to hold 12 troops.
- 1 barrack for a regiment of foot that had been reduced; and this had never been occupied.
- 1 barrack for dragoons, to accommodate 1 troop; but this, though capable of repair, was at the time uninhabitable. It must have been in a very bad state indeed.
- 6 barracks for foot had been evacuated and were derelict.
- 1 barrack for foot had actually been rebuilt, and, what is more, enlarged from two companies to three.

The troubles connected with recruiting in the case of British regiments on the Irish establishment were not little.

A route of the date of 1719 is the only evidence of the whereabouts of part of the regiment during this year. The paper is as follows :—

Munden's. Route for Three Cornets, and ffive Private Men with Thirty Recruit Horses of Brig^{r.} Munden's Regiment from Northampton to Chester. Rugby, Coventry to Rest, etc., Coleshill, Litchfield, Bromley, Stone, Namptwich, Chester, there to Embark for Ireland.

In the Absence of the Secretary at War,

R^{D.} ARNOLD.

WHITEHALL, 9th *October* 1719.

A paper signed " Shannon," and dated from Island Bridge, 19th November 1721, gives some information on this point, which is not without interest.

It appears that when vacancies occurred by "deaths and desertions," it was compulsory to send into Great Britain to raise the necessary numbers to supply the said vacancies.

That the recruiting officer and his party should then return with the recruits after they had been viewed and approved, "so that no other non-effectives be found at any muster but the number usually allowed to make good deaths and desertions." The paper continues: "And you are to give orders to the officers appointed to raise recruits for your Regiment, that they do not only avoid Inlisting any Natives of this Kingdom but likewise Inlisting any man in Ireland on any pretence whatever."

To evade this, it frequently happened thus—Irishmen were enlisted in Ireland, sent over to Scotland, with instructions to return to Ireland dressed in Scottish clothes.

As will be seen later by some returns which will be given, the privates in the 13th Dragoons, and Light Dragoons, as they afterwards became, were at one time nearly all Irishmen.

In 1721 the pay of all the troops on the Irish establishment was less than on the English establishment.

Half-pay in Ireland at this date was: colonel and captain, 15s. 8d.; lieutenant-colonel and captain, 9s. 8d.; major and captain, 8s. 8d.; captain, 6s. 2d.; lieutenant, 3s. 1d.; cornet, 2s. 7d.; quartermaster, 1s. 6d.; chaplain, 3s. 4d.; adjutant (as adjutant), nil; and surgeon, 2s. per diem.

In 1722 the Colonel of the 13th Dragoons, Brigadier-General Munden, was removed to the 8th Dragoons, and he was succeeded in the command of the regiment which he had raised by Brigadier-General Sir Robert Rich, Baronet.

Sir Robert, it may be added, had previously been in command of a regiment of dragoons which had been disbanded.

Brigadier-General Munden did not live long, dying in 1725, when he was succeeded in the colonelcy of the 8th Dragoons by Sir Robert Rich. To the colonelcy of the 13th Dragoons thus vacated Colonel William Stanhope, afterwards the Earl of Harrington, was appointed. Colonel Stanhope, it will be remembered, was one of those to whom a "Letter of Service" was sent on August 18, 1715, empowering him to raise a regiment of dragoons. Stanhope's Dragoons were disbanded in 1718.

For the years 1723 and 1724 there are no records to show where the regiment was quartered in Ireland.

In 1725, "Brigadier Munden's"—the 13th still retained their old name—is found located thus: 3 troops were at Sligo, 1 at Cavan, 1 at Belturbet, and 1 at Colooney. A paper of this date gives details of the barrack accommodation in Ireland. From it we gather that in 1725, 51 troops of cavalry could be quartered in various places. Evidently building operations had been in progress.

In Leinster 19 troops could be housed, Dublin having barracks for 6 troops, and Granard for 2: all the rest being single troop barracks. In Munster only 7 troops could be housed, Clonmell alone taking 2. Connaught accommodated 13 troops, 3 at Sligo, and 2 at Newport. Ulster accommodated 12 troops, 2 being at Ballyshannon, and 2 at Castledawson.

In the regiments on the Irish establishment it would appear that there was a good deal of slackness in this year, as we read: "Officers had left the place where they were posted without licence from the Government, others had overstayed leave to detriment of his Maj$^{ts.}$ Service, and contrary to all good order and decency." In consequence, all officers absent without leave were required immediately to repair to their posts or to take the consequence.

This paper is dated June 8, 1725.

In the year 1726 we find the 13th Dragoons split into three divisions. Three troops were quartered in Dublin, one troop and half of another at Longford, and one troop and the remaining half of the other at Athlone.

In An Abstract of the Army in Ireland as they were reviewed by the General in 1726, with regard to Colonel Stanhope's Regiment the only remark is "no mention of arms." In the rough draft of this abstract which is annexed the wording is: "bad arms = no mention of arms."

This paper is full of interest in an unpleasant way. Nearly every regiment has "bad arms." Many other particulars crop up: "Some horses out of order"; "field officers all absent"; "cloathing of two troops not delivered." "A mistake of 7 men and 7 horses" in one regiment should have read "18 men and 18 horses wanting to complete."

Only Wynne's and Ligonier's Regiments were armed in a satisfactory way.

Apparently the foot were in a better condition of equipment and armament than the horse and dragoons, still they were by no means as they should have been. Who was to blame for these defects does not appear. That the King had been fully aware of the unsatisfactory condition of the regiments on the Irish establishment as far back as 1725 is certain, for a lengthy paper of that date is in existence, formulating rules and regulations which were founded upon a series of rules laid down in 1717.

The paper runs as follows:—

His Majesty, being sensible that many disorders in the quarters and garrisons of his forces in Ireland may be occasioned by the absence of Officers belonging to the same, and it being his Express Will and Pleasure that the Officers of his several Regiments of Horse Foot and Dragoons, in the said Kingdom, should for the future attend their respective Duties in such manner as his Majesty's Service requires, for the keeping of good Order and Discipline in the Army, We have thought fit to settle the following Rules conformably to the orders we have received from his Majesty, founded upon those which were given by his Majesty in England in 1717:—

1. That such a Disposition be made every year by the General or Quarter Master General that the Regiments the most dispersed may be brought together the year following.

2. That no Regiment, nor any particular Troop or Company, do remain two years together in the same quarters.

3. That when the several Troops of any of the Regiments of Horse and Dragoons in this Kingdom shall be quartered together there be always one Field Officer and one half of the Captains present, besides the Field Officers, as always one Commission Officer more besides the Quarter Master present with every Troop.

4. That when a Regiment is divided, and 2 or more Troops are quart$^{d.}$ together, there be 1 Captain at the least always present with each two Troops, and 1 Commission Officer more besides the Quarter Master with such Troops, whereof the Captain shall be present as likewise 2 Commission Officers with such other Troops, whereof the Captain shall happen to be absent.

5. That when a Troop is alone, and the Captain happens to be absent, the Lieutenant or the Cornet shall always be present.

6. That when a Troop is divided in quarters there be a Commission Officer always present with each division.

7. That a Field Officer be always present at the Head Quarters or Other Quarters of the Troops of each Regiment.

The next five paragraphs refer to foot only and are omitted.

13. That no Officer whatever under the Degree of a Colonel be absent above four months in one year, nor no Officer of any Degree do go out of the Kingdom without special leave of the Government, and the General be made ac-

quainted therewith by the Commanding Officer of the Regiment to which such Officer shall belong, or if thought necessary that the Commanding Officer shall first apply to the General, who shall move the Government for such Officer's leave.

14. That the like method of attendance of Officers, as before directed, be duly observed in the march of each Regiment, Troop or Troops belonging to the same.

15. That in Extraordinary Case when the King's Service shall require it, the Colonels or Commanding Officers of the respective Regiments may dispense with the absence of their Officers in a greater number or for a longer period than is specified in the foregoing Rules, but so that the said Colonels or Commanding Officers, who shall take upon them to dispense with the Absence of the said Officers, shall give the General of his Maj^ts. Forces in this Kingdom an account in writing within 14 days or a month of such leave of absence granted, of the service in which such Officer so absent by this leave is employed.

16. The same rule as applied to the Officers of scattered Troops of Horse or Dragoons in which a list is to be forwarded every 14 days or month containing the names of the Officers absent in each quarter, with an account of the time and occasion of such absence, that the Government may be satisfied of the due performance of His Maj^ts. Commands herein, which are hereby directed to be punctually observed.

17. That the patterns of the Cloathing of the Army be brought to the Board of General Officers to be approved of the 1st day of Nov^r.

18. That the Officers be sent into England to recruit before Christmas, that they may return by April with their recruits.

19. That all the Troops do march to their new Quarters in May, so as to be settled and Cloathed by the 28th, by which the Regiments and Recruits may be made perfect in their Exercise, by the time of the General Review of the Army in June or July.

20. That the Commanding Officers of each Regiment do certify to the General Officer that the Regiments are Cloathed by the 28th of May, conformably to this order, that is to say, the Horse and Dragoons to be cloathed every other year and the Foot every year, which certificate shall be sent to the General by the 20th of June that the Cloathing be reviewed by a General Officer before it be sent from Dublin.

21. That the Horse and Dragoons have their Recruit Horses from England by April, which will give the Officers an opportunity if necessary to put the young horses to grass and season them the better for service.

22. That all Captains of Horse and Dragoons be accounted with for their stock-purse money, and non-effectives once a-year, that is, in May; by which time 'tis expected their troops will be complete and in good order, and when so that the Colonel or Commanding Officer of the Regiment do order the Agent to pay the Captains the balance of their abstracts due on all accounts, unless the Government or the General do give order to the contrary.

23. That all Officers of Horse Foot and Dragoons have their Abstracts of Subsistence every month, and their balance paid them unless the Government or the General give orders to the Contrary.

24. Refers to Foot only.

25. That the men be accounted with every two or three months, and what is due paid them.

26. That the Commanding Officers do not suffer their men to wear any Cloaths in Quarters, but such as are Regimental.

27. That the Commanding Officer of Each Regiment do take care that all Officers have Regimental Cloaths, and that no Officer be permitted to mount any guard in Country Quarters, but in Red or Blue Cloaths.

28. That whereas it is necessary for his Majesty's Service and the good of the Troops that there should Constantly be one entire Regiment of Horse or Dragoons upon Duty in Dublin; it be therefore ordered that a Regiment of Horse be Quartered in Dublin for the six summer months and be relieved by a Regiment of Dragoons, which shall continue in Dublin the six winter months, by which no Inconvenience can arise to the Dragoons, they having the summer to put their horses to grass and the Regiment three years in four to do the same if they find it necessary.

A paper dated 1726 gives an estimate of the subsistence of a dragoon, with the "constant and necessary deductions for which he is to be accounted with." The concluding remarks in which it is attempted to show how a dragoon can save are amusing.

SUBSISTENCE.

	£	s.	d.
A Dragoon for the winter six months at $11\frac{1}{2}$d. per diem for 28 days	1	6	10
Subsistence at 3s. per week for 28 days . . £0 12 0			
Forage at $4\frac{1}{2}$d. per diem for do. . . 0 10 6			
Surgeon per week $1\frac{1}{2}$d. ⎫			
Clerk do. 1d. ⎬ is per month . . 0 2 0			
Farrier do. $3\frac{1}{2}$d. ⎭			
Riding Master at $\frac{1}{4}$d. per day is per month . . 0 0 7			
Stableman at 2d. per week is per month . . 0 0 8			
Sheets (washing) 0 0 1			
Remaining to be accounted for 0 1 0			
	£1	6	10
A Dragoon for the summer 6 months—			
Subsistence at 3s. per week for 28 days . . £0 12 0			
Grass at 1s. 2d. per week for 28 days . . . 0 4 0			
Surgeon, Clerk, Farrier and Riding Master . . 0 2 7			
Sheets (washing) and Stableman . . . 0 0 9			
Stock-purse at $1\frac{1}{2}$d. per diem . . . 0 3 6			
Remaining to be accounted for 0 4 0			
	£1	6	10
In Dublin.			
Pay at 30 days, 1s. 4d. per day £2 0 0			
3d. per day additional 0 7 6			
	£2	7	6

Stoppages.

	£	s.	d.
Subsistence	0	13	0
Forage	0	19	4½
Half barrel of bran	0	0	10
Stock-purse at 2d. per month	0	0	2
Troop Clerk, Surgeon and Infirmary	0	0	9½
Riding Master	0	0	7
Stableman	0	0	4
Sheets (washing)	0	0	1
Balance	0	12	4
	£2	7	6

Country Quarters.

	£	s.	d.
Pay at 30 days at 1s. 4d.	£2	0	0
	£2	0	0
Subsistence	0	13	0
Hay	0	7	6
Oats	0	4	0
Bran and Straw	0	1	0
Stock-purse at 2s. per month	0	2	0
Troop Clerk, Surgeon and Infirmary	0	0	7
Riding Master	0	0	6
Sheets (washing)	0	0	1
Balance	0	11	4
	£2	0	0

Computation of the Charges occasioning Stoppages.

	£	s.	d.
Shoeing and Farrying, per annum	£1	10	0
Small Bridle and Bridoon	0	1	8
Curry Comb, Brush, Mane Comb and Sponge	0	3	0
Rubbing Cloth for horse	0	1	6
Washing Buff Belts	0	0	8
Regimental Stockings and Black Garters	0	6	0
Turning old coat into a frock, once in two years	0	5	0
Horse Cloth, once in 4 years	0	8	0
Wallet for horseback, once in 4 years	0	2	0
	£2	17	10

A skull cap, 4s.; powder flask and string, 3s. 6d.; a false scabbard, 1s.; a cockade, 1s. 6d. A goat skin to cover the saddle has been stopped out of troopers' pay, and this is made good out of the same.

When the cavalry grazed horses during the summer months the whole stoppage for the stock-purse was paid during the six summer months from May to October both inclusive, at 4s. per man per month, and a trooper's account for the winter month showed a balance of 12s. 6½d., while for a summer month it was 16s. 6½d.

It is explained that "the Trooper is at little or no charge for shoeing his horse when at grass, and besides saves in the wear and tear of his Clothing, Horse Cloth, Snaffle, Bridle, Curry Comb, Brush and Mane Comb and Sponge, Rubbing Cloth, &c."

On April 23rd, 1726, additional pay to three troops of dragoons doing duty in Dublin was ordered. This amounted to £1, 16s. per troop per day, and was provided for as follows:—

	£	s.	d.
To 3 Quartermasters at 4d. each per day	0	1	0
3 Sergeants	0	1	0
6 Corporals	0	2	0
3 Drummers	0	1	0
15 Officers servants	0	5	0
75 Private men	1	5	0
A further additional allowance of 2d. per diem to each of the six corporals	0	1	0
	£1	16	0

From this it would appear that exclusive of the quartermasters and officers servants the strength of the three troops of the 13th Dragoons, if complete when serving in Dublin, stood at 87 non-commission officers, drummers, and men.

There do not appear to be any facts to be recorded for the year 1727.

A paper dated March 29, 1728, which refers to the augmentation of the pay of troops, is too long to quote in full. An extract therefrom which refers to corporals of dragoons is, however, here given:—

For the Corporals of 5 Regiments of Six Troops, each being sixty in number, at 2d. a day Each Corporal } 10s. for 366 days, £183.

This order took effect from 1st March 1728.

The pay for the regiment this year is given as follows:—

IRELAND.

Field and Staff Officers.

	£	s.	d.	£	s.	d.
Colonel as Colonel 12s., and 6 servants 7s.	0	19	0	346	15	0
Lieutenant-Colonel as Lieut.-Col.	0	7	0	127	15	0
Major as Major	0	5	0	91	5	0
Chaplain	0	6	8	121	13	4
Surgeon	0	4	0	73	0	0
	£2	1	8	£760	8	4

One Troop.
- 1 Captain 10s., 2 Servants 2s. 4d. per week.
- 1 Lieutenant 5s., 1 Servant 1s. 2d. per week.
- 1 Cornet 4s., 1 Servant 1s. 2d. per week.
- 1 Quartermaster 3s.
- 1 Sergeant 2s. 6d., 2 Corporals at 1s. 8d. each.
- 1 Drummer 1s. 6d., 1 Hautboy 1s. 6d., 25 Dragoons 1s. 4d. each.

The allowance for servants to the lieutenant-colonel and major is for some unknown reason not stated in this paper.

It concludes in a not very convincing manner:—

In this Establishment, to the pay of Officers is added the pay of their personal servants, Therefore the number of effective men more plainly appears. All Officers are therefore commanded to see that their respective Troops are kept complete, and Muster Masters are enjoined to particularly note this and report delinquents.

In 1730, Lord Harrington vacated the colonelcy of the 13th Dragoons on being appointed Secretary of State. As Colonel William Stanhope he had been employed on political missions of importance. His successor in the colonelcy of the regiment was Colonel Henry Hawley, an officer from the 33rd Foot—the date of his commission being July 7.

Ever since Lieut.-Colonel Clement Nevill had been removed to the command as colonel of another regiment, the lieutenant-colonel of the 13th Dragoons had been an officer by name Peter Ker, and his tenure of that position lasted until 1739: longer by years than any other officer before or since. The major of the regiment was John Carmichael. This officer either died or left the regiment, as he never became lieutenant-colonel of the 13th. In 1739 Major Shuckburgh Whitney was promoted lieutenant-colonel, and remained so until his death at the Battle of Falkirk in 1746. His widow, Mrs Margaret Whitney, was in receipt of a pension of £100 "during pleasure by the establishment" (Irish), at any rate on October 25th, 1760. The only stipulation was that she should reside in Ireland unless leave was given to her to live elsewhere. Colonel Hawley having been promoted to the rank of Brigadier-General in 1735 and Major-General in 1739, was removed to the Royal Dragoons in May of the following year. He was succeeded in the colonelcy of the 13th Dragoons by Colonel Robert Dalway from the 39th

Foot. Colonel Dalway died in November of the same year, and in January 1741 Colonel Humphrey Bland became the colonel of the regiment.

In the following year the 13th was removed from the Irish establishment and ordered to serve in Great Britain.

There are no records to show in what part of England the regiment was quartered, but Cannon informs us that it was in "South Britain."

In April 1743 Colonel (now Brigadier-General) Bland was removed to the command of the 3rd Dragoons, and was succeeded in the colonelcy of the regiment by Lieut.-Colonel James Gardiner from the Inniskillen Dragoons (6th Dragoons). This regiment was at the time serving in Germany. Colonel Gardiner consequently came over to England to assume command of his new regiment.

CHAPTER IV.

Prestonpans, 1745.

A FULL account of the rebellion in 1745 is not within the scope of this book. A brief account of the events which occurred prior to the battle of Prestonpans is, however, needful.

The British general who held the Scottish command at that time was Sir John Cope, K.B.

The first notice Cope had of an intended rebellion was contained in a letter from the Lord President of the Court of Session in Scotland. This had been rumoured in the Highlands, but the rumour was not credited then. Cope acquainted the Marquis of Tweeddale with the report on the same day, representing that well affected clans were without arms, that arms would be doubtless landed by the rebels for the use of the disaffected, that there were no Magazines of arms available for royalists in the country, that the store in Edinburgh Castle would not be enough for the "Low Country." He finishes by suggesting a supply to be lodged in the Highland garrisons in case of need. The Lords Justices, however, came to no decision. On the 9th Cope states that he had ordered the dragoons whose horses were out at grass to be in readiness to take them up and march at very short warning. He had also ordered as many of the "out-parties" as he conveniently could to draw in.

He had ordered General Preston to repair to his command of Edinburgh Castle.

Cope had projected a tour of inspection, but at this juncture considered it more to the service of the country to remain at headquarters.

13TH DRAGOONS (1742).

(*Lent by* Captain H. J. J. STERN.)

He also suggested a recall of officers to their regiments. The Marquis replied, that ordering the dragoons' horses from grass would alarm the country too much.

The troops quartered in Scotland on July 2nd were as follows:—

Gardiner's Dragoons at Stirling, Linlithgow, Musselburgh, Kelso, and Coldstream.

The 13th may have been quartered at these places then, but earlier in the year some portion of the regiment at any rate was at Berwick.

A paper dated from the War Office, 26th March 1745, gives us this information.

Route for a Quarter Master and 28 men of Col. Gardiner's Regiment of Dragoons from Berwick to Ferrybridge.

Belford, Alnwick, Morpeth, Newcastle, Durham, Darlington, Northallerton, Boroughbridge, Tadcaster, Sherborne, Ferrybridge, there to receive 60 Recruit Horses and then to return by the same Route to Berwick.

In the Absence of the Secretary at War,

EDWARD LLOYD.

The details of the movements of the regiment during this campaign are indeed few. For some reason it seems impossible to ascertain the date of the arrival of the regiment at Edinburgh, as will be seen further on.

Hamilton's Dragoons at Haddington, Dunse, and thereabouts, and the horses of both these regiments were at grass; Guise's Regiment of Foot at Aberdeen and the coast-quarters; five companies of Lee's at Dumfries, Stranraer, Glasgow, and Stirling; Murray's in the Highland barracks; Lascelles' at Edinburgh and Leith; two additional companies of the Royal Regiment of Foot, (St Clair's) at Perth; two companies of the Scotch Fusiliers at Glasgow; two companies of Lord Semple's at Cupar in Fife; three companies of Lord John Murray's Highland Regiment at Crieff. Lord Loudon's Regiment was beginning to be raised, and there were also standing garrisons of Invalids in the castles.

The additional companies of the Royal, Scotch Fusiliers, and Semple's, by reason of draughts made on them and [the difficulties of enlisting men, did not average twenty-five men per company, and these were all newly raised men. The three additional companies of Lord John Murray's were "pretty near compleat." Of these one was sent to Inveraray, the other two which Cope took with him on his march northward "mouldered away by desertion."

By a letter written July 30, and received by Cope on August 3, definite news of the landing of the Prince arrived. The details of this landing as regards numbers and supplies of arms, &c., were much exaggerated; still, the landing was a fact.

Cope now complains that should he have occasion "to make use of any Field Train of Artillery, there were no Gunners in Scotland." He also applied for "Credit" (money), adding, "that though I was not alarmed myself nor endeavoured to alarm others too much, yet I neither have, nor shall omit anything in my Power, to put the few Troops I have in readiness to act against anything that may be attempted in Scotland."

He immediately ordered a concentration of troops upon Stirling: ordered the ovens at Leith, Stirling, and Perth to work night and day (Sundays included) to provide biscuit—a supply not otherwise to be obtained. He contracted for horses to drag four field-pieces (1½ pounders) and four cohorns (mortars); also with a butcher to carry cattle along with the army to kill upon the march. Lord Loudon was actively employed in carrying these orders out, doing the duty of adjutant-general, Major Caulfield was the quartermaster-general; Major Mossman, A.D.C. and "Paymaster of Extraordinaries." Mr Griffiths, a master gunner, was conductor of the train, and commissary of the stores and provisions.

We must now trace the movements of Prince Charles. He landed on July 25, near Moidart, on the coast of Inverness, at a point between the Sound of Arisaig and Loch Shiel. His following consisted of but seven in all, of whom one only, besides himself, had seen service. The Jacobites in England had stipulated for at least a force of 6000 men, and a supply of arms in addition sufficient to equip another 4000. But France did not see its way to provide these. The abortive attempt from Dunkirk in 1643 had cooled the ardour of that Government. At or near Moidart the Prince remained until August 19, occupied in negotiations with his Jacobite friends.

On that date his standard was unfurled at Glenfinnan, a spot some few miles only distant from Moidart, and situated in the immediate neighbourhood of the northern end of Loch Shiel.

On this day Cope left Edinburgh. He had purposed starting earlier, but lack of bread (an absolute necessity) caused the delay. "I go to-morrow to Stirling and the next day to Crief," he writes to Tweeddale on August 18. That he appreciated the gravity of the situation is apparent from the following: "As this affair seems very serious, I need not mention the absolute necessity there is for a re-inforcement of Troops from some part or other." This would have released five companies of Lee's Regiment then at Berwick. But England was comparatively destitute of troops, and Cope knew it. His design was to march on the chain of forts between Fort William and Inverness, "unless," he adds, "I hear anything to make me alter my present Design."

On August 13 the Lords Justices had ordered "all officers belonging to His Majesty's Land Forces serving in England or Scotland to immediately repair to their respective posts." At Crieff he found that none of the Duke of Atholl's men nor those of Lord Glenorchy would join the army. Cope's small body of troops had started with an unwieldy baggage train and also with 1000 stand of arms to distribute to loyal Highlanders. Into the excuses offered for a non-supply of men we need not enter.

Cope's measures before leaving Edinburgh were as follows: He sent two companies of Lascelles' Regiment to strengthen the garrison of Edinburgh Castle; Hamilton's Dragoons were quartered in the Canongate to defend Edinburgh; Gardiner's Dragoons were ordered to Stirling, and two additional companies posted in Stirling Castle; two companies were sent to Glasgow, and one to Inveraray. The command in the "South Country" was given to Lieut.-General Guest.

From Stirling Cope marched with five companies of Lee's Foot, all Murray's Regiment, and two companies of Lord John Murray's Highland Regiment (200 men). He halted at Crieff till the night of the 22nd, waiting for 100 horse-loads of bread. Here eight companies of Lascelles' Regiment joined. The Duke of Atholl's contribution to the army, from which much had been expected, numbered about fifteen men, and after marching a day or two these went home. The difficulties on the march were very great. Horses could hardly be obtained, and to keep them when obtained was almost impossible. They had to be grazed, and there were no enclosed fields. Bread had to be left by the roadside.

On August 23 Cope encamped at Tay Bridge, and was there joined by forty or fifty of Lord Loudon's Regiment. On the 24th he was at Trinisuir, where 200 horses "deserted" in the night.

The next day the force reached Dalnacardoch, and on the 26th arrived at Dalwhinnie. Here Lord Glenorchy proposed that Cope should send back 300 stand of arms, "and he would endeavour to get some of his people to take them." Cope declined. He was urged by Lord Glenorchy to also supply officers — to delay his march forty-eight hours, but Sir John was not to be delayed. His orders were to march north and specially to march on Fort Augustus.

Meanwhile Prince Charles had not been idle. On August 26th he had already taken possession of the passes about Snugborough, a place on the north side of the Corriarrich, over which the direct road to Fort Augustus lay. A cleverly planned ambuscade had been prepared, and there is not a doubt that had Cope attempted to force the pass with his little army, not a man would have escaped death, wounds, or capture. The road here makes no less than nineteen zigzags up the mountain-side, and each is commanded by those above it. The intention was to allow Cope to enter this road, and then having blocked the egress in the rear to annihilate his force. To march thus on Fort Augustus was impossible. Already on August 16 the enemy had captured two companies of the Royals, having killed a dozen of the men. Cope therefore turned aside at Dalwhinnie and directed his march on Inverness. It was either that or a retreat on Stirling. The exact date when Gardiner's Dragoons were moved from Stirling to Edinburgh is unknown. Cope reached Ruthven (not Ruthin as one authority states) on August 27 and passed the Spey that night. He took from the post there a company of Guise's Regiment, and left only a sergeant and twelve men with some invalids in the barrack. The barrack, it may be added, was built to contain but thirty men.

How weak were the garrisons in the Highlands may be gauged from the fact that that of Fort William, which was situated but a few miles from the place where Prince Charles landed on August 13th, amounted to only 130 private men. Cope had, however, done all that he could to strengthen it, and also the other garrisons along the chain of forts. He sent three companies of Guise's Regiment thither. Three he designed for Fort Augustus, two for Inverness, one to Bernera, and an officer and eighteen men to the Isle of Mull. In a letter to Lord Tweeddale he gives details of the whole of his arrangements for the defence of Scotland. To return to Dalwhinnie, when the march of the army was deflected to Inverness, it was found that there was only store of bread for three days—all the rest had either been lost or spoiled.

Cope reached Inverness on August 28. Here he had a reinforcement of 200 men of the Monroes under the command of Captain George Monroe of Calcairn, who agreed to march for fourteen days on the same allowance as they had had in 1719. Owing to their harvest they refused to engage for a longer time.

At Inverness Cope found three companies of Lord Loudon's Regiment, and a fourth company joined him at Aberdeen.

To Aberdeen Cope marched, having ordered transports to meet him there, it having been decided by a Council of War (with one dissentient only) that such a course was "the most advisable Method to be followed." The march from Inverness began on September 4. The army went by the coast road, and a ship was hired "to coast along with provisions under convoy of *The Happy Janet*." At Inverness Major M'Kenzie's company of Lord Loudon's Regiment and M'Intosh's company of Lord John Murray's were left "to compleat them," but Cope took with him another company of Guise's Regiment and two field-pieces and two cohorns. All applications for loyal Highlanders, save the 200 Monroes, were refused, evaded, or disregarded.

The army reached Aberdeen on September 11th. On September 15 it embarked for Leith. The vessels were off the Island of May on the afternoon of the next day, but the wind was light and the fleet made for Dunbar as the nearest place to Edinburgh on the south side which could be reached.

On the 17th a messenger sent in a boat from Dunbar came on board and reported that the city of Edinburgh was given up to the rebels. Later news which reached Cope on landing was that 500 rebels had marched into the city by the Netherbow Gate at 5 A.M. without opposition, and that their main body, having gone round the city to the south, had established the Prince in Holyrood House, encamping themselves in the King's Park.

Cope's troops landed on September 17, and most of the artillery was got on shore the same day.

Brigadier Fowke then joined with Gardiner's and Hamilton's Dragoons. What we do not know is how and when Colonel Gardiner's Dragoons marched from Stirling and arrived in Edinburgh.

It will be remembered that Cope had asked for a reinforcement to Leith to release the troops there. The Dutch Regiment was so ordered to proceed thither, but, owing to contrary winds, did not reach the place. They were driven in to Burlington Bay on September 20.

It is now needful to narrate what occurred to the dragoons posted in Edinburgh, and to give chapter and verse as to their movements between September 15, when Brigadier Fowke reached Edinburgh, and September 17, when that officer and his brigade joined Sir John Cope at Dunbar. As this movement of the Dragoons has been handed down to posterity as "the Canter of Colt-Bridge," it will be well to state what did occur, and the facts here given are based on the sworn testimony of Brigadier Fowke and others,—testimony, it may be well to add, which no single individual at the public inquiry could be found to shake: though Colonel Whiteford did suggest that their retreat had been "precipitate."

On September 15, Fowke, with Lieut.-General Guest, the Lord Justice-Clerk, the Lord Provost, and others, discussed the defence of the city.

Fowke proposed to bring "some part or the whole of the dragoons" into the city to defend it. To this an objection was raised, that it would render "useless so many of His Majesty's Forces," as there were only two days' provisions. After some discussion it was agreed that the dragoons should be "continued upon their Posts at the West-Port on the field near the Colt-Bridge." Early on Monday, September 16, Fowke went to the West Port with Lord Home, Lord Napier, the Hon. Charles Hope, and others, where "on reviewing the Dragoons, I found many of the horses' backs not fit to receive the riders, many of the Men's and some of the Officers' legs so swell'd that they could not wear Boots." All were suffering from want of sleep.

Colonel Gardiner, on the day before his death, made this statement as well as others. This was the first time "I had ever seen the two Dragoon Regiments." On the same day Colonel Gardiner informed the Brigadier "that from the condition the men and horses were in, and in our situation, it would be extreamly right not to wait for Night Work; and that it was absolutely necessary, before it became dark, to retire towards Leith, that we might gain a Passage through, and by the different Stone Walls, during the Daylight." All the field officers concurred in this. It was hoped that at Leith ground would be found to take up post and means to refresh both men and horses. "As this opinion was agreeable to the orders I had received that morning from General Guest, in a message sent by the Major of Brigade, I had the less Difficulty of putting it in Execution. And the Quarter-masters were accordingly sent off to take up the ground, provide necessaries, and other conveniences, both for Men and Horses."

"The advanced guard of an officer and thirty men had my repeated orders to retire slowly and without confusion upon the approach of the rebels moving in a whole body." This movement of the enemy took place at 4 P.M. Fowke marched slowly towards Leith with Colonel Gardiner and the dragoons, when he ordered the Brigade Major to see that the Rear Squadron moved off in order and without hurry, as there were several defiles and stone walls.

On the march the quartermasters returned and informed Colonel Gardiner that they had not been able to find wherewithal at Leith to provide both for men and horses. It was proposed by Colonel Gardiner to continue the march to Musselburgh, and this was done.

At Musselburgh, news arrived that Sir John Cope was off Dunbar. Brigadier Fowke halted the dragoons and sent (with the assistance of the Leith authorities) a message to the Lord Provost, offering to march back into the city with the whole or part of the dragoons. This offer was not accepted, or, at any rate, no reply was received. The march was continued with the design to "lie on our Arms all Night, upon a Piece of Ground Colonel Gardiner would order to be marked out for us near his own House." Colonel Gardiner, it may be remarked, was seriously ill. But he was unlikely to suggest an unsuitable piece of ground seeing that it was close to his own home. A halt was made then for some time, and the dragoons then proceeded to Dunbar *via* North Berwick. At Dunbar they arrived about 11 A.M. on September 17. Now the distance between Edinburgh and Dunbar is about thirty miles and the march occupied nineteen hours, a by no means rapid rate of progression.

To return to Sir John Cope. Sir John marched from Dunbar on the 20th of September. The Quartermaster-General, the Earls of Loudon and Home, and Colonel Whiteford were sent forward to reconnoitre. When they came near Musselburgh the rebels were descried in full march towards the royal army. The Earl of Loudon returned to Sir John to report the fact. Sir John Cope's advanced guard by that time had reached the east end of the plain which lies between Seaton and Preston. Sir John had marched *via* Haddington, avoiding the direct Edinburgh road because of the defiles and enclosures ahead which would have prevented his cavalry from acting. The ground the army was entering, as Sir John says, "being very proper for us, I thought it right to take it." The field was about a mile in length and three-quarters of a mile broad. Bounded on the east by Seaton, on the west by Preston, and on the north by the sea, the village of Tranent lies on the south.

The park walls of Preston stood at the west end, and thence eastward to Seaton was a morass, with a deep ditch between it and the plain, through which there were two very narrow cart-ways.

South of the Preston park walls was a defile leading to Colonel Gardiner's house, from whence there is a road leading to the village of Preston. On the north of the park walls is another defile, also leading to the village, and passing by the house of Mr Erskine of Grange. Beyond this was an open field, lying north and west of it, which was bounded on the north by the village of Prestonpans on the sea shore. Cockenzie or Cockenny House is near the shore, and midway on the north side of the battlefield.

General Cope's original disposition of his force was thus—

Left.	Centre.	Right.
2 squadrons of dragoons (Hamilton's).	R. Lee's Foot (5 companies). C. Lascelles' Foot (8 companies). Guise's Foot (2 companies). L. Murray's Foot (the Regiment).	2 squadrons of dragoons (Gardiner's).

RESERVES.

Left.	Centre.	Right.
1 squadron of Hamilton's dragoons.	Highlanders and Volunteers.	1 squadron of Gardiner's Dragoons.

The artillery was provided for thus—

- 2 pieces between Hamilton's Dragoons and Murray's Foot.
- 2 pieces between Murray's Foot and Lascelles' Foot.
- 2 pieces and cohorns between Lee's Foot and Gardiner's Dragoons.

It was, however, found that there were no gunners, and consequently all the guns and cohorns were massed on the left of the centre. The baggage was placed in the rear.

The ground selected by Sir John was so chosen to give him the command of the outlets from the two defiles, and only through those defiles could he be attacked.

The rebels having approached to about the distance of half a mile, turned off to the right and took ground on the ridge of Fawside Hill, advancing thence to Tranent. "Here I could not attack them," said Cope, "as the ground is so much broken by hollow roads, coalpits and inclosures, that horse cannot act there."

Sir John then changed his position: his right rested on the walls of Preston Park—his left on Seaton or towards Seaton. On his front was "the ditch of the morass." The baggage was moved towards Cockenzie, the artillery remaining on the left. During the afternoon the rebels sent some men down a hollow on the north-west side of Tranent and took possession of the churchyard. Cope advanced two "gallopers" (field-guns), opened fire and dislodged them, killing a few.

An hour before sunset the rebels marched down Fawside Hill and appeared to threaten Cope's right flank, by the defile north of the park walls and the ground north of it. Cope sent his baggage east of Cockenzie and drew up his line obliquely fronting south-west. His right was towards Cockenzie, his left towards the defile leading to Colonel Gardiner's house. This would have compelled the enemy to make a frontal attack. Cope's artillery remained on his left.

The rebels abandoned their design and withdrew the detachment to its original position on the hill.

It was now getting dark. Cope took up his post for the night, forming his line due east and west. His troops lay upon their arms all night, fronting the ditch of the morass with Preston Park walls on the extreme right. "Out-guards" were posted by Major Talbot, who reported to Sir John frequently during the night. Two platoons were posted on the right, in the road that leads to Colonel Gardiner's house. The quarter-guards lay considerably advanced; and the pickets were ordered to support them. On the right, near the defile which lies north of the Park of Preston, "a grand guard of 100 dragoons with a captain and two subalterns" was posted. Another was posted on the left, from which the cornet was to advance with 30 dragoons near to Seaton, the lieutenant with the same number to support him was posted on the side of the morass, and the captain and quartermaster at the entry of one of the roads leading into the morass with 40 dragoons to support him.

These parties patrolled all night across the morass and near to the rebels, who lay on the ground south of the road up Fawside Hill to Tranent.

The baggage and the military chest was ordered to the rear, and the Highlanders were posted on it.

The squadron of Gardiner's Dragoons from the second line was posted near Prestonpans and the corresponding squadron of Hamilton's placed near the point of the plain which ends between Seaton and the sea. To prevent surprise in this direction advanced parties were posted before them.

So matters rested till 3 A.M., the night having been quiet, with the exception of dogs barking loudly between 9 and 10.30 P.M. in Tranent.

At 3 A.M. the patrols reported that the rebels were moving towards the east. At 4 A.M. news arrived that they were moving northward towards Seaton down by the east end of the plain to attack the left flank. Sir John then changed his positon and fronted eastwards. His

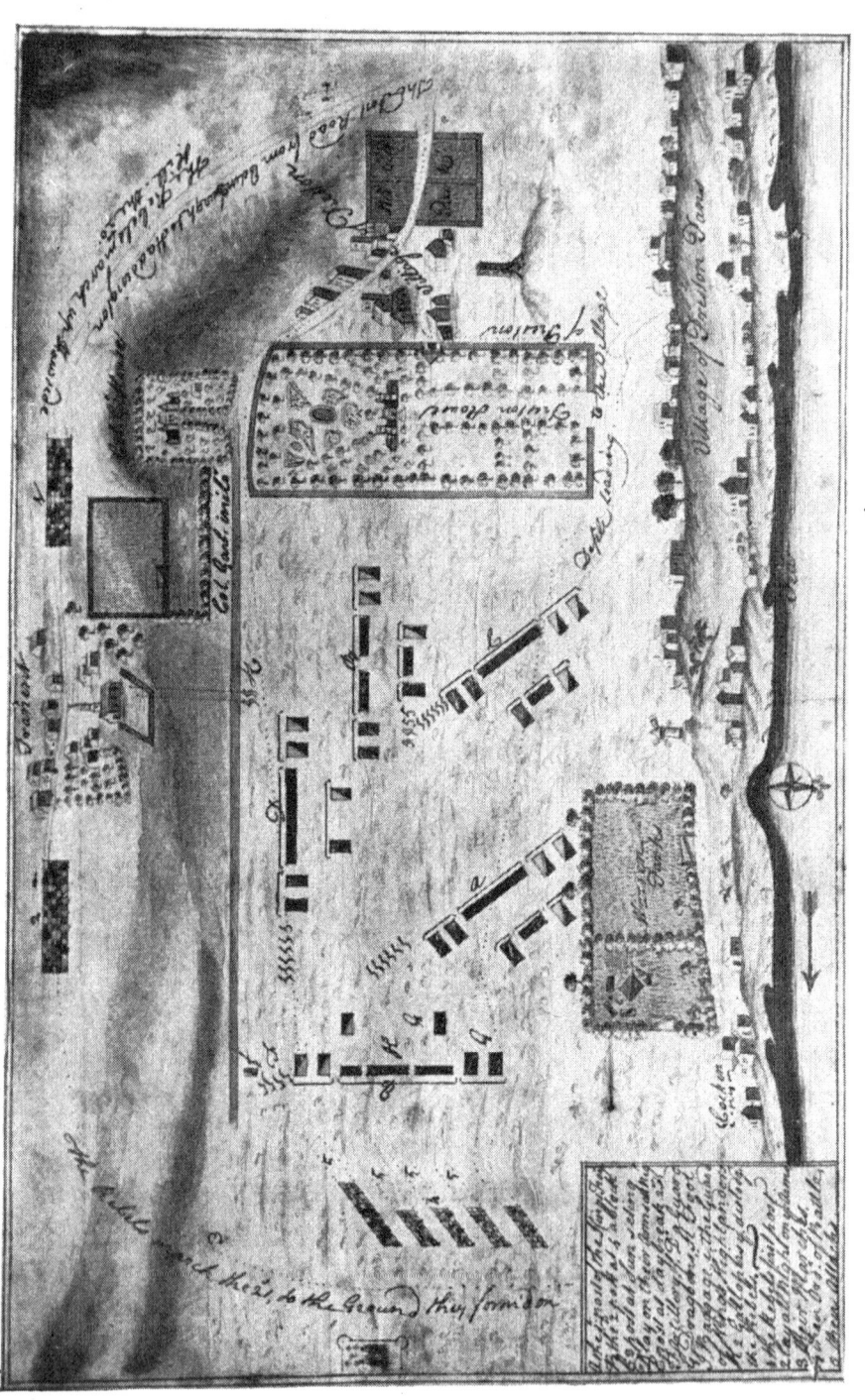

PLAN OF THE BATTLE OF PRESTONPANS.

DRAWN BY A STAFF OFFICER WHO WAS PRESENT.

(By permission of the Secretary, Royal United Service Institution.)

formation was the same as the night before, save that the artillery was on his right, dressed straight with the line. An artillery guard of 100 foot on the right of it. The "out-guard" of the foot being 300, were formed on the right of Lee's five companies. But as there was not enough ground left for Colonel Gardiner's squadron they were formed in the rear of the artillery guard, a few paces behind, ready to sustain it.

Cope's lack of artillerymen has been mentioned. He had applied for them, had been promised them, nay, had even been told they were on their way, but none had arrived. The few cannon-shots which were fired against the rebels were fired by Lieut.-Colonel Whiteford's own hand; and the cohorns, none of whose shells would burst, were fired by Mr Griffiths, an old master gunner. Colonel Whiteford got off five guns but could not fire the sixth, as the men had bolted with the priming horns. This explains why, owing to the absence of gunners, the position of the artillery was changed.

Sir John Cope personally inspected his troops to see that his orders had been carried out. The rebel army advanced in two lines, and it was observed that it greatly outflanked the royalist left.

Major Mossman was sent to Colonel Whiteford for "cannon immediately to annoy them," but the horses were gone off and the guns could not be moved.

Sir John then moved down the line to the right encouraging the men. His reason for shifting from the left to the right was that he perceived the rebels were from the left advancing obliquely with great speed to attack the right.

From line formation they broke into five bodies, of which the one most to the left was the largest, and appeared to be "20 in Front and 30 in Depth." Colonel Whiteford and Mr Griffiths fired as many rounds as they could (eleven in all), when the large body of rebels rushed at the guns. The remaining rebels were firing in an irregular manner as they advanced. Lieut.-Colonel Whitney of Gardiner's Dragoons was then ordered "to march his squadron out of the line, in order to attack them in flank before they reached the guns." He marched out and wheeled his squadron and got within pistol-shot of the rebel flank when the Highlanders opened fire. The dragoons "stopt and could not be got to go farther." The rear rank began to waver and then to run, and the rest followed. Colonel Gardiner's squadron was then ordered to charge the body of rebels that had overrun the guns.

The artillery guard of foot was by this time in confusion, but the rebels were so also, and it was an opportunity in which a cavalry charge would have been most effective. But unfortunately with this squadron the behaviour of the men was the same. A few shot from the enemy, their horses were reined back, and, after a short hesitation—flight. Of the behaviour of the dragoons on the left or of the two squadrons held in reserve there is no more pleasant story to tell. For a few minutes indeed they all tarried at the walls of Mr Erskine's grounds in the rear. Here strenuous efforts were made to rally them, but in vain. By this time the foot had been broken and were also in full flight.

Dawn came on gradually: means of reaching the defile became apparent to the panic-stricken men, and down it the dragoons hurried. Brigadier Fowke attempted to head off the fugitives, cutting their line of flight by taking the south defile. Lord Loudon and Lord Home were both on the same errand. Lord Home, pistol in hand, got to the head of the dragoons at the west end of the village. Lord Loudon turned some of them into a field near the road leading to the village but south of it.

A Mr Drummond, Majors Mossman and Singleton, Captain Wemyss, Captain Forbes, and other officers of the regiments managed to collect some 450 dragoons there, and got them into some kind of formation—one squadron and two smaller bodies. A body of rebels hove in sight, and seeing the dragoons drawn up halted. It was proposed to attack them with the squadron that was formed, but the men could not be brought to charge.

Their officers then removed them farther from the field, or rather attempted to. As soon as the march began, the men began to gallop off. It was found that only "by keeping upon their Head" was it possible to get them to make the semblance of a decent retreat. After consultation with the officers Brigadier Fowke ordered a march on Berwick *viâ* the Channelkirk Road. The dispirited troops then turned south, halted at Lauder to refresh. Thence, says Fowke, "I sent such an account of this unhappy Affair to the Marquis of Tweedale, as I could then give."

The dragoons quartered that night at Coldstream and Cornwall,

JAMES GARDINER
COLONEL 13TH DRAGOONS,
1743 to 1745
SLAIN AT THE BATTLE OF
PRESTON-PANS
Sept. 21st 1745.

and reached Berwick the next day. The two regiments of dragoons totalled 600 when the battle began: of these 450 reached Berwick. Colonel Gardiner, of whose personal bravery all accounts agree, was wounded in the leg at the beginning of the engagement; later, when his squadron refused to charge, he received several other wounds, one of them proving fatal. Removed not to his own house, but to the manse at Tranent, he died a few hours later. Lieut.-Colonel Whitney was also wounded while attempting with Colonel Gardiner to restore the battle. Mention has been made of a sergeant and twelve men who were posted in the barracks at Ruthven. Attacked by a large

Monument to Colonel James Gardiner erected on the spot upon which he received his mortal wound.

body of the enemy they repulsed them with loss. A letter of the sergeant, whose name was Molloy, is extant, in which he reports to Sir John Cope the details of his brilliant little defence. It is most unfortunate that the complete list of the officers in Cope's army who were present at Prestonpans is not in existence; at any rate, from the printed report of the Court-Martial on Sir John Cope, Colonel Lascelles, and Brigadier Fowke, it is lacking. The original was sent to the War Office, and delivered afterwards to the Duke of Cumberland and by him lost.

The complete list of the officers of the 13th Dragoons in the year 1745, with the dates of their rank in the regiment, is as follows:—

13TH DRAGOONS.

Colonel James Gardiner	April 19, 1743.
Lieut.-Colonel Shuckburgh Whitney	June 20, 1739.
Major Lodowick Peterson	Feb. 18, 174$\frac{0}{1}$.
Captain John West	Sept. 1, 1739.
,, Richard Downes	June 20, 1739.
,, John Toovey	Feb. 18, 174$\frac{0}{1}$.
Captain-Lieutenant Andrew Ross	Feb. 18, 174$\frac{0}{1}$.
Lieutenant Charles West	June 20, 1739.
,, William Crofton	July 4, 1723.
,, Francis Turner	Sept. 1, 1739.
,, Edward Vizey	Feb. 18, 174$\frac{0}{1}$.
Cornet John French	Aug. 1, 1741.
,, John Karr (Adjutant)	Feb. 11, 174$\frac{4}{5}$.
,, Thomas Crow	Sept. 1, 1739.
,, John Bland	Feb. 18, 174$\frac{0}{1}$.
,, John Wills	July 1, 1734.
,, Philip Dalzell	June 20, 1739.
,, John Alcock	Feb. 16, 174$\frac{0}{1}$.

Present at the battle was an Irish gentleman of the name of Sadleir, and there is a family tradition that he held a commission in the 13th Dragoons. This, however, does not appear to be the case, though there were officers of that name at other periods. He was the son of Charles Sadleir of Castletown, County Tipperary, who died in 1729 leaving a widow. Seven years later Mrs Sadleir married Cornet Thomas Crow, who ultimately (February 6, 1764) became the lieutenant-colonel of the regiment, from which he retired in the same year.

The circumstances of his marriage with Mrs Sadleir are romantic, and somewhat typical of the customs of those days.

It appears that Mrs Sadleir, having been grossly insulted by a Mr Charles Minchin of Armagh, on her return home wrote him a challenge to a duel, fixing the time and place for a day in the ensuing week. Cornet Crow, who was her first cousin, happened to be staying in the house, and was present in the room when the challenge was written by the high-spirited young lady. Suspecting that something more than ordinary must have happened to so visibly disconcert Mrs

Sadleir, he, by bribing the messenger, succeeded in discovering the source of the trouble. Substituting a challenge in his own name for that sent by Mrs Sadleir he despatched it, and fixed a slightly earlier hour at the same place.

On the arrival of the lady, who drove up in her chariot, and furnished with a pair of rapiers, she found that Cornet Crow had just killed his man. The identical pair of rapiers carried to the ground by Mrs Sadleir were in existence not so many years ago. Shortly after, the marriage between the widow and Cornet Crow took place. Probably it was through the influence of Cornet Crow that his stepson was later put into the 13th Dragoons.

The story of the Sadleir who was at Prestonpans, according to the traditions handed down to his descendants, is as follows:—

At this luckless battle he was taken prisoner by the rebels, who offered him a command if he would join them. This offer he naturally and rightly refused. Apparently the rebels bore their prisoner no malice, nor indeed beyond stripping him of what money and valuables he had on his person did they further molest him. Practically they turned him loose, and while wandering about the young man was taken pity on by a Miss Mary Blair, the daughter of an "upholder" in the neighbourhood of the battlefield. Pity is, they say, akin to love, and Sadleir and Mary Blair contracted a Scottish marriage. The bride, however, lived only a short time, and the widower soon after his return to Ireland married as second wife on 1st February 1750, Abigail, daughter of the Rev. Joseph Green of Ballycommon, King's County. Sadleir was fond of hunting, and a sportsman generally. He was also by no means careful in money matters, and the family estates in consequence suffered very severely. He was accidentally drowned in the lake at Charleville Forest, King's County, October 20, 1756. By his first wife he left an only surviving son Charles, who after graduating M.A. at Glasgow University, obtained a cornet's commission in his father's old regiment, the 13th Dragoons, in 1769, being promoted lieutenant in 1774. He died unmarried in 1787.

The above interesting particulars have been kindly furnished to the writer by Thomas U. Sadleir, Esq., of Dublin, a member of the same family.

The Lieutenant "Grafton" mentioned in Cannon as wounded

should be Crofton. Of the quartermasters, one, by name West, rallied some fifteen dragoons and endeavoured to support Colonel Gardiner in the charge which he made, but the party was overpowered and taken prisoners.

As a matter of fact, the only men who charged, and charged home when ordered to do so, were a small party of eleven under the command of Cornet John Karr (Adjutant). This little band behaved with great gallantry.

The name of another quartermaster—Burroughs—occurs as being wounded, as also does that of Lieutenant Crofton. It is noteworthy that despite the savage slaughter of the rebel onset the wounded were treated with great humanity. Such officers as were taken prisoners were released on parole. The private men were escorted to Edinburgh. As to the causes of this most unfortunate affair they are hardly far to seek. From 1719 to 1742 the 13th Dragoons had been quartered in Ireland. During the whole or nearly the whole of that period it had been split up into detachments. A squadron here, a troop or two there, and half-troops elsewhere. Seldom was the entire regiment collected together. Since Major-General Henry Hawley, their colonel from 1730 to 1740, the regiment had had no less than three colonels,—Dalway for a period of seven months, Bland from 1741 to 1743, and Gardiner from 1744. Colonel Gardiner is stated by Cannon to have been "a most zealous and efficient officer," who "bestowed much care" on the discipline and equipment of the regiment and the condition of the horses. Elsewhere we read that he was at the time of the rebellion most seriously ill, and in fact, as he himself stated at Edinburgh, "not expecting to live long." That he was personally brave is acknowledged by all. It is also stated that he was a man of very strong religious convictions, convictions which he was in the habit of impressing both on his officers and men. Still, certain it is, that the regiment as far as the horses are concerned was in a most unsatisfactory state and the health of the men not in general as it should have been. Whether or no the horses had been broken to fire is not known, but the probabilities are that such training was lacking. Gardiner's statements to Brigadier Fowke all point to a doubt in the colonel's mind as to the regiment being in a well-trained and disciplined condition—yet it was his duty to see that it was both well-trained and disciplined. Doubtless his ill-health had much to do with the neglect of what should have been his chief care. The results we know; and they were most unfortunate.

Prestonpans as a battle is commonly supposed to have been a case in which the royal army was surprised. This is an error. Cope himself in a letter extant distinctly states that it was nothing of the kind. But the method of attack adopted by the rebels was quite unusual in those days. An advance in two lines, which appeared to threaten the royalist left, followed by an oblique attack on the extreme right in five columns, was a method certainly novel; Cope had, as far as the lack of gunners permitted him to do so, drawn up his slender force according to the rules then in vogue. He had taken every precaution possible to guard against surprise, as we have seen, and under ordinary circumstances could reasonably expect to give a good account of the enemy. But the circumstances were not ordinary. The attack was quite unlike the methods of war in which the troops had been presumably exercised, and finally the dragoons, which ought to have constituted his strength, owing to the condition of their horses proved his undoing. The disparity in numbers, though of course a factor in the defeat, had not, it is to be imagined, quite as great importance as has hitherto been ascribed to it.

CHAPTER V.

Falkirk Muir, January 17, 1746.

AFTER the defeat at Prestonpans the 13th Dragoons arrived at Berwick, and were sent thence to join the troops under the aged Field-Marshal Wade, who then lay at Newcastle. In succession to the late Colonel Gardiner, the appointment of Colonel Francis Ligonier was gazetted on October 1, 1745. Field-Marshal Wade was now removed from his command owing to the state of his health. The Duke of Cumberland had hurried south to repel a threatened French invasion.

To the Scottish command succeeded Lieut.-General Henry Hawley. On December 6 the rebel retreat from Derby began. On January 3 the Prince marched from Glasgow towards Stirling. At Stirling he secured a reinforcement of French who had landed at Montrose and also of sundry Highlanders.

His force now amounted to 9000 men, and a siege of Stirling was decided upon. It may be remarked that a battery of heavy guns which accompanied the French rendered this feasible. Lieut.-General Hawley was meanwhile occupied in endeavouring to get his force in condition to take the field. He had three regiments of dragoons, some artillery, and twelve battalions of foot. After most strenuous efforts Hawley was able to march with a view to the relief of Stirling Castle. The Prince, aware of this march, left a small force to maintain the blockade of Stirling Castle, and advanced to meet him. The royal army had arrived near Falkirk, where an encampment was formed. After some preliminary manœuvring on the Stirling side of Falkirk, the Prince marched round to the opposite side of the royal camp and then advanced upon it. Not far from Falkirk is a rough ridge of high ground, and on this the rebel army formed. The precise name of this ridge is Falkirk Muir. In the royal camp the alarm was quickly raised. General Hawley, who was at the time dining with Lady Kilmarnock at Callendar House, near the camp, was hastily fetched, and is reported to have galloped into camp minus his hat. The troops were under arms and were drawn up thus:—

On the extreme left Ligonier's Dragoons (13th), Hamilton's Dragoons on the right, and Cobham's in the centre: all under the command of Ligonier. The infantry was drawn up in two lines, and the above-named cavalry regiments were in advance on the left of the first line. Hawley ordered the dragoons to attack, and this they did in the face of a blinding storm of rain and wind. The charge was delivered, and it is said that the first line of the rebel army was pierced. But on the cavalry reaching the second line of the enemy it was found that it could not be forced. The dragoons fell into confusion and presently retreated. Lieut.-Colonel Whitney of the 13th, who it will be remembered was wounded at Prestonpans, was killed. Hawley now ordered up his infantry, who charged up the hill with bayonets fixed. They were met by the rebels, who advanced. In the royalists' faces the wind and rain still beat fiercely; it is said that the priming of the muskets was drenched and that few went off. The foot wavered, and then, save two regiments, retreated. In their flight many were cut down by the victorious rebels. The two regiments that stood their ground firmly escaped with but little loss. Later, some of the fugitives rallied and retreated in an orderly way. On the whole the casualties were not very numerous, amounting to less than 300. The fate of Colonel Francis Ligonier was peculiarly sad. He had been specially chosen to command the regiment,—the remark of the king on the occasion of his selection being well known. About three days before the battle he was attacked by pleurisy, and having been bled and blistered was confined to his bed.

Ill as he was he rose on the 17th, to command his brigade of cavalry, and led the charge with great spirit. To his exertions after the retreat of the dragoons, in rallying them, and supporting the two regiments of foot that stood their ground, much was due when a general withdrawal to Linlithgow during the night was in progress. But Ligonier's exertions cost him his life; the soaking rain and the winter cold did its work on the frame of a man already ill enough. He died on January 25.

From Linlithgow the 13th was moved to Edinburgh. When the Duke of Cumberland arrived from London and took command of the army, an advance was made against the Jacobite force.

The 13th was, however, left behind at Edinburgh and employed in patrolling the roads leading westwards to intercept any messages passing from English Jacobites to those in Scotland.

On February 17th Lieut.-Colonel Philip Naizon, from the 1st Royal Dragoons, was appointed Colonel of the 13th, in succession to the late Colonel Francis Ligonier. Apparently the lieutenant-colonelcy vacant by the death at Falkirk of Lieut.-Colonel Whitney was not for the time filled up; and it is not until September 19, 1747, that we find a new lieutenant-colonel appointed. His name was John Toovey, and he remained with the regiment till removed to the 1st Royal Dragoons in 1754.

The battle of Culloden was fought and won on April 16, 1746; and for a time rebel hunting, prisoner guarding, and captive escorting were the main occupations of the troops, both horse and foot.

It cannot be ascertained where the regiment was posted during the remainder of its stay in England. In 1748, owing to the Peace of Aix-la-Chapelle, a large number of troops returned to England. Almost directly this had an effect on the Irish establishment, and several changes took place, among them being the return of the 13th to Ireland.

One of the six guns now at Southwold-on-Sea, Suffolk, which were captured by the rebels at Prestonpans, recaptured at Culloden, and presented to the town by the Duke of Cumberland.

CHAPTER VI.

Ireland, 1748-1768.

UNDER date December 25, 1748, we read that Colonel Naizon's Dragoons were placed on the Irish establishment and reduced. The regiment embarked for Ireland in due course, but was prevented from landing for some time owing to contrary winds. Consequently certain troops that were to be disbanded were retained for a time. There is a long paper extant in which the arrangements for the payment of these "shortly-to-be-disbanded troops" are given in detail.

By a chance we have very full information as to the localities in which the regiment was quartered during the next four years, and not only this, but for that period a complete seniority list of the officers by troops; the place at which each troop happened to be quartered being added.

Colonel Philip Naizon Captain-Lieutenant Thomas Smith 3rd Cornet John Karr Quartermaster John King	Hamilton's Bawn.
Lieut.-Colonel John Toovey 5th Lieutenant Ambrose Upton 6th Cornet Richard Gorge Quartermaster Paul Mangin	Killough.
Major Henry Richardson 2nd Lieutenant Philip Delisle 2nd Cornet Ambrose Borrowes Quartermaster Lambert Short	Carrickfergus.

1st Captain William Croffton .
1st Lieutenant George Cumming .
4th Cornet John West .
Quartermaster William Croffton .
} Dawson's Bridge.

2nd Captain Thomas Crow .
4th Lieutenant William Tighe .
5th Cornet Michael Bruce .
Quartermaster John Thomas .
} Hamilton's Bawn.

3rd Captain James Blaquière .
3rd Lieutenant John Alcock .
1st Cornet John Trench .
Quartermaster Henry Young .
} Downpatrick.

The Chaplain was the Rev. Charles Dunster; the Surgeon, Alexander Cuningham; and the Agent, Anthony La Daveze.

For the year 1750 there is similar information. Three of the troops were stationed at Tullamore: those of Colonel Naizon, Major Richardson, and Captain Thomas Crow.

The other three troops were stationed at Phillipstown.

In Colonel Naizon's troop, Cornet King was now second in seniority as cornet.

In Lieut.-Colonel Toovey's troop, Lieutenant Upton now stood third, and Cornet Gorge, fifth.

In Major Richardson's troop the late senior cornet, John Trench, had become fourth in the list of lieutenants, and Cornet Ambrose Borrowes was senior cornet.

In Captain Croffton's troop, a new lieutenant appears, by name Isaac Espinasse, and Cornet John West is now third cornet.

In Captain Crow's troop, Lieutenant Tighe, formerly fourth in seniority, is now second, and Cornet Bruce is now fifth.

In Captain Blaquière's troop, Lieutenant Alcock is now senior lieutenant, and a new cornet has joined, by name, John La Daveze—he was the son of the Agent.

There is a new captain-lieutenant in the person of Philip Delisle, formerly lieutenant in the major's troop.

The name of Dunster now vanishes, the new chaplain being the Rev. Peter Pelissier. With regard to this gentleman, during his long years of office, as will be seen later, he was usually on leave. At last this became so glaring that he was forced to appoint a deputy.

For 1751 the regiment was thus distributed:—

Owing to the death of Colonel Naizon in January a new colonel was appointed in the person of Major-General Sir Charles Armand Powlett, K.B., who came to the regiment from the 9th Foot. Colonel Sir C. Powlett's troop was quartered at Navan; Lieut.-Colonel Toovey's and Major Richardson's at Belturbet; Captain Croffton's at Ballyshannon, as also was the troop of Captain Crow. Lastly, the troop of Captain Blaquière was also at Belturbet. The officers remain the same, except that Cornet Michael Bruce having left the regiment a new cornet, by name Sylvester Devenish, appears in Captain Crow's troop. A new agent to the regiment has also been appointed, by name William Chaigneau. The new colonel dying in November 1757, his successor was appointed from the 34th Regiment of Foot, in the person of Colonel The Hon. Henry Seymour Conway. For this year the regiment was all quartered at one place, Sligo. Among the officers, beyond the fact that there was a new colonel, there were no changes except that Surgeon Alex. Cuningham was succeeded by Surgeon Owen Lindsay, and in the list appears the name of an Adjutant (Francis Campbell). The entire strength of the regiment is also given as 285 (officers included).

Information with regard to the years 1753 and 1754 is lacking, except that Lieut.-General Conway was removed to the 4th Irish Horse (now 7th Dragoon Guards), and Colonel John Mostyn was appointed to the 13th Dragoons.

In 1755 three troops were stationed at Gort, two at Doneraile, and one at Nenagh.

The list of officers for the year 1756 is the same as that for 1755, but the places where the various troops were quartered is not given.

In the year 1757 Colonel Mostyn was promoted to the rank of Major-General. The officers of each troop and the places where quartered for this year are as follows:—

Colonel John Mostyn, Captain-Lieutenant William Tighe, 3rd Cornet Owen Lindsay, and Quartermaster James Seaton, at Phillipstown; Lieut.-Colonel James Johnston, 1st Lieutenant Ambrose

Upton, 6th Cornet John Nattles, and Quartermaster John King, at Tullamore; Major John Balaguire, 2nd Lieutenant John Trench, 2nd Cornet Francis Campbell, and Quartermaster William Karr, at the same place; 1st Captain Thomas Crow, 4th Lieutenant John La Daveze, 4th Cornet John Kelly, and Quartermaster John Thomas, at the same place; 2nd Captain James Blaquière, 5th Lieutenant Sylvester Devenish, 5th Cornet Charles Eustace, and Quartermaster Henry Yonge, at Phillipstown; 3rd Captain John Alcock, 3rd Lieutenant John Karr, 1st Cornet John West, and Quartermaster William Croft, at Phillipstown; the chaplain was the Rev. Peter Pelissier; the Surgeon Owen Lindsay, and the Adjutant Francis Campbell.

For 1758, 1759, and 1760 the places where the regiment was quartered cannot be ascertained.

In 1758 Major-General Mostyn was removed to the 5th Royal Irish Dragoons, and was succeeded in the colonelcy of the 13th by Colonel Archibald Douglas, who was promoted to the rank of Major-General in 1759 and to that of Lieutenant-General in 1761. Colonel Douglas was Aide-de-Camp to the King and also a Member of Parliament.

At this period, from a paper dated April 3, 1760, there was a scarcity of men fit for dragoons in Ireland; and the levy money, £3, 5s., which was allowed was insufficient.

This affected the regiments a good deal in an adverse way, and in addition a commanding officer had to contend with the system which sent the best men and picked horses from a regiment as a draft to another. Only in March of that year 144 men and horses had been drafted from the 1st and 2nd Horse, and 78 horses and men from the 5th, 8th, 9th, 12th, 13th, and 14th Regiments of Dragoons to complete the 3rd and 4th Horse, then under orders for England.

Each trooper was to take with him—

	£	s.	d.
Cloathing—viz$^{t.}$, for a Frock, Waistcoat, Gloves and Hat	1	13	0
And for his horse	35	0	0
	£36	13	0
And for replacing each dragoon—Levy Money	£3	5	0
Cloathing—viz$^{t.}$, Frock, Waistcoat, Breeches, Gloves and hat	1	19	6
And for his horse	27	1	8
	£32	6	2

A paper dated December 2, 1759, may well be quoted at this point, dealing as it does with the proposed conversion of dragoon regiments into light dragoons. It is addressed to

His Grace John Duke of Bedford, Lord-Lieutenant General and General-Governor of Ireland, &c., &c.

THE MEMORIAL OF LIEUTENANT-COLONEL THE EARL OF DROGHEDA.

Humbly sheweth,—

That as Light Dragoons is a Species of Troops intirely new in this Country, Your Memorialist therefore prays Your Grace will take such Method as You shall think proper to procure six Corporals and six Private Men from the Light Dragoons now established in England, as are properly qualified for being Sergeants and Corporals in the Regiment to be commanded by your Memorialist.

Which is most Humbly Submitted,

Drogheda.

The height of recruits at this time could no longer be kept up to the standard. Hitherto 5 ft. 11 in. had been the standard in the Carabiniers. This, in a paper dated January 30, 1760, it is stated to be impossible "without ransacking the whole of Ireland," and "could not be done if the Regiments are to take the Field." During this year Dublin was visited by a severe outbreak of horse sickness. Every horse of the regiment quartered there was sick, and no mounted guard was possible even at the Castle. Writing on April 7, 1760, a man states that though "all possible care is taken of the regimental horses," it would be impossible for the regiment to move.

From 1761 to 1766 there are no records.

On March 18, 1763, dated from the Privy Garden, a paper gives the establishment of Irish dragoon regiments.

It is as follows: "6 Troops, 3 Field Officers, 3 Captains, 3 Lieutenants (including the Captain-Lieutenant), 6 Cornets, 1 Chaplain, 1 Adjutant, 1 Surgeon, 6 Quartermasters, 6 Sergeants, 12 Corporals, 6 Hautboys, 6 Drummers, and 120 Private Effective Men by 20 per Troop, and in all 177 men, officers included."

On July 23, 1763, in consequence of the "Hearts of Oak" rioting, all officers on the Irish establishment were required to repair to their respective posts, notwithstanding leave. All leave was stopped.

The members of the Hearts of Oak Society had a regular military formation, and marched every man with an oak bough. On July 6 no less than 10,000 of these men had been out in one day near Armagh. The Hearts of Oak Society, or Oakboys as they were also called, were Protestants, and were the predecessors of the Steelboys, who rose some eight years later, but for different reasons. The grievances of the Oakboys were various, the chief one being forced labour on the roads which were often private jobs. Much woodland was devastated by the Oakboys, who cut and carried away huge quantities of valuable timber.

In 1767 the regiment if not quartered at Sligo was at any rate assembled there in the month of May. Probably three troops only were at Sligo, and of the other three, one possibly at Newport. From this date there is an almost unbroken series of Inspection Reports, from which not a little interesting matter may be derived as to the condition of dragoon regiments on the Irish establishment. On May 25, 1767, the 13th Dragoons were reviewed by the Right Hon. Major-General Lord Blayney. The total establishment of the regiment present was this: 18 commission officers, 2 staff officers (adjutant and surgeon), 6 quartermasters, 6 sergeants, 12 corporals, 12 drummers and hautboys, and 120 private men; 150 horses were on parade; the accoutrements were reported to be "good," and the majority of the arms, except the pistols, of which 57 pairs were good and 69 bad; the 6 drums dated from 1747; the firelocks and bayonets (126 each) from 1766: there were 132 swords supplied at various times, but which had been all of one pattern since 1754; Pelissier, the chaplain, was absent on leave, and had been so for eight months.

Nearly every man in the regiment was an Irishman, 10 only being Scots and 4 English.

As a regiment the men were tall, the majority being between 5 ft. 9 in. and 5 ft. 11 in. in height.

Ten men had done thirty years' service, 16 had done twenty years, and 26 had done ten.

The horses were almost all either 15·1 hands or 15 hands.

These details are not without interest, and the Confidential Report of Lord Blayney is also worth transcribing :—

The 13th Regiment of Dragoons, Commanded by Lieutenant-General Douglas, are a very good Body of Men, Extremely well sized & tollerably well appointed—their horses, mostly recruited in Ireland—a Troop strong active horse, but not so well managed as ye English horses are in General—they perform'd their exercise very well—the Manuvers mounted with great attention—they had never two Troops of ye long-tailed horses.
Review'd this Reg^{t.} at Sligoe ye 25th of May.   BLAYNEY.

The most remarkable fact about this report is that so large a number of Irishmen should be in the regiment. It had long been difficult to get Protestant recruits from Ulster, the supply having run short by about 1758, and it was absolutely forbidden to enlist a Roman Catholic.

Whether horse, foot, and dragoons on the Irish establishment should or should not be employed to assist the officers of His Majesty's Revenue in the execution of their duties, was raised as a question on May 19, 1768.

This prevention of smuggling and collecting the duties for the Customs and Excise had weighed very heavily on the troops for years. It was now asked what Standing Orders there were in the English army regarding these matters, and whether there existed any English Act empowering the army to be so employed.

The 13th were reviewed at Castlebar on May 28, 1768, by Lieut.-General Robert Armiger.

Apparently a large number of the long-service men had been discharged, as there are only 30 of ten years' service in the regiment. All the horses, save one which was 16 hands, were between 15 and $15\frac{1}{2}$ hands.

112 private men were effective and 110 horses. 4 men were sick and 4 absent.

2 privates were wanting to complete the establishment. Chaplain Pelissier was still away on leave. Complaint is again made of the 69 " bad " pairs of pistols, and it is stated that " some of the belts were 20 years old."

The trumpets had been supplied by the colonel in the preceding year, and henceforward the " hautboy " vanishes.

General Armiger reports that the officers are well armed, and that they saluted well; and he goes on to give certain details as to their uniform which will be treated of elsewhere.

Lieut.-General Armiger specially notices that the officers were "Remarkably well Mounted," but adds, "the Horses want a little Dressing."

The new trumpeters were "young, sounded well, and were mounted on Grey Horses."

The men had "Hats well cocked, Had Black Spaterdashes and Boots."

The horses were "in very good condition—Nimble—Thirty-four long-tailed horses—17 bought since the last Review," of which 6 are "fit for ranks, 11 not sufficiently rode."

He says, "This Regiment Performed very well."

With regard to quarters and barracks the report concludes thus: "The Regiment lays in different Cantoonments and Report all the Barracks good except Gort which is repairing."

CHAPTER VII.

Ireland, 1769-1778.

IN 1769, on June 7th, the regiment was reviewed at Birr by Major-General the Earl of Drogheda.

The report on this occasion was not particularly complimentary.

In the first place, it should however be mentioned that several officers were absent "sick at Castlebar."

The trumpeters did not, it seems, please his lordship, who remarks that they are "young but not perfect in their soundings."

Then he continues: "This Regiment Performed its Movements, Evolutions and Manœuvres, very Indifferently—In other respects it is a good Regiment and fit for Service."

One troop appears to have been quartered at Roscommon and one at Castlebar, where the barracks are at both places reported to be "good." Two troops were at Sligo, and there the barracks are reported as "bad."

On May 16, 1770, the 13th Dragoons were reviewed by Lieut.-General Michael O'Brian Dilkes at Dublin.

The review was held in the Phœnix Park.

The strength of the regiment was 137 men, out of which 126 were Irishmen.

Chaplain Pelissier had at last resigned.

Lieut.-General Dilkes was, like Lord Drogheda, not too complimentary.

The men's uniforms, he remarks, are not well fitted and they do not ride well.

The recruits are "young and of a middling size"—"11 Inlisted since last Review of which 6 In the Ranks, 3 Unfit for the Ranks and 2 Deserted."

His general observation is as follows: "This Regiment is in general good, but not of a good size—Many young men and young horses, and upon the whole, may, by the Next Review, be much improved."

On May 27, 1771, the regiment was reviewed at Clonmell by Lieut.-General Sandford.

He reports another slight change in the officers' uniform, and records that the buttons were "numbered."

The 13th Dragoons mustered 138 men, out of whom 127 were Irishmen.

There were 108 horses, in height between 15 and $15\frac{1}{4}$ hands, and among them 47 long-tailed.

General Sandford says that the regiment is "well disciplined and well appointed—But not so young as they should be after so long a Peace, and far from Complete in Horses, having suffer'd very much by the glanders."

Of the barracks no mention is made.

In this year the apprentices were wont to amuse themselves by enlisting in the dragoons. Having done so, and of course having got the bounty money, they were promptly claimed by their masters. On the claim being made, and the indentures being produced, the young recruit was perforce surrendered. The point, of course, was that he had spent the bounty money and either could not or would not refund it. The system opened a door to frauds of considerable extent, as may easily be supposed.

Lord Blayney reviewed the regiment the next year, the review taking place at Gort on the 19th of June.

The strength of the regiment was 136 men, of which 4 were English and 8 Scots, the remaining 124 being Irishmen.

At the review 124 were effective.

Since the review in the preceding year, Lord Blayney notes that "2 privates had been made corporals from Major (Penefather's) and Captain Hoare's Troops in the Lieutenant-Colonel's (Blaquière) and Captain Douglas's Troops." 70 horses were effective and 44 were required to complete, as 114 were on allowance.

The regiment, Lord Blayney reports, "performed their movements and manœuvres with exactness and attention, and made a pretty good appearance, but from the number of horses wanting, 14 of which were shot, having the glanders, they cannot for some time be fit for service."

Of the barracks the report is, "Indifferent."

It may not be uninteresting here to give a detailed account of what the regiment did on this particular occasion in the way of evolutions, &c.

Regiment pass by in squadrons—Officers salute General—In troops by fours ranking off—Regiment wheel into line, twice to the right, and to the right-about to its proper front—To the left twice, and to the left-about to its proper front—Pass and repass deffiles—Form half squadrons—Form two lines—Charge to the front—Retreat by lines from the line—Wheel outwards by squadrons—Form two columns—Form opposite lines—Charge through the intervals—Form columns to the rear—Wheel inwards by squadrons—Form the line—Charge in four squadrons in line [only seventy horses be it remembered]—Retreat by right files—Wheel to the left by files—Form the line—Form two squadrons—Charge to the front—Squadrons pursue from the flanks—Retreat by fours—Form the line—Regiment charges—General salute.

The above is the usual programme that is to be met with in these reports.

On June 10, 1772, dated from Dublin Castle, a document was issued to this effect.

His Majesty is pleased to direct that for the future the Captain-Lieutenants of the Cavalry and Marching Regiments shall have Rank as well in the Army as in their respective Regiments as Captains. That the present Captain-Lieutenants shall take the said Rank from the 26th Day of May 1772, and all future Captain-Lieutenants from the date of their respective Commissions.

This, of course, involved a change in the price of commissions in the army.

On June 12, 1772, it was proposed to add 3d. per diem to the pay of a private dragoon in Ireland, and thus to put him on an equality with the British dragoon. The officers of dragoons had no compensation, it was alleged, on account of the great advance in the price of forage. To meet this, an extra 1s. per day to a captain and 6d. per day to a subaltern was suggested as meeting the case.

The cost to Government would be £1861, 10s. per annum.

This took effect on April 1, 1788.

"The English dragoon has never less than 3s. 6d. per week for subsistence, or 6d. more than a foot soldier, besides his grass money, which defrays charges for the paymaster, surgeon, and extraordinary necessaries. In Ireland, from the several deductions and various necessaries he is obliged to provide out of his pay, he receives no more than 1s. 9d. for his weekly subsistence, and, of course, lives in the utmost distress."

From papers, the cost of the "Warrant Men" of the 13th Dragoons in 1772, December 1st, may be obtained.

4 "Warrant Men" to each Troop at 1s. 4d. each, £1, 12s. per week, or £584 per annum.
The 5th Regiment of Dragoons having 9 Troops cost £876.

At this time there was barrack accommodation for cavalry in Ireland as follows:—

Leinster, 14 troops, of which Dublin accommodated 3, and all the remaining stations 1.

Munster, 7 troops, of which Charleville accommodated 2, and all the rest 1.

Connaught, 8 troops; and Ulster, 8 troops.

The barracks were supposed to be kept in constant order as to the buildings, walls, roofs, &c.; this being contracted for by the barrack-masters.

The barrack-masters had to supply the non-commissioned officers and men with earthenware, trenchers, &c., subject to breakage.

Bedding, sheeting, and cooking utensils in the Dublin Barracks were under the control of the overseers of barracks who contracted to supply them.

The barrack-masters in the country contracted to supply bedding, sheeting, curtains, and utensils.

The twenty-five barrack-masters in the country cost £50 each. Two inspectors who had to view each of the barracks twice annually were paid £200 each.

The officers of the three troops of dragoons in Dublin received 3d. per day extra for each servant, added to their personal pay in 1772.

The fire and candle allowance varied: For the Dublin Town Guard it was £48; for the Limerick Guard, £48; for the Galway

Guard, £20; for the Charles Fort Guard, £40; and for the Athlone Guard, £10,—total, £166.

Some other accounts dealing with the expenses at this date are not without interest.

The barrack-master in Dublin received £80 per annum, and his assistant £20.

Measuring coals for the Dublin garrison cost £10.

The Surveyor-General and his Extraordinary Clerk, for books, ink, paper, quills, &c., on the barrack account, cost £40.

To the "Register," for his constant attendance at the barrack office in Dublin, £157, 10s.

Five clerks, a door-keeper, messengers, books, paper, ink, quills, and wax, £100.

Council of barracks, £100.

Firing and candles for 37 troops of horse and dragoons and 210 companies of foot, cost £6000.

Straw for the soldiers' beds, to be changed four times a-year, £279, 9s. 8½d.

Watching empty barracks, £400.

Rent of sites of barracks, £68, 8s. 1½d.

The pay for a regiment of dragoons had not been changed.

On May 31, 1773, Lord Blayney again reviewed the regiment, on this occasion at Gort also.

The regiment would appear to have been quartered at Gort, Headford, Portumna, and Loughrea. Except at Gort, where the barracks are stated to be in "bad order," those at the other three places were in good repair.

Eighteen officers were present, of which 4 were English, 3 Scots, and 11 Irish.

Of the 137 men in the regiment, 127 were Irish. There were 108 horses, of which 67 were long-tailed, and are reported on as "good." 29 mounts had been purchased during the past year.

There were 127 effective men at the review and all the horses. The average size of the horses, 15 to 15¼ hands. There must have been something not quite right in the regiment at this time, but it does not seem possible to ascertain who was to blame. All the quarter-masters were absent, "3 trying to sell," whatever that may mean.

A Deputy Chaplain, by name Wilson, had been appointed.

The orderly books are "not certified for, nor do the Government Orders appear to be regularly entered in the several Books of the Regiment."

The writer wishes that at least this Government Order had been obeyed: it would have saved him much vain research. The arms appear to have been kept in good condition, but the dear old pistols are still "bad." The recruits were good and well certified for, this means as regards their Protestantism. "The Manual Exercise," says Lord Blayney, "was by word of command, and 'two' quick, and quite contrary to the King's late order. The officers made a pretty good appearance on Horseback, there are several Old Men in the Regiment—The horses pretty active, but as there are about 30 wanting to compleat, the Reg$^{t.}$ cannot for some time be fit for service."

During the year 1774 the regiment was quartered at Athlone, Loughrea, and Roscommon, and the barracks there are favourably reported on as to condition.

The officer who held the annual review was Major-General James Gisborne, and the function took place at Athlone. The strength of the regiment was 138, of which 129 were Irishmen.

The horses numbered 117, and the standard of height remained the same.

The field strength at the review was 114 men and 93 horses.

Another Deputy Chaplain makes his appearance, the Rev. "Mr" Young.

The arms of the regiment were reported on as being in a disgraceful state as regards utility. All the 132 pairs of pistols were "bad," and likewise 60 firelocks and carbines. All the firelocks had wooden rammers.

It will be remembered that Lord Blayney thought the regiment performed the manual exercise "two" quickly, &c. General Gisborne apparently held an opposite opinion, for he says—

"The Regiment is fit for service, but performs its business rather slow and unsteadily."

With regard to the men, he says that they are "not very young and Ride Indifferently." They are clean and well-dressed but not very steady or attentive.

There are now 82 long-tails among the horses.

Six recruits have been enlisted during the past year, out of which two are in the ranks and the other four discharged.

Major-General James Gisborne reviewed the regiment again in the following year. The review was held on June 5th and took place at Birr.

The strength of the regiment was 136, of whom 128 were Irishmen, 5 Scots, and 3 English.

The men were an even-sized body, nearly every one being between 5 feet 9 inches and 5 feet 10 inches in height. The horses were between 15, 15¼, and 15½ hands in height, no horse was more, and only one was less. 48 firelocks were still "bad," and 85 pairs of pistols also. Nine recruits had been enlisted, but none of them were as yet fit for the ranks. 24 "good" horses had also been purchased since the last review, but these, like the recruits, were not yet fit for the ranks. Among the horses 105 were long-tails.

The exercises, movements, evolutions, and manœuvres performed on the occasion of the review were practically as before, but one novelty was at any rate introduced, and it is an index to the then state of the country: "Street firing and two volleys—Charging to the Front on the Second Volley."

Record of the year 1776 is lacking.

When it is considered how large a proportion of the recruits in the regiment were Irishmen, it is somewhat puzzling to know whence they were derived. That the supply from Ulster of Protestants had been very short for nearly twenty years has been mentioned. But were all the men enlisted Protestants? A paper dated 1776 rather points the other way.

Firstly, it orders that no Roman Catholic should be recruited under any circumstances, and proceeds to mention a case in which a recruiting officer at Sligo advertised, promising Roman Catholic recruits their own chaplain, and offering to accept them on the recommendation of their parish priest.

Lord Harcourt, then the Lord-Lieutenant, and the Colonel of the Regiment, at once repudiated the advertisement as unauthorised, and the offending recruiting officer was threatened with dismissal from the service, and was at once put under arrest.

But from various documents it appears that during both the years 1775 and 1776 recruiting in Ireland was being carried on in the most active manner.

On June 10, 1777, the regiment was reviewed by Lieut.-General James Johnston at Athlone.

It would be interesting were it possible to discover what produced the extraordinary change in the regiment disclosed by the report of General Johnston.

The strength of the regiment is given as 143, 100 of these being under 5 feet 7 inches in height. They were almost all of short service—quite young troops; 110 had served one year only, 13 were either of two or three years' service, 7 of ten years, and 13 of fifteen years.

The horses varied in height between $14\frac{3}{4}$ and $15\frac{1}{2}$ hands, and 26 of them were five years, 21 of them six years, and 19 of them seven years of age. The effective men numbered 103, and the effective horses 76 out of a total of 82. 61 men and 54 horses were wanting to complete.

The field returns show effective men 113, whereas the total should be 174; and 68 horses, where there should be 114.

One captain, 3 subalterns, 2 sergeants, 4 corporals, 2 trumpeters, and 36 privates appear to have been dispersed abroad,—some in England, some in Scotland, with others in Limerick and Inniskillen, besides which 24 were on guard.

Another Deputy Chaplain, by name Gurney, is stated as doing duty.

The arms were as bad as ever, if not worse. 132 pairs of pistols were condemned, and 126 swords were wanting. Similarly, large quantities of accoutrements were required, such as 129 waist-belts, 123 slings, 69 saddles, 69 bridles, and 69 housings and caps.

Two hundred recruits had enlisted since the last review, of whom 2 were dead, 44 deserted, 64 discharged, and 61 drafted. Only 29 were fit for the ranks.

The report is a curious one—

A Squadron of Thirty file was Shewed Mounted and perform'd a few Manœuvres on horseback. Which were those of a Regiment in its Infancy. It was an Exhibition sufficient to prove a foundation well laid for a Good Regiment. But the Corps has no money to buy Horses. Those of the former Establishment being of little value, raised by their sale only a small account.

JAMES JOHNSTON,
Lieutenant-General.

The barracks at Athlone were reported as good.

The date 1783 is that which is accepted as the time when the 13th Dragoons were converted into Light Dragoons. But in Ireland, at any rate, in the case of one regiment, the conversion from dragoons to light dragoons was in process as early as 1769.

In the Confidential Report of this regiment for that year occurs the following passage: "As this Regiment is now converting from Heavy to Light Dragoons it has not been Reviewed. But Copys of the Several Returns transmitted by Lieut.-Colonel Burton are inserted, that the present State and Condition of this Regiment may fully appear."

This regiment was the 12th Dragoons. Now in the Army List for 1778 the 13th is entered as Light Dragoons, and this is the probable explanation of the report for 1777—namely, that the process of conversion had begun. Hence the date 1783 given by Cannon is apparently erroneous. In the year 1778, for at any rate six months during the summer, the regiment was quartered in Dublin. It was reviewed there on August 4 by Major-General Lancelot Baugh. The strength of the regiment was 194 men, of which 170 were Irishmen. Only 16 men were 25 years of age; 47 were 18 years of age, and 118 only 20; the remainder being older. There were but 89 horses, and their ages were 5, 6, and 7 years, height 15 to $15\frac{1}{2}$ hands. The men were mainly short, 140 being under 5 ft. 7 in., 20 were 5 ft. 7 in., and 11 were 5 ft. $7\frac{1}{2}$ in.

116 were of one year's service and 60 of two years.

The effective rank and file were 185, with all the horses. 7 men and 49 horses were wanting to complete the establishment. 105 men had been enlisted since the last review, and of these 20 were discharged, 24 had deserted. 17 horses had been obtained, and 8 had been cast.

The arms were now all reported "good," and only one pair of pistols was wanting. This pair of pistols it appears had been taken from one of the men by the mob.

The accoutrements, with the exception of the saddles of 6 sergeants, were all good, and 2 standards are mentioned. With regard to the clothing of the men, helmets are noted for the first time; and all were reported good.

The movements performed at the review were very elaborate.

They were mainly the same as on previous occasions; but one or two novelties were introduced.

> Performed horse manual—Dismounted and formed battalion—Marched past by divisions—Performed manual exercise and fired a volley—Fired by divisions from centre to flanks—Fired a volley mounted . . .—Charged in line—Pursued and skirmished—Formed two opposite lines—Performed an attack in a wood—Formed two squadrons on the fifteen acres, &c.

General Baugh in his Confidential Report remarks: "This Regiment is in very good Order, and thinks well of itself. Performed their Manœuvres with great Exactness and Rapidity in every respect. Fine Regiment (all that are mounted), very fit for service."

Two prisoners are mentioned; this was a most unusual thing, and hitherto such a fact has never been reported.

Now the fact was that the old Colonel, Lieut.-General Douglas, had died, and the new colonel of the regiment was Lieut.-General Richard Pierson (late of the 36th Foot). He would appear to have been most energetic. General Pierson was created a Knight of the Bath.

CHAPTER VIII.

Ireland, 1779-1795.

IN the year 1779 the North of Ireland was in a disquieted state, several disturbances having taken place.

The 13th Dragoons being ordered to proceed to the scene soon arrived by forced marches. By its presence the troubles were shortly put a stop to.

The next year, in the summer, the regiment marched and encamped with the army in the neighbourhood of Ardfinnan, a place about seven miles from Clonmell.

The regiment was reviewed at Ardfinnan Camp by Major-General Joseph Gabbit on September 30.

The strength of the regiment was 167 men and 127 horses. All were practically of three years' service and under.

137 men were effective in the field and 37 more were wanted to complete. 104 horses were effective and 10 more were wanted.

1 captain, 4 corporals, 24 men, and 4 horses were on duty elsewhere. The report states that the men were rather small; the horses in very bad condition, and rather small. 47 new horses had been obtained, of which 42 were in the ranks and the rest unfit. 31 recruits had been enlisted since the last review, and of these 1 had been discharged, 9 had deserted, 11 were fit for the ranks, and 10 unfit.

General Gabbit remarks: "This is a regiment of rather small men and horses, the latter in very bad condition owing to the long marches they had last spring. But by the apparent Care and Attention of their Commanding Officer they will very soon change for the better and be very Fit for Service."

When this encampment was broken up the 13th moved into quarters, being distributed between Clonmel, Carrick-on-Suir, and Cappoquin.

Here the regiment remained until 1781, when it was moved to Charleville and Bruff.

Lieut.-General Pierson having died suddenly on the 12th February 1781, the colonelcy of the regiment was bestowed on Lieut.-General Francis Craig, who had been Lieutenant-Colonel of the 1st Foot Guards. General Craig died Colonel of the 13th Light Dragoons in 1811.

On September 10, 1781, there was a most serious military riot in Cork.

It appears that on the preceding night a soldier had been murdered by some civilians. The soldiers turned out in force and began to make reprisals, doing a good deal of damage. One of the officers, whose name is not given, turned out with the guard, and by his exertions succeeded in calming the disturbers of the peace and persuading them to return to barracks.

For some years a solitary soldier wandering at night carried his life in his hands.

The record in Kilkenny during one year was sixteen soldiers either killed outright or hamstrung by having the large tendon of their legs cut, being thus crippled for life. All these crimes took place within a short distance from the barracks. Gangs of rioters or seditious persons would lie in wait in any dark spot for a passing soldier, and woe betide the wretched man if they caught him.

As will be remembered, during the autumn of this year a descent upon the Irish coast to the west of Cork by the French was expected.

In consequence the 13th marched into Cork and remained there until the news of Admiral Rodney's victory in the West Indies removed any apprehension of a French invasion.

The regiment was now employed upon a somewhat curious service. It appears that a certain Mr George Robert Fitzgerald had taken possession of his father's house and property near Castlebar, County Mayo. The house he had fortified, and having obtained a dozen large ship guns (6-pounders), had mounted them there with the declared intention of standing a siege. Thither, in order to dispossess the usurper, the 13th, together with some regiments of infantry and detachment of artillery, was despatched. The expedition was under the command of Colonel (afterwards General Sir) Ralph Abercromby.

The expedition duly reached Castlebar late in the evening, and proceeding to the impromptu fort on the morrow discovered that it had been deserted by its gasconading defender. The guns, however, were found and removed to the barracks at Castlebar. The 13th then received orders to send two troops to Ballinrobe and two to Sligo.

Thus split up, the regiment remained in quarters till 1783, when in the spring it was assembled at Belturbet, at which place the summer inspection was held. The inspection concluded, two troops were detached to Sligo, the other four remaining behind.

A few months later, during the winter, the ramshackle barracks at Belturbet fell down.

Two troops were then detached to Cavan till May 1784, when the regiment again assembled at Belturbet for inspection. During June the regiment marched and went into quarters at Athlone, Roscommon, and Clogheen, and at this time the horses of the 13th were turned out to grass for the first time since the peace with America. The quartering of troops, especially of cavalry, in Ireland was at this period managed in this manner.

Here and there in small towns small barracks had been erected. Hotels and public-houses were not so plentiful as in England—at least suitable ones, and billets on private individuals were not found readily, and if found were not usually convenient for the purpose. The system did not work well, as may be imagined. With the troops—nay, of the less than half-troops—of a cavalry regiment in scattered units here and there over a wide district, any real regimental drill became an impossibility, and it often happened that a regiment seldom met in its entirety save perhaps for a brief space on the occasion of the annual inspection.

On June 1, 1784, the 13th were reviewed at Belturbet by Major-General Edward Stopford.

The strength of the regiment was 161 men and 138 horses. 88 men were under 5 ft. 7 in. The horses varied from $14\frac{1}{2}$ to $15\frac{1}{2}$ hands.

The lieutenant.-colonel, Sir James Stewart, Bart., being a Member of Parliament, was almost always in London, at any rate during the session. The major and the other officers, however, would appear to have been zealous. 131 men were effective in the field. 43 men were wanting to complete. 1 corporal and 8 men were absent on duty, and there were no prisoners. 114 horses were effective and none were wanting.

Patrick Doherty, later on the colonel of the regiment, was one of the quartermasters.

The arms were clean and none were wanting, but 4 trumpets, 192 firelocks and carbines, and 192 bayonets are reported as "bad."

The accoutrements were all good and none wanting.

31 recruits had been enlisted, of whom 1 had been discharged, 6 had deserted, and 24 were fit for the ranks.

General Stopford reports: "This Regiment makes a good appearance and is well disciplined. The Horses are thin but hardy and fit for service, the men ride well and the Horses are very well managed."

Of the changes in clothing and equipment, due notice will be taken in a special chapter, when a chronological list will be given with all the details available.

The establishment of each troop of the regiment on the peace with America was as follows: 1 captain, 1 lieutenant, 1 cornet, 1 quartermaster, 1 sergeant, 2 corporals, 1 trumpeter, 19 privates (1 farrier included) mounted, and 11 dismounted men, making a total for the regiment (then 6 troops) of 204 men, including non-commissioned officers and trumpeters, of which 138 were mounted.

On peace being declared, 10 dismounted men from each troop were reduced, by which the strength of the regiment was only 144 men and 138 horses.

The inspection and review of the 13th was held by Lieut.-General Lancelot Baugh.

The strength of the regiment hardly varied from that of the year 1784.

General Baugh reports: "A very good Regiment both of Men and Horses, the latter rather small but extremely active, and the Men ride well. The Appointments are good, and in every particular in good order."

After inspection in June 1785 the regiment marched from Athlone and was quartered at Kilkenny, Ballyragget, and Carrick-on-Suir.

Major-General Charles O'Hara reviewed the regiment this year at Kilkenny on June 8, 1786.

Glancing at his reports on various regiments, he would appear to have been a man not easily satisfied, and given to administering somewhat unpleasant remarks at times. Considering all things, the 13th came off perhaps better than had been anticipated.

Of the report a few things may be noted.

Cornet H. Wentworth Sherston was absent without leave.

5 pairs of pistols were wanting.

126 pouches and 138 bridles were "bad."

The movements, evolutions, and manœuvres performed were more simple than heretofore, and concluded with: "Advanced in a hand gallop—Halted—Volley in the air—Draw swords—General Salute."

General O'Hara's report is very brief: "This Regiment performed their movements slow, Fired Well, Many Horses Slight and of a Bad Kind."

A specimen of what General O'Hara could give in the way of a report is here given. It refers to another regiment, and was dated from Cashel four days later. He had put this regiment through a very elaborate programme, and apparently they had not exactly pleased him. But he attributes any defects there might be to the commanding officer, in the following words: "The Commanding Officer of this Regiment has introduced a frequent shouting of the whole Corps, which he calls a War Whoop, destructive of all attention in the men, the cause of much confusion. *N.B.*—There are 2 grey horses more in this Regiment than in the Establishment."

At this period the cavalry and dragoons generally as to equipment were hopelessly old-fashioned. The old black war horse was extinct. The private soldiers were old, and both the men and the horses were drilled in an antiquated way—year after year in the same evolutions. They could perform these to perfection, no doubt, but the military value of their training was practically nil.

It was suggested that these regiments should take turns in rotation to be quartered in Great Britain, but the "proprietary" colonels objected, and nothing was done. The Commander-in-Chief was powerless.

Colonels were in those days styled "proprietary" because the regiments were in a sense looked upon as their private property. It will be remembered that until the custom gradually died out, regiments were known by the names of their successive colonels; in the case of the 13th Hussars, Rich's (late Munden's), Ligonier's (late Gardiner's) may be cited. Also, a colonel was styled "proprietary" in order to distinguish him from the Lieutenant-Colonel in active command who frequently held full army rank as a colonel,—the "proprietary" colonel being often a Major-General or Lieutenant-General. The system was a bad one. To bad colonels were due the crying abuses of the pay system as well as those of the clothing system—the systematic robbery of the soldier, the mean frauds by which an income was literally swindled out of Government or sweated off the backs of the men; and the abuse of the power of the lash was owing to the same cause.

A colonel might see his regiment once in a year, possibly twice, but how could a wretched soldier bring forward any grievance on such an occasion? the result would have inevitably been arrest for making a frivolous complaint, though, with luck, acquittal might have followed because the complaint turned out to be justified.

True, there was a time when the colonel was the active officer in command, as in Munden's time, when his duties corresponded to the Lieutenant-Colonel of later days, and he was always present (unless on leave) whether at home or in the field.

Of an absentee colonel the case of the commanding officer of the 13th may be quoted, who, being a Member of Parliament, lived mainly in London while the regiment was in Ireland.

Proprietary colonels objected to their regiments being transferred off and on from the Irish to the British Establishment, because there was more to be got out of the clothing and pay when a regiment was serving on the former than when on the latter.

It may perhaps be well to mention that though on paper the pay of a dragoon on the Irish Establishment looks less than that of one on the British, the dragoon in Ireland was in fact better off owing to the peculiar coinage and currency. From 1689 to 1825 the nominal value of the coinage in Ireland was $8\frac{1}{3}$ per cent higher than in England. In the latter year Irish money was reduced to the English standard, from which time the United Kingdom has possessed a perfectly uniform system of metallic money.

Following the inspection in June 1786 at Kilkenny, the 13th was marched to Mallow, Bandon, and Tallow. The two troops stationed at Mallow during the winter of this year were moved into Cork. At this time the lawless proceedings of the White Boys, Right Boys, and Peep-o'-day Boys were a source of great trouble. To suppress their excesses the regiment was employed on constant duty day and night. To arrest the delinquents whose chief desire appeared to be to avenge themselves on the tythe proctors against whom they believed they had real grievances, or at any rate fancied they had, was the chief duty of the 13th. Almost every jail in the county was filled with prisoners brought in by patrols of the regiment, and all to little or no purpose, since for lack of prosecutors coming forward they were released at the following assizes.

In May 1787 the regiment assembled at Cashel for inspection, proceeding thence in June to Maryborough, Mount Mellick, and Thurles.

The review of the regiment was held by Major-General Earl Carhampton on June 7.

The arms of the regiment were in bad order. 123 firelocks and carbines, 119 bayonets, and 38 pairs of pistols were condemned.

The sashes and pouches of the sergeants were also "bad."

19 recruits had enlisted, 5 had deserted, 8 were in the ranks, and 6 were unfit. The horses were in "good condition—nimble." 17 had been bought since the last review, and all of them were in the ranks.

Lord Carhampton gave a very good report of the men as to size, age, and appearance, and concludes: "This is an exceeding good Regiment, and there is no relaxation in point of discipline."

A newspaper cutting, dated June 26, 1788, from Dublin, is not without interest. It is as follows:—

A stranger would imagine we were either in the heat of a war, or on the approach of a rupture. Barracks in every quarter, and others going to be built on the sea-coast. Soldiers without number in the city, and nearly 2000 encamped just outside. There must be an object in all this military preparation—What is it? Standing armies are ever instruments of despotic power, and in a free country to be eyed with suspicion; and the amazing attention bestowed on Mars by nominees augurs a—patriotic administration.

Again on August 26 :—

Dublin looked as if under martial law for some days. Every street and alley was filled with military and police, prepared to pounce upon sundry mechanics. Why this collection of troops took place does not appear. There is nothing in the Annals of Dublin to give a clue to the reason. Possibly the paragraphs were merely journalistic froth.

A change in regard to the warrant men took place in this year :—

The four Warrant Men per Troop which formerly stood upon the Establishment were discontinued, and the following allowances were placed on the said Establishment for the Colonels in lieu thereof—viz., the subsistence of one Warrant Man per Troop, and an Allowance in lieu of the clothing of the four Warrant Men per Troop, which allowances are ordered to be paid to the Colonels half-yearly.

Previous to this change the off-reckonings of these warrant men formed a part of the clothing contract and assignment, but upon the allowance in lieu of the clothing of warrant men being placed as a separate allowance on the establishment, the off-reckonings of the warrant men were no longer assigned in the clothing contract, but were paid to the agents on the part of the colonels half-yearly, as before mentioned.

There was at this time a good deal of dissatisfaction among the army surgeons, and the authorities found it very difficult to get properly qualified men.

In the past £30, 9s. 6¼d.—a strangely odd sum—was allowed as medicine money for each regiment of dragoon guards and dragoons in Ireland. This it was decided in future to change, and to place army surgeons on the Irish establishment on the same pecuniary footing as those in Great Britain.

£8 net was to be paid for each troop when the establishment amounted to forty private men, and an annual allowance at the rate of £6, 4s. net for every troop after they shall be reduced in their establishment below forty private men.

Army surgeons were, however, not permitted to sell their commissions unless they had purchased them. They were to be placed on half-pay for incapacity, old age, loss of sight or limb, or insanity. They were also to be transferred from the British to the Irish establishment, and *vice versa*, at the pleasure of the War Office. These changes had been long in agitation.

The following year the 13th marched in June to Dublin, where it took up the duty from the 2nd Horse, then reducing to Dragoon Guards (now the 5th).

At Dublin the regiment was stationed in the Dublin Barracks till the summer of 1788, when three troops were moved to the Phœnix Park Barracks—then a new Government acquisition, the site having been purchased from Lord Gardiner. Two troops were sent to Navan and one to The Man of War.[1]

Major-General James Paterson reviewed the regiment at Dublin on June 2, 1788.

Sir James Stewart was still absent attending the session of the English Parliament.

There are but few matters to note on this occasion.

The arms were reported clean but mostly in bad condition.

29 recruits had enlisted, and of these 1 had been discharged, 6 had deserted, and 15 were unfit for the ranks.

The report says, *inter alia*, "Horses in good Condition—Nimble —22 purchased, of whom 14 are in the ranks, 6 unfit for the ranks, and 2 dead."

In these quarters the regiment remained till May 1789, when the outlying troops were brought into Chapelizod and the neighbourhood.

Major-General Paterson reviewed the regiment again in the following year, 1789.

Cornet Sherston appears to have at length returned to the regiment, but where he had been, or why he was absent without leave, or for how long he was absent, does not appear.

The strength of the regiment was increased, and it now stood at 143 men with 138 horses. The arms were all reported "good," but as General Paterson "died during his Reviewing Circuit, the Returns are sent without Remarks, &c., &c."

After the annual inspection the troops were changed, and the regiment occupied the same quarters.

---

[1] The Man of War was a townland near Balbriggan, County Dublin, in the Swords Military District, where a small barrack existed as late as 1822, for 3 officers, 40 privates, and 43 horses.

In May 1790 the 13th again assembled as in the previous year, and after the inspection in June marched to Clonmel (3 troops), Clogheen (1 troop), Mallow (1 troop), and Charleville (1 troop), and were quartered in those places until the May following.

On June 2, 1790, the regiment was reviewed in the Phœnix Park by Major-General Charles Wilson Lyon.

The strength was 142 men and 138 horses: 122 of the men were Irish, 6 Scots, and 14 English.

A part of the regiment was at Banbridge with Cornet William Willis in command, and consequently not present at the review.

There are one or two curious facts noted on this occasion.

Three of the quartermasters were without horses, one had been so since 1786, and though ordered to supply themselves for the review had not done so.

Quartermaster Mulholland, who had been six years horseless, was put under stoppages to buy a charger. As the other two had not been more than six months without a mount they were merely warned. Their names were Laurence King and Andrew Newcomen. The manœuvres were more elaborate than usual; among other things they " Formed in Echellon on the Front Squadron."

General Wilson Lyon reports: "The Regiment rides well and is well instructed in the principles on which Cavalry Movements should be made, and they performed their manœuvres on horseback with precision, good judgment, and proper rapidity."

30 recruits had been enlisted; 5 of these were fit for the ranks, 15 were unfit, 4 had deserted, and 6 had been discharged.

"Of 20 seen many too short but very young." They might grow.

On June 8, 1791, the regiment was reviewed at Clonmel by Major-General Richard Whyte.

The strength was 139 men and 131 horses.

One cornet was reported as absent without leave, but the name is not given.

The quartermaster is on Jail guard, but where is not stated.

General Whyte reports: "This is a fine Regiment in every Respect, a Good Body of Men, ride well, well mounted, rapid in their movements, Officers very steady and well mounted, and fit for any Service."

During the winter of 1790 the regiment was called on to furnish a draft consisting of 26 men. This draft, together with others from various regiments, were destined for Jamaica, whither they sailed and eventually formed the 20th Dragoons or Jamaica Regiment.

Having been inspected in June 1791, four troops of the 13th Light Dragoons were moved from the Old Barracks at Clonmel and quartered in the New Barracks there. The remaining two troops were quartered, one at Clogheen and the other at Charleville.

At Clonmel the regiment assembled for the annual inspection in June 1792, and then marched, four troops to Athlone, one to Roscommon, and one to Portumna.

The regiment was reviewed at Clonmel on June 8, 1792, by Major-General Dundas.

Cartridge-boxes are mentioned in the accoutrement return for the first time, and also sword-belts and swivel-belts.

The arms of the regiment were in a very faulty condition, and a Memorandum had been given in to the Lord-Lieutenant for such as were required, the response being "which will be ordered." The three quartermasters were still without horses and the adjutant also.

The standards were getting worn out. They had been in use since 1747.

Twenty-six recruits had been enlisted since the last review, and the General remarks: "On the whole but indifferent, but may improve." 13 were in the ranks, 9 were unfit for the ranks, and 4 had deserted.

In General Dundas's remarks there is a curious entry: "No music—6 Trumpeters." Does this mean that the trumpeters did not sound, or does it point to the beginnings of a band? Hautboys had vanished now for some years.

The Militia Act, now about to be enforced in Ireland, was the source of great trouble.

In Roscommon and Sligo above 10,000 people were up in arms, destroying gentlemen's houses and pulling down churches (Protestant).

One hundred soldiers and as many of the townsmen armed, acted as a guard, night and day, to protect the town of Carrick, when an attack was hourly expected to rescue certain prisoners lodged in the jail there.

On May 28, a magistrate, by name Sir Edward Crofton, with 12 dragoons, went out to quell a disturbance at Lackan and Turrough,

County Roscommon. He tried argument and failed, and then retired. The mob pursued the party, who, facing about, fired, killing seven and wounding sixteen. Nearly two hundred shots were fired at the soldiers, but only one man was wounded by a shot which grazed his eye. One rioter had his arm cut off; another, who fired five times at Sir Edward Crofton, had his nose cut off by the jailer of Roscommon. In another encounter between the rioters and the dragoons, seven were killed, eleven wounded, and one hundred taken prisoners.

In Roscommon, very shortly after in a riot, nineteen were killed by the dragoons, and several prisoners were taken, among them being a ruined gentleman who had made common cause with the mob.

At Manor Hamelin, the mob set on an officer going through the place with a small party of dragoons. The dragoons were forced to fire on the rioters, and killed eighty. Several were wounded, and the rest then fled.

In 1793 the regiment is stated to have been quartered at Belturbet and Sligo, where an inspection was, it is said, held in October.

Towards the end of 1792, or early in 1793, each troop of the regiment was augmented by five men. This augmentation was soon after followed by others, both in men, horses, and troops.

The 13th Light Dragoons were inspected, as usual, in June 1793, but there was no change of quarters till October of that year, when four troops went to Belturbet and two to Sligo.

Late in the autumn the regiment was called on to hand over thirty-six mounted men to complete the cavalry force at that time assembling for foreign service.

The regiments for this force were being assembled in the neighbourhood of Cork, and the transfer of the troops from the 13th Light Dragoons took place at Clogheen.

Early in 1794 the four troops at Belturbet marched to Ballinrobe and Castlebar, two troops being quartered in each place. Two separate inspections were held this year, one for the two troops at Ballinrobe and the other for those at Castlebar. During the summer a cavalry expedition of ten troops was being organised for foreign service.

But there is no record of this review of 1793, nor of a second review of the regiment at Ballinrobe which took place in 1794. However, the report of the Castlebar review on August 23, 1794, is extant.

The reviewing officer was Major-General Charles Crosbie.

The 13th Light Dragoons was now supposed to consist of 9 troops, but 2 of these were at the time vacant.

The regiment had been greatly augmented in strength.

This now stood at 446 men and 393 horses.

Of the men, 263 were under 5 ft. 7 in., 82 were 5 ft. 7 in., and 44 were 5 ft. 8 in.

The horses varied in height from 14 to $15\frac{3}{4}$ hands, but 93 were $14\frac{1}{2}$ hands.

Many arms were wanting—42 firelocks and carbines, 42 bayonets, 336 pairs of pistols, and 243 swords. The supply of accoutrements and horse furniture was also very scanty.

274 recruits had been enlisted since the last review. They were young men and "rather low for the latitude given." Of these recruits, 1 was dead, 9 were discharged, 93 had deserted, 35 were unfit for the ranks, and 136 were fit.

General Crosbie reports that the men were "young, but of an indifferent size, clean, steady, and attentive." The condition of the horses was indifferent, but they were nimble. 164 had joined since the last review, and of these 22 were dead, 20 which were unfit were to be cast, and the remainder were fit for the ranks.

The movements, evolutions, and manœuvres were simple on this occasion.

The report on the barracks and furniture is as follows:—Ballinrobe, Enniskillen, and Sligo were good, but Castlebar was bad.

The report concludes—"This Regiment was merely inspected; the men appeared clean and attentive, the horses young. Their late dispersed situation subjected them to many disadvantages."

The command of this expeditionary force, which amounted to ten troops, was given to Colonel The Hon. George Walpole of the 13th Light Dragoons, and the regiment was called upon to furnish two troops.

In the autumn the regiment marched to Tallow, Mallow, and Bandon, at each of which places two troops were quartered.

CHAPTER IX.

The West Indies, 1796-1798.

IT will be remembered that in the winter of 1790 the regiment had been called upon to furnish a draft of twenty-six men. These twenty-six men were destined for Jamaica, where, on arrival, together with other drafts from other regiments, they formed the 20th Dragoons or Jamaica Regiment. During the autumn of 1793 a further draft of thirty-six mounted men was called for to complete the cavalry force at that time assembling near Cork and destined for service on the continent. The following year the 13th was ordered to furnish two troops for foreign service. The force was to consist of ten troops, under the command of Lieut.-Colonel Hon. George Walpole of the 13th. These two troops marched from Ballinrobe to Dublin, and embarked for Liverpool. The officers who were detached from the regiment on this occasion were Lieut.-Colonel Walpole, Captain Dundas, Captain Blake, Lieutenant Gubbins, Lieutenant Bennet, and Assistant-Surgeon Campbell. The expedition ultimately went to Jamaica, where the Maroons were in insurrection.

These two troops of the 13th Light Dragoons were reviewed at Winchester on April 15, 1795, by Major-General Gwyn. He says, "Two troops of Men, very fine and fit for any Service. The horses that belonged to them, in the care of the 23rd Light Dragoons, very good both in Quality and Condition—one cast and sold."

Of the horses we find that 107 were serviceable, none deficient, and one cast, its disease being "entire decay," and it fetched £5, 5s. This sum was handed to the paymaster of the 23rd Light Dragoons, to be credited by him to Government.

In a letter General Gwyn states that he thought the old horse had "appearances of a bad farcy humour."

Captain LAWRENCE DUNDAS.

(*From a Portrait lent by* Colonel H. J. BLAGROVE, C.B.)

Of the horses of the 13th Light Dragoons he writes, "Those of the 13th Light Dragoons are good horses, almost thoroughbred, and in very good order."

In 1795 the remainder of the regiment was ordered to prepare for service in the West Indies. In the month of June, therefore, it assembled at Mallow. The horses were delivered up to the 22nd Dragoons, who had marched thither dismounted to receive them.

The 13th on the following day marched, dismounted, to Cork to embark. Transports were awaiting them there, but such was the condition of filth, want of proper accommodation, and generally disgraceful state of these vessels, that on the representation of Major Crofton, then in command, Major-General Stewart delayed the departure of the men for two or three days in order to have the transports fumigated and cleaned. The men were billeted in Cork, and though thus dispersed over the city not a man was missing on the day of embarkation, nor, indeed, did any show signs of having been indulging in liquor.

The regiment had a bad passage, but eventually arrived safely at Bristol. There the 14th Dragoons, who were destined for the same service, also arrived, and as well as two mounted regiments which had been brought from Ireland for service in England.

After a few days' delay, during which the men were kept on board, routes arrived. The 13th disembarked, and marched into quarters at Warminster and Frome. Here it remained till July, when it was moved to Salisbury, and thence, a month later, to Winchester. In September the 13th marched to Southampton, where it embarked in transports collected there for the purpose.

The two troops under the command of Lieut.-Colonel Walpole had already sailed for Jamaica, and formed part of the expedition intended to act against the Maroons.

The transports from Southampton sailed as far as Torbay, where they remained at anchor until October. The entire expedition then sailed for Cove Harbour, near Cork, where they arrived towards the end of the month.

At this time the establishment of the regiment was nine troops. A short time after its arrival at Cove the establishment was reduced to seven, but each troop was augmented in strength.

The officers were placed *en second* on the strength of the regiment, and a recruiting troop was ordered to be left at home. The officers left with this troop were Captain Neville, Lieutenant Robbins, and Cornet George Lawrence, all of whom had sick certificates. The necessary non-commissioned officers were also left to carry on the duties. Also, prior to the regiment sailing from Southampton, an order was received to send one captain, one quartermaster, and a proportion of non-commissioned officers to America to purchase mounts for the regiment. Captain Bolton, then the senior captain, went on this service, and shortly after, when a second major was added to the strength of the regiment, he was promoted to that rank.

The expedition did not actually start until February 9, 1796, when a fleet composed of transports, merchant vessels, and a convoy of war ships, amounting to more than 500 sail, weighed anchor. The expedition was unlucky from the outset. A violent storm on the third day completely dispersed it, the vessels taking shelter as they could in various ports, many indeed returning to Cove.

The Headquarters of the 13th was on board the *Concord*, and persevered in the voyage. Unfortunately, when in the Bay of Biscay, a fire broke out, which was only extinguished after most strenuous, nay, even heroic efforts. This fire was caused by an accident while fumigating between decks. This fumigation was in accordance with the orders of General John White, who commanded the entire force, —orders which had been issued before leaving Cove. It was particularly enjoined in case of either a death or of any infectious disease on board. A man died, and the surgeon recommended an immediate fumigation. A "pitch-pot" and heated "loggerhead" was employed. The pitch took fire and blazed up furiously. The ship rolled—the flaming pitch was upset—ran under the men's berths, and a general conflagration was the result. The worst part of it was that, in ignorance, water was thrown on the flaming pitch, and this made matters worse. The captain, who was in his cabin with the first mate engaged in writing, ran on deck with, it is stated, "his pen across his mouth," and dashed through the main hatchway, though the flames were rushing up there. Now the fire happened to be immediately over nineteen casks of powder, and the danger was extreme, as may be imagined.

An officer was sent down to the lower hold to cope with the conflagration, and cover the powder barrels with wet blankets and mattresses. This he did with the assistance of the men, who stuck nobly to their task. "Scores of men with their mattresses held in front of them" threw themselves on the flames, and at length smothered the blaze. By good luck the rigging was not touched by the flames, or nothing could have saved the ship. The officer in the lower hold spread a sailcloth over the barrels, and kept it wet despite the shower of sparks which fell around from the deck above, which was now burnt through. The regimental account of this affair quaintly concludes—"After this escape, fumigation by aid of the tar and pitch-pot was not again practiced."

But the troubles of the *Concord* were not yet over. The ship sprung a leak, and the captain, finding it "impossible to persevere with any hopes of making good his voyage," put about, and made all sail for Cork. Here he arrived after being out for fourteen days.

The *Concord* was the last ship to rejoin, and the rest of the fleet were already then refitted. The *Concord* was, however, hauled up high and dry, and carpenters from the fleet requisitioned. By February 26 the repairs were completed, and the fleet again weighed anchor and stood out to sea.

This time no accidents happened, and the *Concord*, which was somewhat of a slow sailer, reached Bridge Town Harbour, Barbadoes, and dropped anchor on April 1. There all the other transports were found already arrived.

It is now needful to narrate as briefly as possible the state of affairs in the West Indies at that time and to give the causes which led thereto.

Jamaica became a British Possession in 1655, though it was not until three years later that the Spaniards, its former possessors, were finally expelled.

The slaves released by the expulsion of their Spanish masters fled to the mountains, where they herded together and lived mainly by plundering such British settlers and settlements as they could.

These escaped blacks formed two clans—one in the northern part of the island and one in the south. Those in the south threatened Clarendon, then the seat of government, and being a menace had to be dispersed.

Their abandoned territory was seized by others who became a still greater menace, and the planters were compelled to fortify their houses and buildings for protection. Government again took action, and for a time succeeded till a Maroon leader, by name Cudjoe, came to the front. He was a strong man and a strong leader of men. This remarkable savage—for he was nothing more—organised his tribe with a discipline of his own invention. He was joined by the Maroons from the north and by another tribe. His method of warfare was this—never if possible to let one of his men be seen, and never under any circumstances to meet his enemy in the open. The country was such as to favour his strategy and tactics. It was intersected from east to west by a series of deep glens, rocky at the sides, invariably precipitous, and only to be approached by one narrow path along which Indian file was absolutely necessary. These glens were designated "cock-pits." The chain from east to west was connected by narrow passes, and there were certain others running in parallel lines from north to south. The fertile brain of Cudjoe invented a most elaborate system of signals—horns being used. How elaborate this was may be gauged from the fact that it is stated that each man had a separate call. Along the sides of the outlets to the "cock-pits" Cudjoe would post his men in absolute concealment, and some of these outlets were as much as 800 yards in length. Woe betide any force which was caught therein. Each man was marked and shot down by an unseen foe. Still, British modes of warfare at length prevailed, and Cudjoe was driven out from the south. He took refuge in the north-west, in what was called the Trelawney district. Here his fastness was wellnigh impregnable; moreover there was land there which could be cultivated and water to be obtained. For ten years a desultory warfare was carried on with all the horrors of plunder, brigandage, and butchery of wounded and prisoners on the part of the Maroons. At length Cudjoe practically compelled terms to be offered to him, and a treaty was entered into between that worthy and others of his crew (whose names have been handed down as "Johnny," Accompong, Cuffee, and Quaco) and the Government of George II. To the Maroons the terms were distinctly favourable,—absolute independence and self-government, save that they were not allowed to inflict the death penalty, a complete amnesty was assured, hunting rights granted, and 1500 acres of land awarded to them for ever.

All that the Government claimed was a right to send two white residents to Trelawney and that all runaway slaves captured by the

Maroons should be returned. The Maroons also covenanted to aid King George against any enemies.

A similar treaty was made with the other Maroons, and the arrangement worked well till 1795. The Maroons kept to their part of the treaty.

They dwelt in their reserves, some five in number, the chief of which was in the Trelawney district. For amusement they hunted pigs and runaway slaves. From the former, the name "Maroon"=hog-hunters, is supposed to be derived. They were ruled by their chiefs with an iron hand. For religion—if religion it can be called—they practised what remained of their native African god or devil worship. They bred fowls, cattle, and horses, and though negroes, preferred the white men to those of colour, and like white men they both drank and gambled. In 1760 they joined forces with the Government when the blacks rose in revolt, and in 1779-80 made common cause against white invaders of the island. All seemed to point to security.

The restrictions on their intercourse with Jamaica in general gradually relaxed. The Maroon began to wander farther afield and intermarried—if marriage it could be called—with female slaves on the plantations. The chiefs lost their hold on the people and the rod of iron rule was no more. True, the Trelawney Maroons had chiefs, and at length a white man, a certain Major James, who had lived among them most of his life, was elected or appointed to the office. He was not at any time a conspicuous success as chief, and coming into an estate took up his residence there for a good part of the year, leaving the Maroons of Trelawney to take care of themselves. This neither suited the Government nor the Maroons. The latter complained, and Major James was removed from his post. Wroth did he become in consequence, and, such is the perversity of human nature, wroth also became the Maroons. A new resident chief was appointed who was unfitted for the post—a post where a strong man, a man, indeed, capable of physically ruling, was needed. Trouble was brewing, and he was driven from the town. A message came from the now ripe-for-rebellion Maroons that they were ready for war, and that if the white men did not come to fight them they would come down and fight the white men. The then Governor, Lord Balcarres, perceived the gravity of the situation. Already the Maroons had sent their women and children into their fastnesses. They threatened to kill their cattle, and to kill their women and children as well, should these prove an encumbrance. Whether French agents from other West Indian Islands had been at the bottom of the trouble is not absolutely certain, but seems most probable.

And now a new menace arose. On several plantations where the masters and the slaves had hitherto subsisted in such harmony as was possible under the circumstances, unrest on the part of the negroes was apparent and discontent openly expressed. This was also serious. Balcarres endeavoured by diplomatic means to remove the trouble, and indeed persuaded six chiefs to surrender. He then proclaimed martial law, and prepared for military operations on the offensive. The scheme of the Governor was to blockade the recalcitrant Maroons and starve them out. How he expected to blockade forty square miles of most terribly difficult country with the slender force at his disposal effectually, is not easily to be understood.

However, on August 9, the main passes to the Maroon districts were seized. Between thirty and forty of the chiefs surrendered and were placed in confinement. This, however, did not "bring in" the Maroons. As an act of defiance they burnt their towns. War became necessary. Now it is estimated that at this time the Maroons totalled some 1200 men, women, and children, of which half belonged to the Trelawney district. The force at the disposal of Balcarres consisted of detachments of the 13th, 14th, 17th, and 18th Light Dragoons, the 20th Dragoons (the Jamaica Regiment), the 16th and 62nd Foot (about 300 men), and the 83rd Foot. There was also a local Militia officered by settlers, and the number of major-generals among these Militia officers was somewhat remarkable.

We will now return to the 13th Light Dragoons, whom we left at Bridge Town, Barbadoes, on April 1, 1796. Two expeditions were projected—one against St Lucia and the other against St Domingo. On April 21 the force for St Lucia sailed under the command of Sir Ralph Abercromby. On May 2 the troops for St Domingo, under the command of Major-General John White, arrived at Cape Nichola Mole.

The 13th did not disembark, except such detachments as were landed to take over the horses purchased in America by Captain Bolton, until the 27th, 28th, and 29th of July, when the regiment, mounted men and dismounted, were placed under canvas. Already, however, one of the mounted detachments had been employed. Early in June Captain The Hon. John Browne was ordered to parade with the army and march against the town of Bombard, which was then held by some 500 brigands.

The detachment of the 13th, under the command of Captain Browne, consisted of two subalterns and sixty men. The place was only twelve miles away, but owing to various obstacles, particularly the want of water, it took three days to accomplish the distance. All the spare cavalry horses were delivered to the Quartermaster-General's Department to be employed in conveying the commissariat, and to the artillery to drag the guns. The horses were duly harnessed and the army moved on, but "not one horse in ten would draw." A few carts got off towards night, but the sufferings of the troops for want of water were terrible. The first day's march was only five miles, yet thirty-five men perished from thirst.

The fight with the brigands of Bombard did not come off. On the 11th they were "allowed to capitulate, and marched out with the *honours of war!*"

While at St Domingo, with the exception of two or three brushes with the brigands, in one of which a charge was pressed home with effect, the regiment remained under canvas. The men were mainly employed in rearing barracks on the high ground behind Cape Nichola Mole, materials to build these being sent out from England.

Up to this time the regiment had remained in a healthy state. They had not left one man sick behind at Barbadoes, though when they sailed the hospitals there were full of cavalry soldiers. For some time at St Domingo the same favourable conditions were maintained. A note in the regimental records states that this was "generally allowed" to be "principally owing to the wine given by the officers to the surgeon for the use of the men"—the wine, of course, to be administered at his discretion. It seems that a large supply of port and madeira had been laid in. On arrival in hot latitudes the madeira was preferred to the port, and the latter was handed over to the surgeon as stated above. When the supply was exhausted an application was made to the public stores for another allowance of wine, but this was refused; not, as General White said, because he was not "satisfied the wine would only be made use of as intended by the regiment, yet, if he was to do so with us (the 13th), similar applications would come from quarters which, perhaps, would not be equally scrupulous in its distribution."

The regiment was attacked by yellow fever, and its ravages were terrible. "Scores were daily carried off by it, and at length the regiment was so much reduced as to be under the necessity of applying to the 56th Regiment, then in barracks, to bury its dead." The British dragoon regiments who served with the 13th Light Dragoons in this horrible climate, and exposed to this fatal scourge, were the 14th, 17th, 18th, 21st, 26th, and 29th. A list of the officers who escaped and returned to England will be given later.

On December 14, 1796, the remains of the regiment embarked at St Nichola Mole, stopped for a short time at Jerence (St Domingo), and on the 18th arrived at Port Royal, Jamaica, from whence it proceeded to Savannah la Mar and Black River, arriving there on December 31. Four troops were stationed at Savannah la Mar, and two at Black River. Here the remains of the squadron that came out with Lieut.-Colonel Walpole joined the regiment.

We will now continue the narrative of the Maroon War.

The orders given by Lord Balcarres were as follows: Colonel Sandford, with the 16th Foot and the 20th Dragoons, were told off to guard an outlet to the north. Colonel Walpole, with the 13th and 14th Light Dragoons (some 150 men), barred the outlet to the south. Lord Balcarres, with the 83rd Regiment, closed the south-west; while Colonel Hull, with the 62nd Regiment (170 men) and 17th Light Dragoons (one troop), guarded another northern place of egress.

The first blood went to the Maroons, who attacked a Militia post, killing and wounding several men. By the direct orders of Lord Balcarres on the same day (August 12), Colonel Sandford started to take "Old Town," a Maroon village. When well within the pass the column was met by a volley, though not a Maroon was to be seen. A second volley killed Sandford. The officer in command of the cavalry, seeing that a retreat in such a situation would be fatal, dashed right through at the head of his men and managed to rejoin Balcarres. Two officers and thirty-five men were killed and wounded. The local Militia, some of whom had accompanied the column, fled.

Six days later, "New Town," or rather the site of a new town the Maroons were building, was occupied unopposed.

On August 23 a combined movement was made of three columns under Colonels Fitch, Incledon, and Hull. It started at daybreak, and it was proposed to capture "Old Town." The place was taken without opposition, having been evacuated by the Maroons for some days. Lord Balcarres now built a blockhouse on the "New Town" site, and determined to lay waste the Maroon provision grounds.

To his surprise the enemy, whom he thought he had penned in a "cock-pit" to which they had withdrawn, got round some six miles in his rear, plundered a planter's house, and burnt it. Colonel Fitch was now left in command, as Lord Balcarres returned to Port Royal. Fitch was expected to form a complete cordon round the Maroon position, a task which was, of course, beyond him. He was moreover hampered in many ways by the impudence and absolute "impossibility" of the officers of the local Militia, who were even more useless than the men they professed to command. Colonel Fitch did not long enjoy his command. Falling into an ambuscade, he fell, together with two other officers.

The command then was given to Lieut.-Colonel the Hon. George Walpole of the 13th Light Dragoons. On his arrival in the Trelawney district he found his troops suffering from much sickness and the depression which so often accompanies illness and ill-luck combined. There were also signs that the negroes were inclined to join forces with the Maroons, in which case the Government would be face to face with a general revolt of negroes against whites.

The plan adopted by Colonel Walpole was this. He abandoned any idea of drawing a cordon round the district, but he established posts to command all known entrances to the "cock-pits." Here he employed blacks to clear away all jungle both above and below the spots selected. Lastly, he started training some men in, to them, quite a novel manner,—a method, by the way, that he copied from the Maroons themselves. His men always worked in pairs, so that in a precipitous country such as that was one man could climb leaving his arms in the safe custody of the other, who in his turn handed up both weapons while rejoining his companion.

Making every possible use of cover was also assiduously practised. To the surprise of the Maroons they found themselves ambuscaded by the whites. One of their foraging parties was cut off and destroyed utterly.

By a lucky chance, very shortly after, a body of the 17th Light Dragoons were despatched to try and discover from the heights above one of the "cock-pits" the position of the unknown path leading to it. Thirty men of the 17th were engaged, ten having been left behind under a sergeant to act as a support. There was a fierce fight—the supports were called up, and unfortunately the sergeant marched straight into the mouth of the "cock-pit," where he and his party perished. The thirty men on the heights, when their ammunition was exhausted, retreated in good order. Four men were, however, killed, and nine wounded.

Colonel Walpole then succeeded in dragging up a howitzer which he mounted on the heights now cleared of jungle. Shells began to drop into the "cock-pit." The Maroons evacuated it and took refuge in another, where, however, they had no water. Colonel Walpole repeated the operation. The Maroons then betook themselves to high ground, where the howitzer was powerless to harm them. By a lucky chance the path was discovered by one of the 17th, who caught sight of a woman descending to get water and followed her up unseen. The Maroons were driven out and again took refuge in a third "cock-pit" where this time there was water. The abandoned height was occupied. By this time, though the war was not over, it was clear that the back of the enemy's resistance was broken. The original stronghold of Cudjoe was occupied by Colonel Hull and a detachment of the 62nd. The next few months passed in small fights, a particularly brilliant piece of work being on one occasion performed by a non-commissioned officer of the 17th, who brought off his party when his commanding officer had been wounded. This took place about the middle of December. A few days later British and Maroons faced one another on the opposite sides of a deep gorge. In the fight which ensued twelve Maroons fell. They began to blow their horns as if inviting the British to negotiate. Neither side, however, quite knew how to begin. The Maroons feared to be shot. The British felt sure they would be did they show themselves. A young officer, by name Oswald Werge (17th Light Dragoons), climbed down unarmed and succeeded in opening negotiations. This was a most gallant act, as it was 100 to 1 he would be shot at sight. In the event Colonel Walpole was sent for, and to him the Maroons surrendered, on a distinct promise that they should not be deported.

The Government of Jamaica broke this engagement and despatched them to Nova Scotia. To Colonel Walpole the Jamaica Parliament voted a sword of honour. Under the circumstances it is not surprising to read that the sword of honour was declined by its intended recipient.

As will be seen by the foregoing, it was only two troops of the 13th that was employed in Jamaica. But the main interest lies in the fact that not until Lieut.-Colonel Walpole was given the command were the operations against the Maroons conducted with success. It may be with justice said that the credit of bringing those operations to a satisfactory issue is due to the military skill of the Lieutenant-Colonel of the 13th Light Dragoons. The regiment, or what remained of it, was reunited on December 31, 1796. There the regiment remained until May 1797, its numbers being sadly reduced. Fifty-six men of the 17th Light Dragoons were then drafted into the 13th; and a month later eighteen men of the 13th, until then detached at Jeremie in St Domingo, were drafted into the 21st Dragoons.

For about thirteen months the regiment remained at Savannah la Mar and Black River, when orders were received from England to furnish a draft of ninety-five men to the 20th Dragoons (or Jamaica Regiment). The draft was made over on March 25, 1798.

In August 1798 the remainder of the regiment, which consisted chiefly of the non-commissioned officers allowed to be brought home, in all amounting to no more than fifty-two, marched and was embarked for England.

The 13th reached Gravesend on October 31st, 1798, under the command of Licutenant Broome, who had with him Lieutenant Towers, Lieutenant Scully, and Cornet B. Lawrence.

Thence the 13th marched to York and joined that part of the regiment then at York Barracks. It reached York in November, having been absent only two years and six months, during which period 19 officers, 7 quartermasters, 2 volunteers, and 287 non-commissioned officers and men died from sickness. Only 1 man fell by the sword. The following statements give particulars:—

	Men.
Non-commissioned officers and privates sailed from England, including the squadron that went with Colonel Walpole	396
Non-commissioned officers and privates received from the 17th Light Dragoons	56
Total	452

Deduct—

Drafted to the 21st Light Dragoons	18
„ 20th „	95
Died	287
	400

Returned to England, 52.

The following list contains the names of all the officers of the 13th Light Dragoons who went on this expedition, including those who went to Jamaica with Colonel Walpole and those who subsequently joined there and at St Domingo:—

SAILED WITH THE REGIMENT FROM COVE HARBOUR, FEBRUARY 1796.

RANK.	NAME.	FATE.
Major	1. Hamilton L. Crofton	Died on his passage from Cape Nichola Mole, St Domingo, to America, July 14, 1796.
Captains	2. Hon. John Browne	Returned home.
	3. P. Doherty	Returned home.
	4. George Nixon	Died December 22, 1796.
	5. Hon. Robert Fitzroy	Died July 15, 1796.
Lieutenants	6. Christopher Sheares	Died July 25, 1796.
	7. J. S. Bradshaw	Died December 8, 1796.
	8. Arthur Buttle	Died July 25, 1796.
	9. Redmond Morres	Returned home.
Cornets	10. Henry Broome	Returned home.
	11. John Norcat	Died July 14, 1796.
	12. Joseph Faulkner (Adjutant)	Died July 1, 1796.
	13. Joseph Doherty	Died July 1, 1796.
Surgeon	14. Malachy Queely	Died June 26, 1796.
Quartermasters	1. Thomas Freeth	Died July 14, 1796.
	2. John Kelly	Died June 20, 1796.
	3. Wm. Faulkner	Died January 24, 1797.
	4. Brooks Lawrence	Returned home.
	5. William Colligan	Died August 11, 1796.

Sailed with the Expedition to Jamaica.

Rank.	Name.	Fate.
Lieut.-Colonel	15. Hon. George Walpole	Returned home.
Lieutenants	16. Lancelot Gubbins	Died November 25, 1796.
	17. R. Bennet	Returned home.
Assistant-Surgeon	18. J. Campbell	Died November 26, 1796.
Quartermasters	6. Andrew Newcomen	Died November 9, 1796.
	7. Samuel Webster	Died.
	8. Newcomen Wilkinson	Died July 9, 1796.

Joined the Regiment in the West Indies.

Rank.	Name.	Fate.
Major	19. James Preston	Died 1796.
Captain	20. J. Blake	Died August 6, 1797.
Capt.-Lieutenants	21. W. Forbes	Died August 6, 1796.
	22. John Kent	Returned home.
Lieutenants	23. James Towers	Returned home.
	24. D. O'Connor	Died December 28, 1796.
Cornets	25. J. Corbet	Died January 1, 1797.
	26. W. Griffiths	Died.
	27. W. Scully	Returned home.
	28. R. Buchanan	Returned home.
Surgeons	29. G. Ferguson	Died August 8, 1796.
	30. Jordan Roche	Returned home.
Volunteers	1. James Norcat	Died August 8, 1796.
	2. Joseph Faulkener	Died July 5, 1796.

Officers who went to America.

Rank.	Name.	Fate.
Major	31. Robert Bolton	Returned home.
Quartermaster	9. John Gilbert	Returned home.

		Officers.	Quartermasters.	Volunteers.	Grand Total.
Totals	Went out	31	9	2	42
	Died	19	7	2	28
	Returned home	12	2	0	14

Of the fifty-two men who returned to England very many were found on their arrival to be totally unfit for service, and were consequently invalided at Chatham. Of those that joined at York "but few were found useful or serviceable. Completely exhausted and worn out, they were gradually discharged at each succeeding inspection." In these words the regimental record of the 13th Light Dragoons in the West Indies closes.

CHAPTER X.

England, 1798-1809.

MEANWHILE during the month of May His Royal Highness the Commander-in-Chief directed that the regimental recruits at the cavalry depot at Maidstone, as well as all officers of the regiment then in Europe, were to assemble at the Trowbridge Barracks under the command of Lieut.-Colonel Bolton. Owing to the terrible losses by sickness in the West Indies, and the drafts from the regiment into other corps out there, it was practically necessary to raise the regiment anew. The number of recruits at Maidstone was 35, and with these were only 8 horses. Not more than two or three useful non-commissioned officers were to be found among the number. Still, with these a beginning was made to complete the regiment to the establishment ordered—641 men and 641 horses.

Clearly the utmost zeal and labour was required to effect this result. Parties of men under the most active and intelligent officers that could be selected were sent out on this duty, and with such success were their efforts crowned that in a short time the number of recruits obtained was greater than the barrack accommodation for them at Trowbridge, both men and horses being in excess of rooms and stabling. The young regiment in September, therefore, was marched to York: there and on the way more success in recruiting followed, and shortly after the return of the unfortunate relics of the 13th from the West Indies in November the accommodation in York Barracks was insufficient.

By August 1799 the regiment was at its full strength, and routes were received for a march to Weymouth. On arrival at Birmingham orders to halt were received, but in a few weeks the march was resumed, though on a different route, for the regiment was stationed at Coventry, Warwick, and Stratford-on-Avon.

The regiment was now augmented, its establishment being raised to 802 men and 802 horses—nine troops in all.

In the spring of 1800 a part of the regiment (three troops) was quartered in Leicester, and one to Nuneaton, and the establishment was increased to ten troops.

During August and September the 13th were quartered at Norwich, Aylsham, Walsham, Beccles, Bungay, and Wymondham, and remained there till June 1801, another augmentation taking place in March of that year by which the establishment reached 902 men and 902 horses.

In April one troop marched to Attleborough, in June one to Dedham, one changed to Manningtree, and one came into Norwich, four troops marching to Colchester. In October seven troops marched to Ipswich, two to Sudbury, and one to Stow Market and Needham Market. During December three marched to Ipswich and one to Needham Market.

The changes of quarters in 1802 were as follows: January, one troop to Hadleigh and one to Stow Market; February, one troop to Needham Market and one to Stow Market; April, two troops marched to Woodbridge and returned; and in July one troop marched to Boston in Lincolnshire. Meanwhile in May and June two reductions in the establishment took place. By the first the regiment was reduced to 652 men and 600 horses; by the second two troops were done away with, the strength of the regiment now standing at eight troops consisting of 516 men and 436 horses. This reduction was in consequence of the peace with France which followed on the Treaty of Amiens.

In July 1802 the regiment marched into quarters at Romford (barracks and billets) and Hornchurch (one troop).

Later in the year the 13th was moved to Hounslow, Richmond, and Twickenham.

At an inspection held at Hounslow, whither the regiment had been brought for the purpose, the 13th Light Dragoons were for the first time seen by the king. It may be noted that His Majesty made a most minute inspection, and expressed himself as highly pleased with their appearance and performance. The horses he particularly admired. Lieut.-Colonel Bolton on this occasion received great and certainly well-deserved credit.

After the review the regiment returned to Romford and Hornchurch.

But peace was not long to be maintained, and war broke out again in 1803.

The regiment was at once augmented to 604 men and 524 horses. In May it marched to Hounslow (four troops), Windsor (two troops), and Hampton Court (two troops), where it went into quarters. Two months later the establishment was augmented to 684 men and 604 horses.

During this year reviews and inspections were numerous, before His Majesty, the Prince of Wales, and the Dukes of York and Clarence, and a special one also was held by His Majesty's command on Ashford Common, before Elphy Bey, an Egyptian Mameluke and Bey. At this function nearly all the royal dukes and those holding high military command in the country were present. The review was in every way a success.

It will be remembered that England was now threatened with an invasion from France. Napoleon was collecting a huge armament at Boulogne for that purpose. Why the expedition did not start is history, and need not here be recounted. But to aid in repelling this attack, should it ever be made, the 13th Light Dragoons were moved from Hounslow to the south coast during June, and marched to Deal Barracks (four troops), to Sandwich and Stonar (one troop each), and to Ramsgate (two troops). Here the establishment of the regiment was immediately increased to ten troops consisting of 854 men and 754 horses, a further augmentation taking place in December when the strength of the regiment stood at ten troops (1064 men and 1064 horses).

For a year the 13th remained in its quarters, and in December 1805 marched to Canterbury. By this time the scheme for the invasion of England had come to an end, at any rate for the time. The French army had marched into Germany and the apprehension of an immediate hostile attack on our shores had passed away. For 1806 the movements of the regiment were these: in September four troops marched to Deal, two to Sandwich, and two to Ramsgate.

A reduction in the establishment had taken place by the end of the year, and the strength was now 854 men and 854 horses.

On July 23, 1807, the regiment marched from the south coast

through Canterbury to quarters at Kingston, Richmond, Twickenham, and Cobham, remaining in cantonments till August 17, when it was reviewed by the Prince of Wales and the Duke of York. Now at that time orders had already been given for the 13th to move on to Dorchester the next day, but so well did the regiment acquit itself in the field, and so smart was the appearance of the men and the horses, that the marching orders were countermanded. The 13th was in consequence detained and brigaded with the 12th Dragoons, then in Hounslow; the command of the brigade being given to Lieut.-Colonel Bolton of the 13th, to whose soldierly qualities the splendid condition of the regiment was so greatly due. For a month Lieut.-Colonel Bolton exercised the brigade twice weekly, when on September 10 it was again reviewed, this time by H.R.H. the Commander-in-Chief, and received his high approval.

On September 12 the first division of the regiment marched for Dorchester and Weymouth, and was followed by the other divisions on subsequent days, the last division reaching Dorchester on September 24.

The Weymouth troop marched from the Radipole Barracks to Wareham on December 7, the Dorchester troop to Bridport, and three other troops from Radipole went to Dorchester.

A fortnight later a squadron of the 2nd Hussars (King's German Legion) was ordered to Dorchester, and the troops of the 13th there had in consequence to vacate their quarters. They were transferred to Blandford.

On February 8, 1808, one troop marched from Blandford to Trowbridge; and two troops, on February 21, from Blandford to Dorchester. On March 14 one troop went from Wareham to Gosport. Those of the troops remaining in the neighbourhood were reviewed on April 2 by H.R.H. the Duke of Cumberland at Dorchester.

Two troops marched from Dorchester on May 11 and arrived at Trowbridge on the 14th. One went into barracks there and the other into quarters at Bradford-on-Avon. The two troops which were then at Trowbridge marched thence to Dorchester. The establishment of horses of the regiment was now reduced to 754.

During the last days of June and the first few days of July the various scattered troops of the 13th assembled at Exeter for the purposes of inspection and review.

On July 4 it was inspected on foot, on the 11th a review was held, and on the 16th an inspection in marching order, by Major-General Thewles.

Two days later part of the regiment went into cantonments: one troop at Totness, one at Modbury, two at Truro, and one at Taunton. The rest of the regiment remained at Exeter. On August 3 one troop left Exeter for Honiton. During October Major-General Thewles inspected the troops at the several quarters of the regiment, the troop at Truro only excepted.

The movements of the various troops at this time were very involved. The troops from Totness and Modbury marched to Truro and were replaced by two troops from Exeter. Those from Truro marched to Exeter. The Taunton troop changed to Trowbridge late in November, and in February (1809) a troop from Exeter marched to Tiverton and another to Honiton, and a second later to Tiverton. On March 27 the Tiverton troops marched to Taunton.

While the regiment, or rather a portion of it, was quartered at Taunton during this year, a rather serious riot broke out in the town. It seems that a man belonging to the local militia had been placed in the guard-room of his regiment. A corporal and several men attempted his rescue therefrom. The townspeople joined in the disturbance. One of the officers was wounded by the bayonet of one of his own men—a ringleader in the riot. Matters looked very serious until the 13th Light Dragoons, the Taunton Rifle Corps, and various recruiting parties in the town, were called out under arms. Order was then speedily restored.

One hundred horses were now selected from the regiment, and on April 24 marched from Exeter to Plymouth, where they were given over to a detachment of the 20th Dragoons and embarked for Portugal.

The 13th now assembled in Exeter for review by Major-General Thewles. Two troops from Taunton, one from Totness, one from Modbury, and one from Honiton marched into Exeter on April 29, and on May 3 two troops from Truro arrived. The review took place on May 30, an inspection in watering order on the 31st, and on foot under arms on June 2.

The stay of the 13th in the West of England was now ended. On June 22 the regiment began its march from Exeter for "King's Duty," and during the course of July went into cantonments in Hounslow, Hampton Court, Richmond, Twickenham, Chertsey, Staines, and Egham.

The inspection by H.R.H. the Duke of Cambridge took place on Hounslow Heath on July 28, and a review by H.R.H. the Prince of Wales about a month later in the same place. On the last occasion the Dukes of York, Clarence, Cumberland, and Cambridge were all present, besides the Adjutant-General and the Duke of Brunswick Oels.

On November 1 the troops at Hampton Court exchanged quarters with those at Chertsey and Twickenham, and so the regiment remained till just before orders for foreign service in Portugal were received.

CHAPTER XI.

The Peninsular War, 1810.

DURING the first week in February 1810, the 13th Light Dragoons were ordered to prepare eight troops for immediate service. At the time the regiment was stationed at Hounslow, and there the service troops were formed on February 9. Two days later the orders arrived for the regiment to march to Portsmouth, there to embark for foreign service, routes being given. Colonel Bolton left the regiment, and was promoted Major-General on July 25, 1810.

On February 13 the regiment marched in four divisions by several routes—

1ST DIVISION, UNDER THE COMMAND OF LIEUT.-COLONEL MUTER.

1st Division
{ Captain Buchanan's Troop—Captain Buchanan, Lieut. Major and Cornet Garston.
Captain Stisted's Troop—Captain Stisted, Lieutenant Edwards, Cornet King.

2ND DIVISION, UNDER THE COMMAND OF LIEUT.-COLONEL P. DOHERTY.

2nd Division
{ Captain White's Troop—Captain White, Lieutenant Turner, Lieutenant Smyth.
Captain Doherty's Troop—Captain Doherty, Lieutenant Doherty.

3RD DIVISION, UNDER THE COMMAND OF CAPTAIN MACALESTER.

3rd Division
{ Captain Macalester's Troop—Captain Macalester, Lieutenant D'Arcy, Lieutenant White.
Captain Bowers's Troop—Lieutenant Moss, Lieutenant Jeffries.

4TH DIVISION, UNDER THE COMMAND OF CAPTAIN MORRES.

4th Division
{ Captain Morres's Troop—Captain Morres, Lieutenant Taylor, Lieutenant Frederic Geale.
Captain (Major) Boyse's Troop — Captain (Major) Boyse, Lieutenant Drought, Lieutenant Moreton.

Saturday, February 17, the 1st, 2nd, and 3rd Divisions marched into Portsmouth and embarked.

Sunday, February 18, the 4th Division marched in, and a part of Captain Morres's troop was embarked; transport was lacking for the remainder, but this being supplied on the morrow the embarkation was completed.

Major Boyse's troop embarked on Monday, February 26, and Tuesday, February 27.

The entire regiment, consisting of eight troops of 85 men each and 85 horses, was now on board, and it is recorded that no accidents occurred during the embarkation. The regiment was distributed among twenty-three transports.

Lieut.-Colonel Head was in command of the regiment, and, in addition to the officers named, Lieutenant Holmes (Adjutant), Surgeon Roche, Assistant-Surgeon Armstrong, Veterinary Surgeon Chard, and Paymaster Gardiner also embarked.

The troop quartermasters were Murphy, Mitchell, Layfield, Sinclair, and Greenham.

The depot of the regiment was established at Chichester, and thither the two troops which were left at home proceeded.

These two troops were commanded by Captain George Lawrence, and Captain Brooks Lawrence (under the command of the former), the subaltern officers being Cornet Bowers, Cornet Maclean, and Cornet Proby (sick).

Captain Bowers, of the 3rd Division, was a student, and remained at the Royal Military College.

The MS. Records of the Services of the 13th Light Dragoons, compiled by Lieut.-Colonel Patrick Doherty, state that the reception accorded to the various divisions at the various towns and villages *en route* for Portsmouth was most favourable. The war was popular, and the troops were heartily cheered.

The fleets destined for Portugal and Gibraltar weighed anchor on the morning of March 5. Owing to a failure in the wind, however, they were delayed for the night in Yarmouth Roads (Isle of Wight). The voyage was renewed on the morrow, but by 11 A.M. it was again needful to anchor about two miles off the Needles. That evening the fleets put back into Yarmouth Roads. Next day a start was again made, and again it was necessary to return.

From Yarmouth Roads the fleets put back to Stokes Bay, where the vessels remained from 8 P.M. on March 8 until Friday, March 13. At length on the morning of the 14th the regiment fairly started on its voyage. Lisbon was safely reached on March 28 by all, except that part of the regiment which was in the transport *Bulmer*. This, however, arrived two days later.

The troops had been on board for forty days, and during that period had lost seventeen horses.

On the evening of March 28 the men and horses of two transports were disembarked, and marched to the Belem Barracks, situated about four miles from Lisbon.

The following day orders were received to discontinue the disembarkation.

When the *Bulmer*, with Colonel Head and the Staff, arrived on the 30th, the disembarkation was ordered to be resumed, and the men and horses of two more transports proceeded to Belem Barracks. By April 2 all were safely landed. Accommodation for the officers of the regiment was sadly lacking at Belem, owing to the large number of officers of other corps which were there. All hotels were full, and for three or four nights most of the officers of the 13th slept on chairs or on the floor. Permission to put down a mattress on the floor cost half-a-crown. Shoeing the horses, and generally getting into order, and making every necessary arrangement for field service, occupied the next few days. An issue of money to the men, and the cheapness of wine, led to a few cases of excess for a day or two, but "timely notice, a few instances of punishment," soon checked this, and henceforth "the men's conduct was good and soldier-like." Duties went on as if in barracks at home. Parades, mounted and on foot, and, when the horses' hoofs became somewhat hardened, frequent parades in marching order, were held. But it was found that the men carried too much baggage, and it was necessary to reduce the amount. Baggage for each man was cut down to no more "than was absolutely necessary to keep him clean." The rest was packed and stitched in separate canvas bags, duly labelled and placed in store with the heavy baggage.

From the Wellington Despatches we take two brief extracts, dated Viseu, April 5, 1810.

LISBON Police CAVALRY.

LISBON Police Guard.   Armed PEASANT of Algarva

To Col. Peacocke. . . . I beg that, upon the receipt of this letter, one squadron of the 13th Light Dragoons, and 4 corporals belonging to the three squadrons of the same regiment, with their horses, etc., may be embarked to go to Cadiz, as soon as the Agent of Transports shall have prepared vessels to receive them. The 4 corporals must be good horsemen and men well acquainted with the sword exercise; and these men, on their arrival at Cadiz, are to be put under the direction of Maj.-Gen¹· Whittingham, the other 3 Squadrons of the 13th Light Dragoons are to be equipped, and in readiness to take the field, but are to remain at Lisbon till further orders.

To Vice Ad¹· The Hon. G. Berkeley. . . . Direct Agent of Transports to provide transports for their conveyance.

The men were to be sent to Cadiz under convoy "as soon as they shall be embarked."

In consequence of this order a squadron of the regiment, consisting of Captain Morres's and Captain Bowers's troops, began to embark for Cadiz on April 10, but so strong was the wind and so rough was the water that only eighteen horses could be got on board that day. On the 11th the embarkation was safely concluded, and 178 men and horses, exclusive of officers' chargers, were distributed among five transports. The officers sent on this service were Captain Morres (in command of the squadron), and Lieutenants Geale, Moss, and Jeffries, with Quartermasters Murphy and Greenham. On the evening of April 12 the vessels weighed anchor and sailed for Cadiz.

On Wednesday, April 25, Lieut.-Colonel Doherty, Lieut.-Colonel Muter, Captain White, and Captain Stisted went to Lisbon as members of a General Court-Martial, where they remained nearly three weeks, owing to the continued illness of General Leith, the President of the Court.

Meanwhile, on Sunday, April 29, Captain Buchanan's troop marched to Salvatierre. On Wednesday, May 2, Captain Boyse's troop marched to Villa Franca, and Captain Doherty's to Villa Novo. On Thursday, May 3, the troops of Captains White, Stisted, and Macalester marched to Villa Franca also. On May 14, Lieut.-Colonel Muter and Captain White, and the next day Lieut.-Colonel Doherty and Captain Stisted, left Lisbon to join the regiment, having received permission to do so. General Leith was still ill, but it was represented by Lieut.-Colonel Doherty that there were a sufficient number of members on the Court independent of them.

On Wednesday, May 10, the troops of Major Boyse, Captain Buchanan, and Captain Doherty marched for Abrantes. The following day those of Captain White, Captain Stisted, and Captain Macalester left for the same place, where on the 16th further marching orders were received. Captain Buchanan's and Captain Doherty's troops marched for Gaffete. On the 17th Major Boyse's, Captain Stisted's, and Captain Macalester's troops marched for Alpolhoã, and Captain White's troop to Flora de Rosa.

On May 23, Lieut.-Colonel Doherty rejoined and took command of the squadron at Gaffette, and Lieut.-Colonel Muter joined at Flora de Rosa.

Next day the squadron at Gaffete was inspected in marching order by Major-General Fane, who went on thence to inspect the troops under Lieut.-Colonel Head at Alpolhoã.

June 12, Captain White's troop marched from Flora de Rosa to Estremoz. July 11, the three troops at Alpolhoã marched to Portalegre, whither they were followed on the next day by the two troops at Gaffete.

On July 13 the garrison at Portalegre was paraded under arms at 6 A.M., and an hour later marched for Alpolhoã, where the infantry went into bivouac and the 13th into crowded quarters in the town.

Here next day the force was augmented by four regiments of Portuguese cavalry, with Captain Stisted's troop of the 13th. This force was under the immediate command of General Fane.

The Portuguese cavalry marched on to Niza, but Captain Stisted's troop rejoined the regiment.

At 2 A.M. on Sunday, July 15, Captain Macalester's troop marched with General Fane. An hour later the other five troops followed, bivouacking that night for the first time near Povoa, with the exception of Captain Buchanan's troop, which marched to Castello de Vide.

The regiment had never hitherto been in bivouac, and both the officers and men were perfectly ignorant what to do. The horses were tied to trees in a grove where it was intended to bivouac. Nobody knew what was to be done for food, forage, &c. Provisions were served out to the men by the commissary; but how to cook them was another matter. The officers, owing to the way in which the baggage had been reduced, were without canteens or indeed any little comforts.

PEASANT of the Corregimiento of Salamanca.

A PEASANT BOY of Nisa

So the 13th were discovered in the evening by General Fane, who told the men to "hut themselves." It appears that it was not known that to cut down trees or do any injury was permissible. However, in a very short time trees were cut down and huts made and line ropes tied up, so that before dark the bivouac looked comfortable and was complete. Outposts were planted, and a field officer of the day appointed. On the 20th General Fane's cavalry division, consisting of the 13th Light Dragoons and the 1st, 4th, 7th, and 10th Portuguese Cavalry, assembled, and were inspected by the general. Three troops of the 13th with Lieut.-Colonel Head then marched to Alpolhoã, and a squadron with Lieut.-Colonel Doherty to Gaffete. The Portuguese regiments with General Fane moved to Niza. From Gaffete the road to Ponte de Sor was reconnoitred, reports being furnished as to distance, road, and country.

Matters remained thus until August 2, the monotony being only broken by occasional squadron field-days. On that date, at 3 A.M., a move was made, and the troops assembled at Niza. Thence a forward movement began. The Tagus was crossed at Villa Valhe, and the regiment went into bivouac on the road leading to Castel Branco. Next day, starting at 4 A.M., they marched, passing through Castel Branco, and went into bivouac about two miles beyond that place.

On Saturday, August 4, Captain Doherty joined the regiment with a supply of corn which he had with difficulty procured at Ponte de Sor. Captain Doherty had, however, succeeded in purchasing thirty-five mules, which he loaded with corn, brought in, and lodged with the commissary. The next day the regiment marched through a village called Escalos de Cima, and bivouacked a short distance beyond it. Captain White with his troop was, however, sent to Ladoera, to watch the movements of General Regnier's corps. General Fane took up his quarters in the village, while the Portuguese cavalry were distributed either in the neighbouring villages or went into bivouac near.

On Saturday, August 11, the regiment, with the exception of Captain White's troop, paraded at 2 A.M., and marched. At 5 A.M. the whole cavalry division assembled at the village of Malta,—General Fane meanwhile carrying out a reconnaissance in person with three squadrons of Portuguese cavalry.

It had been expected that the cavalry of the enemy would have been met with, but after waiting till 2 P.M., as no enemy appeared, the division marched back to its respective bivouacs. The 13th arrived at about 4 P.M.

During this day Captain White, who with about eighteen men of his troop was out on duty protecting a foraging party, had the good fortune to espy a body of the enemy's cavalry, numbering some 150. He immediately advanced. The enemy retired, and covered their retreat with skirmishers.

Captain White and his men pursued and chased the enemy at a gallop across the plain for some distance. This affair chanced to occur in full view of General Fane, who was out reconnoitring. He was greatly pleased, and on coming up with the regiment he expressed his approbation of it in the handsomest manner.

On August 14 the regiment paraded in marching order, and proceeded to the village of Escalos de Cima to obtain forage. A supply of good hay, sufficient for two days' consumption, was the result.

On the 22nd Captain White and his troop again distinguished themselves. He had marched from Ladoera on a foraging expedition, and fell in with a troop of French cavalry. The two bodies immediately formed and threw out skirmishers. Captain White moved forward to the attack. The enemy then retired, covered by their skirmishers. On Captain White still advancing, the enemy discharged their carbines and again retired. Gradually the pace increased till the pursuit was maintained at a gallop, and so continued for about six miles. Here at the bottom of a hollow way there was a stream of water, and this the enemy crossed and then formed on the opposite side in as wide a formation as the road allowed. Captain White halted his men on the road leading to the water, and formed with a front of threes. When nearly up, the enemy began to retreat from his left flank. Captain White charged and cut completely through the Frenchmen, and so to the head of the column. The affair was short and sharp while it lasted. In the event Captain White captured the whole troop, with the exception of the captain and the farrier, who threw themselves off their horses and escaped in the confusion. The prisoners numbered 2 lieutenants, 3 sergeants, 6 corporals, 1 trumpeter, and 50 dragoons. 58 horses were also taken. Lieutenant Turner, who was with Captain White on this occasion, behaved extremely well.

When the enemy first came in view, Captain White sent a message to a troop of Portuguese cavalry which was stationed with him, but by the time the troop arrived on the scene the enemy had surrendered. Another message despatched to the 13th Light Dragoons at Escalos de Cima brought a troop of the regiment, under Captain Macalester, in support; but as there was nothing to be apprehended the troop returned to the bivouac in the evening. In this brilliant little affair the 13th suffered no casualties. Many of the enemy and their horses, however, received sabre wounds. The prisoners were treated with great humanity, a circumstance that was gratefully acknowledged at General Hill's dinner-table later by a French officer who had been taken in another affair. It appears that the wounded Frenchmen were most carefully tended, and that the prisoners were allowed to retain their packs and personal belongings. A most favourable report of this occurrence was forwarded by General Fane to Headquarters. It is dated from Escalos de Cima, August 22, 1810. The details are in no way different from those already given, but one or two additional particulars are obtained. It appears that Captain White had expressed his obligations to Major Charles A. Vigoureux of the 38th Regiment, who was a volunteer with him. To the information given by Major Vigoureux, then employed on reconnoitring service, was due the discovery of the presence of the enemy. With Major Vigoureux the plan of attack was concerted. The Major, being unmounted, begged a horse, which was supplied. It was one of the largest horses of Captain White's troop. In the charge Major Vigoureux rode with Captain White, and making straight at the French commanding officer, who was leading, that officer, instead of defending himself, dropped his sword to the salute, and turning it, presented the hilt to Major Vigoureux. The sword was afterwards presented to Lieut.-Colonel Brunton, who commanded the 13th Regiment of Light Dragoons in 1831-1833.

From Lazados, dated August 23rd, an order was issued by Lieut.-General Hill intimating his great satisfaction at the report of Brigadier-General Fane, and stating that "the conduct of Capt. White and the officers, non-commissioned officers, and men of the two services (British and Portuguese) engaged in this affair merits the Lieut.-General's best thanks, and he will not fail to lay the particulars before the Commander of the Forces." Brigadier-General Fane has, he says, "much pleasure in communicating the preceding order, and he congratulates the officers and soldiers concerned on having merited the approbation of the Lieut.-General commanding the division." Later (August 28), Major-General Fane, by the orders of Lord Wellington, conveyed "to Captain White and Lieut. Turner of the 13th Light Dragoons, and to Alferes Pedro Raymando di Oliviera of the 4th Regiment of Portuguese Dragoons, and to the non-commissioned officers and soldiers engaged in the affair of the 22nd, near Ladoera, His Excellency's approbation of their conduct, and to inform them that His Excellency will not fail to report his sense of their behaviour in the most favourable terms to His Majesty and to His Royal Highness the Prince Regent." Captain White was afterwards appointed to the Staff of the army. He was killed at the Battle of Salamanca. The captured horses, except those picked out for Portuguese service, were sold by auction on Saturday, August 25, and the proceeds of the sale divided among their captors in the 13th Light Dragoons.

On Thursday, August 23, Lieutenant Doherty, with a party, marched from the bivouac to Malta, where he took charge of the prisoners, who were taken to Castello Branco and delivered over to Lieut.-General Hill.

The regiment now marched from Escalos de Cima to Castello Branco. The baggage started at 4 A.M. on September 5, followed, two hours later, by the troops.

The pickets from the various outposts were collected at 6 in the evening by Lieut.-Colonel Doherty, the field officer for the day, and marched to the same place. Here the regiment was joined by a small draft from England, under the command of Sergeant Brady.

Two days later the troops marched back and took up their old ground near Escalos de Cima.

Hitherto the health of the regiment and the condition of the horses had been all that could be desired, but at Escalos de Cima trouble—and serious trouble—arose. The village was a miserable place; the want of good water was much felt, despite all attempts to obtain a sufficient supply for men and horses.

On Wednesday, September 12, at 1.30 P.M., an order was received

OFFICER, 13TH LIGHT DRAGOONS (1800).

(*Lent by* Lieut.-Colonel A. LEETHAM.)

for the regiment to turn out and march immediately to Castello Branco. One hour later the regiment, with baggage, sick, and wounded, marched off the ground, being joined the same night by Captain White's troop from Ladoera.

The following day the regiment, together with two regiments of Portuguese cavalry, paraded for inspection by General Fane.

On Tuesday, September 18, at 3.30 A.M., the 13th and the Portuguese cavalry marched through an extremely hilly country to Larzedas, where the regiments bivouacked, finding on the ground there some extremely good huts erected by the infantry. The next day the division reached Corticeda, where the quarters were very crowded. On the 20th they arrived at Barca de Codas, near which place they went into bivouac. The following day 135 sick horses and 35 sick men marched from the bivouac, under the command of Quartermaster Mitchell, to Santarem. This was in consequence of a general order that all spare horses and sick men should be sent to the rear. Mention has already been made of the sickness which attacked the regiment near Escalos de Cima, and this was a part of its effect. Fever and ague played havoc with the men, the weather was hot, and the climate most unhealthy. Lieut.-Colonel Doherty tells us that "cart-loads were every day sent off to the General Hospital at Castello Branco; the men's spirits began to flag, fever appeared to possess them to such a degree that, had the regiment remained much longer in that wretched place, the consequences would be lamentable."

At the time the sick convoy started for Santarem, the regiment, with the remainder of the division, marched for Espinal, when the 13th went into crowded quarters, and the Portuguese into bivouac.

This was a most fatiguing march of forty miles. The day was excessively hot, yet the force reached its destination about 4 P.M. The march was resumed on the morrow, through a highly cultivated and what appeared to be a thickly inhabited country. That night the regiment went into bivouac. Marching again on the morrow, a halt for a day was made on the 24th.

On the 25th the division on its march crossed the line of General Hill's division of infantry at Ponte de Murellas, and keeping on its way proceeded till within a league and a half of a French cavalry position. Hoping to induce the French to come out, the division halted for some time, but the enemy declined to stir. The division then retired, the 13th putting up at a miserable deserted village called St Martindo. The Portuguese cavalry was distributed in the neighbourhood. On these marches Captain Doherty had been taken so seriously ill with ague and erysipelas, that he was obliged to be carried on a mule and pack-saddle. The regiment halted during September 26. On that day "much firing was heard" in the direction of Lord Wellington's position. This firing was a preliminary to the sanguinary battle of Busaco.

On the 27th the firing was resumed at daybreak, both cannon and musketry being heard by the regiment, who stood at their horses with baggage packed and loaded, and all things ready to move off instantly if ordered.

From the despatch of Lord Wellington to Lord Liverpool, dated Coimbra, 30th September 1810, and concerning the battle of Busaco, the extract referring to the 13th Light Dragoons is here given:—

> As the enemy's whole army was on the ridge of the Mondego, and as it was evident that he intended to force our position, Lt.-Genl. Hill crossed that river by a short movement to the left on the morning of the 26th, leaving Col. le Cor with his Brigade in the Sierra de Marcella, to cover the right of the Army, and Major-Gen. Fane with his Division of Portuguese Cavalry and the 13th Light Dragoons in front of the Alva [river] to observe and check the movements of the enemy's cavalry on the Mondego. With this exception the whole Army was collected upon the Sierra de Busaco, with the British Cavalry observing the plain in the rear of its left, and the road leading from Montagoa to Oporto, through the mountainous track, which connects the Sierra de Busaco with the Sierra de Caramula.

Thus it happened that it was not the good fortune of the 13th Light Dragoons to be actually engaged in that desperate battle.

Lieut.-Colonel Doherty's manuscript states that during Friday the 28th

> the firing continued at intervals the better part of the morning, and it appeared from such accounts as reached us that the enemy attacked Lord Wellington in his position on the heights of Busaco, both on his right and his centre, with the most determined resolution, and after a great deal of hard fighting, particularly with the bayonet, they were repulsed in all parts with great slaughter. . . .
>
> From a hill in the vicinity of the village (St Martindo), with the help of our glasses, we had an indistinct view of Busaco's heights and of the attacks that took place.

The movement of Lieut.-General Hill alluded to in the Wellington despatch is that in which his line of march crossed the line of march of Major-General Fane's division. It will be remembered that almost immediately on the regiment's arrival at Lisbon a squadron under Captain Morres was detached and sent to Cadiz.

On September 28, this squadron rejoined the regiment and took up its quarters in a village near.

At 6 P.M. the same evening orders were received for the regiment to turn out instantly, and the troops immediately assembled with baggage complete on the alarm post. Here two sergeants of Portuguese cavalry, who were supposed to be well acquainted with the country, were provided as guides. Whether through ignorance, or owing to the darkness of the night, the regiment lost the road and found itself "at one time close upon the French lines, and in a lane so narrow that to get out of it the regiment was obliged to rein backward for a considerable distance. To gain the road the march lay over a rocky and hilly country, the night dark and rainy. In consequence, many accidents occurred both to men and horses. About 3 o'clock in the morning of the 29th, having got on plain ground, the regiment formed in close column of half squadrons—linked [horses]—and men and officers dismounted and lay down to sleep under a rain that fell in torrents."

At 5.30 A.M. orders were received to mount.

The regiment marched, and crossing the Mondego river ascended the opposite mountain by a road so steep that the baggage half-way up had to be unloaded and carried up by hand. This was being done till it was discovered that some distance down the river there was a mule-path leading to the road. On this march the horse which Lieut.-Colonel Doherty was riding was knocked half over a precipice by a wounded led horse ahead which fell. Luckily the colonel's mount managed to regain the path, though its hind legs were down the precipice. The wounded horse rolled over the side and was dashed to pieces. Arrived at the village of St Miguel, the regiment went into bivouac after being in the saddle (with only one short halt) for twenty-one hours. The object of this night march was to intercept a body of the enemy's cavalry. The enemy had, however, marched some hours before.

The following day the regiment returned to St Martindo.

On Monday, October 1, the regiment left its bivouac — four troops with Colonel Head put up at St Miguel, two with Lieut.-

Colonel Doherty at Terrars, and two with Lieut.-Colonel Muter at Vindinha.

The march was resumed next day. Five troops with Colonel Head went to Merianda de Cooa, and the other three troops to the villages near. Here it was ascertained that a considerable number of the enemy's cavalry was hovering about, and a body of them was seen by a Portuguese peasant marching parallel to the right of the 13th. Proceeding on their march, the regiment started at 2 A.M. next day, and arrived at Cabbaio at 4 P.M., where it went into bivouac.

This was a long and trying march.

Thursday, October 4, the division marched at 5 A.M., and on arrival at Thomar the 13th was ordered to fall back. The regiment accordingly did so for a distance of about a league. Pickets were turned out and outposts taken up, the rest of the regiment going into bivouac. Early next morning the pickets were withdrawn, and the regiment again marched into Thomar. There Lieut.-General Hill's division of infantry was found just passing through the town. The 13th linked horses on the parade, and about 4 P.M. put up in quarters. The inhabitants of this town, as of all others, had fled because the French were close at hand, and generally arrived just after our troops had left. Some very great inconvenience was caused to the regiment and the army here owing to an issue of money in dollars by the Paymaster-General. This issue was made because transport for so large a sum was lacking. Officers commanding troops were obliged to give portions of this money to the non-commissioned officers, and also to steady dragoons, after loading their own baggage animals with as much as they could possibly stow away.

In Lieut.-Colonel Doherty's MS. an interesting account is given of an unfortunate English merchant at Thomar, who had laid in an enormous stock of all kinds of goods for the wants of an army. He managed to sell to such regiments as passed as much as they had spare transport to carry, but, lacking transport himself to convey the remainder—and this the greatest part—into a place of safety, was compelled to destroy it all to prevent it falling into the hands of the enemy. Wine was freely given away by the owners thereof to the troops in passing, and the rest ruthlessly destroyed for the same reason.

On Saturday, October 6, the division marched into Gallegon, a town which, like all the rest, was found deserted by its inhabitants. On the march numbers of unfortunate people, some of them of high position, were tramping along the road with perhaps only a few necessaries and articles of dress tied up in a bundle, and endeavouring to keep up with the British troops as a sole means of safety. Mules or horses they had to leave behind. How many aged and infirm men, or delicate women, who, left behind, fell into the hands of the enemy, and what their fate, can never be known,—perhaps in some cases it would be better not to inquire.

On Sunday, October 7, the baggage was sent off at noon, and two hours later the regiment marched from Gallegon. As the British marched out on one side of the town, the enemy's cavalry marched in on the other. The 13th passed through Santarem and another town, in both of which the same scenes were witnessed; the wretched inhabitants by hundreds, with bundles of such things as they could snatch up or that they hoped to be able to carry, making off along the Lisbon Road, and leaving the rest of their property a prey to the advancing French.

On Monday, October 8, under a deluge of rain, the regiment mounted at 2 A.M. At 3 P.M. it reached Villa Novo. During this day's march General Fane had frequently halted the regiment and gave front to the enemy's cavalry who were moving along a road parallel to our line of march and on our right. But the French cavalry declined to come to close quarters. Colonel Head with six troops were put up at Villa Novo, while two troops under Lieut.-Colonel Doherty marched back to a hunting lodge of the Prince Regent. Nearly the whole squadron was required for outpost duty, and any officer not in charge of a picket was on patrol duty throughout the night, for the enemy had strong posts on the road leading to Azambuza.

The next day the regiment marched at 10.30 A.M. and passed through Alhandra, where the British Army was in position under Lord Wellington. A squadron under the command of Lieut.-Colonel Muter was left at Castelheiro to watch the enemy.

At 6 P.M. the regiment arrived at St Antonio de Tozel and put up in quarters. Twenty-four hours later the march was resumed, and the village of Lumiar was reached about midnight. *En route* orders were received to detach a squadron to Alhandra under Major Boyse.

The squadron left on the preceding day at Castelheiro rejoined, the cavalry of the enemy being in possession of that place. Here the regiment halted until October 21.

A note in Lieut.-Colonel Doherty's MS. gives the details of a curious incident which is not without interest. While Lieut.-Colonel Doherty was riding in Villa Nova on October 9, superintending the quarters for his men, he was accosted by a Portuguese gentleman, who, surrounded by his wife and daughters, was standing on a balcony. He offered the hospitality of his house to that officer, an offer which was gladly accepted. Lieut.-Colonel Doherty was treated in the kindest way. It seems that his host, in view of the very rapid advance of the enemy, had determined to flee. His wife and daughters were already equipped for the journey in riding habits, but with, as can be easily understood, hardly more than a few changes of clothing. To Lieut.-Colonel Doherty, however, he handed over the keys of his house, which was full of beautiful furniture and valuables, in the hope that the town would remain in the possession of the British. By good luck, though the 13th marched on the next morning, the house was taken possession of by a British General Officer who was later succeeded by another, and it was so occupied until Massena retired from before the British lines, thus being saved from pillage and destruction.

On Thursday, October 11, one of the officers of the 13th (Lieutenant Taylor of Captain Morres's troop) lost his life through a fall from a window in Lisbon.

At Lumiar, during the halt, the regiment was occupied in getting into order again after the hardships of the last few months. The feet of the horses, which from constant marching were in bad condition, were attended to. Lisbon being near, the men were enabled to obtain such supplies of necessaries as they needed, and welcome these supplies were without a doubt.

On October 21, the regiment marched to St Antonio de Tozel, where it remained until Friday, November 16. Meanwhile Major-General Fane taking with him the 4th and 10th Regiments of Portuguese Cavalry, which were stationed in the villages round about, crossed the Tagus at Lisbon and proceeded into the Alentejo. While

A Portuguese Gentleman

PEASANT of Torres Vedras

at St Antonio de Tozel, the British and Portuguese Army under Lord Wellington was in position and immediately opposite the French Army under Massena. The retreat of Massena began on November 15.

Next day a squadron under Lieut.-Colonel Doherty marched at daybreak under orders to proceed to the quarters of Lieut.-General Hill. By General Hill the squadron was sent on to Alhandra to await further orders there. At 2 P.M. the remainder of the regiment reached that place also, and the whole moved on to Castelheiro. The town of Alhandra had been left a complete wreck by the French, houses plundered and furniture destroyed. In their retreat the enemy had demolished all the small bridges, and hence the march of the regiment, accompanied as it happened to be by a brigade of Portuguese artillery, was much retarded. At Castelheiro the streets of the town were rendered impassable by barricades of furniture so placed as to enable the enemy to gain time in their retreat. The houses in the town were completely gutted, but the regiment managed to get under cover, such as it was. The squadron which was under the command of Major Boyse, however, went forward in pursuit of the enemy, being attached to the division of Major-General Sir William Stewart.

Lieut.-Colonel Doherty gives a most graphic account of the return of a Portuguese officer to his ruined home, which he witnessed. The poor man was distracted with grief. When he had left home his wife and family were there — well, happy, and in affluence. He returned to find that his wife had died, that his children had vanished none knew where, his house and furniture a wreck — not even the feather-beds being spared destruction; and, worse than the loss of goods, all his family papers missing or burnt. Such hospitality as was in the power of the officers of the regiment to offer this poor fellow was freely given, as may be expected, and by dint of sympathetic treatment the unfortunate man was gradually calmed from his frenzied condition.

On Saturday, November 17, the regiment continued its march to Azambuza, crossing many brigades of British infantry who were halted on the road. This was a march of horrible sights — the dead bodies of men, horses, and mules strewing the way, and crushed by the passage over them of carts and waggons. So hasty had the flight of the enemy been, and so hard had the pursuit been pressed, that equipments and stores of all kinds were everywhere found abandoned by the roadside.

On Sunday, November 18, the regiment halted at Azambuza, and during the day numerous brigades of British infantry passed through the place. Azambuza had suffered terribly at the hands of the enemy. The houses were completely gutted, the furniture destroyed, and from the bodies found in the ruined dwellings many murders had evidently been committed.

The next day the regiment, leaving the great road leading to Santarem, turned off towards the small town of Vallada, through which it marched to the banks of the Tagus. Here General Hill's division of infantry were crossing in boats into the Alentejo. The regiment could not cross that day, and was ordered to put up at Vallada.

Vallada was found, as all other towns, a ruin. The wretched inhabitants had fled across the Tagus.

The passage of the British division was effected by means of the boats of the ships of war and transports lying in the Tagus at Lisbon, which had been sent in attendance on the army during its march down the river. These boats were under the command of Captain Beresford, R.N. To transport the 13th over the river occupied most of Tuesday, November 20. The sailors brought planks from some of the villages, and made a platform from which the horses of the 13th could leap into the boats.

Major Boyse's squadron, which had now rejoined, crossed and marched, followed by the others in turn. The regiment put up at Almeria and places in the neighbourhood. In crossing the Tagus only one horse was lost, through its leaping from the boat into the river and being carried away by the rapid current.

On Wednesday, November 21, the several squadrons marched and assembled at Chamusca, where they found the whole of Lieut.-General Hill's division, consisting of seven British regiments of infantry and a brigade of Portuguese artillery. The whole force went into quarters.

The following day heavy firing was heard in the direction of Santarem. Here Marshal Massena had halted and fortified that naturally very strong position. The pursuit was then stopped by Lord Wellington.

Sketch Map showing the principal places to which the regiment went during 1810, from 2nd April to 31st December.

On Friday, November 30, a squadron consisting of the troops of Captain Stisted and Captain Doherty marched from Chamusca, and were distributed among some neighbouring houses (kintas), where they remained until December 4, when they proceeded to Pinhero. The same day Captain Buchanan in command of a squadron composed of his own and the troop of Captain Bowers marched to Carreguira, and proceeded thence on December 19 to the Kinta de Briga.

CHAPTER XII.

The Peninsular War, 1811.

WE left the regiment at Chamusca, where it arrived on November 21. At that place it remained until March 10, 1811. During this period, besides the movements of the two squadrons mentioned in the last chapter, the following took place: January 16, a squadron, consisting of Captain Morres's troop and Captain White's troop, under the command of Captain Morres, marched from Chamusca to Crucifixa, and that under Captain Buchanan came in to Chamusca. On February 18, Major Boyse's and Captain Macalester's troops marched from Chamusca to Carreguira, and Captain Doherty's squadron came into Chamusca. On March 4, under the command of Lieut.-Colonel Muter, the squadron composed of Captain Buchanan's and Captain Bowers's troops went to Carreguira, and Major Boyse's squadron marched into Chamusca.

Two days later, under the command of Lieut.-Colonel Doherty, Captain Stisted's and Captain Doherty's troops went to Carreguira, and Lieut.-Colonel Muter's squadron and that of Major Morres marched to Abrantes.

During this time the enemy was in possession of the country from Santarem on the opposite side of the Tagus.

The Portuguese guerillas acted as scouts, and were most useful in watching the river as far as Abrantes, thus saving the army much labour.

The 13th Light Dragoons had frequent field-days on a large plain near the river, and these were a source of great interest to the French officers. A kind of *entente* had been established. The vedettes on either side had a tacit agreement not to fire on one another, and when the river was low officers from both the contending armies were wont to converse to one another across the narrowed stream,—the first question from a French officer to a British one being invariably, "When are you going to have another field-day?" It is stated that Massena and nearly the whole of his Staff on one occasion were most interested spectators.

The condition of the wretched inhabitants of the district was deplorable in the extreme. Most of them were fugitives from the other side of the Tagus, and to effectively prevent these from perishing from absolute starvation taxed the slender resources of both officers and men to the utmost. Nor were these fugitives confined to the lower class by any means; on the other hand there were many of good if not of very high position. They were stranded in the worst part of the year, without money, food, or shelter, and in most cases with but a slender supply of clothing. Subscriptions were raised by the British officers, and a committee was formed to distribute the money and superintend its expenditure. All the offal of the cattle slaughtered for the army was distributed, and wholesome soup and bread given as far as possible. Every individual gave such articles of his private clothing as he could spare to those most in need, and quarters were provided where buildings were vacant, even though ruinous. Where buildings did not exist huts were erected. Grateful indeed were these poor people for the attempts of our men to alleviate their sufferings. A pathetic story is to be found in Lieut.-Colonel Doherty's MS., which may be briefly given here to show the vicissitudes of a Portuguese family of rank. One evening at the quarters of Lieut.-Colonel Doherty at Chamusca, after dinner, a servant announced that a poor Portuguese man was outside the door wishing to speak to him. The colonel desired that he should be admitted. The man came in almost in rags, approached the colonel, and silently looked him in the face. To all requests for information as to his wants the man was dumb, and presently turned round, and, to the surprise of all, walked to the door. There he turned round again, and on the instant, as in a flash, Colonel Doherty recognised in his visitor one of his former hosts. As far back as the time when he and Captain Stisted had been ordered to Lisbon on a General Court Martial, and delayed there (April 1810), they had been entertained most generously by this gentleman and his wife at Pinhete. They were then on their road to rejoin the regiment.

The Portuguese gentleman on whom, by the way, they were billeted, received them at the head of his staircase which led out of a fine courtyard. Lieut.-Colonel Doherty and Captain Stisted were shown into most handsome and luxuriously furnished rooms. Presently their host returned and introduced his wife and two or three beautiful young children. Every possible attention was paid to the British officers. On the morrow their host accompanied them some distance on horseback, and they parted with mutual expressions of esteem.

The main road at the time being covered with water, the Portuguese gentleman, by means of his local knowledge, was able to guide them by by-paths till the obstacle was passed. And here, within the space of a twelvemonth, was their host an absolute beggar, wretched and nearly famished, with but the tattered remains of a Portuguese cloak to cover him. Colonel Doherty asked after his wife. The man went to the door and brought in one of the most deplorable wretched-looking females that can be conceived. She had scarcely the remains of a shoe to her feet, her hair hung in strings around her neck, and with little more clothing than an old cloak secured at the neck by a wooden skewer she stood before her former guest shivering with cold, wet, and hunger. What a change from her former appearance when, dressed in handsome and costly clothes, handsome in person, she entertained her guests in her splendid house.

Needless to say, all that could be done for these unfortunates was done at once. Like hundreds of others they had been obliged to flee in haste, crossing the Tagus in a boat, and bearing but a small bundle each. They had been some time at Chamusca before they heard mention of the name of Colonel Doherty. Both were sent in a day or two to Lisbon, where the sister of the lady lived. Presumably they were later reinstated in their property, but in all probability only to find their almost palatial house a ruin, since it had been for some time occupied by the French Commander-in Chief, and was later converted into a general hospital.

Towards the end of February the regiment received a remount draft from England under the command of Captain Bowers, who had been left at home on the regiment embarking for the Peninsula. On

Private of French INFANTRY.

A French DRAGOON.
26th Regiment

Sunday, March 10, Colonel Head, with a squadron from Chamusca, and Lieut.-Colonel Doherty, with a squadron from Carreguira, marched to Ponte de Sor, and on the next day to Crato, whence on March 19 they proceeded to Portalegre, where on the 20th they were joined by the squadron under Lieut.-Colonel Muter and Captain Morres, who had marched from Abrantes to Pinhete, and thence beyond Thomar, in pursuit of the enemy. On their return they crossed the Tagus by a bridge of boats and arrived at Carreguira, whence they proceeded to Portalegre *viâ* Ponte de Sor and Crato.

On March 22nd a squadron consisting of Major Boyse's troop and Captain Macalester's troop marched with Lieut.-Colonel Colbourne's light brigade, while the remaining six troops of the regiment went from Portalegre to Assumar.

On March 24th they marched and went into bivouac within about two leagues of Campo Mayor. The division of General Cole joined, and the whole force, under the command of Marshal Beresford, assembled.

CAMPO MAYOR, MARCH 25, 1811.

The position of affairs on this date must be briefly explained. Field-Marshal Sir Wm. Carr Beresford, with a strong body of troops, —among them, as has been related, being the 13th Light Dragoons,— had for some months been stationed at and around Chamusca, his duty being to intercept all communications between Marshal Massena and Marshal Soult. On February 11 the French army retreated from Santarem. When the pursuit of the French ceased, Marshal Beresford's force was detached to relieve Campo Mayor, at that time besieged by the enemy. Campo Mayor, however, surrendered to General Latour Maubourg, who occupied this fortified place. His troops were thus composed:—

2nd Hussars	300 men.
10th Hussars	350 men.
26th Dragoons (Col. Chamorin)	150 men.
4th Spanish Chasseurs	80 men.

making a total of 880 cavalry, of which the 26th were heavy cavalry.

He had also the 100th Regiment of the Line (Infantry), some 1200 strong, commanded by Colonel Quiot, which was a regiment of two battalions, and besides some horse artillery he had a battering train of sixteen heavy guns drawn by mules.

Marshal Beresford came in sight of the enemy's advanced cavalry on the heights of Lopo de Malto, about a league distant from Campo Mayor, on March 25. At that time it was not known whether the French were or were not masters of the place, and if in possession, whether the enemy intended to attempt to maintain it.

Marshal Beresford proposed to post his troops between Latour Maubourg, at Campo Mayor, and the strong fortress of Badajos, at that time held by General Phillipon.

To effect this he gave certain orders to Brigadier-General Long, who was in command of the cavalry.

Now when the enemy's advanced cavalry was first sighted the British began manœuvring on their flank, and some skirmishing took place at the foot of the walls of the town, the enemy having retreated from their advanced post, fearing to be out-flanked.

When Marshal Beresford reached the heights he discovered the enemy's force outside the town. Brigadier-General Long, with the cavalry, was then ordered to "endeavour to turn the enemy's right, keeping out of the reach of the place,"—Marshal Beresford's object being to detain the enemy till some infantry could arrive; but Brigadier-General Long was ordered also to engage the enemy "should circumstances permit." Brigadier-General Long had under his command eight squadrons of heavy dragoons (3rd Dragoon Guards and 4th Dragoons) under Colonel de Grey; two and a half squadrons of the 13th Light Dragoons under Colonel Head, and five small squadrons of Portuguese cavalry under Colonel Otway. We will now turn more particularly to the movements of the 13th Light Dragoons on that day.

At an early hour Captain Morres and his troop marched with directions to place themselves under the orders of Lieut.-Colonel Collins, commanding a brigade of Portuguese infantry. A troop, with Captain Buchanan, and under the orders of Colonel D'Urban, Quartermaster-General to the Portuguese Army, went out on reconnoitring duty, and having obtained the requisite information as to the enemy's movements, retired and joined the regiment. Between 9 and 10 A.M. the regiment received orders to mount and take its place in the column of march.

POPE PIUS VI. BLESSING OFFICERS OF THE 12TH LIGHT DRAGOONS,
VATICAN, 1794.

The second figure from the left is that of Captain-Lieutenant MICHAEL HEAD,
who subsequently joined the 13th.

(*Reprinted from ' The Cavalry Journal.'*)

After going about a league, orders came for *all* the cavalry to gain the front,—the country proving sufficiently open ahead for cavalry operations.

This was done by traversing at a gallop some bad rocky ground. The 13th Light Dragoons, and the 1st and 7th Regiments of Portuguese Cavalry,—these last under the command of Colonel Otway,—on gaining the front, formed contiguous columns of half squadrons at half distance,—occasionally, by nature of the ground, going from either flank by threes, and forming up again. These light regiments were followed by the brigade of heavy cavalry.

The columns moved forward at a brisk trot, and the infantry followed as quickly as permissible. A troop of the 13th (Captain White's), under the command of Lieutenants Moss and Doherty, was detached to skirmish and protect the right flank of the column. The Portuguese and the heavy cavalry also sent detachments on this duty. There was a rising ground on the right of the columns upon which the skirmishers moved.

Until about 1.30 P.M. the columns continued their march, occasionally diminishing or enlarging their front, according as the nature of the ground permitted; and skirmishing on the part of the detached troops went on continuously. At 1.30 the columns ascended the rising ground, and saw, on the plain beneath, the French cavalry formed up and scouting in three bodies of columns of squadrons, and the town of Campo Mayor some 1200 yards distant. By order of General Long, the 13th Light Dragoons instantly formed line, but when this was done it was found that the regiment was too much to the right. Ground was therefore taken to the left, and when opposite to the enemy the 13th was halted, wheeled up, and formed into line. The Portuguese squadrons formed line on the left of the 13th, and were ordered to remain as a support. The heavy brigade was halted, and formed in the rear of the 13th at some distance, and outflanked it on the right. The British and Portuguese infantry and the artillery were also brought up and formed, as fast as they could, on the right of the heavy cavalry, and also at some distance from it. It was clear that the moment for General Long to "engage the enemy should circumstances permit" had arrived, and to Colonel

Head, who was in command of the 13th Light Dragoons, the orders so to do were given.

"Colonel Head, there's your enemy. Attack him." In these words, according to the testimony of Lieut.-Colonel Patrick Doherty, was the order conveyed. General Long also added, "And now, Colonel, the heavy brigade are coming up on your rear, and if you have an opportunity give a good account of these fellows." The reply of Colonel Head was brief: "By gad, sir, I will."

The strength of the 13th Light Dragoons actually engaged in the charge, and their disposition, was as follows: the right squadron consisted of the troops of Captain Bowers and Captain Buchanan, under the command of Lieut.-Colonel Patrick Doherty, and flanked by their respective captains (Bowers and Buchanan), with Lieutenant Jeffreys and Lieutenant Smith serefiles; the left squadron consisted of Captain Gubbins's troop under the command of Lieutenant Major on the right, and Captain Doherty's troop with its captain on the left, the serefile officers being Lieutenant Frederick Geale and his brother Cornet John Geale.

The squadron was commanded by Lieut.-Colonel Muter. Colonel Head placed himself in front of the interval between squadrons, and covered by Lieutenant and Adjutant Holmes.

Just at the moment of charging, the two squadrons were joined by Lieutenant Moss and Lieutenant Doherty, who had been skirmishing with Captain White's troop, as has been stated previously. These officers gathering as many men together as they could bring up, arrived in time for the charge.

Captain White was at the time Assistant Quartermaster-General, attached to the Headquarters, and consequently not present. Captain Stisted had exchanged on February 7, 1811, and his troop was now commanded by Captain James Gubbins. Captain Gubbins, however, had not yet joined; he was still in England, and only sailed for Lisbon on May 12, 1811.

His commission in the 13th is dated February 7, 1811 (by exchange).

The disposition of the French force in its attempt to reach Badajos from the now evacuated town of Campo Mayor was this. The infantry in the centre of the column, at quarter distance, with a squadron of hussars in front and one in rear. The remainder

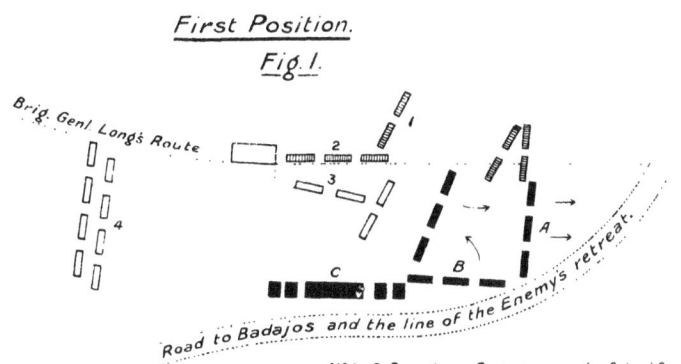

Campo Mayor.

March 25th 1811.

First Position.
Fig. 1.
Brig. Genl. Long's Route
1
2
3
4
A
B
C
Road to Badajos and the line of the Enemy's retreat.
A 3 Squadrons French Dragoons.
B 3 do do. do
C Column of French Infantry, head and rear closed by Troops of Hussars
Nº 1. 2 Squadrons Portuguese under Colonel Otway to cover Genl Long's flank and turn the Enemy's Right.
Nº 2. 3 Squadrons Portuguese to dispose of Corps A.
Nº 3. 2 Squadrons 13th Lt. Dgs. disengaged from rear to dispose of Corps B.
Nº 4. 8 Sqadrons of Heavy Dragoons to support
Second Position.
Fig. 2.
3 Portuguese Squadrons
2 French Sqadrons rallying.
C
French Column continuing its retreat
Road to Badajos
Heavy Brigade Halted
Route of Heavy Brigade under Marl. Beresford
Last Position
Fig. 3.
Portuguese
13th Lt. Dgs. & Portuguese.
Guns
British
French
Road to Badajos
Heavy Brigade
British
Portuguese
French

[From Lieut.-Colonel Patrick Doherty's Manuscript.]

of the cavalry covered the retreat of the infantry, and at the same time secured to themselves the benefit of their co-operation. General Long apparently intended the 13th Light Dragoons to dispose of three of the French dragoon squadrons, while he in personal command of some of the Portuguese cavalry of his brigade (3 squadrons) cut off the retreat of the other three French squadrons and protected the flank of the 13th. The remainder of the Portuguese (2 squadrons), under Colonel Otway, would thus be on his left flank, practically parallel to the head of the enemy's column, and able to check any movement in that direction. The heavy brigade, somewhat in the rear and to the right, was to advance slowly in support of the entire movement. This seems to be the best and most accurate account of what was intended, if one can judge from the sketch-maps of the affair and the somewhat conflicting accounts which have come down to us in many pages of print and manuscript.

For it must be remembered that the "Affair at Campo Mayor" was the subject of a long and most acrimonious discussion, and that even in 1833, when General Long had been some time dead, a member of his family had felt compelled to enter upon a defence of the military conduct of his late relative.

The opposing forces were now some two hundred yards apart. The 13th moved regularly forward by the usual words of command— walk, trot, canter, and charge,—and with a loud cheer the men met the enemy. The enemy cheered likewise, and the two lines crashed into one another. The 13th penetrated the enemy and then wheeled round. The enemy did the same, though not so speedily, and a second charge took place. Man to man with the sabre they went to work, and the 13th used their weapons with great effect. Meanwhile the right squadron of the enemy wheeled to its left, and came upon the left flank of the left squadron of the 13th (Captain Doherty's), and appeared likely to prove troublesome; but they were beaten off. How this happened is thus. By far weaker in numbers than the enemy, the squadrons of the 13th had charged the left and centre squadrons of the French dragoons, the right being left unmolested.

However, in a short space of time the left and centre columns were put to flight, and then, very speedily, the right was induced to follow their example.

Meanwhile the French infantry which were in column behind formed into line, and, as their front cleared of their own cavalry who were put to flight, opened a hot and destructive fire on the 13th who were in pursuit, and caused not a few casualties. Where meanwhile were the Portuguese cavalry?

They were called upon to charge, but did not,—in fact they scampered off. The two squadrons under Colonel Otway, however, rallied them and joined in the pursuit of the flying French dragoons. At first there was some show of resistance on the part of the enemy along the road, but presently they were completely broken; those who could manage to ride off to Badajos did so, those with whom the 13th came up on the road threw down their swords and promptly surrendered. This extraordinary pursuit was continued right up to the bridge head of Badajos, a distance of nearly ten miles. During the course thereof the 13th overtook and captured 16 large pieces of artillery, each drawn by eight mules, numbers of waggons and immense quantities of stores, baggage of all descriptions, provisions, stores, horses, mules—in fact, the whole camp-equipage which had been early that morning despatched from Campo Mayor towards Badajos. The gunners and drivers at first surrendered, but, on approaching Badajos, considering themselves as nearing safety under the guns of the fortress, they endeavoured to make a run for it, but were sabred. Troopers of the 13th were mounted on the mules to bring the guns along.

At the bridge head of Badajos all the officers of the 13th, except Lieutenant Holmes who had been wounded, were gathered together with a number of the men. There were also a good many of the Portuguese. More troopers of the 13th were gradually coming up, but many had been left in charge of the prisoners and the captured guns and stores. It is needless to add that after a couple of charges and a pursuit at a gallop for some ten miles the horses were for the most part blown. The position was now this, as far as the 13th Light Dragoons and the Portuguese squadrons were concerned. They had been ordered to attack a superior force of cavalry, and assured that in the attack they would be supported promptly and effectively by the brigade of heavy cavalry which was backed by a large force of infantry and guns. Sixteen pieces of heavy artillery had been captured, waggons and stores in huge quantities, and the flying enemy had been pursued to within cannon-shot of a strongly fortified place of arms. The gates of Badajos had been opened to admit the defeated remnant of the fugitive French, and this remnant numbered no more than a score of men, so thoroughly had the 13th done their work. At the time of the charge the heavy brigade was at hand, the whole of the British and Portuguese infantry was also nearly up, and with guns. This force was in position practically, and was able to compel the surrender of the entire French force. And, by the way, as was subsequently ascertained, this French force was prepared to surrender. Where were the promised supports? Without a doubt occupied along the road securing their prisoners, and moving towards Badajos shortly to greet the victorious 13th. So thought Colonel Head, and so he had an absolute right to think. As an effective striking force his little band could do no more, and the only course was to retrace their steps towards Campo Mayor, picking up their captured guns, stores, waggons, and prisoners *en route*. Besides, too, British and Portuguese wounded needed to be cared for and transported back. There was little time to decide, and Colonel Head at once decided. Moreover, the batteries from Badajos opened on the little force with grape and canister, and some casualties occurred. Still, there was neither confusion nor undue haste. The men re-formed calmly under fire, and without confusion or disorder began to retire. Prisoners were collected, and by dismounting troopers and putting them to act as drivers on the captured guns and waggons, the victorious little force slowly made its way back along the road towards Campo Mayor, every instant expecting to get news from the British army, and to see ahead of them the promised supports. No message had arrived then, and no supports were visible. On towards Campo Mayor the little force made its way, escorting the fruits of its gallant fight.

Half the distance was traversed when up galloped a trooper of the 13th, sent by Lieutenant and Adjutant Holmes, whose wound had compelled him to remain behind after the charge. His message was somewhat startling, and was to the effect that the entire body of French infantry and the hussars had been permitted to proceed unmolested, and were even now approaching along the road. This news seemed incredible, and that it was at first disregarded by Colonel Head is hardly to be wondered at. It was concluded that by some mistake a support intended for them had been viewed from afar, and that Portuguese infantry had been assumed to be French, probably because both wore a rather similar blue uniform. The retirement along the road was resumed. Then came a second dragoon, also despatched by Lieutenant Holmes in case the first one did not get through, and he brought similar tidings, adding that the enemy's infantry was not only at hand, but supported by a portion of the already surrendered cavalry who, on their approach, had regained their sabres and remounted. This was serious indeed, and coming as it did could not be disregarded. Again Colonel Head was obliged to decide, and promptly, on his course of action. With the horses exhausted as they were, it would have been madness to attempt to resist the attack of 1200 infantry supported by cavalry, and cavalry, too, of probably far greater numerical strength than the sadly thinned ranks of the 13th and their Portuguese allies. It was mortifying to the last degree, but unavoidable. Prisoners, captured guns, waggons, and stores must be abandoned, and by a cross-country detour to the right an endeavour must be made to regain the British army. It had to be done, it was done, nor was it long before they came in sight of the enemy. Pursuing their march in a column of threes over a rough and rocky country, the 13th and Portuguese left the road. Presently the enemy's cavalry appeared in force on high ground on the left of the line of march, and formed up as if to attack. The 13th and Portuguese halted, fronted, and after waiting a few minutes for the enemy to begin, moved forward to attack. The enemy immediately went about and retired pretty briskly. This happened twice. By 6.30 in the evening Colonel Head and his troopers came up with the British and Portuguese army, having had no further view of the enemy.

Up to this point, as far as the proceedings of the 13th and the Portuguese are concerned, there is no conflict as to facts. But as to what orders were or were not given to General Long by Marshal Beresford or by General Long to others, or what messages were sent or reports were made to Marshal Beresford either by General Long or a certain Baron Trip, an officer attached to the cavalry staff, the accounts given vary considerably. But it is possible to state plainly in the first instance what occurred. The charge of the 13th was definitely ordered by General Long, and, strangely enough, he appears

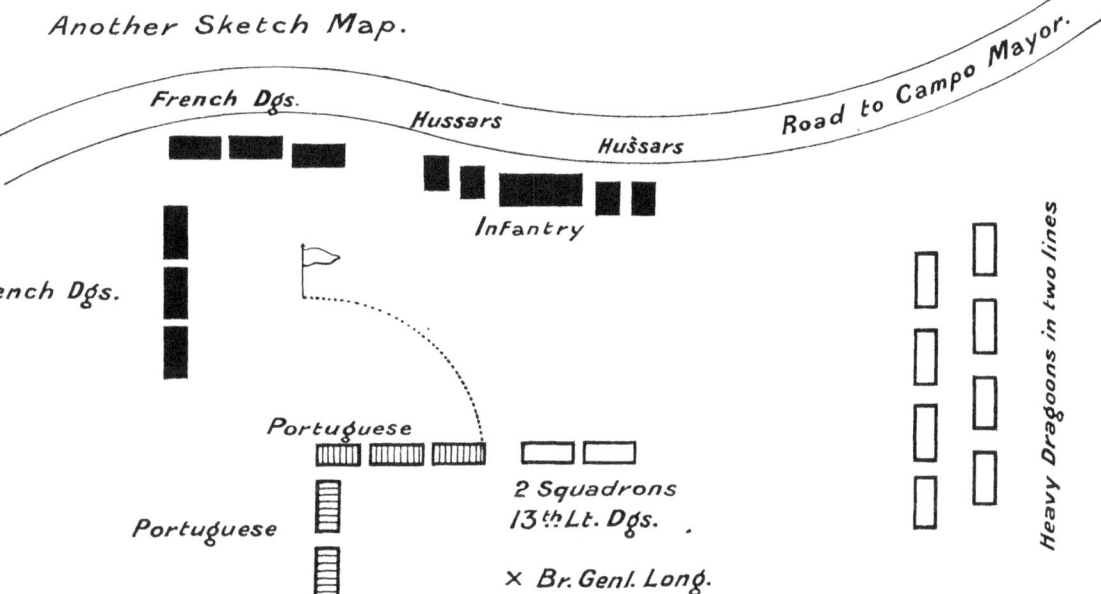
Campo Mayor. March 25th 1811.
Another Sketch Map.
[From Lieut.-Colonel P. Doherty's Manuscript.]

to have been totally ignorant of the effect of that charge. He was with the Portuguese cavalry, who, on being called upon to charge, did not do so, but bolted instead. They were, however, subsequently rallied. General Long had promised to send the heavy brigade in support of the 13th, but he gave no orders to that effect to its commander, and it consequently followed the French infantry, waiting for orders which never came, and doubtless wondering. Somebody—it has never been actually ascertained who—reported officially or unofficially to Marshal Beresford that the 13th had been surrounded and lost. In the controversy which has taken place with regard to Campo Mayor, one side avers that General Long made this report himself; another, that it emanated from Baron Trip. What is more important, however, is that Beresford believed at the time, and apparently on good ground, that such a calamity had taken place.

His cavalry force on this assumption now consisted of the heavy brigade, which could be trusted to be steady, and the three Portuguese squadrons, which by no means could be trusted to be steady,—and they were in fact at the time in a none too orderly condition.

The Marshal declined to risk his only reliable cavalry. Yet the opportunity was one which should have appealed to his military instincts. His own British and Portuguese infantry, some 20,000 in number, were hurrying up, nay, were little more than a quarter of a mile distant. A couple of guns from the German artillery had been brought up and had actually opened fire on the French column, which seemed to be doomed. In addition, the heavy cavalry was close on the column and prepared to attack on the instant, and the three squadrons of doubtful Portuguese hovered about on the other side of the road. All accounts agree that at this moment the entire French force was on the point of surrendering, and this the enemy also admitted. But Marshal Beresford did not compel that surrender. Instead, he halted the cavalry, caused the artillery to cease fire, and permitted the French to continue their retreat without let or hindrance.

Thus it was that the 13th Light Dragoons were deprived of the visible proofs of their gallant performance. But this was not all. Colonel Head, on riding up to Marshal Beresford, was received with coldness and somewhat bitter sarcasm. The report which the Marshal sent in to Lord Wellington elicited from the Commander-in-Chief a severe reprimand for Colonel Head. This reprimand on April 5 was read to the officers of the 13th and to Colonel Otway, who had commanded the Portuguese cavalry. General Long informed them that in a General Order Lord Wellington "censured the conduct of the 13th for their impetuosity on that occasion which displayed a want of the necessary discipline, at the same time giving the regiment credit for its bravery and resolution."

General Long added, that in reading it he had discharged his duty, but "I will never permit it to be entered in the Orderly Book." He continued: "I cannot find words to express my admiration of your gallantry on that occasion, your discipline was most conspicuous; in short, gentlemen, the 13th Dragoons have gained such a laurel on that day as will never fade."

Naturally the reading of this order was felt most acutely, as one of quite a different nature had been expected. A meeting was held to devise means, if possible, to rescue the regiment from the character of improper impetuosity and discipline. That Lord Wellington was under a misapprehension was evident. The affair of Campo Mayor had been under the view of the whole army.

A letter on the subject was signed by all the field officers and carried to General Long, with a request that he would read it and forward it to the Commander-in-Chief. It detailed from first to last the conduct of the regiment—its success, the captures made, and the perfect satisfaction of all that when in pursuit of the enemy not only a support would have been sent forward, which would have secured prisoners and captures left behind, but that there was not anything to be apprehended from the French infantry under the circumstances.

The letter was forwarded, and though the reprimand was not withdrawn by Lord Wellington, who decided that as "it had been issued, it must remain," it is known that had the true facts been before him at the time he would not have issued it. This, though not officially put in writing, was some consolation. Lord Wellington, at dinner, in the presence of Captain Doherty, said as much, and plainly said it. It should be stated also that Marshal Beresford changed his opinion as regards the conduct of the regiment at Campo Mayor, and made a handsome acknowledgment as to their behaviour.

Marshal Beresford ascribed his original attitude to the fact that he had been misinformed by General Long, and appears to hint that

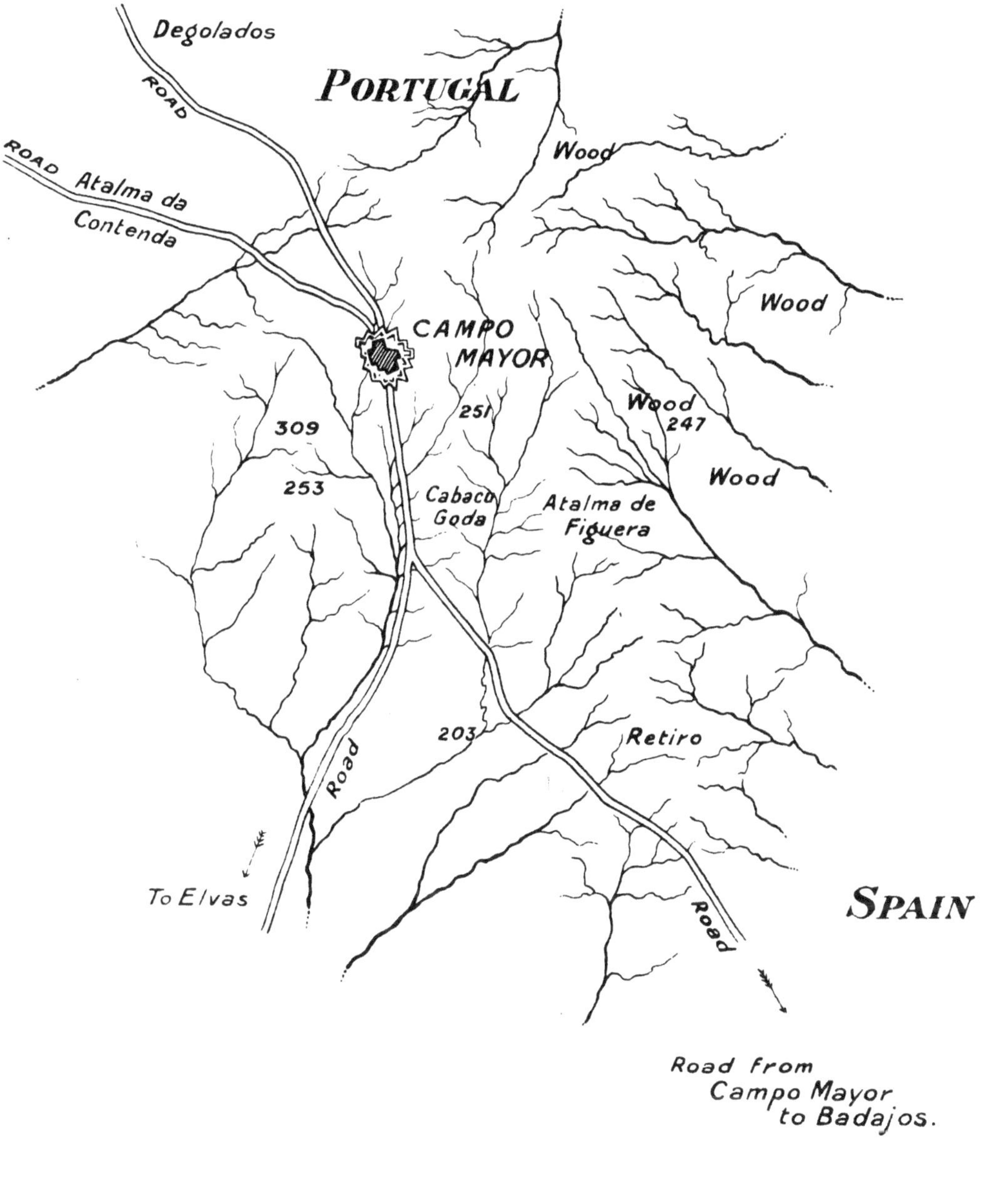

Sketch Map of the country round about Campo Mayor, from the official Portuguese Map, showing the number of streams— a fact which indicates broken ground. Spanish Map not yet published.

Badajos

while General Long verbally praised the regiment after the combat, in his official written reports his opinion of their conduct was adverse. The controversy was long and bitter. Marshal Beresford published pamphlets, Napier attacked Beresford in his Peninsular War, an unknown individual (by some supposed to be Beresford himself) joined in the fray, and finally the matter was taken up by a nephew of General Long. Queries as to facts were sent out to all persons living who were likely to know anything of the matter, but the mystery of who started the rumour that the regiment had been captured was never solved.

There was a considerable divergence of opinion as to the course taken by General Long when ordered to "turn the town of Campo Mayor." Marshal Beresford always averred that that General made too great a detour, and that by so doing he came into contact with the enemy's line of march at a point not intended. Marshal Beresford described General Long's route as "an arc of five miles to a chord of two." General Long and his friends stated that he was never out of range of the guns: the enemy were supposed to be prepared to use these guns. The Marshal's party declared that the ground over which General Long passed was "open and undulating." General Long stated that it was not, and that an "impassable" ravine or defile compelled him to go rather farther round than he wished. One would have thought that a reference to a map would have settled the question, but no such reference seems to have been made. It is just, however, to state that the present official Portuguese map shows a great many watercourses in a very small space of ground around Campo Mayor, and that the contour numbers point to by no means open and undulating ground. You do not meet with a number of brooks close together in level ground or undulating ground, as a rule. As regards the two guns brought up to play upon the French infantry, it has been asked, why not have brought up all and used them? Marshal Beresford averred that the horses even of these two were too distressed to move the guns, and that the others could not be got up. This is greatly to be doubted—as the guns had not been dragged far, or at great speed, and there had been no difficult country to negotiate; moreover, the commander of the artillery, though extremely anxious to bring them all into action, was not permitted to do so.

At the moment the regiment was ordered to charge, its precise strength was as follows: two squadrons of 48 files each, making a total of 192 men. To these must be added the men collected by Lieutenant Moss and Lieutenant Doherty, who were skirmishing. The precise number that were brought by these officers and joined in the charge is not known—we are only told that they collected "as many as they could"; and from this source possibly an addition of perhaps 15 to 20 files accrued. So that at the most the strength of the 13th engaged was between 222 and 232 men. It is strange that on an occasion of this kind no absolute record should have come down to us.

The loss of the allied cavalry on this occasion was—

    1 cornet, 23 rank and file, and 20 horses killed = 24 officers and men, and 20 horses.

    2 lieutenants, 1 staff, 1 quartermaster, 1 sergeant, 55 rank and file, and 35 horses wounded = 60 officers and men, and 35 horses.

    1 sergeant, 76 rank and file, and 108 horses missing, some of the missing men being taken prisoners when wounded near the Bridge of Badajos = 77 men, and 108 horses.

The disproportionate loss of horses was caused by the Portuguese, who abandoned their own weedy mounts in order to secure those of the French, and who made a return of the loss but not of the gain.

The regimental casualties in themselves were as follows—

    12 men and 7 horses killed.

    Lieutenants William Slayter Smith and Frederick Geale, Adjutant Holmes, Quartermaster Greenham, 1 sergeant, and 24 rank and file wounded.

    1 sergeant, 19 rank and file, and 44 horses missing.

Lieutenant Smith received a most dangerous wound in the stomach from a musket-ball. Lieutenant and Adjutant Holmes, while in pursuit of a "hussar" (dragoon?) and in the act of giving point at the body, received a bad sabre wound in his sword hand, which obliged him to retire. How fortuitous this wound was for the regiment, the account makes clear.

Lieutenant Frederick Geale also received a wound in his sword hand when in conflict with one of the "hussars" (dragoons?). Captain Joseph Doherty's sash saved his life: "it was of the hussar kind, with six knobs in front; a sabre cut went completely through the whole of the knobs and part of his jacket, the sash fell on both sides. This

Corporal Logan, 13th Dragoons, slaying Colonel Count Chamorin at Campo Mayor.

happened when he galloped to the assistance of a man of his troop who was defending himself against the attack of three 'hussars' (dragoons?), who were all cut down." But few men were killed in the actual charge and *mêlée;* "the fire of the infantry and that from the fortifications at Badajos took down the principal part of those we know to have fallen." From a Spanish officer who escaped from Badajos a few days later it was learnt that the enemy had fifteen of the 13th prisoners. He also stated that the enemy brought into Badajos upwards of four hundred of their cavalry wounded, and all with sabre cuts. Cannon states that "three hundred French were killed, wounded, and taken prisoners."

The loss of the enemy has been variously estimated. One account puts it as low as 300, another as high as 600. All the men of the French artillery are reported to have been sabred, and a howitzer, a forage cart, and some tumbrils were brought into Campo Mayor. The 26th Dragoons suffered very heavily, losing their colonel and fifteen officers, only six remaining.

Colonel Count Chamorin, of the 26th French Heavy Dragoons, was slain in single combat during the first charge by Corporal Logan of the 13th. Corporal Logan had sabred a Frenchman. Colonel Chamorin singled him out and attacked him to avenge his comrade. Logan was, however, the better swordsman. He cut his opponent twice across the face. The colonel's helmet fell off, and he then received a cut which cleft his skull. Corporal Logan belonged to Captain Stisted's troop, and returned home with the regiment in 1814.

On the morrow a flag of truce was sent out from Badajos, with a request that the enemy might be permitted to bury their dead. This was granted, and our own troops also sent out burying parties. Colonel Chamorin's brother was one of the French who came out on this mission. After a while he found his brother's dead body—stripped by the peasantry. He threw himself on the body in his grief, and was with difficulty persuaded to relax his hold. At length the body was rolled up and carried away. The helmet of Colonel Chamorin was purchased from Corporal Logan by Paymaster Gardiner of the 13th, and his sword was presented to Colonel Head.

A coloured print of this episode in the combat was published in 1818.

In the Diary of Captain James Gubbins (13th Light Dragoons) an entry occurs which bears upon the burial of the dead at Campo Mayor, and shows that it must have been very perfunctorily performed.

"*Campo Mayor, November* 2, 1811.—Rode with G. Doherty over the ground the 13th charged the French upon—skulls and human bones, and remains of the slain."

During the pursuit the men of the 13th had considerable trouble with their Portuguese allies, who could with difficulty be persuaded to give quarter. Many an unfortunate Frenchman's life was saved through the interference of the privates of the regiment.

When the 13th rejoined the army of Marshal Beresford at Campo Mayor, it went into bivouac in an olive grove, distant about a mile from the town. Here it rested till the 28th of March, when it was marched into the town and put up.

On April 1, the regiment marched to Villa Bochin, a distance of 4 leagues; the next day to Villa Vicosa (3 leagues), and thence to bivouac, near Jeremia (3 leagues), where the whole of Marshal Beresford's army had assembled.

Captain Morres had now been promoted Major, and had been succeeded in the command of his troop by Captain William Serle.

On April 5, Major Morres, in command of Captain Serle's and Captain White's troops, marched at 2 P.M., and crossed the river Guadiana. The rest of the regiment, accompanied by General Lumley's brigade of infantry, a park of artillery, and a squadron of Portuguese cavalry, crossed the river Guadiana at 5 P.M. the next day. Flats on large boats had been provided for the purpose —the cavalry going on the flats and the infantry in the bows of the boats. As each squadron got complete on the other side, it moved forward for about a mile on the heath and formed a column of half squadrons — the horses were linked, and officers and men lay down to rest. The left squadron was not up till 2 A.M. on the 7th. Half an hour later firing was heard in the front, and the regiment marched and moved forward in echelon of half squadrons. The infantry all fell in, but owing to the darkness of the night it was impossible to know what was going on. The unfortunate occurrence which took place will be now related.

THE PENINSULAR WAR, 1811.

THE SURPRISE NEAR OLIVENZA.

When the British and Portuguese force crossed the river Guadiana, the enemy were in possession of the town of Olivenza. It appears that there was great delay in making the bridge over the river for the troops to cross.

About 2 A.M. on the morning of the 6th, the enemy advanced with a battalion of infantry, three guns, and about 400 hussars, with the intention of destroying the bridge, they not believing the British to be in force. Now from Olivenza there were two roads to Jeremia: one, the main road, lay considerably to the right of a little wood in which there was a hut; the other lay direct by the side of a small stream with very rotten banks, and passed close by the left of the same wood.

The enemy in their reconnaissance went by the main road, but finding the British had crossed the Guadiana and were so strong, immediately began to retire and took the other road.

It will be remembered that a squadron consisting of Captain Serle's and Captain White's troops, under the command of Major Morres, had been detached on April 5, having crossed the Guadiana in advance of the rest of the army. Their orders were for an immediate advance, and the men had not time to finish cooking before they marched, and consequently went without any provisions.

On the 6th, as the remainder of the regiment was in expectation to move any moment and to join the advanced squadron, no provisions were sent out. Late in the evening, however, when it was known that the army would not advance, an assistant commissary undertook to conduct a train of mules with supplies to Major Morres, though the exact position of the advanced squadron was not accurately determined. He reached Major Morres at about 10 P.M.

The advanced squadron on crossing the Guadiana on the 5th had taken up a position in front of that part of the army which marched with General Lumley, by whom the rest of the British force was joined later. Major Morres placed his vedettes and outposts in the most advantageous positions to watch any movements of the enemy from Olivenza. He continued to hold that post until the evening of the 6th, when he was relieved by a squadron of Portuguese cavalry under Count Penefield, who was accompanied by a British officer, Major Foljambe (20th Regiment), who acted as Assistant Quartermaster-General. Major Morres gave up his posts to the Portuguese and placed their vedettes. From Major Foljambe he received orders to fall back with his squadron and bivouac in the small wood before mentioned. Conceiving that his front was perfectly secured by the Portuguese pickets which were there posted, he only thought it necessary to establish a post on his right flank, which was the most exposed, as that flank of the army was uncovered. Thence he threw out a few pickets with occasional patrolling parties. These arrangements being made, and such others as he deemed needful, the men not immediately on duty tied up their horses, and the officers took possession of the small house or hut which was but a few yards away. At this juncture the Assistant Commissary arrived with the mules and provisions, and by men who had eaten nothing since April 4 those provisions were sadly needed and very welcome. Fires were lighted and food cooked, a meal was eaten, the men lay down by their horses, and the officers in their cloaks occupied the floor of the hut. For his action Major Morres has been blamed, we think unjustly. It has been urged that he should not have permitted fires to be lighted. But what were the facts? He was not on outpost duty. He had been regularly relieved and had fallen back to nearly the position of the army. He had even sent Cornet Macrea to General Stewart with a report of his being relieved, by whom, and the manner in which he had delivered up his post. His men were faint for want of food, and it was impossible to say how soon they might be called upon to turn out again, and to turn out at a time when there would be no chance of cooking a meal. The fires which were lighted were lighted in the rear of his position and towards that occupied by our troops.

Now the enemy in the course of his retirement by the second road mentioned came upon the embers of the camp-fires and speedily located the position of the squadron. In dashed the French cavalry among the sleeping men, and, taking them for Portuguese, used the sabre without mercy. On discovering them to be British, however, they "were less ferocious and more intent on taking them prisoners."

The troopers of the 13th, aroused from sleep, with their sabres hung for the most part on the holster-pipes of their saddles, were totally unprepared for resistance. The officers, aroused from their cabin-floor beds by the cries and shouts, rushed for the door. Lieutenant Doherty and Lieutenant King managed to get outside. The former reached his horse, mounted, gave it its head and the spur, and though pursued by French dragoons dashed out into the night, in what direction owing to the darkness he was unable to determine. By luck he rode towards a British vedette, by whom he was challenged.

In this way the news of the surprise reached the army. Lieutenant Doherty immediately made a report of the circumstance to Marshal Beresford and Sir Lowry Cole, after which he rejoined his regiment. Lieutenant King jumped into the stream near the wood, and though fired at (the top of his cap being pierced), got clean over and escaped. Cornet James Macrea had not returned from his mission and thus escaped.

Major Morres and Lieutenant Moss were taken prisoners, together with 1 sergeant-major, 5 corporals, 2 trumpets, 2 farriers, and 40 privates. Sixty troop-horses and 2 camp-kettle mules were captured. Lieutenant Doherty lost three horses and all his baggage. Lieutenant King a like amount. Cornet Macrea lost two horses and his baggage, and the whole of the horses and baggage of Major Morres and Lieutenant Moss fell into the hands of the enemy. The wife of one trooper was also among the prisoners. Only twenty men escaped, and three wounded were left on the ground.

The alarm was at once raised: before dawn Lieut.-Colonel Doherty with two squadrons of the 13th, one being under the command of Lieut.-Colonel Muter, was ordered forward to reconnoitre. By dawn he had come upon the spot, and was there joined by many of those who had escaped.

The wounded — one of them dangerously — were found on the ground, and scattered about were arms and accoutrements. These last were collected and sent into camp. The two squadrons then separated, each taking a different road towards Olivenza, in search of the enemy. But no enemy was to be seen, as the force, together with its prisoners and loot, had already reached the shelter of the garrison of Olivenza.

The two squadrons of the 13th then returned to their bivouac. During the 8th of April one squadron was sent out, accompanied by a squadron of Portuguese, under the command of Lieut.-Colonel Doherty, to take post in front and on the left flank of the army, and to place the necessary pickets. So exposed was this position that it is recorded that no less than 33 vedettes were found needful. Strong bodies of French cavalry were seen hovering about, and some skirmishing took place with the advanced vedettes. The two squadrons remained in the saddle the whole night.

Next day the army moved forward, and the left flank was covered by the two squadrons that had been on duty the previous night. Passing Olivenza a few shots were fired from the garrison—a man and a horse of the 3rd Dragoon Guards being killed. The army then halted, while a flag of truce with a summons to surrender was sent into Olivenza by Marshal Beresford. The summons was, however, refused. On April 10, the army moved forward, leaving the division under the command of General Cole to besiege Olivenza. Continuing its march, the army passed through Valverde and went into bivouac about a mile beyond. Resuming its march on the 11th, the army passed through the town of Albuera, which, with the exception of the church, was completely in ruins. Not a house in the whole place had either "roof, floor, door, or window."

A short distance beyond the town the army went into bivouac and there remained till the 15th. The length of these marches works out at about 3½ leagues per diem.

The next halting-place was near Santa Martha.

On the morning of the 16th, at 2 A.M., having then resumed its march, and when it was nearing Zaffra, information came that a considerable body of the enemy's cavalry was near Los Santos, where it intended to levy contributions.

When this news arrived the army had halted, while the staff were examining the ground to find a suitable place for a bivouac.

The cavalry were dismounted, and the men slept on the road at their horses' heads.

The order to mount was at once given, and the cavalry moved forward in a column of half squadrons, the 13th in front, followed by the Portuguese cavalry, and in their rear the heavy brigade consisting of the 3rd Dragoon Guards and the 4th Dragoons. Colonel Head was in command of the 13th, while Major-General Long commanded the entire force. Marshal Beresford placed himself at the head of the 13th Light Dragoons.

CHAPTER XIII.

The Affair at Los Santos.

THE columns moved on at a sharp trot, skirting the town of Los Santos, on whose walls the inhabitants mustered in force to cheer their allies.

From a rising ground a view was obtained of the enemy formed up in the plain beneath in three columns of squadrons, one of which deployed into line immediately on the advance squadron of the 13th coming in sight.

The French squadron advanced to attack. The advance squadron of the 13th immediately formed, as did the rest. The disposition was as follows:—

Right squadron (Major Boyse commanding)—Major Boyse's troop and Captain Macalester's troop, having Captain Macalester on the right, Lieutenant Drought on the left, and Cornet Maclean serefile.

Right centre squadron (Lieut.-Colonel Doherty commanding)— Captain Buchanan's troop and Captain Bowers's troop, with Captain Buchanan on the right and Captain Bowers on the left, Lieutenant Jeffreys serefile.

Left centre squadron (Lieut.-Colonel Muter commanding)—Captain Gubbins's troop and Captain Doherty's troop, having Lieutenant Major on the right, Captain Doherty on the left, and Cornet Geale serefile.

Left squadron, composed of the remains of Captain White's and Captain Serle's troops, under the command of Lieutenant Doherty, having Lieutenant King on the right.

THE AFFAIR AT LOS SANTOS.

The enemy moved forward boldly to the attack, being most gallantly led by the officer in command.

The 13th, when formed, were ordered to charge, and with a cheer dashed forward at the enemy.

But the enemy did not wait to close. Their brave leader was cut down; his men went about and fled, but numbers were overtaken and made prisoners, while others were sabred.

The 13th were halted and reformed, and the Portuguese cavalry were ordered up. The Portuguese were hardly formed in line when it was seen that the enemy were retiring under cover of a cloud of skirmishers whose shot reached the British ranks. Again the 13th were launched at them, the left squadron under Lieutenant Doherty being ordered to attack the skirmishers. With their sabres they gallantly charged them, and as this squadron was composed of the remnants of the squadron surprised on the 7th—and by the very enemy before them,—they had an opportunity of paying off old scores. Many were cut down. Lieutenant Doherty's squadron was supported by the left centre squadron. In a very short time the skirmishers were all driven in on their main body, into which the 13th, led by their officers, penetrated.

Meanwhile the other two squadrons, at the head of one of which Marshal Beresford had placed himself, moved forward by threes from the right of squadrons.

The Portuguese horses, unable to stand the pace, fell into the rear.

The heavy brigade at a gallop now attempted by a movement to the right to get into the rear of the enemy.

In this way, for something like nine miles, the pursuit was maintained.

"At first the enemy, having so much ground of us, halted regularly, fronted, and discharged their carbines, and while the 13th were forming up put about their horses and retired at a gallop. But by degrees the 13th closed upon them and their formation was lost; they became completely broken, and a general rout took place. Those of the enemy who, on being overtaken, did not surrender were cut down."

At length Marshal Beresford ordered the pursuit to cease. The regiment was halted and dismounted, and from the Marshal received a handsome compliment on their behaviour.

This was purely a cavalry combat, as the infantry were not up.

Lieutenant King appears to have behaved in a most praiseworthy manner, and was so reported on by Lieutenant Doherty.

The loss of the 13th on this occasion was but trifling—a few men and horses being wounded, and none of these seriously.

Captain Doherty's horse was shot under him at the beginning of the charge, but, managing to mount a troop-horse, he was not delayed.

The losses of the enemy were considerable: 1 officer killed, 2 taken prisoners; 107 prisoners were brought in by the 13th; some Spanish cavalry which chanced to be on the ground collected 170 more.

Many horses and much baggage were captured, mainly by the Portuguese, who were allowed to leave their ranks, while the 13th were not. Among the horses taken, however, were seven belonging to the 13th which had been lost near Olivenza on the 7th. These had on their own saddles and accoutrements.

The heavy brigade and the Portuguese were put up at Los Santos, but the 13th were retired, passing by the town, and went into bivouac a short distance from Zaffra. By eight in the evening, having been eighteen hours in the saddle, they were enabled to get food and rest.

It is stated that the unfortunate French officer who led the charge so gallantly and was cut down by Private Beard of Captain Macalester's troop was to have been married in a few days to a girl of great beauty, the daughter of the Mayor of Zaffra. His death, when the circumstance became known, was even more regretted by the regiment than the death of a brave enemy usually is. In the troop commanded by Captain Macalester there were two privates of the name of Beard, James and John. There is no record to identify the Beard named. Both, however, returned home after the war. A Corporal J. Beard served at Waterloo and returned. The name of the other is not in the lists.

Captain Doherty's horse was struck in the chest by a musket-ball; the animal reared, wheeled round, and fell, lying with his legs stretched out as if dead. He mounted a sergeant's horse and left the man to look after the saddle and accoutrements, for the additional loss of them, situated as the regiment was, would have been very serious. On the return after the charge, to the surprise of all, the animal, instead of being dead, was comfortably feeding in a stable at Zaffra whither the

DRAWN BY COLONEL PATRICK DOHERTY.

sergeant had conveyed it. The ball could not be extracted, yet the horse recovered and seemingly never felt any ill effects from the wound. The strength of the enemy opposed to the 13th on this occasion was upwards of 700 men, and these are stated to have been "of their best cavalry." The presence of Marshal Beresford and his active participation in the operations of the 13th on the occasion of the affair at Los Santos is perhaps worth notice. At Campo Mayor, to pursue a completely routed enemy for nearly ten miles was held to be excessive, while at Los Santos a pursuit of from eight to nine of an enemy which was for a good portion of the distance by no means in complete disorder was not so held; and there were no guns captured. He must, at any rate, have satisfied himself that the regiment was not out of hand on that occasion, if it had been, as has been suggested, at Campo Mayor. But the facts known with regard to Campo Mayor negative the suggestion.

On Wednesday, April 17, the prisoners taken on the previous day were marched through Zaffra to the rear. The weather which had turned to heavy rain caused the bivouac to be broken up, and the regiment went into crowded quarters in Zaffra. On this day eighteen men who had been captured by the enemy near Olivenza rejoined the regiment,—this desirable result was effected through the active assistance of some Spaniards.

The regiment halted on April 18, but at 4 A.M. the following day turned out in the most violent rain; later, they were ordered to turn in again, but to remain ready to mount at any moment.

At Zaffra, the 13th remained in quarters until May 13, during which period the outpost duty was very severe, and the regiment kept at all times on the alert. During this time the British infantry, under General Stewart, marched to Almandrelejo, leaving Zaffra on the 20th of April.

On April 29, a squadron was detached, under the command of Lieut.-Colonel Muter, to join Lieut.-Colonel Colbourne, who, with the light brigade, was sent on a secret expedition. The following day Muter returned, it being found that Lieut.-Colonel Colbourne was junior to him in the service, and the squadron remained under the orders of Captain Buchanan. In consequence of severe illness, on May 4th Lieut.-Colonel Doherty was compelled to leave Zaffra.

Accompanied by Assistant-Surgeon Armstrong of the 13th, he was sent to Elvas in a mule cart. He arrived there on May 7, and was ordered thence to Lisbon. At Lisbon a medical board recommended his return to England. Leave was granted. He sailed from Lisbon on June 23, and arrived at Portsmouth on July 18.

The siege of Badajos was now in progress, and with the intention of relieving that strong fortress the enemy advanced in considerable force on May 12. The 13th continued at Zaffra, awaiting the approach of the enemy, and then retired upon Los Santos, where it went into bivouac. On the morning of the 13th, the pickets under the command of Captain Doherty were attacked by superior numbers and forced to retire. During the night of the 13th, the division retired on Santa Martha, marching on the following day to Albuera, where it went into position, being closely followed by the enemy.

On May 16 the battle of Albuera was fought. There is no need here to enter into a lengthy description of this memorable engagement, and our attention will therefore be merely confined to the share which the 13th Light Dragoons had in the events which occurred.

The regiment, during the whole day, though not very actively employed, was exposed to a most galling artillery fire.

During the action the regiment was divided into two parts. Two squadrons, under the command of Lieut.-Colonel Muter, were placed opposite a bridge, with orders to defend it. These two squadrons had opportunities of making some charges against the enemy's cavalry who endeavoured to ford the river near the bridge, and succeeded in preventing them. The other two squadrons, under the command of Colonel Head, were placed to keep in check a considerable body of the enemy's cavalry in their front, and were exposed to a very severe fire both from infantry and artillery.

As is well known, victory remained with the British and Portuguese. That night the allied army lay on the field of battle, and remained in position during the whole of the next day, neither side seeming desirous of renewing the fight.

On the morning of the 18th it was found that the enemy during the preceding night had begun to retreat. The army advanced in pursuit, during which the 13th Light Dragoons was much employed in skirmishing. The enemy was pursued through Cortes de Pelias

(2 leagues), Almandrelejo (3 leagues), Villa Franca (2 leagues), till on May 23rd they were pressed hard through and beyond Usagre.

During the pursuit numbers of prisoners were made. On the last day of the pursuit the advanced squadron of the 13th were much employed in skirmishing, the rest of the regiment having to act in support of Colonel Silvertop's regiment of Spanish Hussars, who had been driven back by the enemy.

That night the cavalry went into bivouac. On the morrow news was received that the enemy had concentrated and was preparing to advance. The British consequently retired behind Usagre, where they took up a good position behind the town, and there awaited the enemy.

The 13th were posted on a rising ground to the left of Colonel de Grey's heavy brigade (3rd Dragoon Guards and 4th Dragoons), and received orders to act in support.

The enemy brought up four regiments of cavalry, and marched them through the town. They formed outside, and were then and there charged by the heavy brigade in line.

This charge was irresistible. The enemy broke and fled, considerable numbers fell, and many prisoners were taken.

The 13th moved forward to act in support of the charge, but were not required.

The enemy that day made no further attempt, still skirmishing was continuous, and on this duty the 13th was much employed. For two days the British remained on the ground, when a retirement to Robeira was ordered.

Here the regiment took up a chain of posts for about a fortnight, during which it suffered much fatigue from the constant skirmishing and heavy outpost duty.

About June 12th the enemy again advanced to attempt to raise the siege of Badajos. The regiment retired through Villa Franca (1 league) and Azenshall (3 leagues). On the morning of the 16th the British army was again in position at Albuera, and expecting attack.

When the siege of Badajos was raised the army at once withdrew to Elvas.

Here the 11th Light Dragoons joined the army from England, and took over the advanced posts from the 13th Light Dragoons.

The regiment now retired to Barbuera and some villages near, where it was ordered to take a much needed rest. The uncommon fatigues and excessive hard duty which the 13th had lately undergone, added to the severity of the weather, made this absolutely necessary. The horses were so knocked up that they could hardly walk.

After a welcome rest the 13th marched to Assumar, where it remained some five or six weeks. Thence it proceeded to Villa Viciosa, a distance of 5 leagues, and afterwards to Montforte, 4 leagues. At Montforte it went into quarters.

On the night of the 22nd October orders were received to march on the following morning. The route lay through Cordesiera (4 leagues), Casra de Pedro Bueno (4 leagues), Alised (3 leagues), to Malpartida (4 leagues). Here the 13th joined Lord Hill's division. The command of the regiment had now devolved upon Lieut.-Colonel Muter, owing to the absence on sick leave of Lieut.-Colonel Doherty and the illness of Colonel Head. Colonel Head was later sent to Lisbon, and thence ordered to return to England to recover his health.

It should here be mentioned that on July 10th Captain James Gubbins joined the regiment and took command of his troop. We learn this from a most interesting Diary which he kept from May 12, 1811, to May 14, 1812.

Assumar, 12 *o'clock*.—"Called on Colonel Head. Invited to dinner, and was introduced to the officers of the regiment. Heard a good account of my troop." He had travelled up by road from Lisbon, a distance of 120 miles. It seems that the absolute position of the 13th was not known when he started from Lisbon on July 4. The next day he "met a captain of the 7th Fusiliers who had been wounded at Albuera," and was on his way down to Lisbon. On Tuesday, the 9th of July, at Estremoz, he "heard that the regiment was at Assumar," five leagues distant. He left Estremoz on July 10, and reached Assumar the following day.

Throughout the pages of this diary are scattered very neatly condensed remarks on people, places, antiquities, customs, and especially on the landmarks and roads traversed. His first introduction to his troop he records thus: "Went round my stables and found my troop in very good order, only 3 horses sick, the men in good health, and the appointments in as good order as I could have expected after the severe duty they had undergone. Mr Major, my lieutenant, breakfasted with me. Lieutenant L. White dined with me." Of the place he writes: "A walled town of Roman origin, it is very small, and the part without the walls, by far the healthiest, is situated in a flat plain." An entry for July 5 records a visit to Lord Wellington, who was "too much indisposed to see any one." He mentions the pets of a young officer, "Fitzclarence's pets—a young wild boar and a crane."

Tuesday, 16th.—"Called on the 4th Dragoons, and saw all my old friends in that regiment."

Assumar, July 24th.—"16th Dragoons brought over the remounts."

Thursday, 25th.—"Got thorough good horses from the remount."

26th.—"Watering order for Major-General Stapleton Cotton's inspection."

Sunday, 28th.—"Rode to Portalegre (3 leagues). Introduced to Lord 'Tweedale.' Dined with the 24th." Captain Gubbins appears to have contracted a very close friendship with Lord Tweeddale. "Entrance to Portalegre very steep, and bad road; Lord Wellington's headquarters."

Monday, 29th.—"Troop completed their kit. Reported that the regiment was to march on the morrow, but orders were received to the contrary, and the same took place the next day."

Dated Thursday, August 1, Captain Gubbins mentions a visit he paid with Snow Sweetenham, Hay, and Swinfen to see E. Coates at the bivouac, where he "showed me four very good mares. He thinks they stand work better than geldings, and hold condition with less food."

August 5th.—The men are "beginning to show symptoms of sickness—low fevers and ague."

Tuesday, August 13th.—"Received orders to march to Villa Vicosa (6 leagues). The regiment to be halted at Montforte (1½ leagues)."

Wednesday, 21st.—"Horses well put up, shelter, served with forage."

Saturday, 24th.—"Rode to Berba. General Hill saw the two brigades of Portuguese Infantry—viz., 50th, 71st, and 92nd, and a company of Sharpshooters, 70th Regiment, the 6th, 18th, and a Regiment of Cacadores (Light Infantry), Portuguese, the whole having a most respectable appearance."

Thursday, 29th.—" Sent a party with an officer to Casa Forte [?] to patrol to the right and left to . . . [illegible], 2 leagues off."

Friday, 30th.—" Weather getting very hot, men falling sick."

Sunday, September 1st.—" Received orders to hold ourselves in readiness to march. Insurrection in Cadiz in favour of the French spoken of; not believed."

Montforte, Wednesday, 4th.—" Marched from Villa Vicosa at 3, and got here at 9 A.M.; passed Alcaranca, 5 leagues."

Thursday, 5th.—" Provisions of all kinds scarce and dear."

Sunday, 8th.—" Received orders at half past 7 A.M. to go with a despatch from Lord Wellington to General Phillipon, Governor of Badajos. Started at 9 with a trumpeter and a flag of truce; quintas and farms all the way; 2 leagues, a bridge, and a league farther the village of Barbasena; very large cattle fair. A mile on a quinta to the left; bad winter road. A league on you see Elvas and Forte Le Lippe, supposed to be the strongest in Europe, on the summit of a conical hill. It completely commands Elvas. . . . Got to Elvas between one and two. Environs destroyed as a precaution. From aqueduct upon 7 [? 3] brick arches well fortified . . . by Portuguese. The Portuguese General, Victoria de Graciar [?], Marshal of the Portuguese troops . . . very civil. Got a capital billet. Major Dance, 23rd Light Dragoons, commanding the 6th Portuguese Cavalry, called on me, and in a very obliging manner invited me to dinner and offered his services."

Elvas, Monday, 9th. — " Started with Major Dance at 7 for Badajos; passed the Portuguese Brigade half league from the town in a wood; half a league farther passed the patrols and vedettes. Open country within half a league of Badajos; crossed the river Caya, dry at this season; approached the Tête du Pont of Badajos within half a mile, where the guard challenged. Sounded a parley and halted; about 12 of the guard and 2 officers came forward in a slovenly manner, . . . [illegible] as they advanced, delivered my despatch to the officer, who desired us to dismount; tied our handkerchiefs over our eyes, and stood with our backs to the town, altho' we had . . . [illegible] view of the town before for an hour. A handsome town, with a long bridge over the Guadiana, and a strong fort, St Christoval, on the north side of the river, near which they had [thrown?] up a river [work?]. The appearance of officers and men was very [mean?], and indeed [shabby?] and vulgar. He told me Phillipon was [preparing an advance?], which we heard in conversation. He said that Napoleon was coming to Madrid, and that he would be in Lisbon a month afterwards. I told him plainly that 'he was very credulous.' He said Maria (the Empress) was a very beautiful lady, and that Napoleon was very much in love with her. I waited an hour and a half, when I got the Frenchman's answer. When the officer tied my eyes, he told me to stand with my back to the town. I told him it was not necessary, as it was a point of honour that I should not look towards it. However, he said he was ordered to do so. I, of course, submitted, and he touched me to put me in the posture he wanted. I told him 'to speak to me, but not to touch me'; when he begged my pardon. On our return saw the hills of Albuera, where the battle was fought on the 16th May. Before you enter Elvas is on the left a small fort, St Lucia."

This most graphic little description is well worth quoting *in extenso*. Unfortunately a good deal of the Diary has so faded that even with the aid of a powerful magnifying-glass it is impossible to decipher it. Hence the occasional blanks.

Thursday, 12th.—"Rain, with thunder and lightning; after it the air is cool."

Sunday, 15th.—"At night a comet of great magnitude in a north-east direction." This must have been "the grand comet" discovered by Flaugergues at Viviers on the 26th of March 1811.

Montforte, Saturday, 21st.—"Received orders to march on the morrow with a squadron to Assumar and detach a party to Ali-[grede?]."

Sunday, 22nd.—"Marched in at 10 o'clock—place very unhealthy, which the inhabitants imputed to the dragoons burning the stable litter."

The next few entries refer to marches, and the disposition of certain Portuguese troops, and also to the concentration of the Portuguese infantry at Montforte.

Friday, October 11th.—"Dined at Colonel Muter's house; a kind of club dinner. Twenty-two sat down to table. Bowers and F. Geale dressed in masquerade, and performed to admiration."

A further arrival of 1200 Portuguese at Montforte on the 15th crowded the place, and we read "much inconvenience in consequence."

On the 18th a field-day was held at Montforte.

Next day the 10th Portuguese Infantry marched in, "a fine regiment and very strong."

October 21st.—"General Long received orders to march on the morrow. The troops marched and went into bivouac one mile to the left of Cadecera, having left Montforte at 8 A.M., marched by Avronches, a good town, two leagues; crossed the sierra of that name; enter Spain; much rain—a terrible storm. Met the whole division on the march. Everything drenched with rain. Got our tent up. G. Doherty and myself pretty well off for canteen. It rained all night long."

Cadecera, 23rd.—"The troops bivouacked near the town in an olive grove, the officers in the town; got a room for Doherty and myself. Orders to march at 6 A.M. on the morrow."

Thursday, 24th.—"Bivouac near Casa Pedra Bucena; marched from Cadecera at 6 A.M., two miles, cross bridge; bivouacked at 12 o'clock half a mile from Casa—a huge old castle in a wild country, good ground and fine oaks."

Friday, 25th.—"Marched at 5.30 A.M.; fine roads, beautiful country (1 league); cross river Lelor by bridge of fifteen or sixteen arches. Soon after cross a sierra (4 leagues); a large lone house under the sierra; very strong pass through the sierra; bad roads; the town on the other side; overtook 2nd Hussars (Portuguese) and the 9th (Portuguese); had found the Conde de Peraire Morillo and Douny with his Legion in the pass—about fifty men, badly mounted and shabby, and dressed like mountebanks, with lances. Generals Hill, Sir W. Erskine Howard, and Long halted, fed, got our men refreshed; marched again at 4 P.M., two leagues, on the road to Malpartida. The French Corps of Giraud within a league; halted and killed oxen and dressed two days' provisions in the troop; not a tree; linked our horses; got a tent up and took refreshment; laid down for a couple of hours; found a large tarantula (poisonous spider) on my blanket. Sounded to horse at half-past two and marched off immediately—9th Light Dragoons (2 squadrons), 2nd Hussars, 13th Light Dragoons, 2 brigades of infantry, a company of Portuguese artillery, and a brigade of Spaniards."

THE AFFAIR AT LOS SANTOS.

On this march the greatest silence was ordered to be preserved, fires were forbidden to be lighted, and as the weather was very bad indeed the men suffered very much.

The army started again before daylight on the 28th, the directions for silence were repeated, and in addition the men were ordered to "keep their swords in their hands lest the noise of them rattling might be heard."

At dawn the force came in sight of the village of Arroyo Molinos, from which the enemy, about 2000 strong, under General Giraud, were issuing in disorder.

Captain Gubbins of this march writes—

"Very dark; came on to rain hard; passed the fires the French had left at 9 o'clock in the evening before. Formed in two columns of squadrons to the right of Malpartida. Learnt the French were off at 1 A.M. Marched into town between 7 and 8 on the 26th; very cold and wet. A very poor village. Got ourselves to rights with some difficulty. A poor town and wretched inhabitants; half a mile off an old ruined castle and a mill. Orders to march at 6 A.M."

Sunday, 27th.—"Bivouac before Almusar; marched from Malpartida at 6; wet; crossed a very fertile and extensive plain; halted before the village of Casa de Antonio; marched on with the advanced squadron to within a mile of Alcuesca. The whole division encamped there. Came on to rain hard at 9 o'clock; very dark; orders to bridle up and mount at 12; pitch-dark and torrents of rain; marched immediately. Some difficulty in getting the half squadron in column, and men and horses drenched and benumbed. Very bad and deep road; delayed two hours by the oversetting of a Portuguese gun. Learnt that the Frenchmen were in the village of Arroyo del Molino, two leagues off."

Arroyo del Molino.—The 50th, 71st, and 92nd, and 1 company of the 60th Regiments pushed through the village and took many prisoners. The main body of the British infantry moved to the right, to gain the main road to Merida and to cut off the retreat of the enemy. The cavalry in contiguous columns moved on the centre—the 2nd German Hussars on the right, the 9th Dragoons in the centre, and the 13th Light Dragoons on the left. The Hussars, with a squadron of the 9th, attacked the enemy's cavalry and dispersed them, and the 13th moved forward to the attack of a column of French infantry to which Lord Hill had sent terms of surrender, which were refused. The leading squadron of the 13th received orders to charge, and while moving on for that purpose received a countermand, with orders to move briskly to the left and cut the enemy off from the sierras in that direction, which was the only retreat open. The rocky nature of the country prevented the cavalry from acting with much effect when it had arrived at the foot of the sierras; but the British infantry having got round from the high road came up just in time to engage the enemy as he commenced mounting the sierra. A squadron of the 13th, under the command of Captain Bowers, was now ordered to charge the enemy's artillery, which it did in the most gallant manner, and captured two 8-pounders and a howitzer, caissons, &c. The enemy were pursued across the sierra till dark. A troop of the 13th, under the command of Captain Gubbins, supported the infantry. In the evening information was received that a party of the enemy's cavalry was perceived in a wood, and close to one of the advanced posts of the 13th. Captain Bowers was ordered to march his troop in search of them, and on coming up with them he charged, and took the whole of them, consisting of one captain and thirty-three men, and brought them into camp. The loss of the enemy in this affair amounted to about 1500 men, with many officers and the whole of their baggage and artillery.

The British loss was 7 rank and file and 5 horses killed; 1 lieut.-colonel, 2 majors, 4 captains, 4 sergeants, 47 rank and file, 11 horses wounded; 1 general staff missing. Portuguese loss—6 rank and file wounded.

The Spanish infantry was under the command of Brigadier-General Morillo—the Spanish cavalry under Count de Penne Villamur.

The official despatch of Lord Hill states that the British cavalry, owing to the darkness of the night and the badness of the roads, was delayed in its march on Arroyo del Molino, and that the Spanish cavalry under the Count de Penne Villamur "was, upon this occasion, the first to form upon the plain, and engaged the enemy until the British were able to come up."

General Giraud escaped with two or three hundred men, without arms, and was by his A.D.C. (a prisoner) reported as wounded.

The prisoners were sent under escort to Portalegre.

Spanish Military Costume

Light Infantry (Catalonian)   Artillery

Spanish GRENADIERS

Spanish Heavy HORSE

Spanish INFANTRY

THE AFFAIR AT LOS SANTOS.

The account of the affair to be found in the Diary of Captain Gubbins is interesting.

"The battle began by a gun from the enemy; hard rain and a fog. The cavalry formed in a column of half squadrons on the right of the village to cut off the enemy's retreat, and the 92nd Regiment drove them through it at the point of the bayonet. The two squadrons of the Germans [Hussars] charged the enemy, and afterwards a squadron of the 9th [Dragoons], who cut them up. General Hill came up and took our centre squadron with him to charge the enemy's guns. The General, in high spirits, showed us the direction of the French artillery. Charged obliquely; the right of the squadron first up with them; took the guns (2 guns and a howitzer, 6-pounders). General Howard's brigade cheered us in passing. Rode forward and pursued the fugitives. Sullivan only up with me; took 4 prisoners and the horse and baggage of the French Colonel of the 4th Regiment; sent them to the rear. Went with my troop, only 15 rank and file, with Lord Tweedale; crossed the Sierra of Montanches, a league from Arroyo; found the 39th Regiment driving the French fugitives from the sierra and Morillo's men dispersed in all directions; much firing on both sides. Persuaded by Tweedale to go up the mountain against my judgment . . . [very near?] the village of Santa Maria; the French making rapid progress along the sierra, and began to descend. Morillo endeavoured to form his troops in the plain, but in vain. Very anxious myself for him to form; took a position to support him. The 39th, quite exhausted, could not bring up a company. The enemy in the plain formed in close column and retiring with astonishing quickness, covered by their skirmishers. About 500 of the enemy. The Spaniards dispersed in tens and twelves all over the plain and firing to no effect. The enemy still retiring in a rapid and masterly manner. Very anxious to check him; hung upon his flank, constantly showing my front. He gave me some shots. Offered Tweedale to charge him rather than allow him to gain the wood if he would take share in the responsibility; however, he said it would be madness (and indeed so I now think it would, 30 to 500). The Frenchmen gained the wood; Giraud wounded, and his men very turbulent, took the road to Salvaterra; the Spaniards still following him in disorder. Dismounted my troop at 3.30 P.M. Tweedale left me; Lieut.-Colonel Luke, Major of the 39th, came up to me to ask my intentions, which I informed him. I accordingly took my troop to the village of Valdafuentes, and got my men a little bread and the horses some straw. Got a chicken killed, dressed, and eaten in ten minutes [this expression occurs more than once in the Diary, and is not probably expected to be taken literally]. Placed my vedettes, and learned from Colonel Luke that he would keep sentries and a strong guard. The 39th greatly exhausted; got a little wine and bread, which we divided with difficulty. Got straw for the horses, and only one bushel of barley. A peasant brought intelligence that the enemy had halted three leagues off. Offered Colonel Lindsay to march in two hours if he would bring 200 men, which he said he could not do—nor had he orders. Very anxious that he should, but in vain. Wearied and disappointed, changed my linen and got my clothes dried. Gave orders to march in the morning at daylight."

With regard to General Morillo and his Spaniards, Captain Gubbins's account bears the impress of truth; yet in Lord Hill's despatch we read that "Brigadier-General Morillo . . . and the Spanish officers and soldiers in general conducted themselves so as to excite the General's warm approbation."

On the morning of October 29, the division marched to Merida from Arroyo del Molino, where it remained a few days. The object of the expedition was completely accomplished, and consequently it began its retirement on November 1, marching through Puebla de Montejo and Campo Mayor, arriving in Montforte on November 3, where with the other troops the 13th went into quarters. The troop of Captain Gubbins we left at Valdafuentes, a little village. Thence on October 29th he marched at 5.30 A.M. and went to Santa Maria in order to join the Portuguese Regiment. "These not ready to march; got a guide for Arroyo del Molino, who took me up the sierra by a pass beyond description bad and steep; rain in torrents, and high wind. Got the horses up with great difficulty; obliged to make halt every 100 yards. Got to Montanches about 8 o'clock, a neat town in the . . . [heart?] of the Sierra. Halted an hour to refresh my men and horses."

Captain Gubbins graphically describes the kind and hospitable treatment he here received from the Spaniards. Both he and his men were well fed, and in addition four pounds of barley was obtained. He continues: "Found a better road down the sierra to Arroyo Molinos; found General Brun and several French officers prisoners there. Reported to Colonel [Luke?] and marched for Merida."

Passing over the battlefield of the 28th he describes the scene there, which we need not quote. He continues: "A long and tedious march; went the whole way to [Trugellianos?], within a league of Merida; darkness coming on; found a troop of the 9th Light Dragoons there; nothing to be got but a little straw. The troop throughout the whole affair behaved exceedingly well; not a murmur; changed my linen; had my clothes dried. The Spaniards civil, but wretched; got a little bread and chicken. The patron of the house played on the guitar and the girls danced boleros and sang pretty well."

On Wednesday, October 30, Captain Gubbins got into Merida at 7 A.M. and "reported to General Long, who approved of what I had done. Found G. Doherty at my billet; very bad one. The whole division in the town."

On Thursday, October 31, the division marched at 5 A.M. "A beautiful morning; beautiful views along Guadiana. Marched 4 leagues to Puebla de Montejo and Torre Mayor, Perales and Talavera la real." On the other side of the river "the ruins and several fords; good billet at Puebla; civil people. Rouse sounded at 9. Report that enemy had passed the river at Perales. The regiment turned out smart, and found the report false; merely a patrol of enemy; returned to quarters after a couple of hours."

Campo Mayor, November 1st.—"Turned out at 4; waited two hours for the Commissary. The regiment, with 200 British and a brigade of Portuguese infantry, formed the rearguard of the division. Woody country; a league before you pass the high road to Badajos, near which you pass the river Botoa by a deep ford. Quite dark when we got to Campo Mayor after a weary march of six long leagues. 17 hours on horseback. Got a pretty good billet, and some provisions."

Campo Mayor, November 2nd.—"Walked over the works—in pretty good order; some excellent casements [casemates?], the stucco resembling stone and beautifully executed; replenished my baskets; rode with G. Doherty over the ground the 13th charged the French upon.... Marched at 6 by St Olaca to Montforte; got in by 12; took my old billet; gave directions to get troop in order as soon as possible; read General Long's orders thanking the regiment for their conduct in Spain."

The regiment remained at Montforte until the morning of December 26. On November 15th Captain Gubbins met a M. Margane (Captain 34th Infantry), a prisoner taken at Arroyo Molinos. He had been sent to Montforte to be exchanged for Captain Nixon of the 95th Foot. The prisoner and his captors seem to have got on extremely well together. The Frenchman was most communicative as to his career, pay, prospects, &c. He, like most other people, had no high opinion of the Spanish soldiery, and considered Spanish women "of the best families" as "totally devoid of education." He stated that "the surprise at Arroyo Molinos was due to the obstinacy of General Giraud, who was told the night before by General Brun and his aide-de-camp that they had seen the English cavalry and knew them by their short tails, and Giraud replied, 'Ba, ba.' He was also told by a countryman that the English were in force at Alcuescaz, to whom he replied, 'C'est bien,' and said it could not be.

"If we had been ten minutes earlier we should have taken Giraud in bed. The first person who gave intelligence of the approach of the English was a French surgeon who ran through the village crying out 'Chargez vos armes! Chargez vos armes!' He said Giraud was a court favourite and much admired by the women." Captain Margane dined several times with Captain Gubbins or Captain Doherty, and appears to have been a most entertaining companion. He did not seem at all to dislike English fare, though of course different from that to which he was accustomed. He held that all parties were heartily sick of the war. On November 19th he was to have been taken by invitation to Cabeca de Vide to dine with General Long, but on that day "the order arrived for M. M.'s exchange, and that he was to go in the morning in charge of Lieutenant King with a flag of truce."

November 20th.—"Mons. M. called to take leave, and I saw him off with King."

The sad affair which occurred in connection with the exchange of Captain Margane is related both in Captain Gubbins's Diary and in the MS. Records of Lieut.-Colonel Doherty. The story is as follows :—

On the 21st of November an unfortunate occurrence took place

DEATH OF LIEUTENANT S. D. KING, OUTSIDE BADAJOS.

THE AFFAIR AT LOS SANTOS.

in the death of Lieutenant King. A French captain who had been made prisoner at Arroyo Molinos was in the charge of the 13th at Montforte for the purpose of being exchanged for an officer of ours of equal rank who was with the enemy at Badajos.

On the 20th the French officer was marched by Lieutenant King and a flag of truce for this purpose, and that night they halted at Campo Mayor.

On the morning of the 21st they proceeded towards Badajos, and (as it had been previously arranged) about half way they were met by a party from Badajos with the English captain, and the exchange of prisoners took place. Lieutenant King, being very desirous to see the fortress of Badajos, requested and was granted permission to accompany the French officer back. Before they had proceeded far a body of mounted armed peasants was perceived on a hill towards the right. The French officer told Lieutenant King they were guerillas, and that they certainly would not respect a flag of truce. He advised him to quicken his pace and get out of their reach, setting the example by immediately galloping away. Lieutenant King, conceiving that he had only to make them acquainted that he was English, and that they would not then molest him, immediately galloped towards them with his trumpeter (bearing the flag), crying out that he was English. One of them, however, levelled his carbine and shot King through the breast. He fell, and instantly expired. The trumpeter, though repeatedly fired at, escaped by the fleetness of his horse, and joined the French party, who by this time had come up with their advanced post. The picket turned out there and went in pursuit of the murderers, who fled, leaving the body plundered and stripped. The French party brought the body into Badajos. General Phillipon, who commanded that garrison, despatched a letter to the commanding officer of the 13th at Montforte to say that if the body was sent for by 12 o'clock the next day it would be given up, and if not he would have it interred with military honours at Badajos. The peasant entrusted with the delivery of this letter not arriving at Montforte until after the hour stated, General Phillipon assembled the whole of his garrison under arms, and the remains of poor King were interred on the ramparts, with every respect and all military honours which he had in his power to give. He kept the trumpter for the purpose of seeing the respect that was paid to him, after which he dismissed him with the necessary escort to join his regiment.

Lieutenant King was a young man of much promise, a zealous and attentive officer, much beloved by all his brother officers, who most sincerely lamented his untimely fate.

From the Diary of Captain Gubbins one or two details may be added. The horse of the French trumpeter was killed. The guerillas tried to cut off the whole party, and Lieutenant King rode up to them to explain the situation. General Phillipon in his letter "reflected on the British for sanctioning the guerillas, or brigands, as he calls them."

On Christmas Day, 1811, orders were received to march on the morrow to Avronches, and thence next day to Albuquerque. There the regiment joined Lord Hill's division. On December 28th the expedition marched and went into bivouac at La Rosa, a poor village and in ruins. The next day on arrival near La Nava the advanced guard of the 2nd German Hussars (K.G.L.) fell in with a patrol of the enemy—two men—from whom it was learned that part of the enemy was at La Nava. The 13th Light Dragoons and the 2nd Hussars were ordered forward at a brisk trot, and after pushing through La Nava the 2nd Hussars came up with a column of the enemy's infantry. They charged, but made no impression. The enemy continued to retreat in a close and compact body, keeping up a sharp fire on the Hussars and the 13th, who threatened him on both sides of the road, the ground being of such a nature as to render it impossible to charge. Meanwhile artillery was brought up and opened fire on the column, who, notwithstanding, continued its retreat in firm and compact order to nearly half-way to Merida. The ground now improved though still very unfavourable, and orders were given to the 13th and the 2nd Hussars to charge. The ground over which they were ordered to charge was covered with trees, there was consequently considerable opening out of the ranks. The 13th and the 2nd charged more than once, but the firmness of the enemy and the heavy fire he kept up prevented any success. The ground now became still more unfavourable for cavalry, the number of trees increasing. No more attacks were possible, and the enemy made good his retreat to Merida. In these attacks the 13th had eleven men and twenty-two horses badly wounded. Lieut.-Colonel Muter,

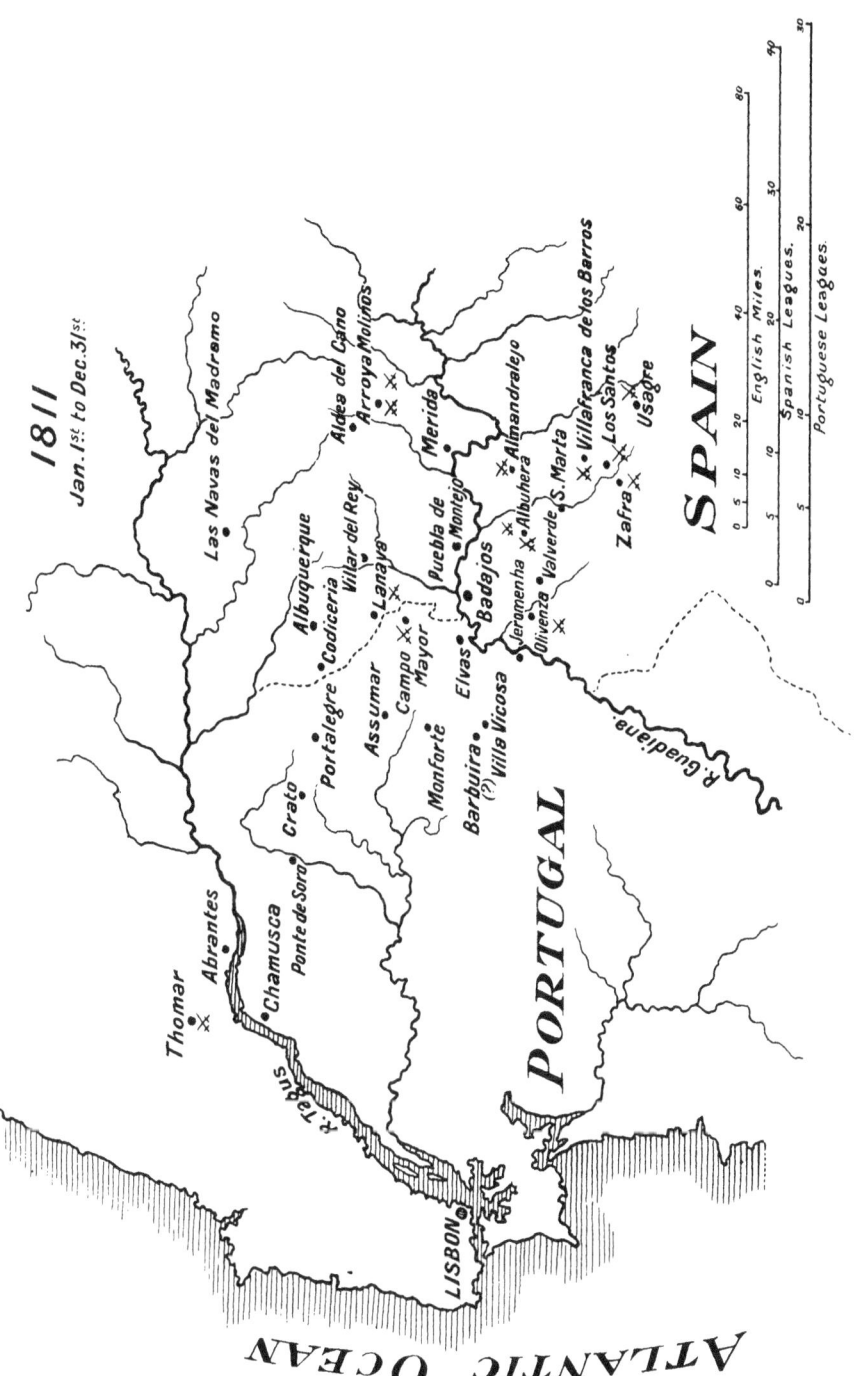

Sketch Map showing most of the places to which the regiment went during 1811. Some of the names cannot, however, be identified, and are therefore omitted.

THE AFFAIR AT LOS SANTOS. 165

Captains Buchanan, Bowers, and Gregory, and Lieutenant Doherty, had horses badly wounded,—the horse of the latter officer received a musket-ball, which went through his body. The account of this affair given by Captain James Gubbins is as follows:—

Sunday, 29th.—" Bivouac half a league from Las Manas [Neanas?]; marched at 7, foggy and cold; at 4 leagues came up with the enemy's vedettes. Within a mile of La Nava halted to inform General Hill. In an hour pushed on, and I found a column of French infantry in good order in the hollow—about 300 men. Smart skirmishing on both sides; the men in high spirits and anxious to charge; the enemy retiring rapidly and in good order, taking advantage of the green ashes [trees] to prevent our charging. A great deal of indecision on our side, and many men and horses struck by shot. The enemy gained the high road. Our German 9-pounder gave him shot. The regiment anxious and in momentary expectation of an order to charge. Received order to follow the Germans [2nd Hussars] and do as they did, marching left in front. The whole thing very badly conducted; the whole affair miscarried entirely for want of decision and proper orders, and the regiment was galloped about in a wild unconsidered way for 6 miles, and then ordered to charge when it was mathematically impossible to obey the order from the situation of the ground and our order of march. Altogether a very bad business owing to want of judgment and indecision in some general or other. All General Hill's Staff reflected on Long, and Offney received General Hill's orders to take the squadron of the Germans on the right and charge, but he failed, and the whole thing was lost by improper management. Extremely vexed and annoyed; lost several men, the man behind me shot through his helmet. Doherty's horse touching me shot through the body; Gregorie's horse killed; Muter wounded in three places, and another in two; Boyce, Buchanan, Bowers, &c., &c., wounded. The enemy had 3 men killed and 13 wounded. The first error was waiting for General Hill, the second indecision and bad order of march in General Long."

On the 30th the division marched and entered Merida, from whence the enemy had retired to Almandrelejo. Resuming its march on the next morning, the cavalry (9th, 13th, and 2nd Hussars) advanced and drove the enemy from thence to Villafranca, and on the following day from Villafranca.

CHAPTER XIV.

1812.

THE division retired to Merida on January 2, 1812, and from thence to Portugal. The 13th arrived at Montforte on January 8, and went into quarters. Captain Gubbins gives details of the events of these few days:—

Merida, December 30th.—"Very wet weather; marched at 7 A.M.; orders to march on morrow."

Almandrelejo, January 1st.—"Four leagues; marched 7 A.M., cold, wet, and foggy—at 2 leagues passed [Torrenaxio?] a village spoiled by the French, and not a soul in it, different articles of furniture broken in the street. A league farther, skirmishing with the enemy, their main body retiring from Almandrelejo, about 3000 infantry and 300 dragoons; drove them all from the town. They retired slowly to Villafranca, 3 leagues off. General Hill ordered our artillery not to follow, as they could play upon the enemy for an hour, supported by the cavalry. Marched in at 6—cold, wet, and dark, and wretched billet. Ordered to keep in readiness to turn out at a moment."

Here there is certainly a discrepancy between the MS. Record of the Regiment and the Diary of Captain Gubbins. Probably, though it is not mentioned in either account, the 13th did not accompany the division, and certainly Captain Gubbins did not reach Montforte till January 16. Equally certain it is that the 2nd German Hussars and the 4th Portuguese Cavalry were with the 13th. From the Diary we get—

Almandrelejo, January 2nd.—"Rouse sounded at 12 o'clock; marched a league towards Villafranca; made patrols up to enemy; returned to quarters at 4 P.M. A good town; found straw that had been concealed, and a quantity of wheat in a church which the French had not time to carry away."

Villafranca, January 3rd.—" Marched at 6 P.M., 2 leagues, the enemy retiring slowly from the town towards Los Santos; halted to reconnoitre; went into the town at 6 A.M.—dark, wet, and cold. A good town, the people put candles at all the doors by way of illumination. Orders to parade at the alarm post at 4 on the morrow."

Almandrelejo, 4th.—" Turned out at 4 A.M., very cold, and torrents of rain with wind—waited there three long hours—drenched with rain, the men and horses almost perished with cold. The 2nd German Hussars and the 4th Portuguese Cavalry charged a squadron of the French and captured 30 men and 2 officers. The Portuguese behaved pretty well. Marched at 7.30 and took up my old quarters. Orders to march on the morrow at 8 o'clock."

Merida, 5th.—" Marched in about 3 P.M.; bad billet, and difficulty in procuring stabling; orders to march with my troop to San Pedro on the morrow at 11."

San Pedro, 6th.—" One league; got in at 12.30; a wretched ruined village; poor billet. Placed my pickets and vedettes in command of roads leading to Truxillo, Medlin, &c."

San Pedro, 7th.—" Rode 2 leagues on Medlin road; crossed the river Burdalo, not fordable in wet weather; a handsome bridge over the Guadiana at Medlin; beautiful plains and very fertile; Cuesta lost a battle here; quantities of game and bustard. Put up a wolf in a coppice."

At San Pedro Captain Gubbins remained till January 12, when he gave orders that there should be a patrol to the picket at Valverde. That night at 11 o'clock he received orders to march to Merida by 8 on the morrow.

Montejo, 13th.—" Six leagues; marched to Merida at 8, and from thence at 11 along the Guadiana to Montejo (5 leagues); good road; large town. Orders to march at 7.30 on morrow. Lately cold weather, with hard frost."

Villa del Rey, 14th.—" Four leagues; marched at 8 A.M.; severe frost. Le Febre's troop of artillery and 9th Light Dragoons joined us. Good road; poor town. Orders to remain saddled and turn out at 6.30 on morrow. This town exhibited the marks of the enormities committed by the French troops. Nine-tenths of the houses destroyed, and it was asserted that about six months ago they ravished all the women in the place and murdered several men."

Cordecera, January 15th.—" Five leagues; at 3 leagues Requella on left. Cross the Gavora rivulet; Albuquerque on sierra on right; the troops bivouacked in the olive grounds adjoining the town. Orders to march at 6.30 A.M."

Montforte, Portugal, 16th.—" Four leagues; marched at 8 through Avronches, 2 leagues; the horses a great deal the worse for the expedition. Took up our old quarters."

From January 17 to January 20, 1812, nothing of importance is mentioned save a report from an officer of the Guards passing through that the French had been driven back in their attack on Tarifa with a loss of upwards of 2000 killed, wounded, and prisoners, 7 pieces of cannon, and 2 howitzers. On the 22nd news was received of the fall of Ciudad Rodrigo—" Great loss on both sides."

On the 24th orders came to march on the morrow for Crato. The route and dates and distances are as follows: Crato, January 25 (5 leagues); Gaffete, January 26 (2 leagues). Here a halt was made till February 9. At Gaffete, on February 6, after dinner with Lord Tweeddale, Colonel Byng, and Lord Guernsey, the latter " shewed us the new Light Dragoon dress; everyone agreed that it was quite shocking."

On February 9th orders were received to march on the morrow at 6 A.M. to Flor-de-Rose and Crato—one squadron (left?) at Flor-de-Rose. "A beautiful old castle and park with fine fir-trees, and a prodigious quantity of storks, a bird respected in Portugal. Orders to march 7.30 morrow."

Montforte, 10th.—" Wet and cold. Took up old quarters."

Captain Gubbins remained at Montforte till the 28th, on which day " Le Febre's troop of artillery, and a Portuguese regiment 1200 strong, marched in, the latter to march on to-morrow."

Montforte, March 3rd.—" Orders to march for Cordicera to-morrow at 7."

March 4th.—" Marched at 7, and went into bivouac close to Cordicera. Orders to march on the morrow at 7."

Villa del Rey, March 5th.—" Marched with the 2nd German Hussars, 9th Light Dragoons, and Le Febre's troop of artillery. Threw out 4 pickets."

March 6th.—" Turned out at 3.30 A.M. with the reserve squadron; returned at 8."

La Roca, March 15th.—" Marched from Villa del Rey; our duty severe there. Orders to march to-morrow."

La Nava, March 16th.—

Merida, March 17th.—" Marched at 7; learned that the enemy has left a squadron in bivouac to the left of the bridge, commanded by Baron St Pol. The 13th crossed the Guadiana half a mile below the bridge. The hussars skirmishing with the enemy on the bridge, followed the enemy 6 miles, who retired in good order—1 officer and 12 men taken in Merida. Marched into the town at 5, called on M. Montenegro."

From the regimental MS. further details of this affair are obtained. On the morning of the 17th, when advancing on Merida, the 2nd hussars fell in and commenced skirmishing with the enemy's cavalry, which they pushed through the town and across the bridge. Whilst this was going forward Major-General Long ordered the 13th to gain the front at a gallop. The enemy being then at the opposite side of the river Guadiana, the 13th received orders to cross, which it did at a deep ford, as fast as the horses could move through, formed up on the opposite side, and charged. The enemy were broke, and fled; the 13th continued in pursuit until nearly dark, constantly skirmishing, when the regiment received orders to cease and return to Merida; a squadron under the command of Captain Bowers was left on the duty of outpost.

On the morning of the 18th the cavalry advanced to Almandrelejo, from whence the enemy retreated, and on the following day returned to Merida, where the regiment continued a few days.

The siege of Badajos was now in progress. The batteries opened there at two o'clock on the 18th of March—60 pieces of heavy ordnance, and on this day the 13th, with the rest of the division except General Hamilton's Portuguese, marched for Almandrelejo. Here they could hear the heavy firing at Badajos.

The 13th were at Merida on the 21st and 22nd of March. Merida was crowded with troops, the inhabitants wretched and starving; bread 10d. a pound. Reports from Badajos stated that all was going well, that the enemy had lost 200 men in a sortie, and that breaching batteries were to open on the 24th.

Captain Gubbins, on the 24th, notes: "Saw Badajos from hills with glasses—very heavy firing."

On March 26th he received orders to march at 6 A.M. on the morrow.

Guareña (Guaranha), March 27th.—"Division marched at 6 A.M., three leagues; a romantic castle one league on the right, on the sierra. . . . Half a league farther cross a branch of the Guadiana—very rich even country. . . . Good town, inhabited by farmers. To march to-morrow at 5."

Don Benito, March 28th.—"Near here Cuesta met the French General Victor, and lost a battle and 15,000 men. Went into bivouac. The 2nd Hussars on picket lost some men by carelessly unbridling to feed; all at once the enemy ran into them."

March 30th.—"Marched back to Guareña."

Merida, March 31st.—"Favourable reports from Badajos."

Merida, April 1st.—"The people here are beginning to gain confidence and the market pretty well supplied, though very dear, bread 10d. per lb."

But the enemy had concentrated his forces and advanced for the relief of Badajos. This compelled Lord Hill to retire.

On April 4th the beautiful Roman bridge of Merida was mined.

Lord Hill's route was by Guareña, Merida, Arroyo, and St Servan, arriving on April 6th at Labon, where on April 7th the news of the capture of Badajos by storm was received.

In consequence the relieving force retreated to Lerida, having their advanced posts at Usagre.

According to Captain Gubbins, on April 7th he was in bivouac near Talavera and remained there till April 12, having visited Badajos, the condition of which place he most graphically describes on April 10, when he delivered letters to Lord Wellington and Marshal Beresford. On April 12th he marched to Almandrelejo.

Meanwhile Lord Hill with his division, according to the MS. Regimental Record, went as far as Villafranca, and he established the cavalry in his front. The 13th were placed on outpost duty at Robeira, round which, being an open country with roads innumerable, the duty was excessively severe. The outposts were so many, the enemy in such force, particularly in cavalry, the country so open, and the roads so numerous, that the utmost vigilance was necessary for security and to prevent surprise. Three troops, independent of the men actually on duty, were kept constantly saddled, and the men kept in such a state of readiness as to enable them to turn out at a moment's notice, either in the day or in the night. Scarcely a day passed but there was skirmishing between the advanced posts of the 13th and the enemy, who generally every morning pushed forward a squadron, and frequently a stronger force, to feel their way. They were always attacked and driven back by the pickets on duty, who were frequently reinforced, according to circumstances, by detachments sent forward from Robeira. The duty of foraging, placed as the regiment was, became an object of much moment. They were obliged to go into the country, cut barley, truss and bring it home, and this in close proximity to an enemy ever vigilant and watchful to seize any opportunity of attacking, which made the duty the more hazardous. However, notwithstanding the severe duty which at this time fell on men and horses, the former continued very healthy, and the latter improved in condition. The arms, accoutrements, and clothing were all got into good repair, and everything, as far as circumstances would permit, was put into the best possible condition for the ensuing campaign, which at this time was every day expected to open.

On Tuesday, April 21, Lieut.-Colonel Patrick Doherty joined from England, and at Robeira took the command of the regiment.

On Sunday, May 3, the regiment marched from Robeira to Palamas, where it continued until the 12th, when at 4 A.M. it marched to Merida and joined Lord Hill's division.

The country here about was infested by robbers. On May 10, Captain Gubbins tells us, a picket of the 13th captured a gang numbering fifteen. Dated May 12, is the last entry in this interesting Diary.

On May 13th the division marched, crossing the river by the bridge at Merida. This bridge, which was mined on April 4, had been blown up, its two centre arches being destroyed. The engineers, however, by means of planks, boards, and cordage succeeded in effecting sufficient repairs to admit of the passage of the army.

While the crossing was in progress one of the baggage mules be-belonging to General Long, heavily laden, jumped into the river. Despite the great height the animal was got out uninjured, and the general's baggage saved. That night the division went into bivouac about six leagues away on the road to Truxillo.

May 14th.—A five-league march in the direction of Truxillo took place, and again the force went into bivouac.

May 15th.—The infantry marched into Truxillo; the 13th went into bivouac near. Truxillo was found greatly ruined. Four companies of the 71st were quartered in the shell of what was once the magnificent house of Pizarro. All along the road, as in the town, the destruction had been the same. Castles, monasteries and nunneries, private houses, cottages, shops, all wrecked. Inhabitants everywhere scarce; those who had remained were poor, wretched, and altogether in a most deplorable state.

At Truxillo orders were received to leave all the baggage behind, except one mule for each field officer and one mule per troop for the officers.

Between one o'clock and two on the morning of Saturday, May 16, the division assembled and marched towards Almaraz, halting between 6 and 7 o'clock and going into bivouac until 10 at night, when the march was resumed. The division passed through Jereźico, and between 12 and 1 o'clock again halted. The cavalry dismounted and lay down at the horses' heads until daylight on Sunday, May 1. It was then found that at about two miles distance the Fort of Castello de Merevalte, an extremely strong position, was opposite, and the fort was held by the enemy. It had been intended to surprise this post during the night, but owing to faulty guides the columns destined for the attack missed their way and did not arrive till daybreak. It was judged better to retire. The troops were ordered to bivouac, and so continued for the whole of the next day. On Tuesday the 19th, at 3 o'clock in the morning, a feint attack was made on Fort Castello de Merevalte. At 6 A.M. a fort on this side of the river Tagus was stormed most gallantly by the 71st and 50th Regiments under General Howard, and carried, despite the strenuous opposition of the enemy. The French had to clear out so rapidly that they had not time to spike the guns. 50 of the enemy were killed and about 300 taken prisoners. Captain Candler of the 50th Regiment, Captain Grant of the 71st Regiment, Lieutenant Thiele of the King's German Artillery, and about 20 men were killed, and 12 officers and 80 men wounded. When the fort was taken its guns were pointed against another fort on the opposite

PORTUGUESE
Officer of ENGINEERS.   Officer of INFANTRY.

Armed PEASANT of the Ciudad Militia

side of the Tagus, and this was in consequence speedily abandoned by the enemy, who fled. Meanwhile the bridge across the river leading to Almaraz was attacked, fired, and entirely destroyed. As the destruction of this bridge was the precise object of the expedition, success was most complete.

From General Hill's despatch, dated May 21, we gather that Major-General Long commanded the centre column, which consisted of the 6th and 18th Portuguese Infantry under Colonel Ashworth, and the 13th Light Dragoons, with artillery. On arrival on May 17 at dawn, they advanced on the highroad to the Pass of Miraleste, the two flank companies being supplied with scaling-ladders. Captain Candler, who fell, left a large family to lament his loss. He was the first man to ascend the scaling-ladder, and fell upon the parapet. Lieutenant Thiele was blown up while destroying the captured fortifications. A very large quantity of provisions was taken.

Almaraz was considered by the enemy to be a most important post, but it was completely destroyed. The towers of masonry of Forts Napoleon and Ragusa were levelled, the ramparts of both destroyed as far as possible and the works near the bridge, together with the workshops, magazines, and even every piece of timber likely to be of use was demolished. A colour of the 4th Battalion of the Corps Etrangers was taken by the 71st Regiment.

On Wednesday, May 20, the division marched on its return, leaving Fort de Meravalte untaken. Its capture would not have been worth the sacrifice of life involved, its value having been completely nullified.

The division marched through Jerezico and went into bivouac. The next day the 13th Light Dragoons put up at a village called Fuerto de Anemy, about one mile from Truxillo. At this place there was good grass and some enclosed land. The horses were therefore turned out for some hours. The baggage of the regiment, which it will be remembered had been left at Truxillo, had meanwhile been sent to Caceres, about nine leagues distant, for security.

The regiment remained in the village till May 23.

The baggage arrived on May 22, in the evening, and the baggage-animals were much fatigued.

On Sunday, May 24, the 13th Light Dragoons marched at 3 A.M. and joined the division near Truxillo. After marching two leagues, information came that General Foy had forded the Tagus, and was advancing hastily with a strong force of cavalry. The 13th was ordered to return and take post near Truxillo, sending out a squadron to reconnoitre and watch the enemy. The regiment therefore returned, Major Boyse having the command of the detached squadron.

Captain Buchanan's troop moved on with General Hill and the infantry. The regiment remained in position until 4 P.M., when the detached squadron joined, having seen nothing of the enemy. The regiment then marched and went into bivouac near Santa Cruz.

May 25, a march of 4½ leagues, and bivouac.

May 26, a march to near San Pedro, and bivouac.

The regiment halted on the 27th. The following day, at 1 P.M., the regiment mounted. A squadron under Lieut.-Colonel Muter marched to Valverde, the remaining squadrons went into San Pedro and put up in quarters. Here the regiment remained until May 31, when, with the exception of Captain Gregorie's troop which was left at San Pedro, the remainder marched at 2 A.M. to Merida. Here it remained until joined by Captain Gregorie's troop on June 4.

On this day it had been determined to give a ball and supper to the people of Merida. It was the second time the regiment had been there, and their reception by the inhabitants had been most hospitable. All arrangements had been made for the festivity, when, to the disappointment of everybody, orders suddenly arrived to parade at 1 A.M. on the morning of the 5th. The regiment marched an hour later to Almandrelejo, and on the day following to Los Santos.

On Monday, June 8, Lieutenants D'Arcy and Turner of the 13th joined the regiment with remounts from England. Lieutenant Smith, who had been absent in consequence of a wound received in March 1811 at Campo Mayor, also joined.

At Los Santos the 13th remained till June 11, when it marched to Bienvenida.

On Friday, June 12, at 4 P.M., the regiment, with Captain Lefebre's troop of artillery, marched beyond Usagre and went into bivouac. Here the 13th was joined by the 9th Light Dragoons under Major Moreland. The two regiments were formed into a brigade under General Long, who had accompanied the 13th. At 11 o'clock that night a squadron under the command of Major Boyse was detached to Maguilla to look after and bring in a number of wounded men belonging to the heavy brigade, who were said to be lying there. It appears that the Royals and 3rd Dragoon Guards had had an encounter with the enemy at Valentia, near Llera. The enemy were put to the rout, but during the pursuit of them the heavy brigade fell in with a fresh body of the enemy and suffered many casualties.

On June 13th the brigade was shifted into a better watered bivouac, near Usagre, where Major Boyse and his squadron joined, after a march of thirteen leagues. He brought with him twelve wounded men of the heavy brigade. The next day at 6 A.M. the brigade and horse artillery marched to Bienvenida, a squadron under Captain Buchanan being detached to Usagre. On Monday, June 15, at 3 A.M., the entire force was turned out and remained under arms at the alarm post till 7 o'clock. The troops then turned in, but half an hour later were again turned out and marched with the infantry brigade to Los Santos. Here General Slade's brigade of cavalry (the Royals and 3rd Dragoon Guards) joined the division.

Resting at Los Santos till the 18th, at 4 P.M. on that day the 13th Light Dragoons, 9th Light Dragoons, 2nd Hussars of the German Legion, and the horse artillery marched to Fuente de Martin, and went into quarters.

The following day they passed through the town of Azenshall, and went into bivouac three miles beyond it. On June 20, starting in the evening, the march was continued, passing by Corte de Pelias, and the troops went into bivouac beyond. Here news came that the enemy was advancing, and was strong in cavalry.

The ground selected for this bivouac was most unfavourable, so its position was changed on June 21st for one where there was better shelter and a more plentiful supply of water and forage.

On this day the baggage and transport animals were nearly destroyed by fire. A widely extended and rapidly approaching blaze was descried. It was supposed that this had been done by the enemy to annoy the British and to conceal their own movements. The grass at the time was very high and very dry. Had the baggage-animals been laden up they could not have escaped, and no attempt was made to load them. Instead, leaving as many men behind as were sufficient to hold the horses, the rest were sent forward, extending the files right and left. Each man had a branch of a tree. They approached within 200 yards of the fire, and then beat down the grass and flattened it, so as to prevent the fire from catching it. By this means the danger was averted, and baggage and animals saved.

On Monday, June 22, the 13th and 9th Light Dragoons, with the 2nd Hussars, marched towards Azenshall. When near the place skirmishers and a flanking party were thrown out to protect the left flank. They soon came in touch with the enemy, and chased him into the town. In the course of the affair Lieutenant Smith was wounded in the shoulder by a spent ball.

When the brigade mounted the high ground over the town the French cavalry were seen drawn up opposite. Their skirmishers were attacked and driven in, and the brigade under General Long began to form up to make an attack. The enemy, however, retreated through the town and formed on the opposite side. The brigade then retired, and at 9 P.M. cooked food on the outskirts of a wood. Three hours later they mounted and retired to a plain, leaving the hussars on outpost duty. The brigade then dismounted, linked horses, and lay down to sleep. At 4 A.M. it was observed that the enemy were in motion, and a squadron under the orders of Captain Doherty was sent forward to support the hussars. The whole brigade was mounted and followed slowly. But the enemy retired, the squadron returned, and the brigade linked horses, and, despite the scorching sun to which they were exposed, continued thus till about 9 P.M. Then, leaving the hussars with a squadron of the 13th to watch the enemy, the brigade marched, and about midnight went into bivouac close by its old bivouac of two days before. Here it remained till June 29, when it marched into Albuera Wood and bivouacked. The hussars were relieved by Colonel Campbell's brigade of Portuguese cavalry.

From Azenshall, however, the cavalry of the enemy advanced and drove back Campbell's Portuguese. Consequently, at 5 A.M. on July 1, the 13th Light Dragoons turned out and advanced on Corte de Pelias, whereupon the enemy retired on Azenshall, and Colonel Campbell resumed his position.

The 13th remained out till 1 A.M., and then retired to bivouac. About 3.30 P.M. shots were heard close at hand, and some Spanish dragoons came galloping in. From these it was ascertained that the Count de Penne was attacked on his march to Fena by a considerable force of the enemy's cavalry, that he was defeated, and that the enemy in hot pursuit was even then in the wood and close to the bivouac. At the instant the regiment was in the act of cleaning their horses, having unsaddled for the first time for some days.

From the events of the morning it had not been anticipated that anything more would occur that night. Some of the men were cooking; nevertheless, within fifteen minutes the regiment mounted, the squadrons were told off and moving briskly forward.

When the regiment cleared the wood it was found that the enemy had been checked by a squadron of the 3rd Dragoon Guards, who had charged them. This squadron had mounted on the first alarm. The enemy retired with considerable haste, so much so that pursuit was given up.

The brigade remained on the ground till near midnight, when it returned to its former position, leaving a squadron of the 13th and the 2nd Hussars on outpost duty.

In their charge the 3rd Dragoons lost Lieutenant Ellis killed, and Captain Watts, who commanded the squadron, wounded. Two or three privates were killed as well. The Spanish cavalry lost about 250 killed, wounded, and prisoners.

On Thursday, July 2, at 2.30 A.M., the troops marched upon Santa Martha, but found it had been evacuated by the enemy the previous night. The British marched through the place and took post beyond it, where, without any shelter and under an excessively hot sun, they remained all day. The regiment slept at the horses' heads at night until 1 A.M., when the army marched. The country was now open, so the cavalry moved in front. Near the town of Villalva the enemy's cavalry was sighted, formed on the plain. The British line was instantly formed. The German 2nd Hussars in the centre, the 13th in column of squadrons on the right, the 9th Light Dragoons similarly on the left, and Captain Lefebre's troop of artillery on the right of the hussars. The infantry in the rear were coming on at a double in columns of companies. The cavalry advanced at a brisk trot. The enemy threw out skirmishers, who were at once attacked and driven in.

During the advance the enemy then put about and retired in haste, and passing through the town took post on the rising ground beyond. The British concealed their strength behind some hills, and the enemy concentrated his force. A river which flowed through the town was between the armies; thus matters rested for three or four hours. The cavalry then mounted and pushed through the town, on which the enemy again retired. At about a league beyond the town the British formed on a plain with the infantry in the rear. The artillery took post on a rising ground on the left. Again there was a wait, when orders came to fall back, each cavalry regiment leaving a squadron on the ground. A position was now taken up close to a river, but eventually orders were received to retire. The river was crossed, and the brigade went into bivouac in a wood. In the evening the enemy were found to be in motion, and orders came to mount, and the brigade with the horse artillery again moved forward quickly and took post on a rising ground. The enemy were on the heights opposite, and the artillery opened a smart fire on them. The fire was returned: one Portuguese was killed, one wounded, and also a horse of Captain Lefebre's troop was shot. The enemy then retired a considerable distance. All firing ceased. The brigade, however, remained in position till it was nearly dark, when it fell back and went into bivouac in the wood.

The army marched on the afternoon of the next day, Saturday, and, reaching the outside of Los Santos during the night, bivouacked.

The following morning, at 3 A.M., the army marched, advancing on Bienvenida,—the hussars in front, followed by the 9th, the 13th, the horse artillery, and the heavy brigade, with the infantry in the rear. Near Bienvenida the army turned off to the left towards Usagre, and soon the advanced guard fell in with the enemy's skirmishers, whom it thrust back. The hussars with the 9th, 13th, and the horse artillery advanced at a gallop; and as the ground permitted, the 9th and the hussars formed into line and advanced up a hill behind which the enemy was supposed to lie. The 13th, meanwhile, in column of squadrons, inclined to the right at a gallop in order to gain the left flank of the enemy.

When the crest of the hill was reached the enemy were viewed in rapid retreat, and protected by a deep ravine which prevented pursuit. But the horse artillery, which was between the 9th and 13th, having gained the hill, opened an effective fire on one of the enemy's columns. The enemy retired through the town, the cavalry and artillery took post on the hill, and the infantry occupied the town. Here, unsheltered and beneath a broiling sun, the cavalry remained until 6 P.M., when it was retired. Foraging parties were sent out, and the men bivouacked in a neighbouring village. It is recorded that the thermometer stood at 96° all this day.

On Monday, July 6, the enemy took the initiative, advancing at 5 P.M. and driving in the outposts. The cavalry were ordered to mount, and the hussars were sent forward. The 9th and 13th followed. Skirmishers were thrown out, who soon fell in with those of the enemy and drove them in. The force of the enemy, which was clearly seen, consisted of three strong columns of cavalry. The British cavalry continued to advance in contiguous columns, and ready to deploy into line. The enemy, however, did not wait, but retired briskly. As a pursuit was not intended, the brigade returned and went into bivouac.

The next day the army marched at 3 A.M., leaving Usagre on the left. The road lay through Villa Garcia. No enemy was visible, and after a while the troops returned to Villa Garcia, where a halt was made. Later they marched again, and went into bivouac nearly.

It seems that an engagement had been anticipated that day, rumours of the intentions of the enemy in that direction being rife. It turned out that it was a ruse. These false rumours had been assiduously circulated by the enemy to cover his retreat—a retreat which began on the previous night.

The army therefore continued in its bivouac during July 8th and July 9th.

At 1.45 A.M. on the morning of July 10th the cavalry and artillery paraded, and were joined by the whole of the infantry from Villa Garcia. After some little delay the whole force moved off in the direction of Maguillan, under the command of Sir William Erskine. The line of march was, however, soon deflected to the right towards Bolanja. During the march artillery fire was heard on the right, and this proved later to proceed from the army under General Hill, who had that morning marched from Llerena. On the way he fell in with a body of French cavalry who soon retired.

The march of Sir William Erskine was uninterrupted as far

as the town of Arioles. Near this town a halt of two hours was made and the regiment dismounted. Resuming its march, when approaching Bolanja the French were descried retiring therefrom. The British marched past the town, and in a wood about a league beyond dismounted and gave the horses forage.

The enemy then appeared in force on the high grounds in the front. A squadron of the heavy brigade was sent out to reconnoitre. On this the enemy retired. That night the horses were linked, and officers and men, momentarily expecting to be called out, lay down at their horses' heads and slept till 2 A.M.

Saturday, July 11, at 2 A.M., the army got under arms—and the cavalry formed in contiguous columns of squadrons near Bolanja. At 6 A.M. the infantry began to retire, an hour later the cavalry followed, and the whole force returned to the bivouacs it had occupied before this forward movement. The excessive heat and entire want of shelter on these two days were most severely felt by the men and horses.

On Sunday, July 12, at 3 A.M., the brigade, consisting of the 9th, 13th, the 2nd Hussars, and Captain Lefebre's troop of horse artillery, marched towards Arioles. Near that town news came that the enemy's cavalry were in force and near the front. General Long immediately formed the brigade. The 9th Light Dragoons and the 2nd Hussars in line in front. The 13th Light Dragoons formed a second line, with the horse artillery also in line in the centre. Parties were also detached to the right and left. In this order the brigade moved forward till from some high ground the cavalry of the enemy came fully into view. But instead of being near, as was expected, it was drawn up in line on the heights beyond the town of Bolanja, but immediately over it. The heavy brigade was formed up at some little distance on the right, and their skirmishers had already engaged those of the enemy and driven them in. The enemy got into motion. The British halted to see what was intended. The enemy moved forward in columns of squadrons—halted, deployed, formed columns again, took ground to the right, and then went briskly off by threes from his left to his rear, and disappeared. The British remained in position for about two hours, when, finding the enemy did not mean fighting, the two brigades retired to a village called Anoles, in the street of which the horses were linked, and the men took shelter in the houses. Here they remained till 7 P.M., when the brigade mounted and marched back to their old bivouac, arriving at 1 A.M. on July 13. After a march of at least forty miles, both men and horses were greatly fatigued. Three days' rest, however, followed.

On July 16th the brigade went into quarters at Villa Garcia and remained there till the 21st, when it marched to Usagre and thence on the 22nd to Villafranca, halting on the 23rd.

On Tuesday, July 25, while the regiment was mustering in watering order, it was reported that the enemy were advancing in force from Robeira, and orders to turn out on the instant were given. Already all the posts occupied by the Portuguese cavalry had been driven in. The regiment was very quickly on parade, and at a brisk trot moved forward, taking post on the outskirts of an olive-grove.

A reconnoitring party was sent out and soon returned with the information that the enemy were advancing and driving in the Portuguese skirmishers in all directions. By this time the entire brigade had assembled, and General Long with it. The force moved forward to support the Portuguese; upon which the enemy began to retire. The brigade continued to advance till near Robeira, and then halted at the foot of a hill. Lieutenant Turner of the 13th was now sent by General Long to apprise Sir William Erskine, who was with his heavy cavalry brigade. Lieutenant Turner rode across country with as much speed as possible and delivered his message. The heavy brigade started. General Long waited till he thought the support from Los Santos ought to be well on its way, and then formed up his brigade. The 9th on the right, the 13th, 2nd Hussars, and horse artillery in the centre, and the Portuguese cavalry on the left. The brigade moved forward in contiguous columns of squadrons at a brisk trot.

The enemy was now discovered to consist of seven squadrons. The horse artillery pressed forward and opened fire on two bodies of the enemy, one near the town and the other on the Lleira Road, and the guns being well served did much execution. The skirmishers then dashed into those of the enemy with the sabre, and headed by Lieutenant Edwards of the 13th drove them all in. The enemy now began to retreat in haste. The brigade pursued across the country, with the horse artillery at a gallop. Gaining some rising ground, the enemy was again in view, and again the horse artillery opened on him. While the artillery played, the cavalry moved at a gallop in pursuit over the lower ground. The enemy had now had enough. All semblance of order was lost, and he retired in confusion at a gallop. The pursuit was continued for nearly six miles, when General Long halted the brigade. Presently they retired, and having marched a short distance dismounted. The heavy brigade here came up, but unfortunately for themselves too late. The fact was that the distance was too great to be done in the time, and General Long perhaps a trifle hasty in ordering the advance. The heavy brigade then returned to Los Santos. Great praise is due to Captain Lefebre for the splendid way in which he fought his guns. The enemy lost in this affair 39 men killed, a great many wounded, and 18 prisoners and many horses taken. The loss of the 13th was one man and two horses wounded.

The regiment remained at Villafranca during Saturday, July 25. On the following day the 13th alone marched thence at 2 A.M., reaching the bivouac of Colonel Campbell and a regiment of Portuguese cavalry at daybreak near Robeira. The object of this march was to relieve this advanced post. The 13th accordingly took up the posts, and the strength required for this duty amounted to 2 subaltern officers and 94 non-commissioned officers and men. When this was done the remainder of the regiment marched into Robeira about 8 A.M. Here, having regard to information obtained as to the strength of the enemy and his situation with respect to the regiment, it was deemed needful to send all the baggage to the rear, and it was consequently remitted to Villafranca. The regiment continued saddled and prepared for any emergency at a moment's notice. During the day, from the information obtained both by parties sent out for that purpose and from the alcades (magistrates) of the various towns near, it was seen to be absolutely necessary for the regiment to go into bivouac. Consequently in the evening near Robeira the 13th formed a close column of squadrons on the high ground, and the men lay at their horses' heads all night.

On the next day, after the outposts were relieved and reports from the district received, the regiment marched into Robeira. Information arrived during the day that the enemy had received a great increase in strength of cavalry, artillery, and infantry during the night, and that these reinforcements were distributed in the towns of Hornaches,

Palamas, and Llera—towns situated on the front and left flank, from about two to four leagues distant. That night the portion of the regiment not on outpost duty again went into bivouac, but not at the same spot.

On Tuesday the 28th the same routine was gone through. In the evening the 9th Light Dragoons arrived and took up the outpost duty, the 13th falling back to a wood some distance from Robeira, where officers and men lay at their horses' heads all night. The next day the position in the wood was changed for one where the water-supply was more accessible, and that night the baggage came in from Villafranca.

Early on July 30th the regiment turned out and formed outside the wood in consequence of a report that the enemy's cavalry had advanced on Robeira. It would appear that at some period during the last few days the remainder of the brigade had joined the 13th, for Colonel Doherty mentions that after the 9th Light Dragoons had repulsed the enemy from Robeira the *army* returned to bivouac.

On Friday, July 31, the brigade (9th Light Dragoons excepted, who remained on the outpost duty) marched into Villafranca, into which the 71st Regiment this day marched, and the whole went into quarters.

There seems to be a little confusion here in the MS., but there are no means of disentangling the matter: and it is not really of great importance.

Early in the morning of Saturday, August 1, the 9th Light Dragoons were relieved by the 2nd German Hussars. Very shortly after they had taken up the duty, five strong squadrons of the enemy from Hornaches moved on Robeira. They marched through the place, but on the other side found the 2nd Hussars awaiting them. The 2nd Hussars gallantly charged them, broke them, and took 20 officers and 31 men prisoners. A fresh body of the enemy's cavalry, however, arrived, supported by infantry. The 2nd were compelled to retire, and being hard pressed lost the whole of the prisoners they had taken and eleven of their own men besides. One of their officers (Lieutenant Grueber) was killed and two men. News of this reaching Villafranca, the 13th, the 9th Light Dragoons, the 3rd Dragoon Guards, and the horse artillery were at once moved quickly forward towards Robeira. After having gone some distance, the whole brigade with the exception of the 13th was halted on the road, and the regiment received orders to push forward to Robeira to the support of the 2nd German Hussars. After some skirmishing the enemy were driven off, retiring pretty briskly, and leaving a good number of dead and wounded behind them. Lieutenant Smith of the 13th had the good fortune to be present and to join in the charge, as he had been sent to the hussars with some order during the morning. He is reported to have behaved remarkably well. As nothing more was seen of the enemy, the 3rd Dragoon Guards were ordered up to Robeira, where a squadron of the 13th was also left on outpost duty, and the rest of the brigade and the artillery returned to Villafranca and went into very crowded quarters, crowded because during the day three regiments of British infantry had reached that place. On Sunday, August 2, Lieutenant Grueber's body was buried with full military honours—all the officers attending the funeral.

The next day the regiment marched out of Villafranca and went into bivouac in a neighbouring wood, having sent forward a squadron to Robeira to relieve that doing outpost duty there with the 3rd Dragoon Guards. The 13th during this and the next day remained in bivouac, having the charge of all the outposts.

On Wednesday, August 5, being relieved, the 13th marched into Villafranca, remaining there till the 11th, when it marched and took up the duty of the outposts from the 3rd Dragoon Guards and 2nd Hussars, performing those duties until the 14th, when being relieved by the 9th Light Dragoons it returned to Villafranca.

Lieut.-Colonel Doherty was on the 15th ordered to sit as a member of a General Court-Martial which assembled at Fuente del Maistre.

Outpost duty was shared between the 3rd Dragoon Guards, the 9th and 13th Dragoons, and the 2nd Hussars of the German Legion, from the 15th to the 28th of August. Regiments relieving each other every alternate day. Want of water both in Villafranca and in the bivouac was now greatly felt, the more so as the weather was excessively hot.

One or two skirmishes and alarms occurred, and during one on the 19th Lieutenant Strenuitz, A.D.C. to Sir William Erskine, was taken prisoner.

Lieutenant Smith now became seriously ill and was compelled to leave quarters.

The General Court-Martial was ordered to transfer its sittings from Fuente del Maistre to Los Santos, as the garrison had left the former place. When the members met at Los Santos an order arrived to adjourn till further orders, and for the members to proceed to their various regiments.

For several days the army was almost constantly on the march; their movements, however, need only be recorded in brief.

August 28th.—3rd and 4th Dragoon Guards and the Royals under General Slade; 9th and 13th Light Dragoons, 2nd Hussars, and Captain Lefebre's Horse Artillery under General Long; 50th, 71st, and 92nd Regiments under General Howard, from Villafranca to Usagre—General Slade's and General Long's going into bivouac near.

August 29th.—Heavy cavalry brigade to Llerena; light brigade to Villa Garcia.

August 30th.—Whole army to Berlanja, whence the enemy retired on the previous night. Cavalry in bivouac.

August 31st.—Light cavalry marched into Berlanja and halted till September 2.

September 2nd.—Light cavalry and horse artillery to Maguillan.

September 3rd. — Campillo. *4th,* Zelamea, crossing the sierra by "most infamous roads." Halted on 5th.

September 6th.—Light cavalry and horse artillery to Camponarco; good roads and a pleasant country. Very well received by inhabitants. The Court-Martial which had been adjourned was ordered to assemble at Don Benito, where, on the 7th, it was closed.

September 11th.—General Long inspected the 13th in watering order.

September 13th.—Madrigillas; 14*th,* Eriegula; 15*th,* Truxillo; 16*th,* Torrecillas and Aldea Nueva; 17*st,* halted; 18*th,* Delitosa; 19*th,* through El Camillo and Mesa de Ibor to Ellbonal; 20*th,* Arcobisco—completely in ruins; 21*st,* Talavera de la Reyna, also considerably damaged. Halted on 22nd and 23rd. Colonel Doherty with several officers inspected the battlefield there, and specially the ravine where the 23rd Dragoons suffered so severely. Even then the bones of the men and horses that had fallen were lying where they fell, all mixed together. Colonel Doherty by experiment proved that it was absolutely impossible to see the ravine until just upon it. This the French infantry knew, and hence the terrible slaughter.

September 24th.—The 9th and 13th marched to Puebla Nueva, a town which had not been injured by the French, owing, it is said, to a voluntary contribution having been raised on any approach of the enemy, and paid over to the officer in command as a price for forbearing to quarter troops there. This savours of the free companions of the middle ages. Here the brigade remained during the 25th, 26th, and 27th, with the exception of the 2nd Hussars, who moved on to Malpiscea.

Monday, September 28th.—Navalmoral de Toledo; 29*th*, Galves; 30*th*, halted.

October 1st.—Sonceia; 2*nd*, Yeavenos; 3*rd*, Madrelejos; 4*th* and 5*th*, halted; 6*th*, Villacana; 7*th*, the 9th and 13th marched into Coral de Almagesta.

During the whole of this time the British troops were received with acclamations, ringing of bells, and the utmost hospitality—the inhabitants voluntarily entertaining in quarters as many men and horses as they could accommodate.

October 17th.—Lieutenant D'Arcy, Sergeant-Major Taylor, and seven men left the regiment sick. The next day Captain Bowers and Lieutenant Jeffreys, 13 men, and 17 horses sick were sent to the rear.

The brigade was now in close proximity to the enemy, and on the 19th a squadron under the command of Major Boyse, and consisting of his own troop and that of Captain Macalester, marched to Quintana to watch the motions of the enemy. In consequence of the advance of the enemy in force, the 9th and the 13th (with the exception of the squadron with Major Boyse) marched from Coral de Almagesta to Villa Tobas on October 21, and next day to Oceana, when Major Boyse's squadron fell back to Villa Tobas. The regiments now halted for two days.

Early in the morning of Sunday, October 25, the enemy advanced on Villa Tobas with a considerable body of cavalry. Major Boyse with his squadron slowly retired. On reaching the open country the enemy sent strong detachments on his flank to outflank him and get into his rear.

Meanwhile their main body was moving forward. This obliged Major Boyse to increase his pace, and he retired by alternate half squadrons, covered by skirmishers under the command of Lieutenant Doherty. The skirmishers were fully employed and had frequently to charge those of the enemy. Thus, though severely pressed, the squadron continued to make good its retreat till a squadron of the 9th arrived in support. This squadron of the 9th lost eleven men taken prisoners, the enemy having managed to outflank them. The

13th had two men taken prisoners owing to their horses falling while skirmishing.

By this time news of the advance of the enemy had reached Sir William Erskine. The cavalry, who were just then engaged in cooking their food, were ordered out, and took up a position on the other side of Oceana, where a body of Spanish cavalry and a brigade of Portuguese cavalry were also assembled. Here they were joined by the two retiring squadrons of the 9th and 13th. The horses of the latter were so fatigued from the length of the retirement and the pace at which it had to be performed to avoid being outflanked, that orders were given to Major Boyse to fall slowly back on Aranjuez. The enemy took up a position on the farther side of Oceana, but in the absence of precise information as to the strength of the force near and what other forces might be advancing, Sir William Erskine did not order an attack.

The brigade remained on the ground until the evening, and then marched to Aranjuez, arriving there about 10 P.M.

With difficulty could the troops get quarters here, as the great majority of the inhabitants had deserted it, and in addition had left their houses so bolted, barred, and locked up that admittance could be only obtained with great difficulty — often indeed only by using force.

On Monday, October 26, the brigade marched at 1 A.M., and after crossing the bridges preparations were made to destroy them. The destruction of these bridges at Aranjuez was most important. Unfortunately on this occasion it was not carried out effectually.

Not far from Aranjuez the brigade turned into a field, formed contiguous columns of half squadrons, linked horses, placed a few vedettes, and officers and men lay down to sleep. Later in the day the bridles of the horses were removed, in order that they might feed more freely on some straw which had been found in a neighbouring house.

The bridles were placed on the holsters. While thus occupied it seems that an order had arrived for the 2nd German Hussars to join Lord Wellington.

The 2nd Hussars mounted and filed off. Now this regiment had served with the 13th for a long period both in England and later in the Peninsula. As they passed, up sprang the men of the 13th to give their old comrades a parting cheer. They did, cheering most heartily, and this so terrified the horses that four troops broke loose, and despite all the efforts of the regiment, aided by their old comrades the hussars, the frightened animals broke away and got clear off into the open country, where it is said "by squads they took various directions" and dispersed at a gallop. Bits, swords, carbines, and pistols were scattered by them as they went in every direction. How serious the matter was may be gauged by the fact that at that very moment the enemy, and a force particularly strong in cavalry, was pouring into Aranjuez, the town they had not long left, and hardly more than six miles distant. In addition to this, the river was known to be fordable in several places, even if the bridges were destroyed, which happened not to be the case. The remaining squadrons of the 13th mounted instantly, as did the 9th Light Dragoons, and off they started in pursuit of the fugitives and to recover the arms and equipments. A long line was formed of single files at double distance across the country, following up the tracks of the horses, and small parties were thrown out on the flanks to make inquiries. By the evening all the horses but twenty-seven had been recovered. A special search-party, under Holmes the Adjutant, then started to endeavour to retrieve them. By good fortune the runaways were found in the safe custody of some Spaniards, who had caught them and hidden them from the French in a house some five leagues distant. The arms and accoutrements found were brought in during the evening, and when each troop had received its own it was found that 1 bridle, 2 swords, and 1 pistol only were missing. The horses, too, had all escaped uninjured.

That night the regiment put up at a house called Cortejo Real—a place where the royal wine was stored for the king. The 9th Light Dragoons and the artillery marched farther up the river. When the outposts were placed that night the river in front of the post occupied by the 13th was found to be fordable for cavalry in more than one place. It was known that Aranjuez was full of the enemy, and particularly of the enemy's cavalry. Now, in consequence of the numerous outposts taken up, the regiment, as a regiment, was considerably weakened, so much so that it became absolutely necessary to ask for a reinforcement. Colonel Doherty therefore applied to Colonel Skerret, who was commanding a Brigade of Guards, and who had just arrived. Colonel Skerret immediately sent 100 men with the necessary proportion of officers. These were placed in fitting situations on the outposts, with a few of the 13th with each party. By this means the chief part of the men on the detached posts were brought in and the regiment strengthened.

Next evening the horse artillery returned to the position occupied by the 13th the night before. The enemy advanced and made an attack on one of the bridges. This bridge over the river Jeremia was defended by the 95th Regiment in the most gallant manner, and every attempt made by the enemy to cross failed. One officer of the 95th was most seriously wounded, and was carried into the post occupied by the 13th.

On Wednesday, October 28, information came that the enemy intended to ford the river at some spot with his cavalry, and preparations were at once made to prevent it. The whole brigade with the artillery assembled at the ford which was thought the most likely to be the scene of the attempt. The main portion of the British force was concealed.

After waiting a long time no enemy appeared, and the report was evidently false, so the brigade retired to Cortejo del Real.

Thursday, October 29th.—The brigade marched, crossing the river Jeremia by a bridge, which the engineers were then ordered to destroy, arriving at quarters at Cimperzula at 7 P.M.

Next day the baggage of the brigade arrived at about noon; two hours and a half later it was ordered to be sent away instantly to Arrevena. At the same time the brigade was ordered out and marched back to the bridge it had crossed the day before, and which the engineers had failed to destroy effectually. The enemy was attacking the bridge in great force, and the bridge itself was being defended by our infantry. The brigade formed on the high ground above the river. The attack on the bridge was very determined. Guns were brought to bear on the bridge by the enemy, and their men several times assailed the defenders at the point of the bayonet. Every attack was, however, repulsed, and the British infantry held the bridge till night ended the conflict.

The British loss was between seventy and eighty men killed and wounded. On the withdrawal of the infantry, which took place during the evening, cavalry pickets took their posts. At midnight all the outposts were withdrawn, and the brigade marched, covering the retreat of the infantry, towards Madrid.

Next morning at daybreak a squadron of the 13th was detached to the rear to watch the movements of the enemy. The brigade continued its march to within a league of Madrid, when it took up its position and halted. The enemy also halted. The brigade resumed its march, passing close by Madrid, and went into bivouac at Arevena, where the baggage had previously been despatched. During the night the detached squadron joined, and at daybreak on November 1st the whole army got into position and awaited the attack of the enemy. The enemy, however, declined to attack, and the army then began a retreat on the Escorial. On the road thither the infantry went into bivouac, while the brigade continued its march, going into quarters at the Escorial that night. The army marched on November 2nd to Villa Cartia, where the infantry went into bivouac and the cavalry into quarters. Marching the next day, the infantry turned off on the Salamanca Road, while the cavalry followed that leading to Valladolid as far as Martinmunez, where it went into quarters. The next day, November 4, the cavalry halted and was joined by the baggage and convalescent horses. On November 5th the brigade marched going into bivouac at Fonte Veras, and here the enemy was very close in the rear. For the next three days, marching by day and going into bivouac by night, the brigade proceeded, till it arrived near Alba de Tormes. Here a halt was made, and after some few hours orders were received to march back and relieve the 2nd Hussars, who had hitherto been acting as rearguard. Accordingly the 9th and 13th retraced their steps as far as the village of Garcia del Almonda. Here, when the inhabitants learned that the enemy was approaching, they fled in the utmost consternation, carrying with them in bundles such of their possessions as were portable. Outposts were placed, and the 9th and 13th remained ready to mount at a moment's notice. On Monday, November 9, the cavalry of the enemy advanced in force, the outposts were all driven in, and the brigade formed, and having thrown out skirmishers slowly retired on Alba de Tormes by alternate half squadrons, contiguous columns of which were formed. At Alba de Tormes the brigade went into bivouac—the enemy did the same, and the hostile pickets that night were in close proximity.

The next morning the army marched, and crossing the river Tormes by the bridge took post on the other side. The enemy advanced in considerable force of cavalry, infantry, and artillery, and took post on the heights above the town. Alba de Tormes was occupied by General Howard's brigade of British infantry (50th, 71st, and 92nd Regiments), with a brigade of Portuguese infantry, the whole under the command of General Hamilton.

CHAPTER XV.

Alba de Tormes, 1812.

ON November 10, at about 2 P.M., the attack of the enemy began with a most tremendous fire from twenty heavy guns, under cover of which his infantry attacked the outworks which were defended by the British infantry brigade. All attacks were repulsed, and repulsed with considerable loss to the enemy. This went on without intermission until dark. At one time the enemy's guns were turned on the cavalry brigade, which in consequence of the shot passing through the ranks, was retired to the neighbourhood of Terredelos, a small village. Here the cavalry bivouacked. It is recorded that on this occasion the Portuguese artillery was remarkably well served and did considerable execution. An hour before dawn on the 11th the cavalry brigade mounted and moved forward again to the high grounds, where it formed, and at daybreak the attack of the enemy was resumed. The artillery fire continued till noon, when it slackened, during which time repeated attacks on the outworks and town had been made with great fury. All these attacks, as on the previous day, failed, several being repulsed by the bayonet. Strong pickets and supporting pickets of cavalry and infantry were then placed along the banks of the river, particularly at the fords, where, as the water was then low, there were many places fordable.

In the evening the brigade returned to its bivouac.

Next morning the brigade resumed its old position on the heights, and the onslaughts of the enemy were as furious as ever, and were repulsed as before. On the 13th the firing ceased.

Early on the 14th the enemy succeeded in crossing the river Tormes by means of the many fords. A detachment of Portuguese infantry was left in Alba de Tormes, and subsequently surrendered. All the British posts were forced, and the pickets retired, with the exception of a Portuguese infantry picket, which, being surrounded by the enemy's cavalry, surrendered. The British Army slowly withdrew. During the retirement the 9th and 13th frequently formed line in expectation of an attack by the enemy's cavalry, but though there was some skirmishing no attack was made.

That night the army went into bivouac, near a small village, under torrents of rain.

On Sunday, November 13, both armies manœuvred around the Arapiles. The cavalry was this day under the command of Lord Combermere.

Positions were repeatedly changed, but no attack took place. The 13th was much employed in skirmishing, and the enemy employed a device which may be mentioned. Mounting their sharpshooters, they brought them forward behind the skirmishers for a certain distance, and then dismounted them. To rid themselves of these, the skirmishers of the 13th had repeatedly to charge with the sabre.

Towards evening both armies took up positions, and the British opened a heavy artillery fire which, while it lasted, did considerable execution.

Darkness now came on and the British retired. The cavalry brigade went into bivouac near the village of Calvaraso. During the whole day rain had fallen in torrents, the men had had no food and the horses no forage. On the top of this came the serious intelligence that the commissary with his brigade of mules had been surprised by the enemy in one of the neighbouring towns whither he had gone for supplies. This occurred just as he was in the act of loading up; and the muleteers had cut away their loads and made off when they could, the remainder being captured. Thus the whole mule brigade was dispersed, and there was no chance for the unfortunate wearied troops or horses getting any supplies.

Before daybreak on November 16th the brigade paraded on the outskirts of a wood. For three days no provisions had been received by the men, and this was brought to the notice of Sir William Erskine. He appreciated the exigencies of the situation, sanctioned the sending out of flanking parties during the day's march, when practicable, to collect and drive forward any cattle that could be obtained.

The 2nd Hussars (King's German Legion) this day formed the rearguard and had the best opportunity for carrying this into execution. Twelve bullocks were collected and driven into the bivouac, which was in a wood. As a spot for a bivouac it was not by any means of the best. At all times marshy, the ground from the torrents of rain was exceedingly wet. The horses were tied up and the men employed in collecting such dry wood as could be got and in kindling fires. It looked as if a square meal for the famished men was in the immediate future. The adjutant took a carbine and, having selected a bullock, fired. The animal was only wounded. Mad with pain or terror, it dashed into the wood. The next followed its example, and the whole of the hardly gained food-supply vanished. The adjutant and twelve dragoons mounted,—the party who had brought the beasts in had not unsaddled. Off went the pursuers at a gallop. The chase was continued for some leagues, but the herd could not be headed, nor could even one be cut off.

Crestfallen, weary, and starving, the party slowly returned. On the road their luck changed, for a flock of sheep was met with and as promptly annexed. Driving the animals before them, they reached the camp, to be hailed with joy by the half-famished men. There was no ceremony in the slaughter that began, for the men waited not for the professional services of the regimental butchers. Anybody who listed selected his sheep and slew it. The fires burned brightly and cooking operations were in progress everywhere. The camp-kettles were there, for the baggage was with the regiment. The meat was nearly cooked and the soup nearly boiled, and dinner momentarily expected, when up galloped Lieutenant Doherty, who at the time was acting A.D.C. to Sir William Erskine. This officer brought orders for the regiment to mount immediately and move forward to meet the advancing enemy.

It appears that by a rapid advance in force the French cavalry had forced back the 2nd Hussars, who were that day acting as rearguard. Nor was this all the order, for the general directed that the baggage should be immediately packed and sent off some miles to the rear. Instantly the camp-kettles were emptied, the regiment mounted, the baggage-animals were loaded, and the whole moved off. Hardly had the regiment gone a hundred yards when a countermand came. It appears that the Hussars had rallied, had attacked the enemy, and had driven him back, killing a dozen and taking twenty-seven prisoners. The regiment again put up, the camp-kettles were again filled, and a plentiful supply of mutton was soon prepared. The horses were less fortunate, for there was neither grass nor forage, and the only feed obtainable was by means of cutting down the branches of such trees as at that season happened still to have a few leaves.

On the morning of November 17, before daybreak, the brigade marched, starting in torrents of rain. When near the village of San Munez the enemy were reported as rapidly advancing in considerable strength. The cavalry was at once pushed forward and took possession of the heights. These they held for some time till orders came to retire, to cross a ravine and river near the place, and to take post on the opposite bank. The river was in flood and the banks steep and rotten, but no casualties occurred. The brigade got over and formed. Meanwhile the infantry was moving along the great road.

On the right flank severe skirmishing was kept up between the light troops of both armies.

While the cavalry were crossing the river the enemy took possession of the heights and planted thereon no less than twenty-five pieces of heavy artillery, with which a tremendous fire of grape, canister, round-shot, and shell was maintained. The missiles fell around and behind the brigade from 2 P.M. to dark.

The British artillery was brought up and posted in front of the cavalry and opened fire in reply, but owing to the height of the hills did not seem able to harm the enemy, though they themselves suffered considerably.

Here the cavalry had to remain exposed to protect the guns, for a body of the enemy's cavalry appeared on the right, near the village, where there was a bridge, and threatened them.

The brigade (9th and 13th) on this occasion were posted in a ploughed field which, owing to the rain even then continuing to pour down in torrents, was so soft that the horses stood knee-deep in the mud. However, one good effect came from this—the shells sank in so far that when they burst they did no more injury than showering mud about. The round-shot, as a rule, went over the men's heads, but did some execution among the brigade of mules nearly three-quarters of a mile in the rear, and supposed to be beyond the reach of fire. A few horses of the 13th were wounded, but not in a serious way.

After dusk, when the firing had ceased, the regiment marched towards a village near which it was supposed forage might be obtained, and left a squadron under the command of Major Boyse behind to take up ground for a bivouac. At the village a scanty supply of straw was obtained—the regiment returned to the bivouac, where the horses were up to their knees in mud, and a man lucky enough to find a tree root or trunk to sit on was to be envied.

This evening, while on the expedition in search of straw to the little village mentioned, Captain Gubbins had an amusing though somewhat embarrassing adventure. In the place he saw a light in the window of a decent-looking house. Anxious to get shelter while the search for forage was in progress, he rode up, dismounted, and knocked at the door. The door was opened by a young man dressed in a blue cloak, whom Captain Gubbins conceived to be a commissary or one of the clerks in that department. Accosting the young man in quite a free and easy manner, he was invited to enter. He did so— he was cold, wet through, and hungry, and intimated as much. His host was hospitality itself, and for campaign fare did him well— beefsteak and good wine. Presently the Sergeant-Major arrived with his report that the troop was ready.

Captain Gubbins prepared to take leave of his host, and when expressing his thanks trusted that he should at some future time be able to return the hospitality he had received. Now, curiously enough, all this while he had not discovered nor had inquired the name of his entertainer. He asked it, and received for reply, "The Prince of Orange"! Captain Gubbins was for the moment considerably taken aback, but recovering himself apologised at once for the familiarity with which he had addressed his unknown host.

The Prince in the most good-humoured way accepted what was said, and with a neatly turned compliment quite set his guest at his ease, on departure shaking hands in farewell, and despite the weather attending him to the door and remaining till Captain Gubbins rode off. Colonel Doherty relates this incident at some considerable length and with evident enjoyment in his diary.

During the day the infantry had been heavily engaged in repelling the attacks of the enemy who were endeavouring to cross the river.

The loss was but trifling, however—a few stragglers from the infantry were taken, and General Paget, missing his way, was made prisoner in a wood.

Before daylight on the morning of November 18th the brigade mounted, and the 13th received orders to form the rearguard and cover the retreat of the army.

The brigade moved out of the muddy morass in which it had passed the night and gained the main road, leaving a squadron under Captain Doherty to form the rearguard.

At daybreak the cavalry of the enemy advanced and threw out skirmishers. Captain Doherty did the same, and as the orders were to retire gradually a constant skirmish was kept up. The squadron retired by alternate half squadrons, while the brigade slowly maintained its retreat by the high road, picking up here and there such infantry soldiers as from sheer exhaustion and privation had fallen by the way. And of these there were not a few. At the village of Cabrillas a halt was ordered to enable the infantry to make headway. The cavalry of the enemy not seeming anxious to advance, the retreat was again resumed,—the brigade passing through Aldea Albo, Beca Cara, and Santa Spirito, beyond which it went into bivouac after this long and harassing march. The situation of both men and horses was wretched—of the horses specially so; for by good fortune eight bullocks were met with, driven in, and this time slaughtered. How acceptable these supplies proved will be understood seeing that no provisions had been served out to the men since November 16.

But the case of the horses was nearly desperate. For them no other food could be obtained save the withered leaves on the branches of such trees as still retained them. Here and there a little withered grass could be found by the roadside. It is not to be wondered that many horses died in the course of the night.

At daybreak, however, on the morning of the 19th of November, the brigade resumed its march, passing through Samara and Attalaya, on the route crossing the 2nd and 4th Divisions of infantry, and then went into bivouac. By this time the condition of the horses was even more deplorable. On the morning of the 20th the painful duty of shooting many of the poor animals was carried out. The wretched creatures could not rise from the ground—even those that did rise were scarcely able to crawl. In this condition the brigade marched—marched over stony mountain tracks across the sierras till a miserable village called Serradilla de la Reya was reached, and there with great difficulty the horses of the 13th got under cover. The 9th went into another village near, which was equally wretched. At Serradilla enough straw to last two days was obtained, and from a distant commissary about two pounds of wheat for each horse.

As the enemy had ceased to advance, the 13th remained in the village till the 27th. The problem was, how to keep the life in the horses, and this is how it was solved. In Serradilla there was no forage; the country round about was equally destitute. Hence each man took out his horse every morning and led him round the ditches and the roots of the trees—wherever, in fact, a blade of grass was to be found. The ground beneath the chestnut-trees was also hunted carefully, and all stray nuts secured and given to the luckless animals. In fact, the whole, or nearly the whole, of the time of the men was given, and given willingly, in an endeavour to save their horses. Yet despite all this, when the order to march came on the 27th, in so famished a state were the horses still, that the next morning, when a start should have been made, it was with difficulty that a sufficient number were found to mount the sick or such convalescents as were unable to walk. All the rest had to be led. And in this condition the 13th, after all its labours, began its retreat towards Portugal.

On the first day the march was long and fatiguing—the roads were bad and rocky. Fifteen led horses fell, and being unable to rise again were destroyed. The regiment halted at Songa, where old thatch from the roofs of houses was the only forage obtainable.

On the 29th the regiment reached Peraparda, by roads equally bad, and under the same conditions. But here for the first time since the 17th a sufficient supply of straw was found, and three pounds of Indian corn and one or two pounds of potatoes for each horse. But four more horses had fallen and died on the road that day. It is morally certain that had not supplies been obtained that night at Peraparda, the remainder could not have marched another day. On November 30th the brigade crossed the Sierra Gata to the town of Gata, and there

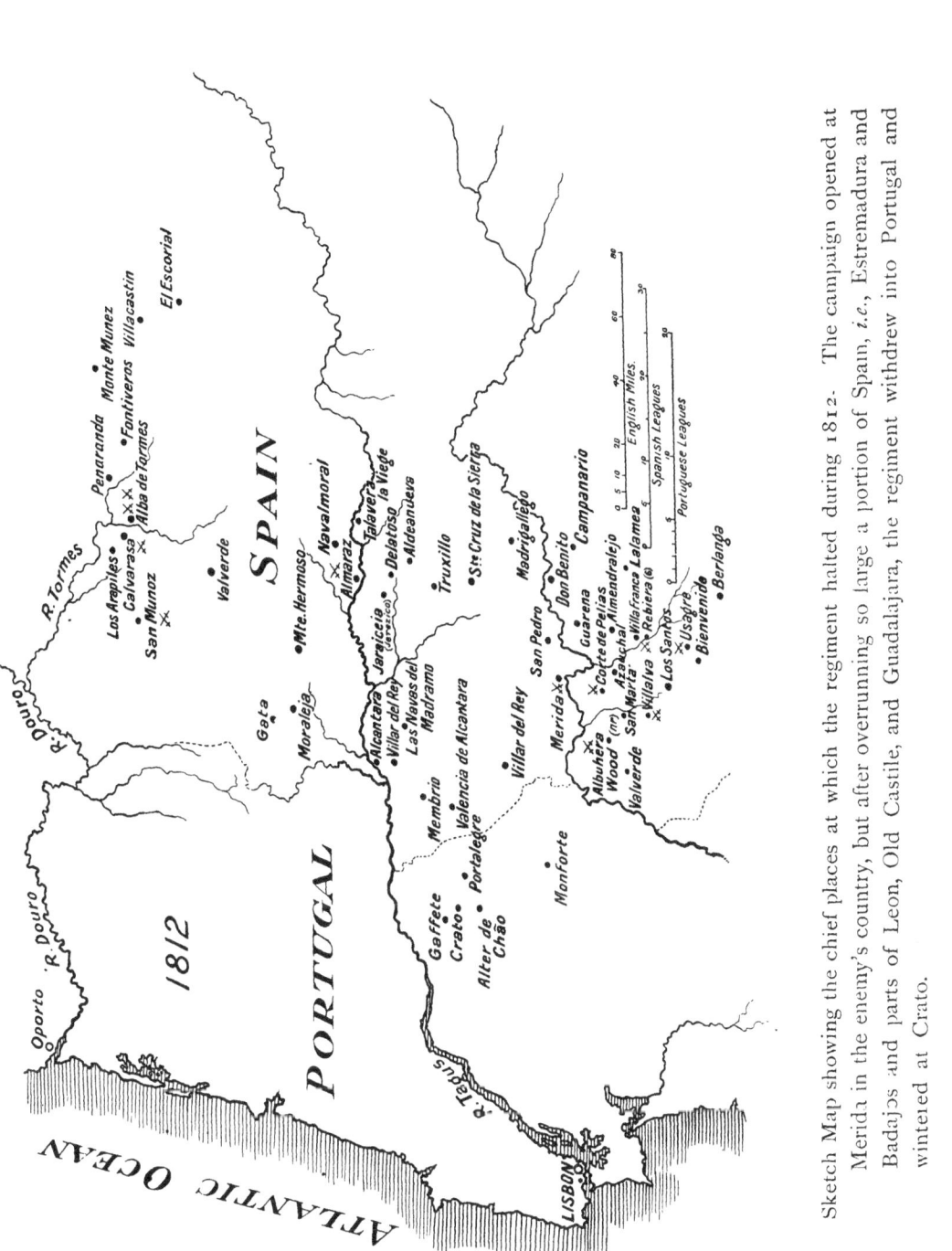

Sketch Map showing the chief places at which the regiment halted during 1812. The campaign opened at Merida in the enemy's country, but after overrunning so large a portion of Spain, i.e., Estremadura and Badajos and parts of Leon, Old Castile, and Guadalajara, the regiment withdrew into Portugal and wintered at Crato.

halted till December 4. At Gata there was little straw, little or no corn, but as luck would have it, a large supply of chestnuts, and on these the horses lived.

Friday, December 4, marked the breaking up of the brigade. The 9th Dragoons marched for Cabeia de Vide in Portugal, and the 13th for Monte Hermosa, where it went into quarters. But the forage difficulty pursued them here, and it was necessary to make a representation to Sir William Erskine respecting it. The corn supply was most scanty—there was but little straw, and that bad. It was a place that was impossible, under these conditions, for cavalry. But here the regiment remained till December 9, when it moved on to Calzedilla. On the 10th it reached Morolejo and Don Gomez, next day arriving at Zaza la Mayor, and on December 12th at Alcaulara. Here, however, the bridge had been blown up and the ruins were impassable; so the regiment put up in two villages near, while the bridge was repaired. By the next day it was possible to get the men and horses over the bridge, and they crossed, marching to Alcantra, where the Regimental Quartermaster Lawrence joined the regiment with a most seasonable supply of necessaries for the men from Lisbon. How they were needed after such a campaign, and how welcome, can be easily imagined. On Monday, December 14, Membrio was reached by means of one of the worst and most rocky roads possible. After a day's halt, on the 16th the regiment marched to Valentia de Alcantara, and on the following entered Portugal at Portalegre, "over sierras and horrible roads, through torrents of rain." Here the regiment halted for a day, and on December 19th marched to Crato, the cantonment fixed on for winter quarters.

At Crato the regiment was joined by a party of remounts from England, under command of Captain Macalester, who had had many and most fatiguing marches to discover its whereabouts.

From the 12th of May to the 19th of December 1812, the regiment had marched 388 leagues, which, taking an average of $4\frac{1}{2}$ miles each, gives a total of 1746 miles—and this besides fighting—in seven months.

CHAPTER XVI.

Vittoria, 1813.

THE regiment, after its arduous campaign, was now in quarters for the winter. During the period before active hostilities again began, there was much to be done. Every exertion was needed to get the horses into condition—the arms, accoutrements, &c., completed and in perfect repair for the ensuing campaign. A party of remounts from England had arrived during December; another arrived from England on Tuesday, January 12, under the command of Cornet Willis, who also brought on a detachment of recovered men and horses from Lisbon. Cornet Willis was promoted lieutenant during this year, and died at Rita on October 30. On January 27th Lieutenant Doherty went on three months' leave of absence to England.

At Crato the supply of forage was found to be very scanty, and a representation to this effect was made. After the hardships and starvation the animals had undergone, to set them in a place where forage was scarce seemed hardly prudent. This the authorities recognised, and an order was received to move to Montforte. The regiment accordingly marched to that town on January 30. There it went into quarters, and forage was found to be better in quality and more abundant as well.

On February 9th Colonel Head joined and resumed command of the regiment.

On February 24th 156 horses from the 9th Dragoons were drafted into the regiment, the remainder going to the 14th Dragoons.

This was the outcome of the men of the 9th Dragoons being ordered to England. The transfer of the horses took place at Frontera.

A Private of the 13th Lt. Drags. in the present Costume.

DRAWN BY COLONEL PATRICK DOHERTY.

VITTORIA, 1813.

Colonel Head did not remain long in command, and his ill-health was unfortunately again the cause. On April 2nd he left the regiment and went to Aller del Chao; thence he was sent to Lisbon, and afterwards to England. In England he was promoted to Major-General on June 4.

A Staff Corps was now being formed under the command of Lieut.-Colonel Scovel. To join this a sergeant and ten men mounted marched towards Trenada on April 18, this number being the proportion the regiment was ordered to furnish.

At Montforte the 13th remained until April 28. Meanwhile a most minute inspection was made by General Long, which lasted two entire days. Every part of all the arms and accoutrements were most carefully and particularly examined, and their condition was most highly approved by the General.

The first issue of the clothing of the new pattern was here made to the men. Thanks also to the neighbourhood of Montforte having afforded grass of fair quality, the condition of the sickly and weak horses was much improved, and the horses of the regiment were in a fairly good condition when the order to take the field arrived. It may be well here to enumerate the changes in the command of the regiment since it left England.

Colonel Head, who sailed with it on March 5, 1810, commanded until October 1811, when, owing to ill-health, he was obliged to leave. The command of the 13th then devolved on Lieut.-Colonel Muter, as Lieut.-Colonel P. Doherty was also on sick leave.

Lieut.-Colonel P. Doherty joined on April 12th and commanded until February 1813, when Colonel Head returned and resumed command, retaining it until April 2, as has been mentioned already. From that period, in all the subsequent operations in which the regiment was engaged, and until its arrival in England, Lieut.-Colonel P. Doherty was in command.

On Wednesday, April 28, the regiment began its march for the campaign of 1813, in two divisions. The first, consisting of the right and centre squadrons under the command of Lieut.-Colonel P. Doherty, reached Aronches the same day. The second division (the left squadron), under the command of Major Boyse, remained at Montforte till the following day. What might have been a most serious affair, which might even have imperilled the efficiency of the 13th as a cavalry regiment during the campaign, took place on April 27, the day on which the orders to march arrived.

The horses of the regiment were all turned out to grass. When the orders arrived the men went to take up their horses; but before they reached the ground a most terrific thunderstorm broke over the district. This so terrified the horses that they stampeded in every direction over the open and unenclosed country. So completely did they disperse, that, as Colonel Doherty puts it, "I was apprehensive we never should be able to collect them; however, with infinite labour and exertion we succeeded in the course of the day, the evening, and night to secure the whole."

The following table will give in brief the routes traversed by the two divisions of the regiment on this march to the front:—

Date.	Right Squadron.	Centre Squadron.	Left Squadron.
April 29.	Cordeseira.	Cordeseira.	Aronches.
April 30.	San Vincente.	San Vincente.	Cordeseira.
May 1.	(halted)	(halted)	San Vincente.
May 2.	Membrio.	Membrio.	(halted)
May 3.	Alcantara.	Villa del Real.	Membrio.
May 4.	(halted)	Alcantara.	Alcantara.
May 5.	Lazza la Mayor.	Lazza la Mayor.	(halted)
May 6.	Morelejo.	Morelejo.	Lazza la Mayor.
May 7.	Cassilius.	Calzadillo.	Morelejo.
May 8.	(halted)	(halted)	Casas de don Gomez.
	(A halt until May 16.)		
May 16.	Guijon de Coria.	Accytura.	El Campo.
May 17.	Aygel.	Aygel.	Obedia.
May 18.	Regiment halted.		
May 19.	Regiment halted.		
May 20.	Guaradilla.	Guaradilla.	Hervas.
May 21.	Hervas.	Hervas.	(halted)
May 22.	Regiment marched to Pena Cabalera.		
May 23.	Marched to the front of Peramingo and went into bivouac.		

The regiment was now in the neighbourhood of the enemy, and outpost duty began.

On May 24th the march was continued to the front of Fuente Robled, when the 13th went into bivouac. Next day the regiment reached Calzadilla de Mondiger on the Salamanca Road, and again went into bivouac. The enemy was now very near, and great caution was observed on the march.

The distance covered by the regiment between Montforte and Calzadilla de Mondiger is approximately 207 miles. At daylight on May 26th the regiment marched, proceeding through a wooded country, and on the way passing a corps of Spanish infantry under the command of General Morillo. Very shortly after, the advanced guard fell in with a body of the enemy's cavalry, numbering about sixty. The 13th attacked them, routed them, and briskly pursued them for a short distance, when the fugitives joined a column of infantry. The ground was rocky and bad, in what force the enemy might be was unknown, and as the spot was near to Alba de Tormes it was conjectured that reinforcements from thence would speedily come up. The regiment was therefore halted to await the arrival of the Spanish infantry with General Morillo. These were not long in arriving, and speedily drove the enemy to the bridge, which, by this time, was held in force.

Also, the enemy had some 1000 men on the hills above the town. The walls beneath the castle as well as the outworks were manned. General Morillo had some artillery with him, and brought it to bear on the bridge; a small fire of musketry also began. Meanwhile the 13th were moved briskly to the right to look for a ford. A ford being discovered, the regiment crossed the river, formed on the other side, and advanced swiftly. By this time the enemy had been driven from the bridge, and were retiring. The 13th dashed into the town on one side, the Spaniards entered on the other. The 13th were then pushed forward at a smart trot to gain the high ground lately occupied by the enemy. They did so, but beyond a few stragglers who were cut off, nothing more of the enemy was to be seen. Thus did the strong position of Alba de Tormes again fall into the hands of the allies.

It will be remembered that in the preceding November, when held by us, it had withstood for three whole days the attack of the entire French Army in those parts—and an attack aided by twenty-five pieces of heavy artillery. The casualties of the 13th in this brilliant little affair were no more than two horses killed.

The regiment put up at a ruined convent near the town, the Spaniards occupying the town itself. Towards night, the former inhabitants of the place came flocking in with their movable goods, from the different places in which they had taken refuge since the town had been occupied by the enemy. As usual, they hailed the British as their friends and deliverers.

On the following day the regiment marched to Machicão, passing through Caravassa de Aribo and Caravassa de Aboxo, and there halted till between 7 and 8 P.M. on the 30th, when orders were received to march immediately to Aldea Lingua.

The 13th crossed the river Tormes at night—though broad, and in many places deep—without accident. On arrival at the village at about 1 A.M. the place proved to be in such a state of ruin that there was no cover for the horses. A bivouac was sought, and when found, horses were linked, and men and officers lay down to sleep. Here the regiment remained till June 2, when it marched, and went into bivouac in front of Orbida. The Blues and Life Guards here joined the division for the first time, and went into bivouac.

At 3 A.M. on the 3rd of June this cavalry joined the army. The 13th formed the advanced guard, and were followed by the cavalry consisting of the 1st and 2nd Life Guards, the Royal Horse Guards Blue, the Royal Dragoons, and the 3rd Dragoons, with the 6th Regiment of Portuguese Cavalry. The artillery followed, with the 2nd Division of infantry under Lord Hill.

After marching seven leagues and passing through many villages, the army went into bivouac near Toro. Resuming its march at 4 A.M. on the next day, the cavalry forded the Douro without loss, though the river was broad, deep, and rapid. One horse of the Life Guards was nearly swept away, but Lord Tweeddale at much risk succeeded in cutting away the saddle-girths and saving the animal.

On this day the 6th Portuguese Cavalry under the command of Lieut.-Colonel Diggins were placed in brigade with the 13th, and with General Long. The brigade that night put up in the village of Padrossa del Rey.

Of the route followed by the regiment a list may here be given, as beyond the fact that every town and village through which they passed had been wrecked, that everywhere they were received with acclamations, bell-ringing, &c., and that the retreating enemy was often only a few hours ahead, there is nothing to recount save that on June 8th the bivouac was visited by a terrific storm of rain, thunder, lightning, and wind, which blew down the few tents they had.

June 5, Torrelobatum; June 6, Cegales; June 7, Duennas; June 8, Torquemado; June 9, Dela *Zazza* de Rivella Valligera; June 10, Nostroso; June 11, after lying at the horses' heads from 3 A.M. to 5 A.M., the brigade marched by a bad road and went into bivouac in the evening near the magnificent ruins of a destroyed and plundered convent. At 4.30 A.M. on June 12th the brigade again marched, and on arriving near the village of Estafere came at length in view of the enemy drawn up in considerable force on the heights between the British and the town. Lord Hill's division, to which the 13th belonged, was at this time in front of the enemy's left. Lord Wellington manœuvred and succeeded in turning the enemy's right, thus throwing them into confusion, and they retired. The 14th Dragoons got a chance of a charge, and took a 6-pounder.

The cavalry brigade was meanwhile employed in making a bridge across the river, as the enemy had destroyed the bridge which previously existed there. The brigade crossed and moved forward briskly for some three miles.

The enemy rapidly retired, night began to fall, and General Hill ordered the brigade to retire and take post for the night. The spot selected was the site of the bivouac of the enemy's cavalry on the preceding night. Here an ample supply of forage was found scattered about on the ground. From the peasants it was learnt that King Joseph had been there on the previous night, and that he had at least 20,000 men. The enemy continuing to retire, the army followed with what speed it might.

On June 13th the regiment bivouacked in front of Villarejo. Next night it lay near Monetaia; on the 15th at Cerenegula; next day crossing the Ebro at Puente Arenas, where it went into bivouac that evening. Medina was reached on June 16. On the 18th, after a long and most fatiguing march through La Corca, Villamor, San Martin de Losa, and other places, it again bivouacked. On June 19th the regiment marched through certain villages to near Puente Lara, but retired in the evening for some distance and bivouacked.

Selenus, so famous for its salt-pans, was reached the next day; the army passed through it and went into bivouac in the neighbourhood of Vittoria, where the French were known to be.

Vittoria, June 21, 1813.

Approximately the distance marched by the 13th between Calzadilla de Mondiger and Vittoria amounted to 333 miles. For the greater part of the way the roads had been very trying and the hours that the men were in the saddle very long. The weather was at times most inclement. Quarters, when they could be obtained, were by no means good, and for nearly the whole of this long march the regiment bivouacked at night in consequence. It will be easily understood that the nature of the ground traversed by the army since it passed the Ebro was such that the columns had necessarilly extended, and with the main army there was a halt on the 20th in order to close up. The left of the army then moved to Margina.

Briefly now let us describe the position of the enemy. On June 19th Joseph Buonaparte, with Marshal Jourdan, took up his position in the evening in front of Vittoria. On the 21st June, Reille, facing north, formed the extreme right defending the Zadora river where the Bilboa and Durango roads crossed it by the bridges of Gamara Major and Ariga, about two miles to the north of Vittoria. The Zadora here flows nearly east and west, and continues in the same direction for some seven miles. To the west, near the heights of Margarita, the river makes a sharp bend to the south, and flows to the defile of Puebla, about five miles away. Covered by the Zadora, the King placed his centre and left on the heights on the left bank of the river. This front, which was facing west, extended from the heights of Margarita, in front of the village of Asinez, across the main Vittoria-Miranda road, across the rocky ground behind Subijana de Alava to the spurs of the Puebla mountain. His extreme left was protected by Maransin's brigade posted on the mountain. The bulk of the cavalry and the King's Guard were held in reserve behind the centre of this front, near the village of Gomecha. We thus see his front was some fourteen miles in extent, but that it included a gap of about five and a half miles between his right and his centre. The part which the regiment took in the battle is as follows: The cavalry brigade marched at an early hour in the morning, and at about 9 A.M. joined many other cavalry regiments on the left of the great road leading to Vittoria. The cavalry were formed up in close columns of half squadrons.

A part of Lord Hill's division, consisting of General Morillo's brigade of Spanish infantry, was then moved forward to attack the extreme left of the enemy's position on the heights of Puebla de Arlazan. Immediately on the Spanish advance the enemy despatched considerable reinforcements to this part of the field, and a most stubborn fight took place there. The allies, however, gained possession of the heights, and despite the strenuous efforts of the enemy to recover them, and despite the fact that more and more reinforcements were hurried thither for that purpose, the position won was maintained.

The 13th were ordered to take post on the right of the great road and nearer to the town of Vittoria. The next order to the regiment was to move briskly to the right, and take post on a rising ground which was indicated. Trotting up to this position, Lord Wellington galloped by and called out, "13th, keep your horses in wind, we shall shortly want you." From their position on this rising ground the regiment could see the entire force of the enemy, "almost blackening the plain below," with infantry, cavalry, and artillery all drawn up in order of battle. Guns were now ordered up to the hill, an officer of the 13th being sent for them, and Captain Bean's troop of Horse Artillery came up at a gallop, unlimbered, and instantly opened fire with murderous effect on the masses of the enemy in the plain beneath.

The 13th were now ordered to descend the hill on the left and form beneath the guns, ready to act as opportunity might afford.

The regiment descended, and formed, and awaited events. Very shortly the fire from Captain Bean's troop produced an impression on the enemy, and he began to move. The 13th then went forward in line to the charge, but was much hampered by a ravine which crossed their front, and which was concealed by standing corn. This ravine was, however, luckily perceived in time, though not until the regiment was close upon it. It was not impassable, fortunately, and a crossing was effected in several places. The 13th got over, formed again on the other side, and again charged. Two more ravines, equally deep, occurred to hamper their movements—both had to be, and were, negotiated, though with difficulty. But the enemy by this time had begun to break. On towards Vittoria the regiment pressed, and, nearing the town, perceived ahead the royal carriages and equipment of King Joseph under a cavalry guard.

General Long immediately ordered a squadron to attack and capture them. Captains Doherty's and Gubbins's troops, under the command of the former, went on this duty. Around the carriages a sharp conflict took place with the guard. The officer in command of the guard behaved most gallantly on the occasion. He first ran through the body Trooper Westerholm of Captain Doherty's troop, who, though apparently slain, eventually recovered and rejoined the regiment some months later. The officer next turned his attention to Trooper Michael Sullivan, with whom he had a fierce single combat which ended in his death. Trooper Michael Sullivan belonged to Captain Gubbins's troop, a fact which Lieut.-Colonel Doherty omits to mention, though the honours of the contest certainly lay with him.

From the roll of the regiment one is glad to read that Sullivan returned home at the end of the war in safety. Trooper Sullivan brought in the horse of the officer he had slain. The carriages of King Joseph were all captured.

Meanwhile the remainder of the regiment had moved forward and formed line in a field. Opposite to them was a body of the enemy as yet unbroken; but between the 13th and the enemy lay a high ditch (wall or bank). The enemy—infantry—at once threw out a number of skirmishers, who advanced right up to the ditch and thence poured in a heavy fire on the regiment. At this juncture Captain Doherty, seeing the regiment formed in line, and as though preparing to charge, placed Sergeant Scriven and twelve dragoons in charge of the captured carriages, and with the remainder of his troop and that of Captain Gubbins rejoined the regiment at a gallop. Galled by the fire of the enemy's skirmishers, the 13th, and with them now the 6th Portuguese Cavalry, sent forward skirmishers to clear the ditch. This was soon done—gaps were found, or places where the obstruction could be passed, and the skirmishers of the 13th and 6th charging with the sabre cut down many and drove back the rest. The regiment now moved off the ground in column of threes in pursuit of the enemy, which by this time was in active flight in all directions.

The pursuit was rapid and continued until nightfall. Although the capture of the royal carriages was the act of the regiment, a curious circumstance occurred. An infantry officer with fifty men came to the sergeant of the 13th who had been left in charge by

CAPTURE OF KING JOSEPH BONAPARTE'S BAGGAGE AT VITTORIA

Captain Doherty and stated that he had Lord Wellington's orders to take charge of them. The sergeant gave them over accordingly, but foolishly took no receipt—nor did he even ask the name of the officer or notice (for he would not need to have asked) the regiment to which he belonged, but simply surrendered the prizes.

In the pursuit the regiment joined with the heavy brigade, and had it not been for the numerous ravines with which the country was intersected, would have had many more opportunities of acting with effect. The cavalry went into bivouac that evening in an adjoining wood. Parties were detached to obtain forage and water. By midnight the tired men had attended to their horses and to their own needs, and, lying at the horses' heads, slept till dawn, when it had been ordered that the pursuit should be resumed.

The enormous amount of war material captured from the enemy in this glorious victory included 151 pieces of artillery—which was the entire number of the enemy's guns, save one and a howitzer; 432 ammunition waggons and carts, and all the treasure, clothing, &c. The marshal's baton of Jourdan even was among the spoils, and King Joseph himself narrowly escaped being taken prisoner.

The retreat of the enemy towards France by the high road was cut off by the troops under Sir T. Graham, who held Gemarra and Abahnes. Consequently the best line of retreat was towards Pampeluna, and this was the direction taken by the defeated army.

At the battle the whole of the Armies of the South, and of the Centre, and of four divisions, and all the cavalry of the Army of Portugal, and some troops of the Army of the North, were present with King Joseph and Marshal Jourdan.

The division of the Army of Portugal commanded by General Foin was near Bilbao. General Clausel, who commanded the Army of the North, was near Logrono with one division of the Army of Portugal commanded by General Topin, and General Vandermasen's division of the Army of the North. These were not present at the battle. Of the allies, the division under the command of General Pakenham was absent, being detained at Medina del Pomar for three days to cover the march of the magazine and stores.

The rearguard of the enemy reached Pampeluna on June 24th with only the howitzer, as the last field-gun had been captured by the advanced-guard of the allies.

General Clausel approached Vittoria on the day after the battle, but finding General Pakenham's division just arrived, and having heard of the battle of the preceding day, promptly retired upon La Guardia, and later upon Tudela del Ebro.

At daybreak on June 22, the day following the battle, the men of the 13th stood at their horses' heads awaiting the signal to mount. Thus were they kept until between nine and ten o'clock, when the cavalry moved forward through the town of Salvatierre, and went into bivouac at some distance beyond it. The baggage was still in the rear.

In the bivouac they halted till the evening of the 23rd, when the baggage came up. The discomforts of this bivouac were intense. Rain poured incessantly, and in such torrents that the bivouac became nearly knee-deep in mud.

Next morning the 13th marched into a small village called Monice, while the infantry with Lord Wellington pushed on to Pampeluna. Here a halt was made for two days. On the 27th the regiment marched to Thurmendi, the next day to Yzurdiage, and the day following to the villages of Lagarette and Sueste and Zya.

On this day a troop of the 13th under Major Boyse, and a troop of the Royals, together with a brigade of infantry—the whole being under the command of General Byng—proceeded to secure the pass at Roncesvalles.

Pampeluna was within sight at about a distance of three miles. The regiment halted on June 30th and July 1st. On July 2nd it marched and occupied the villages of Salina, Espartes, Arlezinand, and Tajoner, remaining there until July 18, when it marched and occupied Larasoin, Urdanez, and Zurain.

The enemy were now threatening General Byng's force at Roncesvalles. Thither as a reinforcement, therefore, Captain Doherty was sent on the 23rd. The next day the enemy showed a disposition to attack the pass, and on the following day did so in considerable force. General Byng's brigade of infantry and the two troops of the 13th made a most spirited resistance, but eventually the pass of Roncesvalles was carried by the enemy, who greatly outnumbered the British.

The force then fell back slowly, skirmishing; Major Boyse's troop being considerably harassed on this occasion by the enemy.

Early on the morning of July 26th all the cavalry in the valley of Zibri was ordered to fall back and to retire immediately beyond Huerta, there to await orders. At the moment this order arrived the 13th were out foraging by troops in various directions in the neighbourhood, where it seemed probable supplies would be obtained. Orders for the assembly of the regiment at Larasoin were therefore sent out, and as the several foraging parties came in they got ready and mustered on the alarm-post. The baggage of the infantry came pouring in and in some confusion. The 13th assisted in getting the baggage train in order, and for some time moved in its rear, eventually taking post beyond Huelva, on the road to Pampeluna. The enemy meanwhile advanced and our troops retired.

On the following morning the squadron from the pass of Roncesvalles under Major Boyse joined. This squadron had had a very rough time, having been on severe duty for sixty-four hours without food. Every horse was laden with wounded infantry soldiers. These wounded were at once mounted on fresh horses, and the regiment began retiring beyond Pampeluna in obedience to orders.

The road was for some distance very narrow and scarped along the mountain-side. It was also exposed to the fire of the batteries on the walls of Pampeluna. The regiment in single file had to run the gauntlet of this fire, and though shots went above and below, by good fortune there were no casualties.

Prior to this march, the troop under the command of Captain Gregorie had been sent to make a demonstration in front of Pampeluna, where the enemy had been employed in making sorties against the Spanish posts.

During the day Captain Gregorie's troop was engaged in some smart skirmishing with the enemy, and five men and four horses were so badly wounded as to require to be sent to the rear. At the same time it was determined to send away all the wounded infantry from Roncesvalles. These were therefore placed in some houses in a village some four miles in the rear of Pampeluna and on the Vittoria road. The escort of the wounded men was furnished by the 13th, who, when their charges were safely housed, rejoined the regiment. A welcome supply of forage was obtained at this village, and seeing that the horses had been fasting for twenty hours they needed food badly.

Towards evening on July 27th an officer of the 13th was sent to

Villaba to inquire if there was any officer of rank there to give orders, and if so to receive them. The officer returned about 6 P.M. with orders from Lord Wellington to return and take post at Villaba. It was nearly dark, and a severe storm of thunder, lightning, and rain broke and continued for the better part of the night. The regiment on this occasion, instead of taking the narrow mountain-path they had previously used that morning, took a lower one, and actually marched silently close by the walls of Pampeluna. That town was illuminated in expectation of speedy relief.

The 13th was halted in an open space, but this was found to be commanded by the guns of the fortress; consequently fresh quarters were sought, and under the guidance of a Spaniard, by midnight the regiment reached a straw-yard where the horses having been linked, men and officers lay down to sleep. Between 3 and 4 A.M. on the following morning orders were received for the regiment to mount and follow the march of the heavy brigade (3rd Dragoons and 5th Dragoon Guards).

After a short march the heavy brigade were ordered to move off and put up in some villages, while the 13th was to remain; later it was sent back again to Villaba, one squadron being detached towards Ortiz to watch the movements of the enemy's cavalry. Before 2 P.M. the other squadrons were ordered to mount and march immediately to the support of the 6th Division, under Major-General Pack, which was then engaged with the enemy.

The 13th proceeded at a brisk trot, and formed in rear of the infantry, who were most heavily engaged: during this operation the squadron detached in the morning came up.

CHAPTER XVII.

Pyrenees. 1st Battle, July 28, 1813.

THE First Battle of the Pyrenees was contested on both sides in the most determined and desperate manner. The nature of the ground was such, that to turn the enemy out of the positions which he occupied required repeated charges with the bayonet, and these combats were most sanguinary. Eventually the French were compelled to give way, and took post in a village on the heights, also occupying the heights above and beyond it on either side. A most severe musketry fire was continuous between the enemy in the village and the allies outside, who were pressing their attack with vigour, and also between the main bodies of both armies who crowned the stupendous heights and the precipitous mountain-sides where posts had been taken up. Throughout the day the fire was most heavy and continuous, nor did it slacken till the evening, when, with the approach of darkness, it gradually died away. On the narrow roads and on the sides of the precipices, as will be understood, any opportunity for action on the part of the cavalry was wellnigh, if not absolutely, impossible. But as a support and protection to two or three of our guns which had been brought to bear on the village, the 13th were able to do service. These guns were towards evening threatened by a body of the enemys' cavalry, who made a demonstration on the right of the line, and appeared prepared to advance to the attack. Finding, however, that the 13th were ready to receive them, they did no more than threaten. During the day the regiment was never out of range of the enemy's guns, and was continuously the objective of artillery or other fire, but beyond a few men and horses being wounded suffered no loss.

When darkness came on, the 13th was ordered to retire to Villaba, from which place they had marched in the morning. Here the town was already crowded with wounded men, who had been brought down, and more were momentarily coming in. In consequence, with great difficulty quarters were found. With daylight on the following morning a squadron was detached under Major Boyse to occupy the post which had been held by the regiment during the engagement of the previous day.

The battle can hardly be said to have been renewed on July 29, for though there was firing at intervals between the opposing armies, the attention of our infantry was turned to getting up guns, and putting them into position on the heights, the nature of the ground being such that manual labour was necessary for the purpose, and horse or even mule traction wellnigh impossible. The wounded, too, in Villaba were ordered to be removed to the rear of Pampeluna. To effect this, the commissariat mules of all the regiments were requisitioned and given over to the Medical Department.

In the absence of any information tending to show that this order was unnecessary, it must be assumed to have been deemed absolutely imperative, but the tortures inflicted on the wounded officers and men during the operation of placing them on these animals, and their terrible sufferings in transit, were excruciating. It is stated that the impression produced on the minds of those that witnessed the scene was one of pain which could never be effaced.

By daylight on the morning of the 30th of July, the squadron under Captain Doherty was ordered to the position which had been occupied by Major Boyse on the previous day. The comparative lull in active warfare of the last twenty-four hours had ceased, and with but little delay the 2nd Battle of the Pyrenees was in progress.

Pyrenees. 2nd Battle, July 30, 1813.

Quickly a most active musketry fire developed all along the line— a musketry fire broken only by repeated and most sanguinary charges with the bayonet. The regiment was called for, marched to the ground, and received orders to support General Pack's 6th Division.

By this time the fruits of the toil of the day before, when the guns had been so laboriously dragged up, became apparent. From their lofty positions these opened fire on the enemy, and, coupled with constant attacks by the allies with the bayonet, at length, gallant though the resistance of the enemy had been, they began to waver. The French were first driven from the village, only to take up a position on the heights. The attack was pressed on and on. From mountain to mountain the foe was successively driven—each time the retirement was less orderly than the last—disorder supervened—and then a general rout. With the rest of the allies the 6th Division pressed forward, the 13th continuing to advance in support.

But as far as active cavalry movements were concerned, the ground traversed made such impossible. Presently a column of the enemy numbering 1454 men was met descending the mountain-side, and prisoners of war under the escort of their captors. Others of the enemy were in full flight over the mountains, in places where men could clamber but cavalry could not act.

The 13th was then ordered to move along the road through Ortiz, and when a short distance beyond that place it was halted and went into bivouac. The detached squadron under Captain Doherty, however, continued to advance, being attached to the brigade of Sir John Byng. During that evening Sir John Byng's brigade had a sharp encounter with a considerable body of the enemy who, rallied by their officers, took post on a hill and stood at bay.

General Byng moved up his brigade, and at point of bayonet captured the position, taking numerous prisoners. It should be mentioned that the sides of this hill were exceedingly steep, in some places even almost perpendicular. Following on this success, Sir John captured a considerable quantity of baggage, provisions, and stores, which he found on the opposite side of the hill. Captain Doherty's squadron, though much exposed to fire throughout the day, escaped casualties.

To return to the regiment. From the bivouac beyond Ortiz it was ordered to march at 5 A.M. on July 31, and still to act in support of the 6th Division. At Olaque directions were received to move upon Enqui, where on arrival a staff-officer brought orders to march upon Lanz, and there to await further instructions. Near Lanz the squadron under Captain Doherty joined, and towards evening the regiment went into bivouac.

On August 1st the 13th marched to Olaque, putting up there and in the villages round about. Here a halt was made until August 3, during which time prisoners of war that had been taken after the second battle, during the pursuit, were marched through under escort *en route* for Vittoria.

The regiment was now ordered to render every possible assistance to prevent the enemy from escaping from the fortress of Pampeluna, at the time being blockaded by Spanish troops left for the purpose under the command of Don Carlos D'España. But before this order came into effect the movements of the 13th were as follows:—

August 3, marched to Lanz, next day to Arroyos and Oroones, halting on August 5 and 6. On the next day four troops returned to Lanz and two put up in the villages near.

August 8, two troops marched to Lizoain, two to Viscaret, and two to Mezquinez, halting on the 9th. On August 10th one squadron under the command of Captain Buchanan marched to Espinal, and one with Major Boyse to Erro. Forage in these Pyrennean villages was scanty, and a representation was made on the subject to Lord Hill. From him permission was received to move from village to village at discretion, provided that all changes made were reported to the Assistant Quartermaster-General. By this expedient the horses were the better supplied with forage. Captain Buchanan's squadron consequently shifted to Garralda on the 12th, and the right squadron to Arietta and Pueblo Novo.

With a view to acting in conjunction with the Spaniards before Pampeluna, small posts were established between the headquarters of the blockading army and that of the regiment. It was supposed that the garrison of Pampeluna meditated an attempt at an escape from the beleaguered place, and this was of course to be prevented if possible. If the enemy surrendered, the regiment had orders at once to march to Elezonde. But Pampeluna gallantly held out till October 31, marching out with the honours of war on the following day, when, having surrendered their arms, the garrison was despatched to the rear as prisoners of war. The men were, however, allowed to keep their knapsacks, and the officers their private property. It will be admitted that the garrison well merited the consideration thus shown them. Lord Wellington had meanwhile thrust his left across the Bidassoa and entered France. It was not, however, possible for him to enter upon more active operations until the surrender of this gallantly defended fortress took place.

Meanwhile, in pursuance of the policy of shifting squadrons to places capable of or better able to provide forage, numerous moves were made. The regiment remained at Garralda, Arietta, and Pueblo Novo until September 5, when the right squadron moved to Ardaiz and Uricelque; and on September 8th the left squadron, which had been at Erro, moved to Garralda, the centre squadron shifting to Negore.

On September 12th Captain Lennox and Lieutenant Doherty arrived from England, and on the same day thirty-nine remounts with twenty-three men. The rough work over rocky places that the horses of the regiment had done since the campaign started had told upon the horses' shoes. The regimental stock of iron was exhausted. By good fortune at a foundry near Roncesvalles, where a party of the regiment was stationed with Lord Hill, a most welcome supply of bar-iron was discovered. The horses of the regiment were all new shod, and, moreover, each man was supplied with enough of the raw material to make another set.

On September 23rd the right squadron shifted from Ardaiz and Uricelque to Lizoain and Redin. On October 11th the centre squadron marched to Ordanez. The party at Roncesvalles had now been increased to an officer's detachment. News that the garrison at Pampeluna, numbering about 3000 men, had capitulated, was received on October 31.

On November 1st the right and centre squadrons marched into Huerta and the villages around, and witnessed the capitulation. Many of the officers visited Pampeluna, finding it a well-built town with wide streets and well-paved, lofty houses, fine public walks and buildings, handsome squares, and fortifications of the first order and in good repair. The British officers were received by the inhabitants with much enthusiasm. It is recorded, and is a somewhat unusual fact, that the enemy "left the town clean and every part of it in good order."

On Tuesday, November 2, the right and centre squadrons marched to Olaque, where they halted till the 6th, when they marched to Almandoz and Irneta, arriving on the next day at Los Carus in the neighbourhood of Elizonde. Here the left squadron joined, and the regiment now entire halted for a day.

On November 9, at 4 P.M., the regiment marched into Elizonde, where it was joined by the 14th Dragoons, thereby forming a brigade.

This brigade was under the command of Colonel C. Grant.

General Long, having received an appointment to a command in England shortly after the battles in the Pyrenees, had left.

In a brigade order, dated St Estevan, August 12, 1813, and also in a private letter to Lieut.-Colonel Doherty, General Long, on severing his connection with the 13th, expresses most handsomely his appreciation of their conduct while under his command, and his best wishes for their prosperity and continued success. He concludes with a desire that the officers, non-commissioned, and men will "accept his best thanks, and be assured of the continued and deep interest he must ever take in their welfare, credit, and prosperity."

At Elizonde, Colonel Grant assumed the command of the brigade, and marched towards a pass in the Pyrenees known as Maya. The pass was traversed during the night by the brigade, and it proceeded thence towards the town of Urdax (variously written Ardox, Urdache, Ordache).

Urdax is on the river Bidassoa, the frontier between France and Spain.

During the night of November 9th this river was crossed, and after a tedious night march over the mountains for six leagues the brigade went into bivouac at 3 A.M.

France, November 10, 1813.

After a few hours' sleep, the brigade mounted and advanced with the infantry. It was not long before the latter were in touch with the enemy's outposts. These were attacked and driven in. Advancing, the army came in view of the position which Marshal Soult had taken up. This was entrenched, fortified by numerous redoubts, and most heavily armed with guns.

Soult was persuaded that his position thus fortified was impregnable, and proposed to pass the winter months there. His

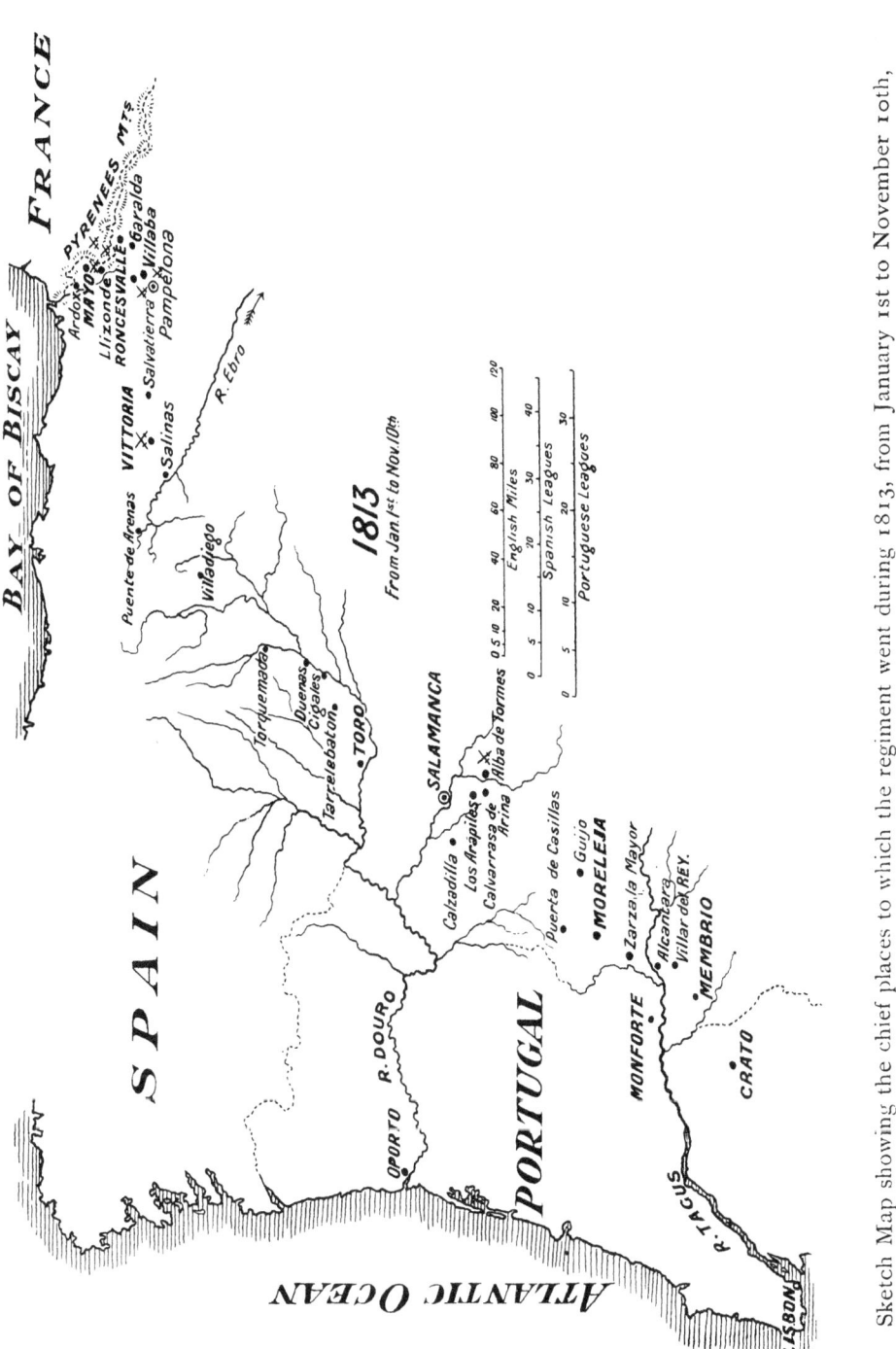

Sketch Map showing the chief places to which the regiment went during 1813, from January 1st to November 10th, on which date the French frontier was crossed. It has not been found possible to locate numerous small villages and farms, hence they are omitted.

men had in fact erected huts, and the whole army was under cover. How was it possible for the British to force such a position in the face of the weight of metal which could be brought to bear on any attack? But his confidence was not based on sufficient grounds. The infantry, with the utmost hardihood, make attack after attack, and mainly with the bayonet. One position after another, one hill after another, the entrenchments, the redoubts, and the forts, all were carried, despite the efforts of the numerous and determined men who attempted to defend them. At length the battle was lost, and Soult and his army fled in all directions, with the infantry in hot pursuit.

In support of the infantry, the cavalry brigade (13th and 14th Light Dragoons) moved throughout the day exposed to cannon shot and musketry, compelled, owing to the nature of the ground, to be spectators. It was only possible for cavalry to move on the road, or would have been, had not the enemy taken the precaution to fell trees across it and otherwise obstruct the passage. During the engagement, Colonel Grant from illness was obliged to quit the field, and the command of the brigade devolved upon Lieut.-Colonel Doherty. At length, after succeeding in getting round or through the various obstructions on the road, open and flat country was reached, and in the pursuit of the enemy the brigade took many prisoners. When the pursuit ceased, the brigade fell back and went into bivouac in a wood.

During the course of the fight the 13th unfortunately sustained a most serious loss, a loss which was shared by the officers of the 14th and others of the division. This was no less than the baggage belonging to eight officers of the 13th; the paymaster and pay-master-sergeant were also taken prisoners with all their baggage, books, papers, and a considerable sum of public money. In fact, the personal belongings of nearly every officer of the division whose baggage had crossed the pass fell into the hands of the enemy.

How this occurred is as follows: The baggage, with the paymaster and paymaster-sergeant, chanced to be on the right of the British army, on which side the Spaniards were posted. The enemy attacking the Spaniards drove them in, and the baggage of the unfortunate British officers became in consequence the spoils of war. The loss, as may well be imagined, was most serious.

As an instance of the methods employed by our Spanish allies while in an enemy's country, the following account is not without interest, as a contrast to the behaviour of the British troops at Hasparen shortly afterwards.

Before the orders to retire and put up in bivouac were received, a squadron under the command of Captain Doherty was detached on reconnaissance duty with directions to proceed with all necessary caution towards Espinelle, and to observe the movements of the enemy. On arrival near the town it was found that the hedges leading to it were filled with the enemy's sharpshooters. But as the object was, if possible, to find out whether the town was in the possession of the enemy, Lieutenant Doherty with six men went forward across country and galloped into one end of Espinelle as the enemy was retiring from the other.

The little party was not only exposed to fire from the sharpshooters, but also from the rear-guard of the enemy. When Captain Doherty learned that the evacuation had taken place, he marched his squadron into the place, and having planted an outpost under Lieutenant Doherty, retired in the evening and went into bivouac. Sometime after dark, a body of Spanish infantry arrived for the purpose of levying a contribution on the unfortunate inhabitants. Now most of the inhabitants had deserted the place, and those who remained were quite unable to make up the sum demanded. Consequently the Spaniards set fire to the town in many places, and it was only by the exertions of the squadron with Captain Doherty and some British infantry which were sent forward on his representation that the town was saved. Some of the incendiaries were arrested by Captain Doherty, and subsequently brought to trial before a court-martial by order of Sir William Stewart. General Stewart thanked Captain Doherty, the officers, and squadron for their timely assistance and exertions.

On the morrow the brigade marched to Anina, where the inhabitants were rather "more hospitable in the distribution of brandy to the men than could be wished for." About 4 P.M. the regiment turned out and went into bivouac near Espilotte. Colonel Grant having somewhat recovered, resumed the command of the brigade.

Next day the 13th marched, going into bivouac on an advanced post some distance to the front. During this day cannon-shot and musketry fire were frequently exchanged on the banks of the river near Cambo. At dusk the allied infantry was retired, but no orders to do so reached the 13th, who in consequence remained in position—a position which was not a little exposed. However, a brigade of Portuguese infantry which happened to be the last to retire approached the bivouac. The officer in command (General Buchan) halted his brigade and took post in the rear to act as a support to the 13th should it be attacked. The troops this night were most miserably circumstanced. Early in the evening a terrific storm of rain and wind set in, and continued all night without ceasing. Men and horses, drenched with the downpour, were soon up to their knees in mud. The next morning the regiment marched into Espilotte, leaving one troop at the bivouac on outpost duty. The infantry, as on the previous day, returned to the banks of the river Nive and took up its old position. Lieutenant Buchanan now joined the regiment (by purchase September 2), succeeding Lieutenant Jefferies who had retired.

On the 14th the regiment halted, marching again on the following day, when one squadron went to Osteritz and two to Larasor. The squadron from Osteritz on the 16th marched to Larasor, and the two at Larasor proceeded to Soraide.

Four days later Colonel Grant was compelled to relinquish his command owing to his continued ill-health and left for England. He was succeeded by Colonel Vivian on November 27. During its stay in these cantonments the regiment suffered a good deal from lack of forage; but despite this had to remain in its cantonments until December 9, when at 2 A.M. it marched, and long before daybreak had reached its appointed position near the river Nive.

At daylight the forcing of the passage of the Nive began. Fords in front of the allied army were numerous, and though these were stoutly defended by the enemy, a passage was made good. The 13th and 14th Light Dragoons forded the river beyond a bridge over which the infantry passed. The cavalry brigade formed on the other side, the infantry advanced, and attacking drove the enemy from any positions occupied by them. In support of the infantry the cavalry brigade continued, for owing to the enclosed nature of the country it was prevented from acting to any great extent. Still, the squadron under Major Boyse being detached to reconnoitre, happening to fall in with a detachment of the enemy's cavalry attacked them, routed them, and chased them through and beyond the town of Hasparen. This done, the squadron returned and joined the regiment. Two other parties were also detached to reconnoitre, one under Lieutenant Major and the other under Lieutenant Doherty. That under Lieutenant Doherty also fell in with a party of the enemy, who were treated much in the same way as the others had been by Major Boyse's squadron.

That evening the regiment moved towards Hasparen, halting outside the town. An officer with the regimental quartermaster and a sergeant from each troop were then sent forward to requisition the mayor for quarters. This was the first French town into which the regiment had entered, and rules had been drawn up in order that no cause of complaint should be given. Among these was that thoroughly British custom of paying for all supplies. The mayor came out on his part to learn what composition in cash he would have to levy on the inhabitants, naturally supposing that the British would in such a matter comport themselves after French methods in foreign countries during a state of war. He was indeed hard to be persuaded that the proposal to pay by weight for all forage and pay with cash was serious. In fact, not until the money was actually paid on the following morning could he quite credit the matter. Surprise and pleasure were expressed by the town's folk, and the regiments of the British Army were received with the utmost hospitality. Posts were put out, and at Hasparen the regiment remained till December 11, when it marched and went into quarters in detached houses on the right and rear of Vieu Mouguien. The advanced posts of the British were now close to those of the enemy on the side of Bayonne. During the night there was a good deal of firing. The outpost duty was severe, requiring no less than 100 men. The remainder continued with their horses saddled and with their accoutrements on throughout the night. The following day the quarters of the left squadron were shifted, but the regiment still continued in a very scattered position.

CHAPTER XVIII.

Bayonne, December 13, 1813.

BEFORE daybreak on Monday, December 13, the regiment concentrated by order on the road leading to Vieu Mouguien, all the baggage being sent to the rear. On assembly the 13th was directed to move on with the infantry and to act in support of the brigade commanded by General Byng, which was then on its march towards the high grounds above Bayonne.

Shortly after it was light Marshal Soult moved his army out of Bayonne, massed in columns. The British force consisted only of General Hill's division (the 2nd), composed of British and Portuguese troops, and the 13th. The infantry was formed in line on the high ground, and had there to withstand the most desperate and often-repeated charges of the enemy. These charges were ineffectual, and at the point of the bayonet the heavy attacking columns of the French Army were driven back with slaughter. For some hours this sanguinary engagement was continued with great loss of life. The 6th Division, under Lord Wellington, now arrived, and the repulse of the enemy was complete. The beaten troops of Marshal Soult were finally driven back and compelled to take refuge behind the batteries in front of Bayonne. The heaviest loss fell on the 50th, 71st, and 92nd Regiments of British infantry, all of which earned well-deserved laurels in this fiercely contested battle.

It is recorded that on the arrival of the 6th Division, the brigade of British infantry consisting of the 50th, 71st, and 92nd Regiments, who had borne the brunt of the day's fighting and had suffered very severely, were ordered to the rear. Retiring, they took post some little distance in the rear of the 13th. The men were black with powder, and quite exhausted. They lay down on the ground and remained there till the action was over. When the 13th received orders to retire and put up for the night, the regiment passed by the wearied men, who instantly sprang up, seized their arms, and gave the regiment three cheers,—cheers which were as heartily returned. It is quaint to read that their bands at the same time played that then popular air, "The Downfall of Paris."

A trooper of the 13th, by name James Armstrong, and belonging to the troop of Captain Bowers, greatly distinguished himself during the battle. He was one of a small party of the regiment placed on the right of the line for the purpose of communication. During the battle some skirmishers of the British infantry had been driven back from Vieu Mouguien by those of the enemy. Armstrong rallied these, led them forward again, attacked and drove back the enemy, cutting some down and making prisoners of others. This gallant exploit came under the personal observation of General Hill, who not only mentioned it on the field to the Commanding Officer, but directed the Adjutant-General to write officially that evening recommending the man for promotion. James Armstrong was accordingly promoted to the rank of sergeant. It would be interesting to know exactly what became of this good soldier, but that cannot be told with certainty. In 1810 there was a Sergeant Armstrong in Captain Stisted's troop. To this troop Captain Gubbins succeeded in 1811, and presumably the same Sergeant Armstrong is the man who returned from Spain with the regiment and acted as sergeant of the same troop at Waterloo, from which campaign he also returned. In the roll of the regiment made on its return after Waterloo, the name of James Armstrong occurs, but as a private, and his death as a private is recorded as taking place August 13, 1815. There was a William Armstrong, a private in Captain Bowers' troop in 1815. Armstrong may possibly have declined promotion, or he may have received it and subsequently have been reduced. The regiment at dusk received orders to retire. On the morrow, at daybreak, the troops resumed the positions they had held on the previous evening and awaited events till past noon. The enemy, however, showed no disposition for further hostilities that day. Consequently the army moved off the ground, the 13th returning to the cantonments it had occupied the two previous nights.

The next morning the regiment, with the exception of Captain Gubbins's troop which remained, marched to Urguit and the neighbourhood. Hardly had it arrived when information came that the enemy were crossing the river in large flat-bottomed boats, and in force, apparently with an intention to attack. All the baggage was consequently sent to the rear—the troops saddled and remained ready to mount. The enemy, however, did not cross the river,—either the information was false or the design was abandoned. At Urguit a number of young French conscripts, accompanied by their parents, all in much dejection, were found assembled. On the morrow they were to have been delivered over for service in the French Army. When the British arrived these youths were informed that they were free to return to their homes, to the delight of themselves and their parents. In the exuberance of their joy many fell on their knees, invoking blessings on their deliverers.

The regiment halted on the 16th, sending forward on the morrow a troop under the command of Captain Buchanan on outpost duty near Bastide. This troop was relieved on the 20th by a picket, which on the 21st was relieved by a picket of the 14th Light Dragoons. On the 22nd, Captain Gregorie's troop relieved the picket of the 14th. Thus engaged on outpost duty the regiment remained until January 3, 1814. During this time frequent attempts were made by the enemy to cross the river in boats, but always unsuccessfully. In the skirmishes there were a few men and horses wounded, and one man killed. On the evening of that day a trooper of the 14th galloped in, with orders for the march of the regiment forthwith to a position chosen, of the locality of which the messenger had been already made acquainted. The trooper was sent as a guide thither. It happened that at the moment the message arrived the annual inspection of accoutrements, &c., was in progress. However, the regiment quickly turned out and marched to the appointed spot—high ground, about two leagues in front of Briscous. Here General Fane met the regiment and issued his instructions to Lieut.-Colonel Doherty. The service upon which the regiment was now engaged was important, and in the performance of it much suffering to both horses and men was entailed through lack of forage and provisions. Heavy rain also added to the discomforts of the 13th. The ground was flooded and so soaked that the whole place became a sea of mud,—mud in which the horses stood knee-deep, and in which the men, wet and ill-fed, had to sleep. For to light fires was an impossibility, and such provisions as they had were perforce eaten uncooked. In their front was a small river which flowed through a ravine, but which was fordable in several places. This river divided the outposts of the 13th from those of the enemy. On the arrival of the regiment on the spot selected, outposts were immediately chosen and fixed, and the utmost vigilance was enjoined. The task was to prevent the enemy from crossing the river in force. What the actual strength of the enemy might be was then unknown. The outposts being fixed, the regiment retired a short distance to go into bivouac in a somewhat less exposed situation. Before a site for the bivouac could be selected shots were heard in the direction of the outposts. The 13th put about and moved forward, one squadron being sent ahead at a brisk trot. This soon fell in with the pickets, which had been driven back by two squadrons of the enemy who had forded the river in the dusk, attacked the posts, and forced them. The advanced squadron immediately attacked these, the remainder of the regiment moving on to support if necessary. The enemy was routed and driven back across the river again, our posts being resumed but strengthened. In addition, a troop was left in the rear of the main picket as a support, should other attempts be made by the enemy. The rest of the regiment retired to a small field where they formed a close column of half-squadrons, the horses were linked, and the men lay down at their heads in a torrent of rain, which continued without a break throughout the night. Lieut.-Colonel Doherty mentions the soldierly behaviour of Lieutenant Phillips, who was detached from Captain Gregorie's troop in charge of a picket. This officer seems to have displayed much "prudence and presence of mind" in retiring his men, thereby baffling the enemy in more than one attempt to surround him.

Captain Gregorie also retired his troop with much circumspection. It was now ascertained that no less than seven regiments of French dragoons, under Soult (the younger), lay on the opposite side of this little river. It should be mentioned that had a reverse happened to the 13th it would have been a most serious matter, as the only line of retreat open to them in their rear was a pass by a mill-dam, where but one horse could cross at a time.

Before dawn on the morning of January 4th the regiment mounted and moved forward, taking up a position in the rear of the outposts, though some little distance away. General Fane came up and remained some time with the regiment. Throughout this day, too, the rain descended in torrents. Towards evening the outposts were relieved, others posted, and another supporting troop left as before, while the remainder of the 13th retired and went into bivouac near the spot where they had passed the previous night.

The next day passed as the day before, rain, cold, mud, and semi-starvation, no fires, nothing but a very small quantity of biscuit with spirits and water for the men, and scanty, very scanty, forage for the horses. To supply the latter want, parties were sent out to forage. A small supply was obtained by them, and for even this they had literally to fight, as parties of the enemy were also astir and required to be driven back. That night the 14th joined the regiment. Now, during the day Lord Wellington had ridden by the post, and had observed the wretched state to which the brigade was reduced. As things were, it would not have been either wise or indeed safe to remove the brigade, and the only alternative was therefore to force the enemy from his position. At daylight on the morning of January 6th the brigade formed as usual in its accustomed place. About 3 P.M. Sir L. Cole's division, with that of Sir Thomas Picton, came up. These two divisions should have arrived hours before, and Lord Wellington was on the ground early to meet them, but the state of the country from floods, and the continual rain which fell, had prevented greater despatch.

The attack began at once, all the posts of the enemy being simultaneously assailed. These having been driven in, the action became general along the line. The British pressed on, the enemy retired, first in an orderly manner, but soon in great confusion. It is stated that Lord Wellington exposed himself no little on this occasion; he seemed anxious as to the result, and pressed forward in the middle of the skirmishers, urging them on. It was rumoured that a musket-ball hit the heel of his boot. The British sustained no loss on this occasion. The country in this district is very hilly, it is much enclosed and also intersected by deep ravines, the water-courses too were much swollen. In consequence the cavalry brigade could not act in a body, but detached parties were employed with effect. When the enemy retired, the brigade, having posted the necessary outposts, found shelter in some ruined houses near. Scanty supplies for the horses were found with difficulty.

On January 7th the infantry retired, and the 13th received orders to march to Briscous while the 14th went to Urt. Here men and horses got once more under cover, and the baggage came up. The effects of the severe fatigue the regiment had undergone during the last five days were very manifest, and every exertion was made to repair damages.

In this place the regiment remained until February 11, occupied with outpost duty. The duty was severe, and rendered even more so by the lack of food and forage. Many small affairs of outposts took place, especially when foraging parties were out. These had to journey over rather a wide stretch, for the country near was completely exhausted, and neither straw nor corn could be procured. Often the wearied troopers had to return disappointed in being unable to get anything for their wearied and worn-out horses. The roads were execrable, nay even dangerous, so deep was the mire. Furze, though only in its winter foliage, had to be resorted to as forage for the horses. This pounded, an Irish custom by the way, was, when reduced to a sort of paste, the only food obtainable for the last fortnight. The horses, whose condition was already low enough, under this diet showed signs of farcy. Yet all that could be done for the animals was done; all men not otherwise employed led their horses along hedgerows and lanes seeking a chance supply of grass for them however small, or indeed anything else that they might eat.

On February 11th the regiment received orders to march to St Pé —a distance of six leagues, over execrable roads. How it ever got there, under the circumstances, is almost a mystery. Here it went into quarters, and a small supply of corn was received for the horses. Now it was ascertained that supplies of various kinds and new clothing for the men were at Bilbao; and as the regiment stood in great need thereof, the quartermaster and a sufficient number of mules were sent to bring them up. It was hoped that the regiment would be left at St Pé till those supplies came up, as it appeared that it had on that account been sent thither. But this was not to be—on February 13th orders to march arrived, and before daybreak on the 14th the regiment had started for Urrcuerage, over wretched roads. Beyond Urrcuerage the 13th were halted. Thence they marched towards the great St Palais road. This road they reached, and had proceeded along it for about a league, when orders arrived to halt and await orders. During the halt the regiment witnessed the gallant way in which the infantry stormed a strong position which was held by the enemy in considerable force, and drove them therefrom. Fighting continued till dark, when the 13th were ordered to retire and put up in the village of Maniondie. On the morrow at daybreak the regiment marched, proceeding along the St Palais road, where they were joined by the 14th Light Dragoons. As the country was unfit for cavalry operations the brigade went forward in rear of the infantry. Soult, who commanded the French army, disputed every mile of the way with the greatest obstinacy, but the infantry was not to be denied. From every position the enemy was thrust back, often at the point of the bayonet. Towards evening the enemy halted and took up a position on three mountains over Garis, the centre mountain being crowned by a fort. Soult got his guns up and his men, his army literally appearing to cover the hills in serried masses. It was truly a formidable position. Night had now come on, but despite the darkness General Sir William Stewart, who at the moment commanded the British and Portuguese, halted the Allied army. The position of the enemy was reconnoitred. The requisite orders to officers commanding brigades and regiments were issued, and an immediate attack was determined on. The brigades advanced, but before they could reach their several points of attack darkness had come on. Then as they came within range the enemy opened fire, and from the crests of the mountains and their sides flashed guns and musketry. The night was clear, the stars shining brightly. By the flashes of the guns it could be seen that the allied attack was succeeding at all points. Our troops were pressing upwards and the enemy retreating. Shortly the British cheers, as regiment or brigade won its way to the tops of the mountains, echoing from mountain to mountain, proclaimed victory. But while the battle lasted it had been contested with the greatest stubbornness on both sides. The bayonet was freely used, and the carnage terrible. It was rumoured that the distribution of brandy among the French troops by Soult's orders immediately prior to the attack was not without effect in stimulating, if not courage, at any rate ferocity.

The loss of the enemy both in killed, wounded, and prisoners was very considerable, particularly in the last named. When the positions were won the squadron commanded by Captain Macallester was pushed forward and took post beyond the heights from which the enemy had been driven. The remainder of the cavalry brigade went into bivouac on the ground they occupied during the battle. Next morning the brigade marched, crossing the scene of the last night's engagement. So crowded was it with dead that the horses could with difficulty find room to pass without trampling on them. The detached squadron of the 13th was moved on, an advance from it with Lieutenant Doherty in command being sent forward to reconnoitre. Lieutenant Doherty proceeded as far as St Palais, from which he found the enemy had retired after having blown up the bridge over the river. The party with Lieutenant Doherty, however, discovered a ford and crossed the river. Still following up the retreating enemy, it had not proceeded far before it fell in with a detachment of French cavalry which formed part of the enemy's rearguard. This detachment Lieutenant Doherty's party charged, and having driven them in on their supports then retired, being followed by the enemy. A body of infantry of the allied army now coming up, and with them presumably Sir William Stewart, Lieutenant Doherty fronted his party, charged the enemy again, routed them, and pursued them. The enemy's cavalry after this second experience did not again rally. Lieutenant Doherty moved on and established the necessary outposts in front of the allied army. In the course of the evening fresh detachments of the 13th being advanced, he was relieved.

It is related that during the second brush with the enemy a trooper of the 13th, named Owen Shreeman, behaved with great gallantry. He was attacked by two French dragoons—one he slew and the other he brought in prisoner, together with both the horses. Sir William Stewart who witnessed the action was so pleased that, pulling his purse from his pocket, he insisted on the man accepting it. All that can be found out about this brave man's career is as follows:—

He was in the troop commanded by Captain B. Lawrence at the depôt, and did not sail for Portugal with the regiment. How he got to the Peninsuala, or when, we cannot learn. His name does not occur in any of the lists of the remount drafts—lists which seem to be carefully kept and dated.

In the lists of casualties at Waterloo, however, we find his name as of one missing and supposed to be killed, and therefore struck off the strength of the regiment.

The 13th was ordered to put up at St Palais, but on arrival the town was found to be so crowded with Spanish troops that a bivouac in a neighbouring wood was adopted as preferable.

The 14th Light Dragoons remained at Garis.

On the next day (February 17) the regiment advanced, and on gaining the great road received orders to march with and protect the guns.

The country still being unfavourable for the action of cavalry, the allied infantry marched in front; but after traversing some two or three leagues the ground opened, on which the 13th and the guns were ordered to the front, as the enemy were in view, strong in force, and particularly in cavalry.

CHAPTER XIX.

Affair near Sauveterre, February 17, 1814.

THE cavalry brigade and the horse artillery having gained the front, the guns were speedily brought to bear on the enemy and as speedily replied to. For some time the cavalry brigade was exposed to this cannonade. A gun laid by Captain Bean of the horse artillery dismounted one of the enemy's pieces, and the rest were at once withdrawn. Two of the guns of the allies were posted on the left, and to support these a squadron under the command of Major Boyse was detached. By this time the infantry had come up and were moved forward to attack a village in their front, but on the opposite side of the river. Here there had been a bridge, but this had been destroyed by the enemy. The 92nd Regiment dashed into the river, and supported by others crossed, and forming on the other side rushed on to the attack. They drove the enemy out of the village after an obstinate conflict, and pursued them towards the town of Sauveterre.

On the advancing British the batteries in the town immediately opened. One of the first shots mortally wounded Lieutenant Frederick Geale, carrying away his shoulder and part of his neck. He was removed from the field and died during the evening. Major Boyse also received a ball through his chaco. The detached squadron was at this moment acting in support of the infantry attack, having by order forded the river and formed on the plain beyond. When the retreating enemy took refuge beneath the guns of Sauveterre the advanced squadron received orders to retire. It retired, established outposts, and went into bivouac in a neighbouring wood, a troop under the command of Lieutenant Doherty being detached to find out and establish a post on the great road from St Palais to Jean Pied de Port. Two other incidents occurred during the engagement which may be mentioned. General Hill's horse was shot under him, a cannon-ball going through it, the general being uninjured. A shell struck the mare of Sergeant-Major Rosser, and burst inside the animal, the rider being unharmed though the poor beast was literally blown to pieces. The adventures of Sergeant-Major Rosser were not yet over, for being detached with a party of twelve troopers on reconnoitring duty, he fell in with a party of the enemy's cavalry more than double his number. He charged with his men three times, cut down three of the enemy himself, and brought in four prisoners and three horses.

Thomas Rosser joined the regiment in 1798, and was appointed acting non-commissioned officer in 1799, continuing so to act till 1818. He went out with the regiment to Portugal in 1810, being then a sergeant in the troop commanded by Captain Bowers. The date of his promotion to sergeant-major is not given, but as sergeant-major he served in the troop commanded by Captain Macallester at Waterloo. He was appointed cornet in the regiment in 1818, acted as adjutant from October 29, 1818 (in succession to J. Lawrence) until September 8, 1831. Lieutenant in 1819, and captain, September 8, 1831 (without purchase *vice* Maclean), he retired by the sale of his commission on January 8, 1841.

In this affair the loss of the 13th was one killed (Lieutenant F. Geale), four men, and five horses, wounded.

On Friday, February 18, early in the morning, the funeral of Lieutenant Geale took place and was attended by all the officers off duty.

The regiment later forded the river and took post on the other side. Here it remained during the greater part of the day, mainly employed in skirmishing. The quarters of the 13th that evening were in a wretched village near, where sufficient corn for the horses could hardly be obtained.

Next day orders were received to march to Navas and the neighbourhood, where the Spaniards under General Morillo lay. The duty of the regiment was to cover the front and right flank of this corps. A squadron was detached on this duty under the command of Major Boyse, and the remainder of the regiment, having established posts on the right of the Spaniards, took refuge in wretched detached cottages outside Navas, that town being crowded with Morillo's men.

The position this night was one of some anxiety, as information was received that the enemy were strong in cavalry and distant not more than a league and a half, though their exact *locale* was not to be ascertained. It was then past eight o'clock at night, the weather was very severe, with rain and snow. The roads were bad and deep with mire, and it was a matter of considerable doubt as to whether the outposts taken up were correct or not, since the definite position of the enemy was unknown. At daybreak on February 20th the outposts were all examined, and such changes made as seemed necessary in those on the right of the Spaniards. On arrival at the outposts established in front, it was found that General Morillo's troops were retiring. The outposts of the 13th were therefore withdrawn, and some of the Spanish troops having been sent away from Navas, the regiment on arrival there obtained rather better quarters. To give some idea of the extensive character of the outpost duty on this occasion, it may be remarked that it employed no less than 102 non-commissioned officers and men of the regiment. At daybreak on February 21st the regiment marched, and fording the river which was so swollen that the water came up on the saddle skirts, arrived at the ground on which the brigade was to assemble. To this spot came the 14th and the Spanish troops under General Morillo. Hither also came General Hill, who, taking with him 1400 Spaniards and a squadron of the 13th, went to make a reconnaissance towards Navarens. A little skirmishing took place on the road, but as the orders were not to press the enemy, no casualties occurred. The object of the expedition being attained, the force returned and the squadron joined the regiment.

Captain Doherty was now detached with his troop to take post at St Palais. He was relieved on February 23rd by a troop commanded by Captain Lennox (recently promoted). The next day the troop commanded by Captain Gubbins was detached to join General Morillo's corps.

The remainder of the regiment (four troops), together with Captain Bean's troop of artillery and the Light Division, crossed the Gave de Oleron at Villeneuve. Here the 14th joined. The enemy was in the neighbourhood. The force advanced against them and the enemy retired. On this day the advance-guard was furnished by a squadron of the 13th. Towards evening a small detached party of the regiment, under command of Lieutenant Nesbit, was sent out to reconnoitre a road on the right of the line of march. A party of the enemy's infantry happened to be lying in a small village. Lieutenant Nesbit having discovered their whereabouts, instantly attacked them and put them to flight. Seven prisoners were taken and brought safely in. During the march that day the 14th had a small affair with the enemy, when Captain Townshend of that regiment attacked and made prisoner a French cavalry officer, who with one or two others was brought in. That evening the brigade bivouacked on each side of the road, the 13th planting posts on the right, the 14th on the left flank, while the squadron of the 13th in front established the necessary posts in that direction. The weather was extremely cold, the troops suffering from a severe frost. Forage, too, was very scarce, and after darkness had fallen parties were sent out to obtain a supply. After some hours they returned, but it had not been possible to find more than a very limited quantity.

On February 25th the regiment marched, and on arrival on the high ground over the town of Oris, by which runs the river Gave du Pau, descried the enemy on the opposite bank in considerable force—cavalry, artillery, and infantry. The guns of the Allies were brought up and opened with effect. Shortly the baggage of the enemy was seen to be moving off, covered by four squadrons of cavalry. The enemy's infantry, followed by the rest of the cavalry, was the next to retire, but the artillery remained. Towards evening the regiment was ordered to put up in the village of Brion, which was close to the river. As the enemy's artillery was within half cannon-shot of the village, the position of the regiment was much exposed, and naturally it was expected that the guns of the French would make things unpleasant during the night. The utmost vigilance was therefore exercised, specially, too, as it was discovered that the river was fordable in several places—outposts were placed with care but not until after dark, when proper positions for them under the existing circumstances were selected. The brigade turned out before daybreak and formed on the alarm-post, but finding that the enemy was disinclined to attack, again turned in at 8 A.M. At noon, movements on the part of the enemy were again observed, and again the brigade turned out, continuing at the alarm-post till 6 P.M., when as everything remained quiet it again put up.

CHAPTER XX.

Orthes, February 27, 1814.

BEFORE daybreak the brigade assembled, and between 9 and 10 A.M. received orders to advance. The passage of the Gave du Pau was forced, and the army moved forward to attack the French army under the immediate command of Marshal Soult. Soult had taken up a strong position over the town of Orthes.

The strength of the 13th on this occasion was only three weak troops, since one troop was detached on duty at St Palais, another with General Morillo's Spaniards, and a third on picket and not yet joined. Various other small detached parties were also out in different directions.

Marshal Soult's army was estimated to amount to more than 50,000 men.

The 2nd Division with Lord Hill advanced rapidly to attack the enemy's left—a strong position. This, after an obstinate defence, was carried.

Meanwhile the 13th was ordered to cover and protect Captain Bean's troop of horse artillery. The guns were thrust forward on to a rising ground whence they opened a well-directed and destructive fire on the enemy massed beneath them.

While this was going on, a movement among the enemy's cavalry was observed, and Sir William Stewart in consequence ordered the 13th to proceed for some distance along the road on the right of the guns, the 50th Regiment of infantry being ordered as a support.

Having thrown out an advance-guard the 13th proceeded along the road. Very soon it was found that the enemy's cavalry were advancing in considerable force and at a brisk pace. The road was sufficiently wide for the regiment to form in a column of divisions. This was done, and the 13th trotted off to meet the enemy's advance.

The French cavalry met them at a gallop headed by their commanding officer.

The 13th charged, headed by Lieutenant-Colonel Doherty, Captain Doherty, and Lieutenant Doherty, three abreast.

The French commander singled out Lieutenant Doherty, and when a few yards distant let out his horse, making a lunge at him with his sword. This Lieutenant Doherty parried, but his horse received a deep wound in the neck. Lieutenant Doherty returned the thrust by a sabre cut which caught the Frenchman between the bottom of his chaco and his collar, instantly killing him. The opposing cavalry met; the front ranks of the enemy put about, but as there was a bend in the road, the rear, unable to see this, still pressed forward, and they became wedged together. The 13th used their sabres with great effect, and the enemy gave way. Pursuit for about three-quarters of a mile was continued, and then a halt was called, it not being deemed prudent to proceed farther without support. The routed French cavalry farther down the road rallied and formed behind a body of their infantry. In this affair the regiment took many prisoners, mostly wounded, among them being two officers, a number of horses, and several mules.

Sir William Stewart on his arrival on the scene handsomely complimented the regiment on what it had done. The loss of the 13th in this attack amounted to two men, Trumpeter Sincock and Private William Freeling killed, and two horses,—Sincock belonged to Major Boyse's troop, and Freeling to that commanded by Captain Doherty. A sergeant was badly wounded, on the first attack being run through the body. He, however, subsequently recovered and did duty with the regiment. Lieut.-Colonel Doherty gives the name of this man as "Masculine," but no name of the kind can be traced on the rolls of 1810 or 1816. Besides these casualties only three or four men were wounded, and six horses. Lieutenants Mill and Nesbit, who were with the advance-guard, are recorded as having behaved well. The latter was severely wounded in the breast by a musket-ball, which was subsequently cut out near his collar-bone. Captain Doherty's horse was shot under him.

This incident of the three Dohertys charging abreast is incorrectly stated by Napier to have taken place at St Gaudens.

The strength of the French cavalry which were opposed to the 13th on this occasion amounted to nine troops. The death of Trumpeter Sincock is related to have taken place in the following manner. It appears that while fording the river in the morning, as the stream was very rapid, numbers of the infantry soldiers laid hold of the swords of the cavalry troopers or of other parts of their equipments, to enable them to keep their feet. Two or three took hold of Trumpeter Sincock,—the strength of the river carried them off their feet, and the trumpeter was unhorsed. All were, however, safely got across.

The weather was very cold, there had been frost in the night, and Sincock was drenched. A trumpeter of the 14th proffered his canteen, and Sincock presumably took a longer and stronger pull at it than was wise. At any rate, when the regiment was ordered to charge and the trumpeters in front ordered to the rear, Sincock, instead of obeying, when near the enemy let out his horse and sword in hand dashed into the front ranks. He was instantly sabred, receiving a blow across his face which struck him between nose and mouth and nearly severed his head. His horse got among the enemy and was never recovered. On his holster he carried Colonel Doherty's light great-coat, the pockets of which contained a number of memoranda and orders which, from the unsettled state of the regiment and the absence of baggage, it had been impossible to arrange and put up. These, too, were all lost.

Meanwhile the battle was fiercely contested all along the line. After a severe struggle the enemy was driven back from all his positions.

The 13th received orders to make a detour to the right, in order to intercept some of the fugitives. Passing at a gallop for some two or three miles through a woody country, the 13th gained the great road. Here the regiment passed the Household and Hussar Brigades. Proceeding along the road, still at a gallop, the 13th gained the summit of a hill, whence the enemy were seen massed in the plain beneath, but in confusion, and endeavouring to gain a village in the front. The regiment was ordered to halt. Artillery was brought up and played with great effect on the confused masses of the enemy beneath. However, when the enemy gained some rising ground in the rear of the village, they appeared to rally, and even brought up some guns and opened fire.

Meanwhile the 14th had joined the 13th.

The brigade, when the artillery opened on them, received orders to retire and take post behind some rising ground. The enemy's guns did them no more harm than inflicting slight wounds on a few men and horses. This was the last effort of the French that day, as they shortly afterwards retired in confusion in all directions. The British Army went into bivouac on the ground, after a victory as complete in its way as that of Vittoria. The loss of the French in killed, wounded, and prisoners, amounted to between eight and ten thousand men.

At daybreak on Monday, February 28, the brigade mounted, and with the horse artillery marched by bad cross-country roads till it gained the great road.

Passing through the town of Coudures, beyond which at some distances some scattered houses were found, the brigade and artillery put up, two squadrons being placed on outpost duty.

During the day a considerable number of prisoners had been taken, and these were at once sent under escort to the rear.

On Tuesday, March 1, the brigade assembled at daybreak and marched by bad country roads to the river Adour. Having forded the river, they proceeded for some time along the great road. An order to countermarch was then received, the brigade retraced its steps, reforded the river, and after a dreary wait was ordered to find quarters under cover wherever possible. Two squadrons under the field officer of the day were sent on outpost duty, but as all the villages were full of infantry it was not till after it became dark that the brigade got under cover in detached houses. This had been a most fatiguing march. It had rained in torrents throughout the day, and the rain continued all through the night.

Ayre, March 2, 1814.

At daybreak on Wednesday, March 2, the brigade mounted and proceeded to the place appointed for assembly. On arrival they were ordered to advance and head the infantry who were then marching upon Ayre. Having gained the front, a squadron furnished by the 14th acted as advance-guard. These, on arriving on some high ground overlooking Ayre, found that not only had the enemy not retired from the place, but that he was in position and in force in front of it. General Hill reconnoitred the position, and then ordered the infantry to attack. The attack was successful, and the enemy were driven out of all their positions, and ultimately out of Ayre.

Meanwhile the 13th had been ordered to make a demonstration on the right. Having crossed a deep ravine and a river, they gained the opposite heights, from which heights the enemy had been driven at dusk. The enemy were even then retiring in all directions.

To the 13th orders were then given to protect the front, and for those men and horses who were not on duty to take refuge under cover if possible. A large house was found—the only one available. The horses were tied up within and around it, and a squadron was pushed forward on outpost duty. Hardly were the men dismounted when firing was heard in front, and some of the advanced squadron came in wounded, with the information that the enemy had rallied and were advancing. The regiment instantly mounted and moved forward, a message being sent to some light companies of British infantry in the rear. These, despite the darkness and torrents of rain which were coming down, soon arrived. The enemy was attacked and driven off, the posts were resumed, and the regiment again put up, but in great discomfort, for all were drenched to the skin, there was no baggage up, so no change of clothing could be obtained, and cloaks and clothing were soaked. Hence men and officers had to content themselves with lying down on some straw which was found, and there they remained till morning.

In 'Trifles from my Portfolio; or, Recollections of Scenes and Small Adventures,' by A Staff Surgeon, the following anecdote is given :—

At Ayre on the Adour.

One morning when I was quitting the British Hospital a cart was driven to the door from the 2nd Division, then 5 or 6 leagues in front, containing a French and an English Dragoon: the latter, being the worser case, was attended first. This man, Corporal James Buchanan of the 13th Light Dragoons, carried with him a written certificate from his Commanding Officer stating that he had been attacked, the day before, by three French Dragoons, whom he fought individually, slaying one outright, putting the second to flight badly wounded, and wounding and capturing the third, who came with him in the cart. Buchanan had received fifteen wounds, in the Head, Face, arms and body: His nose was cut off and one bone of the forearm cut through. It is needless to add that I paid the tenderest attention to this glorious fellow—patched up a jury-nose for him as well as I could, and I am happy to say left him convalescent and in the best intelligence with his prisoner who slept in the bed by his side.

This extract is "certified" by W. Henry, D.I.G., Fort Pitt, Chatham, 19th November 1850.

Next morning, in the still continuing rain—rain now mingled with snow—the regiment marched and put up in a commune called Legos, where, though the troops were widely extended, yet they were all under cover. Outpost duty here on front and flanks required 38 men.

Here the regiment remained during the 4th, 5th, and 6th, parading daily on the alarm post at daybreak, and putting up again about 9 A.M.

The baggage now came up, and on the 7th the regiment marched to Garlin, a post in front of, and between two or three leagues distant from, the army. Here, owing to the number of roads all round, it required nearly half the regiment on outpost duty. About 4 o'clock that afternoon the enemy pushed forward a body of cavalry from Conches and drove in the advanced posts, whereupon the main picket under Lieutenant John Geale turned out and advanced. Thereupon the enemy halted and retired. The advanced posts were again resumed. Two horses were this day wounded by the enemy. About 1 A.M. next morning news came to Lieut.-Colonel Doherty that a considerable body of the enemy's cavalry had marched out of Conches, and that it was supposed they meditated an attempt at surprising the 13th at Garlin, and that their commander was a man of enterprise. Hardly had this news come in when a trooper arrived dismounted. He was one of a party of four men who had been sent out with a sergeant, by name Grey, on patrolling duty.

Sergeant Grey sailed with the regiment in 1810, was promoted corporal in Captain Bowers's troop, returned home after the war, served at Waterloo, returned home in 1816. The intelligence brought by the trooper was to the effect that the enemy had got in the rear of the patrol and captured them, but that managing to climb a high ditch he had escaped in the darkness. He reported that the enemy were on the great road, were advancing towards Garlin, and were no great distance away. Instantly the troops were turned out, the more quickly as all the horses were saddled and the men sleeping in the stables. The regiment formed on the alarm post. The baggage which had only come in late that evening was sent to the rear, and all necessary arrangements were made to repel an attack. Small parties were sent out to reconnoitre, and from these it was reported that the strength of the enemy was considerable, but that he was halted. Later it was ascertained that the trumpet sounding "to horse" had warned them that the 13th were prepared, and despite the fact that their strength amounted to two regiments of cavalry, they did not deem it prudent to proceed farther. The regiment continued at the alarm post until daybreak, the enemy retired, and the posts were relieved. So severe, however, was this duty, that not only was every man not on duty employed, but some of those who had been on duty all night had to do a double turn. A careful inspection of the country next morning revealed a narrow path or lane overgrown with bushes, leading from Conches to the great road, which had been overlooked. By Indian file the enemy had passed along it. The spot where Sergeant Grey and his patrol were placed was on the great road beyond. The enemy came on his rear, and so he was captured.

On March 8th, General Hill visited the post, and on consideration of its exposed situation saw the advisability of strengthening it. Accordingly he despatched thither three companies of the 57th British infantry, who, taking up those posts nearest the town, considerably eased the duty of the regiment.

The 13th remained at Garlin until March 10, when it marched to the village of Tadusse, a post even more advanced, closer up to the enemy, and still more difficult to guard than Garlin, for the country was close and woody, and the number of roads and paths innumerable. Again, too, the regiment was acting independently of infantry, and consequently nearly two-thirds of the men were required on outpost duty.

Two troopers were taken prisoners on the day the 13th reached Tadusse, while patrolling. The whole of the next day was employed in reconnoitring the country, examining roads, paths, and woods; arranging the outposts and concentrating quarters as far as possible, for greater security.

On March 12, the regiment marched and gained the great road leading to Lambage, when a squadron under the command of Captain Gubbins was ordered forward to reconnoitre towards that place. Some time afterwards Captain Gubbins sent back for support, as the enemy were in sight. The remainder of the regiment moved forward briskly, and met the squadron returning after having fulfilled its mission. Captain Gubbins had ascertained that the enemy appeared in considerable force, and had outside the town over eight hundred cavalry.

The regiment then returned to Tadusse and put up. On the morning of the 13th, while yet on the alarm post, at which the regiment generally paraded an hour before daylight, it was discovered that the enemy were advancing in very considerable force of all arms on the great road leading from Lambage to Conches. The posts on that road were driven in, the picket in that direction, under the command of Lieutenant Mill, being retired in a most soldierlike and prudent manner, moving slowly, often fronting, and repeatedly skirmishing. The regiment at once moved along to gain the great road leading from Conches to Garlin, throwing out a squadron in advance, upon which Lieutenant Mill and his picket from Conches retired. It turned out that the whole of Soult's army was advancing—a force of seventy thousand men. From the enemy a column of infantry was sent forward and threw out their sharpshooters. The 13th slowly retired, halting and fronting occasionally. It will be remembered that there was no British infantry at hand. Slowly retiring, halting and fronting, the regiment went doggedly till nightfall, when orders were received to get under cover anywhere, in any convenient houses, leaving a squadron on the road on outpost duty. After some difficulty, about half the horses were housed, the rest being tied up round cabins and huts. During the day a few men and horses had been wounded, some of the latter badly.

Lieutenant Maclean, who had been sent on reconnoitring duty by General Fane, with a small party, was wounded and taken prisoner, and with him a private by name Nicholas Boddy, who had joined the regiment with the 1st remount, arriving in Portugal, September 8,

1810. He was at the depot during the Waterloo campaign, and belonged then to Captain M'Neil's troop.

The rest of the party escaped, thanks to the goodness of their horses, and rejoined the regiment.

The mishap to Lieutenant Maclean was due to the closeness and woody nature of the country. His party fell in with a body of the enemy's cavalry. In defending himself Lieutenant Maclean was wounded; he put his horse at a leap which it failed to clear, and fell. When taken prisoner he was at once plundered, and among other things taken from him was a gold watch he very much valued, it being a family relic. Wishing to recover it if possible, when in the evening he was brought into the quarters of Marshal Soult he applied to his A.D.C., offering a draft on the paymaster to the dragoon who took it for its value on restoration of the watch. The A.D.C. assured him he would get it, and that it should be returned. Later that evening he brought it, but instead of giving it to Maclean, calmly took from his fob an old silver watch which he offered him, saying, "This will do you just as well, and as I fancy you will shortly be exchanged and may in all probability again be captured, this will be better to lose than your gold one." He then deliberately put Maclean's watch in his pocket and walked off.

Before daylight on the morning of March 14, the regiment assembled and formed on the ground it had occupied the preceding evening. At daylight, the infantry of the enemy advanced, covered by a cloud of sharpshooters. Thereupon as on the previous day the 13th began to retire slowly, halting and fronting occasionally. On the arrival of some Spanish infantry they were ordered to the front, and the regiment was sent in support, being instructed to keep as much out of fire as possible. The behaviour of the Spanish infantry nullified this, as they continually fell back before the enemy, and never halted until just close to the front of the 13th. Thus retreating the Spanish and the 13th arrived quite near to Garlin, during which the regiment from its exposed situation lost some men and horses badly wounded.

At length the British infantry arrived, and among them the 28th Regiment. This regiment was sent forward, and without delay charged the sharpshooters, and at the point of the bayonet drove them in.

The rest of the British infantry was then sent forward, with the result that the column supporting the sharpshooters was thrown into confusion. Shortly after the entire force of the enemy was driven back, and the victorious British took possession of the heights lately occupied by the French, and established themselves thereon.

The 13th were ordered to march and take up a post on the great Pau road, where it remained until dark, when it was instructed to put up at Garlin.

The 14th Light Dragoons on this day had two affairs with the enemy in which they manifested their usual bravery, but unfortunately Captain Babington of that regiment was wounded and taken prisoner, sharing the fate of another captain of the 14th, by name Townsend, who, a day or two previously, had met with a similar misfortune.

On the next morning the regiment turned out and marched to the rendezvous on the Pau road. Here it was joined by the 14th and General Fane. Amid a terrific storm of rain and snow the brigade remained until between 3 and 4 P.M., when the 13th returned to Garlin. Here it was found that a brigade of infantry had arrived, and the place was so crowded that with great difficulty the horses were got under cover.

On the following day precisely the same events occurred, and the weather was equally unpropitious. In the evening the regiment again returned to Garlin, and hardly had the horses been housed when orders were received to detach a squadron immediately to Torniquet and another to Claracq, and to relieve the 14th on the Pau road.

Next morning the 13th paraded at the usual hour on the alarm post, and there remained until 2 P.M., when orders were received to shift the squadron then on the Pau road to Ribborony (?) while the other two squadrons remained on duty. Of the detached squadron the advance-guard under the command of Lieutenant Doherty fell in with one of the outposts of the enemy, which was attacked and driven in. But the main body of the enemy was in close proximity to the village, and roads around the place so numerous that more could not be attempted. The outpost duty was very severe for the detached squadron.

On March 18th two squadrons marched and took post at St Jean Page, the advance squadron of which *en route* fell in with an outpost of the enemy which was attacked, driven in, and pursued until it reached its support—a body of infantry and cavalry. Captain Doherty was in command of this squadron.

The support was posted near to the village of Lalongue. It was drawn up outside the place, and consisted of four companies of infantry and two strong squadrons of cavalry.

The 13th were then ordered to march and gain the great road leading to Lambage. On arrival there, instructions to return were almost immediately received in order to take post at a village called Vallier, whence a close watch on the enemy at Lalongue was to be maintained.

For this purpose one squadron was posted close to the village, supported by two companies of Spanish infantry which had been sent forward specially for that purpose and posted in the rear of the squadron.

Meanwhile the infantry on the left were warmly engaged with the enemy. Ultimately the latter were driven from all their positions, and the two armies that night went into bivouac close to each other.

On March 19th the regiment paraded at the usual hour—an hour before daybreak—on the alarm post. Reconnoitring parties were then sent out, by whom it was ascertained that the enemy had retired during the night from Lalongue. The 13th then received orders to march and join the army on the Lambage road. Thence on arrival a squadron was detached to Sevignac under the command of Captain Doherty to watch the movements of the younger Soult, who was in the neighbourhood in command of a body of the enemy's cavalry.

On arrival near Sevignac, Captain Doherty learned that the enemy had evacuated the town—at least so he was informed. Luckily before seeking information he had concealed his squadron in a wood as evening fell. As to the truth of his information he had doubts, and with a small party went out to personally investigate the report. As he suspected it proved to be false. The enemy to the number of 800 was still in the town. Captain Doherty's squadron therefore went into bivouac in the wood, of course taking every precaution against surprise. However during the night the enemy did retire.

As Captain Doherty's squadron marched on this duty, the squadron under the command of Major Boyse, which had been detached, rejoined the regiment, and the two squadrons moved on with the army, marching through Lambage. Here they were but a few hours behind the enemy.

The 13th were halted a short distance from Vig Bigorre. Against this place Sir Thomas Picton advanced with the 3rd Division, and drove out the enemy in gallant style from the vineyards over the town.

On the march the 14th joined, and the brigade once more together went into bivouac that night in a neighbouring wood with neither tents nor baggage. Officers and men lay down and slept in their cloaks. During the night the Heavy Brigade, consisting of the 3rd Dragoon Guards and the 1st Royal Dragoons, arrived, under the command of Lieut.-Colonel Clifton of the Royals. This body of cavalry now forming a Division under the orders of Major-General Fane was formed into a Light and Heavy Brigade. The command of the Light Brigade was given to Lieut.-Colonel Doherty of the 13th, while Lieut.-Colonel Clifton continued to command the 3rd Dragoon Guards and the 1st Royal Dragoons.

CHAPTER XXI.

Tarbes and St Gaudens, &c., March 20, 1814.

ON the morning of March 20, at 6 A.M., the Division marched towards Tarbes, flanking the infantry on the right. Beyond Tarbes the cavalry forded the Adour, while the infantry crossed that river by the bridge. On the farther side of the Adour the cavalry formed in contiguous columns of half squadrons, covering the crossing of the infantry. On the heights the enemy were in considerable force. The infantry formed up and moved on to the attack, being supported by the cavalry. But the ground was by no means favourable for the action of mounted men. However, the enemy were attacked with great vigour, and in a short time driven from all their positions. Slowly retiring, the defeated French fronted whenever the nature of the ground permitted, until the evening closed in. Again both armies went into bivouac close to each other. In Lord Wellington's despatch, dated Tarbes, 29th March 1814, he mentions the gallant conduct of one squadron of the 13th on March 16, and that of two squadrons of the 14th under Captain Mills of the 14th, who took a great number of prisoners. What these affairs were do not appear from the papers of Lieut.-Colonel Doherty, or from the Regimental Record. On the day that the battle of Tarbes was fought the regiment marched five and a half leagues.

On the 21st of March the cavalry, owing to the open nature of the country, were enabled to march in front and across the ground. At night, after having proceeded five leagues, the Light Brigade put up in the village of La Bartha and the Heavy in some neighbouring villages.

St Gaudens, March 22, 1814.

At an early hour in the morning the army marched, the cavalry being in front, and on this day the 13th formed the advance. From the regiment, a squadron under the command of Captain Macallester, consisting of his troop with Lieutenant Drought and Captain Gregorie's troop under the command of Lieutenant Doherty, was sent out as an advance-guard. The day was extremely wet, nor did the rain cease for five minutes.

Towards evening the 14th Light Dragoons received orders to put up in a village which appeared in view on the right. The Royals were similarly sent to another, and the two regiments filed off.

The 3rd Dragoon Guards, being at the rear of all, were at some considerable distance. A long gap was thus existing between the 13th and the 3rd. The regiment continued to advance, when a report came in from Captain Macallester that he had fallen in with the enemy's advanced posts. Skirmishing then took place, and the enemy's posts were quickly driven in on their supports, which consisted of a squadron drawn up on the St Gaudens road. General Fane then ordered a halt, and endeavours were made to learn the strength and position of the enemy.

Ahead lay St Gaudens, a town built on the top of a hill. On one side, by means of glasses, two strong squadrons were discerned in formation. On the other side, the rain prevented objects from being accurately viewed, but something was made out which was concluded to be infantry. Meanwhile General Fane had ordered the 3rd Dragoon Guards to mount the heights on the left for the purpose of ascertaining whether any of the enemy lay beyond. A detachment from the supporting squadron of the 13th, under the command of Lieutenant Major, as Captain Doherty's squadron which was detached on the 19th had not rejoined, was sent to cover the right flank and to reconnoitre. By these means the strength of the regiment was reduced to three weak troops. The cavalry of the enemy now filed off and marched into St Gaudens, his rear squadron following. The 13th and its support moved on. The enemy quickened his pace, and the 13th followed suit, till at a gallop they went up the hill and dashed through the streets of that badly paved town. Colonel Doherty states that the inhabitants from their windows acclaimed the British troops, waved their handkerchiefs, and wished them success as they galloped by. A little way beyond the town the 13th came up with the enemy, who had fronted and were formed up in good order on a wide road. The 13th pulled up and formed a front of sixes, the road allowing it. Then, having given their horses a brief breathing time, they charged the enemy. At once the enemy fired a volley from their carbines, which did practically no damage. Then the two bodies of cavalry met, and the enemy broke and fled. The 13th pursued till they were stopped by the road being completely blocked up by the number of the enemy's men and horses which lay in it. This had to be removed, and during the time thus occupied the enemy employed themselves in halting, fronting, and forming. The 13th did the same, and a second charge was delivered, with the same result, and again an obstruction (this time a wine cart) put a period to the pursuit. During this charge Lieutenant Lawrence was in a most uncomfortable and perilous situation, for his saddle turned under his horse. But assistance was given him, and he was extricated.

The large wine-cart—a cart nearly as large as an English brewer's dray—having been removed so as to permit the passage of more than one man at a time at one end, the regiment again formed up, and by this time the enemy were again prepared to make a stand. A third charge was delivered, and with the same result. The enemy broke and fled, nor was there any impediment on the road to check the pursuit this time, and the routed French cavalry were chased until it was deemed prudent to sound a halt.

The enemy did not attempt another formation after their third encounter. They were completely broken and went off at a gallop. The squadron of the 3rd Dragoon Guards which had been detached on the left now joined, and the whole retired back to St Gaudens over a road some three miles in length, which was strewn with dead and wounded men and horses and all kinds of cavalry arms and equipments.

The troop of the 13th which had been detached to the right succeeded in gaining the road during the conflict and pursuit, and gave great assistance in securing the captures.

One hundred and ten prisoners and sixty horses were taken. The number of dead was considerable on the side of the enemy.

The British casualties were one man badly wounded and six others slightly. The horse of Lieutenant Doherty received a bad sabre wound on the head, and one or two troop horses were also cut about. The strength of the enemy on this occasion consisted of one regiment of chasseurs, having three squadrons each of one hundred men. This regiment had been left as a rear-guard by the younger Soult, who had marched from St Gaudens a few hours previously with six regiments of cavalry. General Fane most warmly congratulated the regiment on its gallant performance.

That night the 13th put up in the village of Villeneuve, distant some two miles in the rear of St Gaudens.

During the combat Lieut.-Colonel Doherty nearly lost his life at the end of the first pursuit. It will be remembered that the pursuit was checked by men and horses of the enemy that had fallen across the road.

One man who had fallen in the ditch, raised himself as the colonel galloped up, and deliberately taking aim at the officer fired. The ball passed through Colonel Doherty's cloak and under his left arm, just grazing his jacket. The men were so exasperated that despite the colonel's efforts to save the fellow he was immediately sabred.

Lieutenant Doherty, observing one of the enemy making his escape on foot across a field, whom from his dress and appearance he supposed to be an officer—a richly laced jacket, laced overalls, bear-skin cap with rich tassels,—gave chase. The fugitive was making his way to a ditch on the other side, near to which Lieutenant Doherty having cleared that at the road caught his man. Summoned to surrender, the Frenchman gave up his sword and was conducted back to the road in triumph. But it was only the Trumpet-Major, and not as supposed either the commanding officer or even a commissioned officer of any rank.

Captain Macallester who commanded the advance on this occasion evinced signal gallantry, and was rewarded in consequence with the rank of major in the army.

It is stated that the enemy belonged to the 10th French Hussars, and that they were nearly cut to pieces. Lieut.-Colonel Cadell remarks in his narrative of the campaigns of the 28th Regiment: "When we came up, the sight was truly melancholy: throughout the many actions in which we had taken share we never had seen men and horses so dreadfully mangled. The horses were sold next day; but the best brought very little." Besides the officers already named, Major Boyse, Lieutenant Lawrence, and Brigade Major Dunbar were also present on this occasion.

On March 23rd the regiment halted for a day. In fact, after the exertions of the last few days and of the 22nd in particular, many things required to be put in order. The horses' feet, from constant marching on roads all day and every day, needed shoeing badly. However, from out of the captured animals twenty were selected with the approval of General Fane for the use of the regiment. It chanced that the division of General Hill was marching by, and the General with his staff rode up to the field where the 13th were and desired to see the officers who had been present at the affair of the previous day. They were accordingly presented to him, when he thanked them for their bravery and paid many handsome compliments to them and to the regiment. In the evening General Hill issued an order highly complimentary to the regiment and to the officers engaged. Of the affair at St Gaudens, Lord Wellington's despatch contains no more than a bare mention.

The squadron under the command of Captain Doherty which had been detached joined the regiment the day after the affair at St Gaudens, having made long and forced marches to come up with them.

This conclusively shows that it could not have been at St Gaudens that the "veteran Major Doherty" charged with one son on either side of him at the head of the leading squadron.

Of the prisoners, 76 were sent to the rear under an infantry escort and 30 were left in hospital at St Gaudens.

On March 24, the regiment and the Heavy Brigade marched through St Gaudens to Marthias. Here they put up but found the place much crowded. They gathered from the people that numerous wounded men who had escaped from the sabres of the 13th at St Gaudens had passed through the place, and that a captain had died of his wounds there the preceding night.

Apparently the 14th Light Dragoons joined the brigade here, for we read that on March 25th the 13th put up at a village called Payssies, while the 14th and the Heavy Brigade were located in some villages near.

On March 26, after parading on the alarm post at daylight in drenching rain, orders were received to turn in again and remain ready. About noon orders came to march, and the whole division joined the 13th on the great road leading to Toulouse—the regiment marching in front. The 13th marched through the large town of Murat, where the rest of the cavalry were halted. To the regiment, however, orders were given to move forward and "to establish the headquarters of the regiment at Roques, then in possession of the enemy, to force the enemy from some villages in the neighbourhood, and to push the advance posts as near Toulouse as possible." All the baggage of the regiment was at once sent to the rear. An advanced squadron was as usual in front, and this on arrival near Roques fell in with the advanced posts of the enemy. These were attacked and driven in on their main body which was formed near the village. The main body was then attacked and retired on Portet skirmishing. From Portet the enemy was then driven and retired on Toulouse. By dark all the advanced posts were established and vedettes posted on the road to Toulouse. Posts were also established on both flanks, and a squadron was left on the road to support them. The rest of the regiment retired to Roques, in obedience to the orders previously received, and there put up. The vedettes left on the road were not more than a mile and a half or two miles from Toulouse, and close to those of the enemy.

On the next day, March 27, the regiment mounted before dawn, and marched to near where the squadron had been left in support. All things were found to continue as on the evening before. After remaining some time, as all was quiet, the regiment returned and put up at Roques. About noon orders came to turn out again, the regiment mounted, and while proceeding along the great road to Toulouse was joined by the remainder of the cavalry brigade and also the horse artillery. After remaining for some time on the road, during which time the squadron of the 13th was relieved by one of the Royals, which regiment took up the duty for the day, the regiment and the horse artillery marched, putting up that night at Villeneuve, while the remainder of the division took shelter in neighbouring villages.

At daybreak on March 28, the regiment assembled on the alarm post, and after some time was ordered back to quarters and to remain ready. The baggage now came up. March 29th was passed in precisely the same way. Next day, however, the regiment was ordered to march at daybreak, to relieve the regiment on outpost duty in front of Poiret; and in consequence the baggage was sent to the rear.

On March 31st the regiment was relieved by the 5th Dragoon Guards at 5 P.M., and marched, crossing the river by the pontoon bridge which had been thrown over. By midnight the village of Miremont was reached, and there the regiment put up.

On April 1st the 13th marched before daybreak and formed on the great road, with the rest of the division and the artillery.

Here it was halted until ordered to return. This order was given in consequence of the state of the roads, which owing to the incessant rain were in such a condition as to prevent the expedition which had crossed the river from proceeding. The 13th accordingly returned to Miremont, where it remained until 7 o'clock that evening, when in obdience to orders it turned out and marched to the spot on the main road it had left that morning. From thence the regiment proceeded to the river, crossed it by the pontoon bridge, and marched to Villeneuve, at which place it arrived at one o'clock on the morning of April 2. At Villeneuve the regiment remained until 1 A.M. on April 4, being during the whole of that time prepared to mount and march at a moment's notice.

At 1 A.M. on April 4th the 13th marched, with orders to join the 2nd Division of Infantry on the great road leading from Corneaux to Toulouse. On the junction being effected, the regiment marched in front till it arrived on the high ground before Toulouse and within a mile of that city. The 13th was then halted and took post, remaining exposed to a blinding and continuous deluge of rain until 4 P.M. Orders were then received to relieve the 15th Hussars who were then on outpost duty.

To effect this, and to supply the other detached posts, required nearly sixty men and a proportion of officers. The posts having been established, the remainder of the regiment marched to St Martino, in and around which place they put up. For five consecutive mornings the 13th paraded on the alarm post near Toulouse before daybreak, the infantry being also there under arms. In this position the force remained till noon each day, when all returned to quarters.

Forage by this time had become very scarce in the district—

no hay, very little straw and that bad, and hardly any corn could be obtained. Frequently the foraging parties had leagues to go after dismissal from the alarm post, and were then obliged to be content with bringing in rotten straw collected from old thatched houses.

The horses were mainly tied up in wine-houses and wine-cellars, where a most abundant supply of wine was to be found,—the horses of the commanding officer, the staff, and one troop occupying houses in the village. But although an abundance of drink was obtainable by the men for the asking, it is to be recorded that not one case of drunkenness, nor even of a man appearing to be in liquor, was observed during these days. This fact is one which reflects the greatest credit on the regiments.

CHAPTER XXII.

Toulouse, April 10, 1814.

BEFORE daylight on the morning of April 10, the 13th and 14th paraded on the alarm post as customary, and awaited the expected battle. About 8 A.M. the British attack began on the right of the enemy's position.

Here the enemy was very strongly posted, having taken possession of large houses which were loopholed for musketry, and moreover protected by artillery. At these Lord Wellington directed the attack. The conflict, while it lasted, was sanguinary, but at length the enemy was driven from all his positions and rolled back upon Toulouse. The attack on the left flank of the enemy was equally successful. During the morning the brigade was engaged in driving in the outposts of the enemy in front of Toulouse, a duty which gave it plenty of occupation, as they were numerous. When these posts had been driven in, the brigade formed on the plain in front of Toulouse, and within range of the guns there, which did not neglect to open fire.

Later, the 13th was ordered to take up a position covering some of the British guns, which were pounding away at a battery near the town. One of the British guns, however, was dismounted by a shot, and the rest were then withdrawn, but the 13th remained in the position to which it had been sent and exposed to the fire from the battery.

Here it remained without any opportunity of acting until dusk, when it marched back to its old cantonments at St Martino and the neighbourhood, and put up for the night. It is a somewhat remarkable fact that the 8th and last party of remounts from

England joined the regiment during the course of the Battle of Toulouse.

This draft was under the command of Captain Goulburn, and consisted of Sergeant-Major King, Sergeant Lawlor, and thirty-four rank and file, with seventy-four horses.

Of these, Sergeant Lawlor died within a month, and two troopers, William Goscombe and Thomas Cleverly, died, one on May 14 and the other on June 19.

On the morning after the battle the regiment turned out as usual at daybreak, but as nothing occurred it later returned to quarters.

During the night of April 11, Soult with the remainder of his army evacuated Toulouse. When the brigade paraded the following morning at daybreak on the alarm post, the intelligence of this event was made known.

During the day the division of cavalry under the command of General Fane assembled and took part in the formal military entry into Toulouse of the victorious Allies.

Through the streets the victors passed with swords drawn, trumpets sounding, and all the pomp and show of a military parade.

The inhabitants filled the windows and crowded the streets, greeting the British troops all along the line with acclamations.

The Bourbon white cockade was everywhere in evidence. A large statue of Napoleon was ignominiously hurled out of the window of the Municipal Buildings in the square, and was shattered to pieces on the pavement below—a rather childish performance this. The Bourbon white flag was hoisted on the responsibility of the French, and not by the act of the British. The authorities were warned, as a matter of fact, that any revolutionary act they might commit was at their own peril. Through the town in long line passed the cavalry brigade and out into the country beyond. To the infantry, who followed, the occupation of Toulouse was intrusted. Four leagues beyond Toulouse information came to the cavalry brigade that a body of the enemy's cavalry was posted to the left of the road, and beyond a canal which ran parallel to it.

The division halted, as did the artillery which had accompanied it on the march.

As the enemy had destroyed the bridge over the canal it was needful to construct one temporarily, but of sufficient strength to permit the passage of cavalry.

The 13th and the artillery were employed on this, and by the aid of peasants who brought timber with great willingness for the purpose, a bridge was soon constructed and the regiment crossed, its orders being to make for a village which appeared in the distance.

On the way thither another branch of the canal was discovered, and a canal which was possessed of very steep banks. This, however, the 13th managed to ford, and then formed up on the opposite side. Here information reached them that a squadron of the 1st Hussars (King's German Legion) without supports was engaged with the enemy's cavalry on the farther side of the village. The right squadron of the 13th, under Captain Doherty, was at once sent briskly forward, the rest of the regiment following in support. The Hussars, however, as was to be expected, had repulsed the enemy before the 13th arrived, having charged their opponents, broken them, and pursued them for some distance, capturing thirty or forty prisoners, and nearly as many horses.

The 18th Hussars now came on the scene with Sir Stapleton Cotton, and the 13th was then ordered to recross the canal and put up in any convenient villages which were found. Towards dusk that evening the regiment reached Montesquieu, where news came that the enemy's cavalry were not far distant. In consequence the 13th remained in the village street till nearly nine o'clock, when, having established the necessary posts to ensure security, it got under cover.

On April 13, after the usual daybreak parade and subsequent visits to the outposts, intelligence was received that Colonel Cooke had, during the night, passed through the lines on his way to Marshal Soult to announce the Abdication of Buonaparte and the Recall of Louis XVIII. Hostilities were to cease, and an immediate peace to ensue. Among the peasants in the locality it is said that this news was received with the most extravagant demonstrations of joy. But Marshal Soult was not at first disposed to accept the situation—he, at any rate, held out for his fallen master to the bitter end, and with undeniable fidelity.

On the cavalry division marching that day, the 3rd Dragoons

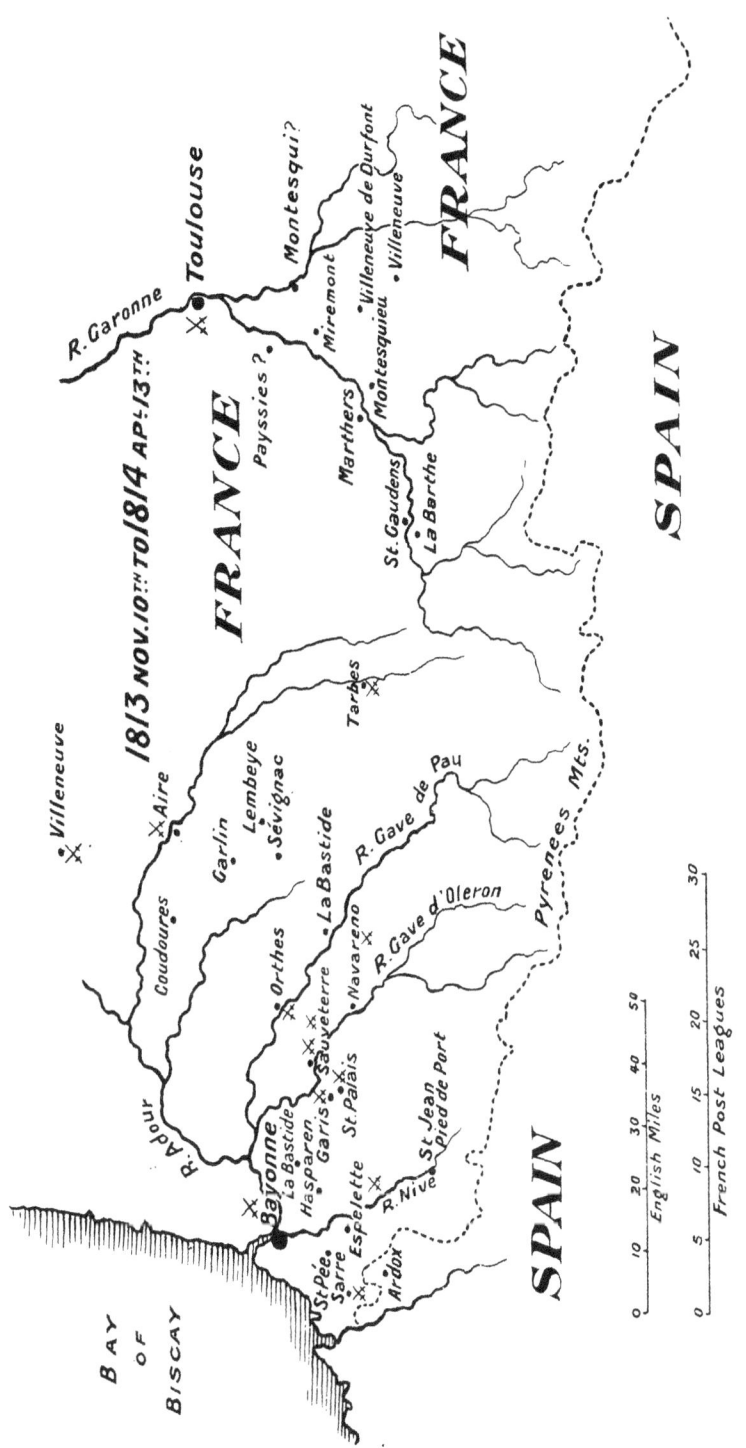

Sketch Map showing the chief places at which the regiment was from November 10th, 1813, until April 13th, 1814, when peace was declared

in front, it approached the town of Villeneuve and was fired upon by the batteries. A halt was called, and a flag of truce was sent in. After a parley, and much communication between the British headquarters and Soult, the latter had to agree to an arangement as follows: three days were allowed the marshal to make up his mind—he wanted time to send a messenger to Paris and obtain thence an answer, professing to doubt the possibility of either the abdication of Napoleon or the restoration of the Bourbons. This Wellington refused, and stated that on the expiration of the three days Soult would be at once attacked.

Posts were established on the great road, and so near one another were the vedettes of both armies that French and British officers often met and discussed the situation.

Early on the morning of the 14th of April the regiment marched. Two of the squadrons put up at Villefranche and the third relieved the 3rd Dragoon Guards of their outpost duty. Villefranche was full of infantry, and stabling for only one squadron could be obtained there—the horses of the second squadron being tied up under the Town Hall, in a place used as a market.

At 3 A.M. on April 15th a communication was received stating that hostilities had not ceased, and directing the regiment to turn out immediately and move to the front. Colonel Doherty was also directed to forward this order to all the cavalry regiments and to the artillery in the neighbourhood.

The regiment turned out and assembled with the infantry on the alarm post. A reconnaissance revealed that, except a few changes in the position of the French infantry, everything continued unchanged.

The British remained under arms till between 8 and 9 o'clock, when they were ordered to turn in again, but to remain ready to act at an instant's notice.

Towards evening the 13th was ordered out to relieve the Royals on outpost duty. A squadron was therefore put on the great road, various posts were taken up, and the rest of the regiment put up at scattered farmhouses.

April 16. Two squadrons paraded at the alarm post at daybreak— at 9 A.M. turned in again and relieved various posts.

April 17. On the usual daybreak parade it was ascertained that a French officer of distinction, accompanied by a British officer, had passed through the lines during the night bearing despatches from the French Government to Marshal Soult. It was reported that Napoleon had left Paris for Elba, that the Empress had left to join her father, and that Louis XVIII. was recalled and proclaimed King.

On April 18th two squadrons marched into Villefranche, while the third squadron relieved the 3rd Dragoon Guards on outpost duty. This day an announcement that hostilities had ceased appeared in general orders to the army, but that no further communication was to be between the armies "than what is permitted by the laws of war."

Next day the French posts in the front were all withdrawn. The 13th marched from Villefranche and returned to its former quarters in the farmhouses, where it remained till April 22.

On April 22nd the brigade consisting of the 13th and 14th received orders to march under the command of Lieut.-Colonel Doherty for Aire. The 13th marched to Tournefuile, viâ Toulouse, and the 14th to Columniez. On the 23rd the brigade marched to Isle de Jourdain, the 24th to Ginion, the 25th halted, the 26th to Auch, where the 14th put up while the 13th went on and put up near Ordain. During this day's march the Duc d'Angoulême was met by the brigade and received with the salute due to his rank—an attention which he appreciated greatly, tendering his thanks. On the 27th the brigade reached Vu Fuezensac, the 28th to Nigora, and on the 29th arrived at Aire, where orders were received to continue the march to Monte Marsan, and there the brigade went into quarters. The distance marched amounted to thirty-four and a half French leagues.

At Monte Marsan the 13th remained until May 23, and the halt was indeed welcome. As no clothing had been issued to the men the previous winter, what with the effects of the weather and the constant duty by night and day the condition of their garments and the appearance of the men can be more easily imagined than described.

Overalls patched with cloth of all sorts of colours and most frequently with red oilskin,—fragments of the baggage wrappers, by the way,—were universal or almost so.

Supplies of all kinds were, however, to be obtained at Monte

Marsan, and each man soon received a good strong pair of grey overalls, other necessaries being also supplied.

The want of forage had told terribly on the horses, farcy made its appearance, and numbers were in consequence destroyed. The losses of the officers in horses were particularly heavy through this disease.

On May 6, Lieutenant Moss, who had been a prisoner of war ever since April 7, 1811, joined the regiment. Two days later Lieutenant Maclean, who was taken prisoner on the 13th of the previous March, arrived.

On May 13th the 14th Light Dragoons received orders to march to Bordeaux, and started on the following day. Thus these two regiments, who had served so long and so gloriously together in a series of most arduous campaigns, at length separated, and the " Ragged Brigade " ceased to be.

On May 23rd the 13th began its march for Bordeaux, and that night reached Roquefort. The three next days Capticox, Bazas, and Langan were the stopping-places, where a halt was made on the 27th. On the 28th the regiment reached Castres, where Paymaster Strange, who was taken prisoner with the baggage on November 10, 1813, joined. The next day Bordeaux was reached, and on the 30th Carbon-blanc, where, having crossed the Garonne, the regiment went into quarters.

On June 2, Lieut.-Colonel Doherty was appointed to the command of the 4th Division of the left column of cavalry, consisting of the 14th Light Dragoons, Field Artillery, and Waggon Train. In consequence the command of the 13th devolved on Major Boyse.

Next day the 13th began its march homewards, reaching St André that night. The route was as follows :—

June 4, Montlieu; June 5, Barbezieux; June 6, Angoulême and neighbourhood; June 7, halted; June 8, Mansle; June 9, Ruffec; June 10, Coutré; June 11, Poictiers; June 12, halted; June 13, Châtellerault; June 14, St Maures; June 15, Tours; June 16, halted; June 17, Château-Reynault; June 18, Vendôme; June 19, Cloye; June 20, Bonneval; June 21, Chartres; June 22, halted; June 23, Epernon; June 24, Houdan; June 25, Mantes; June 26, halted; June 27, Gisors; June 28, Gournay; June 29, Neufchâtel; June 30, Blanges; July 1, Abbeville; July 2, halted; July 3, Rue; July 4, Montreuil; July 5, Boulogne.

The regiment immediately embarked, and on the 6th, 7th, and 8th of July arrived and landed at Ramsgate.

It may be well to briefly sum up the performances of the regiment during the war.

It was absent from England for four years and five months.

During that period the regiment marched 1506 leagues, which may be estimated as about 6024 miles.

The 13th was engaged in twelve battles and in thirty-two affairs, many of these being most sharply contested. Lieut.-Colonel Doherty gives fifty-two as the number of "other affairs," stating dates, places, officers concerned, and all.

During this period the regiment was one hundred and ninety-seven nights in bivouac.

The casualties amounted to six officers and 274 men. These figures include killed in action, death from sickness, and discharge.

Only four privates were discharged during the war, and one was invalided.

The loss in horses amounted to 1009.

A careful analysis of the regimental rolls discloses the fact that during the whole of this arduous campaign, when hardships were many and there was a by no means hostile reception awaiting a deserter among the enemy, yet only seven men were guilty of this crime. From three of the squadrons no man deserted.

This immunity from so serious a military offence deserves to be put on record as being an additional proof, were one needed, of the honour and loyalty of the 13th Light Dragoons.

For some reason, for which an explanation is entirely lacking, although the regiment was designated the "Thirteenth Light Dragoons" as far back as 1784, Lieut.-Colonel Doherty more often than not omits "Light"—and the same thing occurs in official despatches. A similiar lack of uniformity is to be found in Cannon's 'Historical Record.' In the earlier portion of Lieut.-Colonel Doherty's papers—those concerned with the period between 1790 and 1810, "Light Dragoons" is the style adopted. The dropping of the word "Light" begins as early as March 1811. Other Light Dragoon regiments have also a similar alteration or omission. As Lieut.-Colonel Doherty's first commission dates from long after 1784, it could hardly be owing to a memory of the original style of his

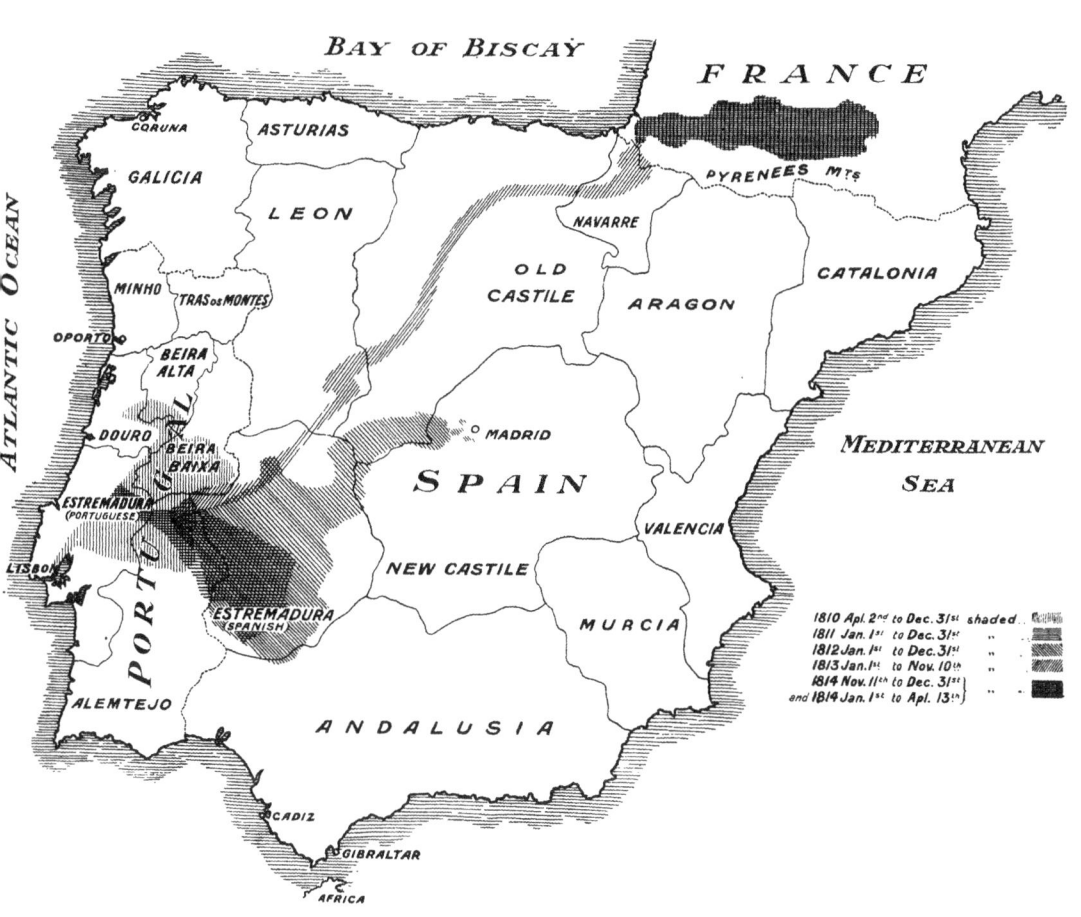

Sketch Map showing approximately the ground covered by the regiment during the Peninsula campaign.

regiment. It could hardly have been carelessness in a man whose painstaking attention to details is evidenced on each page — and there are nearly 300 pages folio, closely written.

A list of the commissioned officers and quartermasters during 1810-11-12-13-14, may well here be given under the following headings:—

SAILED WITH THE REGIMENT, FEBRUARY 1810.

Lieut.-Colonel Head	Returned home.
Major P. Doherty (Lieut.-Colonel)	Returned home.
,, Muter (Lieut.-Colonel)	Promoted to 6th Dragoons.
Captain Morres (Major)	Promoted to 9th Dragoons.
,, Boyse (Major)	Returned home.
,, Buchanan	Retired.
,, White	Killed in action (General Staff).
,, Stisted	Exchanged.
,, Doherty	Returned home.
,, Macallester	Returned home.
,, Whittingham	Spanish Staff.
Lieutenant Taylor	Died October 9, 1810.
,, Moreton	Promoted in Life Guards.
,, Major	Returned home.
,, Turner	Returned home.
,, Moss	Returned home.
,, Doherty	Returned home.
,, White	Retired.
,, F. Geale	Killed in action.
,, D'Arcy	Returned home.
,, Drought	Returned home.
,, Edwards	Returned home.
,, Jefferies	Returned home.
,, Smith	Returned home.
Cornet Graston	Returned home.
,, King (Lieutenant)	Killed November 21, 1811.
Adjutant Holmes	Returned home.
Surgeon Roache	Promoted Staff Surgeon.
Assistant-Surgeon Armstrong	Returned home.
Veterinary-Surgeon Chard	Died October 15, 1812.
Paymaster Gardener	Exchanged.
Regimental Quartermaster Minchin	Returned home.
Troop Quartermaster Murphy	Returned home.
,, St Clair	Returned home.
,, Mitchell	Returned home.
,, Layfield	Returned home.
,, Greenham	Returned home.

OFFICERS LEFT IN ENGLAND.

Captain G. Lawrence.
„ B. Lawrence.
Lieutenant Lennox.
„ Considine.
„ Bowers.
„ Podmore.
Cornet Proby.
„ Bowers.
Assistant-Surgeon Dillon.
Regimental Quartermaster Lawrence . . Promoted Adjutant.

STAFF.

Colonel Craig.
Lieut.-Colonel Bolton.

JOINED FROM ENGLAND.

Captain Bowers . . . . . . Returned home.
„ Lennox . . . . . Returned home.
„ Gubbins . . . . . Returned home.
„ Goulburn . . . . . Returned home.
„ Gregorie . . . . . Returned home.
Lieutenant M'Crea . . . . . Returned home.
„ Nesbitt . . . . . Returned home.
„ Mill . . . . . Returned home.
„ W. T. Buchanan . . . Returned home.
„ Willis . . . . . Died October 30, 1813.
Cornet M'Crea . . . . . . Returned home.
„ J. Geale . . . . . Returned home.
„ A. T. Maclean . . . . Returned home.
„ Phillips . . . . . Returned home.
„ Pymm . . . . . . Returned home.
Surgeon Logan . . . . . . Returned home.
„ Caldwell . . . . . Returned home.
Assistant-Surgeon Dillon . . . . Returned home.
Paymaster Strange . . . . . Returned home.
Quartermaster Lawrence . . . . Returned home.

OFFICERS GAZETTED TO THE REGIMENT; PUT ON STRENGTH; DID NOT JOIN.

Lord March.
Captain Searle.

Cornet Harris.
Surgeon Piper.

It is interesting to record that a veteran of the name of David Westall survived till 1873, dying in the September of that year at North Shields, aged eighty-seven. When the Peninsula War broke out he was a private in the troop commanded by Captain B. Lawrence, 13th Light Dragoons, at the depot.

Westall embarked on April 24, 1812, with the 4th Remount, and joined the regiment at Los Santos on June 8. He was present at Albuera, Vittoria, Nive, and Toulouse, and later at Waterloo.

Westall had the Peninsula medal with four clasps, and also that for Waterloo. At Waterloo he belonged to the troop commanded by Captain Gregorie.

CHAPTER XXIII.

England and Ireland, 1814.

THE 13th Light Dragoons marched from Ramsgate on the day of arrival, July 8, *en route* to Hounslow, reaching that place and stations in the neighbourhood on July 14.

Here Colonel Doherty, who had been promoted to the rank of Colonel, joined and resumed command.

Four days later the regiment was inspected by H.R.H. The Commander-in-Chief, and then marched in two divisions for Weymouth, arriving there on July 28th and 29th.

On July 25, and apparently while on the march, a reduction took place in the establishment of the regiment. It was in future to consist of eight troops, containing in the whole 549 men and 453 horses.

At Weymouth the regiment remained until 11th October, when orders were received to march to Plymouth *en route* for Ireland. But the regiment was, of course, to be no longer on what used to be called the "Irish Establishment," that having ceased to exist.

The 13th marched in four divisions.

On October 11th the 1st division marched to Plymouth, and consisted of the troops commanded by Captain Gregorie and Captain Gubbins.

On the three next days the 2nd, 3rd, and 4th divisions followed, being those commanded by Captain Holmes and Captain Bowers; Captain Doherty and Captain Lennox; Major Lawrence and Major Macallester, both now promoted. This last division was under the command of Major Lawrence, as Colonel Doherty and Lieut.-Colonel Boyse were both on leave which had been granted prior to marching orders being received. Major Boyse, as will be seen, had been promoted to lieutenant-colonel.

Captain Holmes succeeded Captain White without purchase on September 10, 1812, being then adjutant. Captain White, it will be remembered, distinguished himself when in the 13th in the affair near Ladoera, August 28, 1810. He was subsequently appointed to the Staff of the army, and fell at the battle of Salamanca.

Captain Goulburn, who commanded the draft which arrived from England during the battle of Toulouse, had retired on half-pay.

The regiment arrived at Plymouth on the 17th, 18th, 19th, and 20th of October, embarked on the 29th and 30th of October, and on the 7th and 8th of November reached Cove, near Cork, where disembarkation took place, Major Lawrence being in command, as both Colonel Doherty and Lieut.-Colonel Boyse were still on leave.

Upon the day of disembarkation the 1st division marched to Fermoy, and upon the same and the next days the remaining three divisions marched into Cork.

On November 14th Major Lawrence's troop marched to Mallow, and Captain Bowers's troop to Bandon. Next day the troops commanded by Captain Doherty and Captain Holmes marched into barracks at Cork.

On November 17th Major Macallester's and Captain Lennox's troops marched to Fermoy. On the next day Major Macallester's and Captain Gregorie's troops marched for Limerick. Meanwhile, on November 12, the troop commanded by Captain Gubbins marched from Fermoy to Clogheen. There were no further changes of quarters until February 15, 1815, on which date Captain Holmes's troop marched from Cork for Gort, and Captain Lennox's troop from Fermoy to Cork. On February 20th Captain Gubbins's troop marched from Clogheen to Mallow, and on March 18th Captain Doherty's troop marched from Cork to Limerick. Two days later, on March 20, Napoleon escaped from Elba.

On the 9th of April Colonel Doherty joined at Cork, and resumed the command of the regiment. War was again imminent.

On April 6, 1815, in commemoration of the services during the late war in Portugal, Spain, and France, the regiment received the royal authority to bear on its guidons and appointments the word "PENINSULA," in addition to any other badges or devices.

The notification was made to the regiment on the above date, the honour had been "approved" on March 27, *vide* 'Submissions to the Sovereign,' vol. ii. Colonel Doherty received the medal commemorative of the battle of Vittoria, February 28, 1814. The bar (gold) for Orthes, to wear upon the medal ribbon as an additional mark of distinction, was not bestowed on him until 1st July 1815.

CHAPTER XXIV.

The Waterloo Campaign, 1815.

ON April 20, 1815, orders were received at Cork to prepare six troops of the regiment for immediate service.

The regiment on this date was in decidedly scattered quarters, as will be seen from the following. One troop was at Cork, the headquarters, one each at Mallow, Bandon, Tallow, and Gort, three at Limerick, in addition to which there were various detachments spread about from the several out-stations.

Five days later, by order, the regiment was augmented to ten troops, the whole to consist of 895 men and 775 horses.

The same day the troops from Bandon, Tallow, and Mallow marched into Cork, and were completed for service by Captain Lennox's troop.

On the 28th of April the troops from Limerick marched in, and on the following day were completed for service by Captain Holmes's troop, who marched in from Gort.

At 4 A.M. on April 29th Captain Bowers's troop and a detachment of Captain Gubbins's marched to Cove and embarked.

On May 1st the same took place with the remainder of Captain Gubbins's troop and a portion of Captain Gregorie's. Three days later Major Lawrence's, Captain Doherty's, Major Macallester's troops, and the remainder of Captain Gregorie's, marched and embarked.

The entire embarkation was effected without any accident. The first two detachments sailed at once for Ramsgate, where they were reshipped and sent to Ostend.

Colonel Doherty tells us that the arrangements for the horses on board the ships at Cork were by no means good. The vessels were very small, the horses were very much crowded, and there were but few mangers, while the animals were generally tied up to the sides of the ships.

The regiment now on board consisted of the following numbers, forming six troops. Each troop had 1 troop sergeant-major, 4 sergeants, 4 corporals, 1 trumpeter, 2 farriers, and 59 privates with 66 horses.

The following lists show the officers who sailed with the regiment, those who subsequently joined at Ostend, and those who remained in England:—

Sailed.—Colonel P. Doherty, Captain (Major) B. Lawrence, Captain (Major) Macallester, Captain C. Gregorie, Captain M. Bowers, Lieutenant G. Doherty, Lieutenant J. Drought, Lieutenant C. Bowers, Lieutenant Maclean, Lieutenant R. Nesbitt, Lieutenant J. Geale, Lieutenant H. Acton, Lieutenant J. E. Irving, Lieutenant J. Wallace, Cornet J. Wakefield, Surgeon T. G. Logan, Assistant-Surgeon A. Armstrong, Veterinary-Surgeon J. Constant, Quartermaster W. Minchin, and Paymaster A. Strange.

Officers who joined at Ostend.— Major (Lieut.-Colonel) Boyse, Captain J. Doherty, Captain R. Goulburn, Captain J. Gubbins, Lieutenant J. J. Moss, Lieutenant W. Turner, Lieutenant J. Pymm, Lieutenant J. Mill, and Lieutenant George Pack.

Officers who remained in England.—Major G. Lawrence, Captain S. Holmes, Captain J. Considine, Captain H. M'Neil, Lieutenant W. D'Arcy, Lieutenant J. Major, Cornet J. Trood, Cornet J. Maitland, and Adjutant J. Lawrence.

Later, Lieutenant R. Adams, Cornet J. Atherton, and Cornet J. Ryan, joined from England with a draft of men and remounts.

Adjutant Lawrence was sent out afterwards to join the regiment.

Twenty-eight women and nine children sailed with the regiment.

On May 9, 1815, the vessels weighed anchor and put to sea, but owing to contrary winds and continued bad weather a part of the fleet of transports put back and arrived at Cove on the evening of May 11.

On the 13th the vessels again sailed, this time with better success, as they reached Ostend on May 22.

The headquarters ship, the *Wellington*, which held on its voyage in the first instance, arrived at its destination on May 17,—the troops and horses it carried being immediately disembarked and marched up the country.

On the 22nd the entire regiment, with the exception of the men and horses with Major B. Lawrence who were in the *Prince of Wales* transport, having arrived were similarly landed and despatched up country.

Major B. Lawrence was delayed and did not join the regiment until May 31, on which day Captain Goulburn from England also joined.

Meanwhile the regiment had marched through Bruges, Ecklau, and Ghent to Drongen, in and around which place it went into cantonments.

On May 26th the 13th marched again through Ghent, and in the evening went into cantonments in the villages of Nieuroc, Kerchen, Haelters, and Erembodeghem.

Two days later it changed its quarters to Castre, Herffelinghe, Pepinge, Bogaerden, and Hauteroix.

Next day the 13th marched to Scendelbeck, where the whole of the British cavalry and artillery were assembled under the command of the Earl of Uxbridge. Exclusive of the artillery there were 6000 sabres present.

Here the force was inspected by Lord Wellington, who was accompanied on the occasion by the Prince of Orange and his brother, the Duc de Berri, the Duke of Brunswick-Oels, Field-Marshal Blucher, the Prussian Ambassador, and many other distinguished persons. The army was drawn up in three lines, and having been inspected marched past in parade order, after which the various regiments returned to their several cantonments.

Things remained quiet until June 10. On this date another inspection and review took place, for which purpose the regiment assembled and marched to a plain near the village of Scendelbeck. Here there were also assembled the 11th, 12th, 16th, and 23rd Light Dragoons.

Lord Uxbridge most minutely inspected this fine array of men, and then ordered the performance of a large number of movements. These were done in such a manner as to cause him to express his complete satisfaction, and by his direction a perfect appreciation both of the appearance and the performance of the regiment was communicated in the strongest terms both to officers and men.

Late that evening the regiment returned to cantonments.

Again all was quiet—a quiet which lasted till June 16.

Between 3 and 4 A.M. on the morning of that day orders were received to march to Enghien. The 13th started, but on the road an order arrived to change the route through Briane le Comte to Nivelles.

On arrival at Nivelles the regiment was at once sent towards Quatre Bras.

About one hour before midnight a halt was ordered, and after a twelve-league march the 13th went into bivouac in a wheat-field.

Colonel Doherty, on the morning of the 16th, was so ill with fever and ague that he was utterly unable to leave his bed when the order to march arrived. About noon, however, he managed to mount his horse, and with Assistant-Surgeon Armstrong in attendance made an endeavour to follow the regiment in the hopes of being able to join. He succeeded in reaching Briane le Comte that evening, but in such a state of exhaustion that he was totally unable to proceed. During the night the fever increased, and Assistant-Surgeon Armstrong, taking into consideration that the state of the country was so disturbed and his patient so ill, came to the conclusion that for Colonel Doherty to remain there was not only not calculated to restore him to health, but extremely dangerous. He therefore urged most anxiously that Colonel Doherty should be removed to Brussels. This course was pursued, and by the morning of June 18th he with his patient arrived in that city.

In consequence the command of the regiment devolved on Lieut.-Colonel Boyse.

At daybreak on June 17th the 13th was ready to mount, but not until 8 A.M. did it receive orders to march. The regiment was then directed to join the brigade under Major-General Grant, a brigade consisting of the 7th and 15th Hussars, and posted immediately behind the wood where a severe affair had taken place the previous evening.

It was now ascertained that the British and their Allies were retiring, and that the brigade was employed in covering the retreat.

The infantry, &c., now began to move to the rear. The cavalry brigade continued on the ground until nearly three o'clock, when the enemy were observed debouching from a large wood in heavy columns of cavalry. On these columns the artillery played as long as practicable, and the brigade then began its retreat.

The rear-guard on the road to Brussels was commanded by Major-General Dornberg, and consisted of the 7th Hussars, the 23rd Light Dragoons, and the Life Guards. Major-General Grant retired by another road parallel to the Chaussée; and passed through Lillers, towards Brian le Lend.

When the cavalry arrived on a line with Genappe, the enemy were seen passing through that town. As soon as the French cleared it, Lord Uxbridge attacked them with the 7th Hussars, having the 23rd Light Dragoons in support and the Life Guards in reserve. The fight was for some time obstinately contested, but such a large force of cuirassiers and lancers was brought up by the French and hurled at the 7th Hussars and 23rd Dragoons (who had been joined in the attack), that these regiments were compelled to give way, and they retired behind their reserves.

The Life Guards then moved forward, and charged the enemy in the most gallant manner—broke him, and pursued him for some distance, when they halted, formed, and retired.

The enemy having rallied, again formed and advanced. The Life Guards then delivered a second charge, and for the second time broke and routed the enemy. After this they again retired in admirable order, during which they were exposed to a violent and severe artillery fire. When the 13th and 15th arrived at the Chaussée leading from Brussels to Nivelles with General Grant, a troop from each regiment was detached to cover the march of some baggage which was on that road. Between these two troops and the enemy some skirmishing took place, but the French did not press their attack here, and there was but little molestation during the retreat.

June 18, 1815.

At daylight on the morning of Sunday, June 18, the brigade consisting of the 7th Hussars, 13th Light Dragoons, and 15th Hussars, under the command of Major-General Grant, moved to the right centre of the position occupied by the army, and took up its post on the left of the road leading to Nivelles, in rear of the brigade of Guards commanded by Major-General Byng. A portion of the Guards brigade occupied the house and gardens of Hougomont, and in the rear of this and the orchard, where others of the Guards were, the cavalry brigade took post.

Between 10 and 11 A.M. the furious attacks on Hougomont began, and most sanguinary conflicts took place. But despite the attacks of the enemy again and again renewed, the Guards held their ground and the French were repulsed. Meanwhile the cavalry brigade was exposed to a most heavy artillery fire, which, coupled with musketry, lasted until between 3 and 4 P.M. During this time many casualties took place, men and horses being killed and wounded.

About noon Lieut.-Colonel Boyse had his horse killed under him by a cannon-shot, and in the fall was so severely bruised as to be compelled to leave the field.

The command of the regiment therefore devolved on Major B. Lawrence.

Lieutenant Packe and Lieutenant Irving were about the same time wounded, the former by a splinter of a shell which struck him in the hip, and the latter by a spent ball which hit him in the jaw. Both of these officers were removed to the rear.

The brigade had not, however, been stationary during these long hours. It had been moved more than once, but hitherto no opportunity had arrived for more active operations. However, the enemy now pushed forward two strong columns of cavalry supported by infantry, in an endeavour to force the British position. The cavalry brigade received orders to charge. It charged, and the charge succeeded. The enemy broke and were pursued until the approach of a fresh body of the enemy's cavalry on the left flank was detected.

The brigade then retired and formed in the rear of the infantry. Shortly after the regiment was brought on to the attack by Lord Uxbridge and Lord Hill, and charged a square of the enemy's infantry, which it completely broke, routed, and dispersed. There were several other attacks, till at length the enemy were completely driven from the position. But the losses of the regiment had been most severe. The continual artillery fire of round-shot, shell, and grape, besides musketry, had sadly thinned the ranks. Captain

Captain JAMES GUBBINS.

Killed at Waterloo.

(The uniform is that of his former regiment.)

(*From a Miniature lent by* Major R. R. Gubbins, D.S.O.)

Gubbins was killed by a cannon-shot, Lieutenant Geale and Lieutenant Pymm had both been mortally wounded by musketry fire, while Captain Gregorie and Lieutenant Mill, though with sabre wounds in their hands, yet were able to continue with the regiment in the field.

The afternoon passed, and towards evening the enemy in their last endeavours renewed their attacks, and renewed them with redoubled fury. Forward were sent their massive columns of cavalry and infantry—columns which were received with the utmost determination by the British, and, as all know, repulsed. Lord Hill again ordered up the brigade and also that commanded by General Dornberg, which was formed up on the left. Cheering them on, the two brigades were launched against a heavy column of infantry. At it they rode, delivering their charge amid a most severe and galling fire. But the cavalry brigades were not to be denied. The charge was perfectly successful. The enemy faltered, gave way, and was routed. It was the beginning of the end. In this desperate attack the casualties were also numerous. Lieutenant Doherty received a severe wound: a grape-shot contusion in his groin, which only missed killing him owing to his watch. The watch, a doubled-cased one, was flattened. He was also severely wounded in the head by a musket-shot. Lieutenant Bowers was similarly shot in the head. For nearly three months these two officers lay sick at Brussels, and even when they did join the regiment were not completely cured for some time after. Captain Doherty received a wound in his hand, another a musket-shot in the arm and a contusion in his side by a blow from a sabre. Despite this he did not quit the field. The losses in horses too were heavy. Major Lawrence lost three killed and wounded, and hardly an officer escaped having one at least.

The final period of the battle is too well known to need repetition in anything but the most brief manner. The Prussians arrived, taking the French perpendicularly on the right flank. Against it and the Germans the French could only oppose scattered regiments of the Imperial Guard and the 6th Corps under Lobau. Although these troops fought splendidly, all other organised resistance turned to confusion—confusion which is so often, nay almost always, the precursor of a total rout. The Emperor was finally forced to take refuge in one of the squares of the Guard, and was carried by them safely off the field. The total rout ensued. The British pursuit began, and there is no more than a catalogue of disaster to relate.

Throwing away their arms, their accoutrements, abandoning their guns, caissons, baggage, ammunition, and stores, the vanquished French made the best of their way from the field. After a pursuit of some three miles the brigade was halted and went into bivouac. To the Prussians was committed the duty of keeping the conquered on the run. It was well for the Frenchman who could keep on—he met with scant mercy if overtaken.

Here a letter from Lieutenant William Turner, 13th Light Dragoons, which gives a most graphic account of the Battle of Waterloo and the march to Paris, may well be inserted. It confirms in its main narrative the story of the battle as told in the regimental records and in Colonel Doherty's papers, but it also adds other details which are full of interest.

The letter, which is a long one, runs as follows:—

VILLEPEUT, near PARIS,
3rd July 1815.

MY DEAR BUSBY,—I assure you it is with the greatest pleasure I can find time to inform you I am perfectly sound and in good health and spirits. We marched into this village last night from near Louvres, and are only nine miles from Paris and can distinctly hear the firing, which takes place at Paris, between the Prussian advanced posts and the French. This war cannot possibly last long, for every town and village is completely ransacked, and pillaged by the Prussians and neither wine, spirits, or bread are to be found. The whole country from the frontier to Paris has been laid waste by the march of troops, and the crops nearly destroyed, we are waiting for the Prussians when that infernal City Paris will be attacked and no doubt pillaged, for it is a debt we owe to the whole of Europe, all the inhabitants for leagues round here have taken themselves and their effects into Paris, so that it will be worth taking if we loose 20,000 men. You have no idea of the enthusiasm of the troops and their determination to carry before them everything in their way; the Prussians are also determind soldiers and I expect in one week Paris will be completely sacked and perhaps burned. Our Rocket Brigade went to the front yesterday, and Blucher is much exasperated because they have detained the flags of truce. I will as shortly as possible give you some particulars of what I have seen since I wrote to you at Ghent, three days after I joined the Regiment at Castrés near Grammont, where we were quartered for some days and had a review by Lord Uxbridge with the other Cavalry Regiments. On 15th June I rode to see the City of Brussels 16 miles distant, it is a handsome and pleasant place, returned in the evening home (very fortunately); at 7 next morning 16th instant was rousted out of my bed by a Sergeant to say we were to march immediately, soon turned out but owing to the Regiment being so distributed about the country we were not able to march before 11 A.M., we then marched by Eughien [Enghien], Brainale, Cante and Nivelle and arrived on the field of battle near Genappe about 10 P.M. just as the battle ended, (nothing to eat all day), bivouacked all night in corn, at 3 A.M. turned out, had . . . at 10 A.M. rode over the field of battle which was covered with dead, went to the front when I was near being shot by four Frenchmen, whom I took for Belgians, they all fired but luckily missed me . . . and the officer who was with me retired, and soon after began the retreat. The Cavalry in the rear went slowly, the French followed the Hussars and Life Guards on one road, we and the 15th on the other were about 300 yards distant when the 7th charged and the Life Guards charged in support. We then continued retiring and one of the heaviest showers I ever felt made us wet to the skin, we halted close to the village of Mont St Jean with the whole Army, it was a dreadful rainy night, every man in the Cavalry wet to the skin and nearly all the Infantry as bad; nothing to eat all day, being without rations and our baggage at Brussels. At 4 A.M. on the memorable 18th June turned out and formed on the field of battle in wet corn and a cold morning without anything to eat, nothing but some gin, which I purchased from a German woman, saved and enabled me and three other officers to stand the fatigues of the day. About 10 A.M. the French began to move large columns of troops in our front, and about half-past eleven the Battle began, we were put with the 15th and commanded by General Grant, we were on the right of the great road and nearly the right of our line, we covered the Artillery of Captain Macdonald's troop who behaved well, before two o'clock we had three officers and several men killed by Cannon Balls and Shells, we were then put close to some Belgian Artillery, to keep them to their guns and there we suffered from musketry and round-shot; we then moved to the right of the line to charge the French Lancers but they retired. We then came back to our place close to the Artillery which the French Imperial Guard à Cheval and Cuirassiers had taken, we immediately formed up in line with the 15th, gave three cheers, and went at them full speed, they retired immediately and we charged after them all down their position up to their Infantry, when we were ordered to retire, which we did but in confusion, we formed and told off again having lost a good many men; I shot one Frenchman with my pistol but did not use my sword, (I had the misfortune to break the double barrelled one in marching up the country or else I should have shot two); at 4 P.M. the French Cavalry came up again but on our trotting to meet them they immediately retired, we then came back on our side of the hill beyond our guns; the Battle was now most dreadful and the field covered with dead and dying in all directions. Lord Wellington repeatedly passed us, when we Huzzared him; the French Cavalry advanced again to the muzzle of our guns, the Gunners were ordered to retire and we charged them again in the grandest style between our masses of Infantry; they retreated and we charged them close to their Infantry, who were formed in Squares the same as ours; in this charge I am sorry to say the black mare I purchased from Paddock, got two musket balls in her close to my leg just behind the shoulder joint, it was with difficulty I got her to the rear of the Artillery when I dismounted and sent her to the rear by a Dragoon, whose horse I mounted as he was; we still continued retiring on guns when the havoc amongst us was dreadful, one cannon-ball killed General Grant's horse, Col. Dalrymple's horse and took off his leg, it then passed between Wallace and me, we remained here still exposed, every minute some man or horse falling, Captain Goulburg (Goulburn?) at whose side I was, had just mounted a trooper after having had his horse wounded, when he was knocked off by a spent ball but fortunately without injury, about half-past six we charged again down the hill and then retreated to our guns; again about 8 P.M. the great attack was made when the French were repulsed, we were immediately ordered to charge as our Infantry were . . . General Hill came in our front and called out "now 13th come on" he took of his hat with several other Generals we immediately Huzzared with the whole of the Infantry and charged, the French retired in the greatest confusion, our Infantry advancing kept us at a trot for three miles when we with the whole of the Cavalry pursued them about three miles further when darkness, at 9 P.M. put an end to the slaughter, the last charge was literally riding over men and horses, who lay in heaps; such is the account of the battle I myself saw and can vouch for the general particulars you have in the despatches and newspapers. I assure you our Regiment had been without rations since Thursday, and it was not till Monday evening June 19th that we got our meat, I luckily had one fowl and some mouldy bread in four days. We bivouacked for the night and next day advanced and have continued to do so (except one day) ever since we crossed the frontier (near B——) on the 21st June, the Cavalry have advanced here chiefly by cross country roads through the fields as it is not enclosed as in England. I have heard since of the Black mare and find she is in Brussels and hope she will recover but have no great hopes, she is an excellent charger. Our loss in Officers is Captain Gubbins killed, do. Pym (Pymm), do. Gale (Geale), the two former by cannon-balls, two Lieutenants severely wounded and five slightly, seven or eight Officers had their horses shot and wounded under them, and General Grant had five horses shot under him. When the Regiment mustered after the action at 10 P.M., that night we had only 65 men left out of 260 who went into the field in the morning, the rest were either killed, wounded, or missing, the 15th have also suffered most dreadfully as well as the whole of the Cavalry, and yet notwithstanding such losses we are as ripe and anxious to try our fortune once more at Paris and settle the peace of Europe. You may expect and depend upon everything from the English and Prussians who will go hand and heart together as brothers. I must finish for the Bugle sounds for . . . but I hope not to march this day.

In the official list of wounded occurs the name of Captain William Moray, 13th Light Dragoons, extra A.D.C. to Major-General Grant, severely. His name is not, however, included in the Regimental List of Casualties.

LORD HILL AND THE 13TH LIGHT DRAGOONS AT WATERLOO. "DRIVE THEM BACK, 13TH"

In the Roll of Depot Troops, however, we find that Captain M. M'Neil remained in England in command of a troop when the regiment sailed on May 9th for Ostend. He exchanged into the 17th Light Dragoons on 29th June 1815 (Army List).

William Moray was a lieutenant in the 17th Light Dragoons, 19th October 1804; Captain, 11th February 1808; exchanged into 13th Light Dragoons, 29th June 1815; Major, 13th Light Dragoons, 21st June 1817; exchanged into the 19th Light Dragoons later, and retired on Irish half-pay as a Major in 1822.

In the Regimental Record of "Succession of Captains" the name of Captain Moray is numbered 53, and the date of his Regimental Commission is marked "unknown." In the list of "Succession of Majors" his name does not occur.

Probably Captain Moray never either joined at the depot or did duty with the regiment before the campaign, but by influence went out to the campaign as A.D.C. to General Grant. Hence he is not mentioned by Colonel Doherty.

The following are the names of the officers who were present and fought with the regiment at the battle of Waterloo:—

Major (Lieut.-Colonel) Boyse, Captain (Major) B. Lawrence, Captain Doherty, Captain (Major) Macallester, Captains Bowers, Gregorie, Gubbins, and Goulburn; Lieutenants Moss, Doherty, Drought, Bowers, Maclean, Nisbett, Turner, Pymm, Mill, J. Geale, Packe, Acton, Irving, and Wallace. Cornet Wakefield was with the baggage.

Of the staff there was with the regiment in the field Surgeon Logan, Veterinary-Surgeon Constant, and Regimental Quartermaster Minchin.

Six officers were slightly and two severely wounded.

Three sergeant-majors and six sergeants, two corporals and two trumpeters were wounded, and fifty-two privates.

Eight privates were missing, and of these only one — William Rapier — joined; the remaining seven, being presumably killed, were struck off the strength of the regiment.

Twelve privates were killed on the field of battle; two reported only wounded were afterwards found to have been killed. Three of those reported wounded subsequently died of their wounds.

The following table shows the loss sustained by the regiment at Waterloo:—

	Officers.	Sergeant-Majors.	Sergeants.	Corporals.	Trumpeters.	Privates.
Killed	3	...	...	...	...	12
Wounded	8	3	6	2	2	52
Missing	...	...	...	...	...	8
Total	11	3	6	2	2	72

Horses killed, 15; wounded, 46; missing, 52; total, 113.

Grand Total: 96 men and 113 horses.

After the death of Captain James Gubbins and the disablement of the other officers of the troop, the command devolved upon Troop Sergeant-Major Edward Wells. His gallant conduct on the occasion was particularly remarked, and in the following year he received a commission.

The date of his enlistment in the 13th does not appear. He was a sergeant in Captain Stisted's (Gubbins's) troop in 1810. Between that date and 1815 he must have been promoted to Troop Sergeant-Major.

Edward Wells was gazetted Ensign in the 2nd West India Regiment, June 26, 1816; Lieutenant in the 54th Regiment, December 25, 1823; Captain in the 54th Regiment, July 1, 1836; and he retired from the service in 1841.

For its gallant service at the battle of Waterloo the 13th Light Dragoons received the following honours:—

By royal authority the word "WATERLOO" was in future to be borne on the guidons and appointments.

Every officer and soldier present received a silver medal, and the privilege of reckoning two years' service for that day was also conferred on the troops.

Colonel Patrick Doherty and Lieut.-Colonel Shapland Boyse were both made Companions of the Bath.

On June 19, the day following the victory at Waterloo, the regiment continued in pursuit, or rather in pressing on in the wake of the defeated and retreating French army—an army that had during the night suffered much at the hands of the pursuing Prussians. That evening, after a march of eight leagues, the 13th went into bivouac near Nivelles. Next morning the march was resumed, and that night the site of the bivouac was near Binch. On June 21st the regiment marched five leagues to a bivouac near Gommeyries. The next night the bivouac was near Montaige—a shorter march of only three leagues. The distance covered on the 23rd to a bivouac near Beaumont was four leagues, and then the regiment halted for a day. Resuming the march on the 25th, the 13th arrived near Beaurevon, a distance of six leagues, and again went into bivouac. The same distance was covered on the 26th, when the regiment bivouacked near Betham Court. Six leagues next day brought the 13th to a bivouac near Armancourt. After a march of seven leagues on the 28th the neighbourhood of Latouce was reached, on the 29th to near Equippe, and on the 30th to near Boisseau, distances of six and nine leagues respectively, and the 13th went into bivouac each night. After a halt on July 1st the regiment marched two leagues till it had arrived near Villa Puite, where going into bivouac a halt was ordered which lasted until July 7. On that day the 13th marched nine leagues, and arrived at Genevillier, where it went into quarters and remained until July 30.

During its stay at Genevillier detachments from the regiment were employed daily in and around Paris, where numerous posts had to be taken up and a share of the duties of the Army of Occupation to be performed. Reviews and inspections of the British troops and their Allies were also held by the allied sovereigns then in the city.

On July 30th the regiment marched daily until August 4, the halting-places being Lazarches, six leagues; Clermont, six leagues; Breteuil, six leagues; Amiens, four leagues; Flexieurt, five leagues; and Abbeville, five leagues.

Here the regiment was distributed in the town and the neighbourhood. Captain Doherty's troop was stationed at Abbeville, the troops of Lieut.-Colonel Lawrence and Captain Gregorie at Gemashe; those of Major Macallester and Captain Bowers at Halincourt, and the troop of Captain Goulburn at Mayeuville. But these quarters were very wide of each other, and the arrangement was found to be most inconvenient.

On August 9, Colonel Doherty arrived at Abbeville from Brussels and resumed the command of the regiment. The 13th was then brigaded with the 1st Hussars of the King's German Legion, and the brigade placed under the command of Colonel Baron Sir F. Arentschildts of the latter.

Next day the troop commanded by Major Macallester marched to Huppy, and that of Captain Goulburn to Peuffle.

The inconveniences attaching to the division of the regiment now led to representations being made on the matter to the civil authorities of Abbeville. In consequence some large houses were fitted up for the regiment as barracks in the town, and a riding-school was converted into a stable, which with the stables already occupied was sufficient to accommodate all, and the 13th was soon brought together again. The troops of Lieut.-Colonel Lawrence and Captain Gregorie marched in on August 25, those of Major Macallester and Captain Bowers on September 2, and that of Captain Goulburn on September 8. The officers now for the first time had an opportunity of forming a mess. Here the 13th remained brigaded with the 1st Hussars of the King's German Legion until December 3, when it marched to Trevent *en route* for St Pol. On the same day the German Hussars started for Hanover.

Prior to the march the half-yearly inspection was held by Colonel Arentschildts.

The march on the 3rd was a distance of nine leagues, over an extremely bad road.

On December 3rd the regiment arrived at St Pol, marching five leagues, and the troops were distributed in St Pol and the neighbouring villages of Marquet, Hernicourt, Croix, Braile, and Hentecloque.

On December 6th thirteen horses were received from the 23rd Light Dragoons, and one from the Waggon-Train, a receipt for which was passed. Thirty-one horses cast from the 13th Light Dragoons by order of Lord Combermere were delivered to the 23rd Light Dragoons.

Two days later forty-seven horses from the Royals, twenty-nine from the Greys, and thirty-three from the Inniskillings, were received by the regiment.

On January 9, 1816, Lieutenant Adams, Cornets Ryan and Atherton, with a detachment consisting of one sergeant and seventy-six rank and file, joined the regiment at St Pol from the depôt in England.

Major-General Grant having gone home, the command of the brigade, now consisting of the 11th, 13th, 15th, and a troop of horse artillery, devolved on Colonel Doherty, in consequence of which Lieut.-Colonel Boyse took the command of the regiment.

On January 12th the regiment and the horse artillery marched to Lilliers, a distance of six leagues, and continuing the next day arrived at Hazebrouck, seven leagues beyond. Here the 13th was cantoned as follows. The troops of Major Macallester and Captain Goulburn at Bailleul, that of Captain Doherty at Steenworde, that of Captain Bowers at Morbeck, that of Captain Gregorie at Castre and St Silvestre, that of Lieut.-Colonel Lawrence at Berguin and in the neighbourhood. Hazebrouck was occupied by the staff and headquarters. The horse artillery moved to Cassel and went into quarters.

On January 18th the troop of Lieut.-Colonel Lawrence marched to Steinbeck. Having got a monastery fitted up by arrangement with the civil authorities as barracks at Hazebrouck, the troop of Captain Doherty, with the addition of the young and awkward men and horses of the other five troops, marched in and were quartered there. On February 2nd Captain Goulburn's troop marched to Borr and proceeded on the 4th to Merville. The troop of Major Macallester was also moved on the 2nd, marching to Oxillare.

Thus the regiment rested until March 20, when General Grant joined, having returned from England and resumed the command of the brigade. Colonel Doherty in consequence reverted to his regimental command.

The time for the regiment to return to England was now approaching.

On April 17th two sergeants, two corporals, one farrier, and eighteen privates mounted were delivered over to Major During for the service of the Staff Cavalry Corps. There were already three men from the regiment employed on that duty.

Orders for England having arrived, the regiment on May 6th was inspected by Lord Combermere, and certain horses were by him selected for transfer to other regiments.

Fifty-six horses went to the 11th Light Dragoons, one hundred and twenty-four to the 12th Light Dragoons, and eighty-one to the 15th Hussars,—making a total, when the twenty-six already transferred to the Staff Cavalry Corps are included, of two hundred and eighty-seven horses.

On the 7th May the 13th marched from Hazebrouck, on its return to England, putting up that night at the villages near St Omer. It appears that the French did not admit any troops into their garrison towns. The baggage was, however, passed through, and sent by boats from St Omer to Calais.

Next evening the regiment put up in the villages between St Omer and Calais.

It had been intended to embark on the next day, but the weather was so tempestuous that no embarkation could possibly take place. However, on May 10, 1816, the regiment proceeded on board at Calais. The horses were placed in Dover Packets accompanied by the men to whom they belonged; the dismounted men being conveyed in transports. And here, cooped up on board ship, the regiment had to remain until May 13, as the weather rendered it quite impossible to proceed to sea with any probability of making a passage.

On the 13th, however, at 3 P.M., the vessels weighed anchor and put to sea. The first vessel reached Dover in four hours, the last at 11 P.M. that night. On the next morning the regiment disembarked at Dover, after an absence of a little more than a year.

During that period it had been through a most arduous though brief campaign. It had marched 234 leagues (French) or 702 miles. It had lost in killed, died, and discharged in consequence of wounds, three officers, sixty-five men, and two hundred and four horses. To other corps it had transferred twenty-six men and two hundred and eighty-seven horses. From France only sixty-two horses were brought back to England.

CHAPTER XXV.

England, 1816-1818.

IMMEDIATELY after disembarkation on May 14, 1819, the regiment marched to Canterbury, proceeding on the following day *en route* for Romford, Essex, where it arrived on the 20th.

The depôt of the regiment being quartered there in consequence joined.

Ten days later an order arrived for the reduction of the 2nd Lieutenants.

The following officers were therefore placed on the half-pay list, though they were kept upon full pay until July 24: Lieutenants W. T. Buchanan, Henry Acton, John Wallace, J. Æneas Irving, J. H. Maitland, and John Trood.

Lieutenant J. Æneas Irving, however, returned to the regiment in 1816, *vice* Adams.

A reduction of ten horses per troop also took place almost immediately after the arrival of the regiment in England, the establishment of horses now standing at 501.

On June 3rd the regiment was inspected by H.R.H. The Commander-in-Chief, attended by the Adjutant-General, the Quartermaster-General, and Major-General Bolton, the Inspector-General of Cavalry (formerly Lieutenant-Colonel of the 13th Light Dragoons, 1797-1799). On this occasion the regiment was headed by its Colonel, The Hon. Sir Henry George Grey.

Next day Colonel Doherty went on leave, and the command of the regiment devolved on Major Lawrence, as Lieut.-Colonel Boyse was also absent.

Marching orders having arrived, the regiment left Romford on the 5th June, with the exception of the troop commanded by Captain Moray, which marched on the following day. York was the destination of the 13th, and it proceeded thither in this order.

The troops commanded by Major Macallester and Captain Considine were timed to arrive at Newmarket on the 8th; those commanded by Lieut.-Colonel Lawrence and Captain Doherty to reach Bury St Edmunds on the 8th; those commanded by Captain Gregorie and Captain Bowers to reach Ely on the 9th. The troop commanded by Captain Holmes was due at Peterborough on the 12th.

When or where Captain Moray joined the regiment, unless he was commanding a troop at the depôt, does not appear, but he marched thence for York on the 6th, being timed to reach Cambridge on the 9th.

In consequence of disturbances taking place in the neighbourhood of Bury, Ely, &c., this arrangement was not adhered to.

On July 6th the squadron which had reached Bury St Edmunds marched for Cambridge, halting one night at Newmarket and reaching Cambridge on the 7th. On the 11th three squadrons continued their march to York, where the 1st division, consisting of the troops commanded by Captain Holmes and Captain Moray, arrived on the 18th. The 2nd division, consisting of the troops commanded by Major Macallester and Captain Considine, arrived the next day. The 3rd division, consisting of Lieut.-Colonel Lawrence's and Captain Doherty's troops, arrived on the 20th, and two days later the 4th division, consisting of the troops commanded by Captains Bowers and Gregorie, marched in.

On the 23rd Major Macallester's troop marched from York for Carlisle, and the troops of Captains Gregorie and Moray for Newcastle-on-Tyne.

The next day Captain Bowers's troop marched to Tadcaster.

On July 27th a detachment under the command of Lieutenant Turner, and consisting of one sergeant, two corporals, and twenty-eight privates mounted, marched for Stockton-on-Tees.

The troop from Tadcaster returned on August 9th and went into quarters.

On the 14th September, on the requisition of the Mayor of Hull, who was apprehensive of serious riots in that place, a mounted detachment with Captain Holmes, Lieutenant Major, Cornet Ryan, and forty men proceeded thither, returning to York on the 23rd.

On October 1st Captain Doherty's troop marched to Pontefract, where it went into quarters.

In November the troops commanded by Lieut.-Colonel Lawrence, and Captains Bowers, Considine, and Holmes, were inspected at York by Major-General Sir R. Bolton. A few days previous to this inspection orders had been received for a reduction of the establishment of the regiment, which was in future to consist of 509 men and 333 horses. The recruiting parties were also withdrawn.

Early in December a detachment under the command of Lieut.-Colonel Lawrence, and consisting of Lieutenant Doherty, Cornet Handcock, forty men and forty horses of Captain Bowers's and Lawrence's troops, marched to Tadcaster to wait orders from the magistrates of Leeds, who were apprehensive of serious riots in that place.

This detachment returned on December 11.

1817-1818.

During the first half of 1817 detachments of the regiment were sent from York to aid the civil authorities in various places. Such was the unsettled state of the country that disturbances and riots were of most frequent occurrence. Robbery, violence, arson, and murder, were committed by the mobs who collected. Arms were looted from the gunsmiths' shops, even in London. By means of the enrolment of special constables it was possible for the civil authorities at times to cope with the disorders, but more frequently mayors and magistrates invoked the assistance of the military forces.

However truculent the mob might be in presence of the local authorities, or the special constables, or even of the militia, the appearance of a detachment of light dragoons was generally sufficient to disperse any seditious gathering.

It is undoubtedly true that times were what is called "bad." Works and collieries had closed, furnaces had shut down, the introduction of machinery had lessened the demand for labour, and, above all, bread was terribly dear. People who suffered, and had suffered for no little time under such conditions, were ready to listen to agitators and ripe to fall in with their views. They must, of course, be blamed; they can, however, be pitied.

In 1816 five men were condemned at Ely, and hanged—the Government made an example of them; but it was merciful enough to refuse to prosecute some 65 or 70 others who had been arrested at the same time. To act on the requisition of the mayor or magistrates, under such circumstances, was a duty, and as such had to be performed, but acting in aid of the civil power was even then most unpopular among the soldiers so employed. In these days to "call out the military," as the phrase goes, is a rare—a very rare—event. In those it was comparatively a common occurrence. In these days troops are only employed as a rule on such service when all other means have failed, and after much damage has been done, and probably many persons injured. In those, the authorities, policeless as they were, summoned the troops to their aid when they anticipated, or thought they anticipated, trouble. They had, indeed, no other course they could pursue, as no force existed save the military, to stand between peace-loving and law-abiding citizens, and law-breaking though maybe deluded mobs of riotous rogues.

The list of the various expeditions made during 1817 by detachments of the 13th in aid of the civil powers is as follows:—

February 9th.—Captain Holmes, Cornet Morris, and 48 men and 40 horses, marched to Beverley, as the magistrates of Hull anticipated a riot there by the fishermen of the Greenland Fishery (whalers). This detachment did not return till May 9.

March 8th.—Major Lawrence, Lieutenants Doherty and Turner, and Cornet Handcock, with 115 men and 100 horses, marched to Leeds, serious rioting being apprehended. This display of force was sufficient to overawe any intended evil-doing, and within six days it was back again at York.

March 28th.—Lieut.-Colonel Boyse, Lieutenants Major, Doherty, and Nisbett, with 89 men and 82 horses, marched to Wakefield on similar duty, and returned on April 4.

May 10th.—Captain Doherty's troop, which had been at Pontefract since October 1, 1816, joined at York. This troop returned to Pontefract on May 15, having only marched to York for the purpose of being inspected together with the troops of Lieut.-Colonel Lawrence, Captain Bowers, Captain Considine, and Captain Holmes. The inspecting officer was Major-General Sir John Byng.

June 7th.—Captain Bowers, Captain Holmes, Lieutenant Turner, Cornet Stones, and Cornet Morris, with 102 men and 100 horses, marched to Leeds, where serious trouble was expected. Captain Bowers, with 51 men and 50 horses, returned to York on June 20; Captain Holmes, with the remainder of the detachment, proceeded from Leeds to Huddersfield and did not return till July 1.

On July 9th Captain Gregorie's and Captain Moray's troops marched into York from Newcastle-on-Tyne. The 13th was now under orders to proceed to Brighton. On the same day (July 9) the troops commanded by Lieut.-Colonel Lawrence and Captain Considine marched from York for Brighton.

Next day the troop commanded by Captain Doherty left Pontefract, and that commanded by Captain Bowers left York, for Brighton. On the 18th the troops commanded by Captain Gregorie and Captain Moray marched for Brighton, and on the following morning the troops commanded by Major Macallester and Holmes went thither. Nine days later, four troops, those commanded by Lieut.-Colonel Lawrence, Captain Bowers, Captain Doherty, and Captain Considine, were inspected on Wimbledon Common by Major-General Sir Robert Bolton.

On July 29th Captain Doherty's troop left Kingston for Brighton, and Captain Bowers's troop marched to Chichester, Lieut.-Colonel Lawrence's troop proceeded to Hastings, and Captain Considine's to Eastbourne. On July 31st the troops commanded by Captains Gregorie and Moray marched to Brentford, and Captain Doherty's troop arrived at Brighton. On August 1st Major Macallester's and Captain Holmes's troops marched to Richmond.

Four troops were now near London, and these were inspected on Wimbledon Common by Sir Robert Bolton on August 4. They were the troops commanded by Major Macallester and Captains Gregorie, Holmes, and Moray.

Next morning the two first-named troops marched to Brighton from Richmond, Captain Holmes went from Richmond to Arundel, and Captain Moray from Kingston to Brighton.

These three troops reached Brighton Barracks on August 7.

At Brighton the greater part of the regiment remained until December. An inspection of the troops of Captain Doherty, Major Macallester, Captain Gregorie, and Captain Moray, by Major-General Sir R. Bolton, took place on November 24; and on December 3rd these four troops marched from Brighton for Hastings, Arundel, Chichester, and Eastbourne respectively, replacing the four troops who had been there in quarters. These returned to Brighton, arriving on the 3rd, 5th, and 6th. On December 29th an order was received to transfer twenty horses to the Cavalry Staff Corps at Frome in Somerset.

During March 1818, the four troops in Brighton changed with those in Arundel, Chichester, Eastbourne, and Hastings, where they remained until May, with one brief change, when orders were received for the regiment to proceed to Manchester.

On May 23rd the troops of Lieut.-Colonel Lawrence and Captain Bowers marched to Manchester; the troops of both the Captains Doherty—G. Doherty having been promoted—marched from Arundel to Chertsey; while Lieut.-Colonel Lawrence and Captain Bowers halted at Weybridge.

These four troops, on May 26, marched thence to Hounslow Heath, where they kept the ground on the occasion of a review of the Life Guards, the Blues, the 10th Hussars, and the 19th Lancers. On the following day they continued their march to Manchester.

June 1st.—The troops of Captain Considine and Captain Moray marched from Arundel and Chichester to Manchester, and were followed on the next day by those of Major Macallester and Captain Gregorie.

The first detachment of four troops reached Manchester on June 11, whence on the 14th Lieut.-Colonel Lawrence's troop marched to Kendal. On June 18th Captain Considine's and Captain Moray's troops arrived at Manchester Barracks.

On the 25th Lieut.-Colonel Lawrence's troop returned from Kendal. Four days later Major Macallester's troop joined, and on the 30th Captain Gregorie's troop arrived. The regiment being now together, it was inspected by Major-General Sir R. Bolton.

In consequence of riots taking place in Stockport, Captain Considine's troop marched there on July 16. A part of the troop returned to Manchester on the 23rd. One month later Captain

Bowers and a detachment were sent to the same place, but returned to Manchester on the same day.

On the last day of August the regiment was inspected by Major-General Sir John Byng. A few days later the following changes took place. Major Macallester's troop marched to Blackburn, Captain J. Doherty's to Bolton, and thence to Preston, while Captain (now Major) Moray's proceeded to Bolton.

Orders were now received for the regiment to proceed to India, and in consequence the establishment of the 13th was augmented on October 25th to 701 men and 701 horses.

Towards the end of December, the outlying troops from Blackburn, Bolton, and Preston marched in to Manchester, where the regiment was inspected by Major-General Sir R. Bolton on December 29. On December 31st the regiment left Manchester in two divisions.

The first division, consisting of the troops commanded by Lieut.-Colonel Lawrence, Captain J. Doherty, Captain G. Doherty, and Captain Gregorie, marched on that date, arriving at Romford Barracks on January 16. The second division, consisting of the troops commanded by Major Macallester, Captain Considine, Captain Bowers, and Captain Moray, started on January 1, 1819, and reached Romford Barracks on January 18.

A transfer of horses prior to embarking for India took place. 133 were delivered to the 18th Hussars, 133 to the 7th Hussars, 31 to the 19th Lancers, and 23 were cast and sold.

On February 8th the regiment marched from Romford to Tilbury and embarked for India, sailing the next day.

CHAPTER XXVI.

India, 1819-1840.

AFTER a voyage lasting from February 9 to June 13, the regiment on that date arrived at Madras. On disembarkation it was marched into Fort St George, where it remained until the 10th of July.

Marching for Arcot on that day, the future station of the 13th Light Dragoons was reached on July 19.

In the preceding pages the history of the regiment has been traced from its raising. The story of its two campaigns against the Jacobite rebels has been narrated, the disastrous losses of the regiment by yellow fever in the West Indies have been recorded, and the hardships and glories of the Peninsula and Waterloo campaigns have been dealt with in detail. We now arrive at a period of no less than twenty years' duration, when no call was made on the 13th to display its proved prowess in the field on active service. For it was not until March 1839 that any portion of the regiment was employed in forming a part of an Expeditionary Force. For all these long years of peace—inspections, reviews, the joining of remounts, the transfer of horses, and similar notices, are the only events which exist to be chronicled. As a catalogue, they cannot be said to be interesting, still, for the sake of accuracy and continuity, the record of them must be duly set forth here; though with the brevity which their absolute lack of interest warrants.

On July 30, 1819, the regiment was inspected at Arcot by Major-General Browne—and similar inspections took place on October 13 and 14.

The 21st Light Dragoons during September were presumably

under orders for England, and from that regiment thirteen privates volunteered and joined the 13th.

During October 389 men volunteered from the 22nd Light Dragoons and joined the 13th.

On October 24th eighty remount horses joined.

During October and November two very large drafts of horses were made over to the regiment from the 22nd Light Dragoons, amounting to 415 and 120 respectively.

From the Army List we find that the 21st Light Dragoons were disbanded at Chatham in May 1820, and the 22nd in July of that year, and at the same place.

On February 1, 1820, the 13th marched from Arcot for Bangalore, at which station it arrived on February 19.

During May, on the 3rd, 6th, and 13th, the regiment was inspected by Major-General Hare.

A remount of 191 horses joined the 13th from Koongul on June 15.

On July 4th a review of the regiment was held at Bangalore by Major-General Sir W. G. Keir.

A draft of nine men from the depôt in England joined on September 27.

The regiment was inspected by Major-General Sewell at Bangalore on the 28th and 31st of October, and November 1.

There is no entry until May 1821, when on the 14th, 15th, 16th, and 18th, an inspection was held by Lieut.-General Bowser.

On June 14th six men joined at Poonawallee from the depôt in England.

Inspections by Lieut.-General Bowser were held at Bangalore on October 24, 1821, and May 9, 1822.

On July 31st seventy remount horses joined from Koongul.

On September 23rd forty men joined the regiment from the depôt in England.

Inspections were held by Lieut.-General Bowser on October 4, 1822, and on May 15, 1823.

On June 19th twenty-two men joined from England, and on August 3rd forty-six remount horses were received from Koongul.

Lieut.-General Bowser inspected the regiment on December 12, 1823, and again on May 18, 1824.

For the next three years there is absolutely nothing to record.

Men joined the regiment at intervals and in numbers varying from two to forty. Horses were received from Koongul as remounts, and some were transferred to the 2nd Light Cavalry, to the "Horse Brigade," and to the 1st Light Cavalry.

The inspecting officers were Major-General Jewell in May 1825, Major-General Sir T. Pritzler, K.C.B., in December 1825 and in May 1826, while in December 1826, in May 1827, and again in December of that year, the inspecting officer was Major-General Sir John Doveton, K.C.B.

In all, 152 men joined the regiment from England, 159 horses were received from Koongul, and 105 horses were delivered over to regiments of native cavalry.

On July 15, 1826, the 13th Light Dragoons marched from Bangalore to Arcot.

Between January 1828 and April 1829 the history of the regiment may be summarised as follows:—

Seventy-nine men joined the regiment from England, three having died on the voyage; 258 horses were transferred to native cavalry regiments, 90 were cast and sold, and 250 joined from Koornul and Oossoor, of which 90 were young horses.

Major-General Sir John Doveton, K.C.B., inspected the regiment on May 1, 1828, and also on December 30th and 31st of that year.

Owing to the cholera which prevailed in the cantonments at Arcot, the regiment marched out and went into camp on February 15, 1828, and proceeded on March 3rd from that encampment to cantonments at Arnee, where it arrived on the following day. Here the regiment remained for a year, when it returned to Bangalore, arriving there on April 8.

On May 27th the regiment was inspected at line duties by Major-General Sir T. Pritzler, K.C.B., and three days later dismounted by the same officer.

Between August 4, 1829, and December 31, 1830, one hundred and sixty-six men joined the regiment, all of whom came from England, except nine who volunteered from the 47th Foot. Forty-seven remount horses joined from Oossoor. On December 30, 1829, the regiment was inspected by Colonel Armstrong commanding at Bangalore.

An inspection in marching order and ball-practice was held on

OFFICER, 13TH LIGHT DRAGOONS (1832).

(Scarlet Tunic.)

(*Lent by* Lieut.-Colonel A. LEETHAM.)

January 14, 1830, and on the following day the regiment was reviewed by the same officer.

On May 27, 1830, and the two following days, Major-General Sir T. Pritzler, K.C.B., held inspections of the regiment, dismounted and at riding drill, followed by a review.

For four days in December the same officer held inspections and a review, dismounted (December 8), riding-school order (December 10), review (December 13), and ball-practice in marching order (December 15).

During 1831 forty-four horses were cast and transferred to the Commissariat, and one hundred artillery horses were received from Oossoor. Thirty men joined from the depôt in England. During May, Major-General T. Hawker inspected the regiment—dismounted, saddlery, accoutrements, barrack-rooms, and horse lines. He also held a review on December 1, and on the following day examined the saddlery, cloaks, hospital, canteens, barracks, &c.

In addition to these inspections, His Excellency Lieut.-General Sir George Walker, G.C.B., K.C.I., Commander-in-Chief of the Madras Army, reviewed the regiment on September 13, and early in October held an inspection of the barracks, school, canteen, stores, &c., and the regiment dismounted.

The Mutiny at Bangalore.

In the month of October 1832 the existence of a plot to mutiny and murder all the European officers and soldiers in Bangalore was discovered.

As no account of this serious matter is to be found in histories, and as the destruction of the 13th Light Dragoons formed part of the conspiracy, the details may well be inserted here.

The mutiny was timed to break out at midnight on the 28th of October. Up to the morning of that day no suspicion even was entertained by either European officers, soldiers, or officials.

The mutineers were Mussulmans, and if the outbreak at Bangalore had proved successful, it was to be followed by similar outbreaks at Bellary, Jaulnah, Hyderabad, and Nagpore. Doubtless, too, it would have spread far and wide.

To Major Inglis, commanding the 48th Native Infantry, however, on the morning of October 28th came Jemadar Emaun Khan, a native officer of his regiment, and to the astonishment of his commanding officer revealed the whole plot. Prompt measures were at once taken, the European regiments then at Bangalore, the 62nd Foot and the 13th Light Dragoons, were immediately warned. Parties were sent out, and all those named by the Jemadar were immediately arrested. The ringleader was a certain Hyder Ali Khan, who liked to be styled the "Nawaub," and who lived in the Pettah of Bangalore. With him were associated Syfut Ali Shah, a fakir who pretended to be an alchemist, and who promised those who joined the conspirators pecuniary rewards in this world and rewards of another, but equally satisfactory, nature in the next. A Mussulman buttermerchant was also deeply implicated.

Had, however, the sedition been confined to these civilian natives, it would not have been particularly formidable, but unfortunately several havildars and sepoys of the native horse artillery, and certain regiments of native infantry and cavalry, had been seduced from their allegiance, and, what is more, would probably have received a certain amount of support from their comrades when once the trouble had begun.

A court of inquiry was held on Tuesday, October 30, and continued its sittings till Sunday, November 4.

The story of this plot is as follows: For some little time Hyder Ali Khan, the "Nawaub" as he pleased to call himself, had lived in the Pettah at Bangalore. He appeared to be well supplied with money, and exercised not a little hospitality; his main endeavour being at first to attract to his house as many sepoys and native officers of the Company's service as he could, particularly those of the Native Horse Artillery. He had also entered into communication with, and enlisted in his design, a goodly number of disbanded troopers and discharged sepoys who had formerly been in the service of the Rajah of Mysore. Some two or three hundred Pindarees, too, were prepared to join when the signal of revolt was given. It happened, too, that certain details of light cavalry had left Bangalore for Mysore on the 25th under the command of a subadar major. Arrangements had been made to intercept this force, and with the aid of certain mutineers who belonged to it to murder the officers if true to their salt, and then to return and join their comrades at Bangalore. If the subadar chose to throw in his lot with the mutineers, all the better. The Vakeel of the Coorg Rajah also had promised 12,000 horse and 7000 foot to be at Bangalore by daybreak on the 29th, provided he received news that the mutiny had really taken place.

By means of a clever ruse a havildar favourable to the conspiracy had been appointed on the Mysore gate at Bangalore for that night, and his task was to open it and admit the mutineers. How this appointment was managed is worth relating. It appears that his brother, also a mutineer, met the havildar major coming out of the Adjutant's quarters. To the havildar major he presented a couple of silk handkerchiefs which had been provided for the purpose by the "Nawaub." The handkerchiefs were accepted and the traitor then proceeded to ask a favour. "As my child's ear is diseased," said he, "and the doctors tell me that the blood of swallows is good for it, if you will put my brother on the Mysore gate he will be able to get some for me." The petition was granted, and Shaik Ismael, havildar in the 9th Native Infantry, was duly posted on the gate. The mutineers designed to divide themselves into three bodies. The first was to be admitted through the Mysore gate, where the arsenal and magazine were to be seized and arms distributed, the European guard having been killed. Next the European Main guard was to share the same fate, after which the garden of the general commanding the district (Major-General Hawker) was to be surrounded, and that officer murdered. A gun was then to be fired from the ramparts, and a green flag displayed. This gun was to be a signal for the other two parties of mutineers to get to their allotted work, and to warn the Native Horse Artillery as well that their time for action had arrived.

Now at Bangalore there was a detachment of European artillery, and the European gunners were to be butchered. Then the guns, with their draught bullocks, were to be carried off, and together with those of the Native Horse Artillery were to be trained on the barracks of the 62nd Regiment and of the 13th Light Dragoons. Immediately the head and foot ropes of the dragoons' horses were to be cut, and the animals mounted by the Pindarees. Then the guns were to open fire on the barracks of the 13th and 62nd.

A third party of mutineers was told off to take the barracks in the rear. It was calculated that if grape-shot was well plied into the barracks there would be little chance of the Europeans escaping, roused as they were in the dead of the night. The officers in general, who lived in bungalows apart and in a rather scattered way, were destined to be shot or cut down as they rushed from their dwellings.

The plot had every, or rather many, elements of success in its conception, and even assuming that in the long-run the mutiny had been suppressed, it is morally certain that a great deal of bloodshed would have occurred.

The "Nawaub" purposed to install himself as King of Bangalore, with one Seyd Tippoo, a prominent mutineer, as his Prime Minister.

Twenty-three native soldiers were brought before the Court of Inquiry, and some forty scamps from the bazaar. A court-martial was held later, which began its sittings on December 19. Four of the accused were sentenced to be blown from guns, and some others to be shot. Several more were sentenced to death, but the sentences were commuted to transportation for life.

The executions duly took place at Bangalore, in presence of the garrison, on December 24. Rewards were given to the loyal native officers and sepoys who gave information — several did so, but a few hours later than the time the Jemadar of the 48th came to Major Inglis.

A searching investigation was made to find out the full extent of this conspiracy, but not much came to light. In the house of one of the rebels, a certain Abbas Ali, and in his own handwriting, was found a draft proclamation and a part of a fair copy thereof; but all other documents had been destroyed. The whole affair is remarkable in a way. There was no grievance of any kind among the native sepoys. Some of those condemned had even been years in the service—one as much as nineteen—several had had fathers and other relatives who had died in battle honourably.

Rewards were given to all who had given information, promotion in all cases, and sometimes in addition a pecuniary grant of 500 Rs.

Forewarned, it was easy to nip this mutiny in the bud—but what if the warning of trouble had been withheld?

During 1832 twenty-four men joined from England, thirty-eight horses were cast and delivered to the Commissariat, and seventy-three remount horses were received from Oossoor. The regiment was inspected by Major-General Hawker on May 2; reviewed on December 3, and the saddlery, cloaks, arms, &c., inspected on the following day; the canteen, school, and hospital were inspected on December 5; in marching order, at carbine and pistol practice, on December 6; the horses proposed to be cast and the remounts on December 7; and the riding-school on December 8.

Besides this His Excellency Lieut.-General Sir R. W. O'Callaghan, K.C.B., reviewed the regiment on September 7, and a week later inspected the riding-school, young horses, barracks, horse lines, &c.

During 1833 seventeen men joined from England, ninety-two horses were cast and transferred to the Commissariat, and seventy-seven remount horses joined from Oossoor. Reviews and inspections were held by Major-General Hawker in May and December.

For 1834 similar reviews and inspections were held by Major-General Hawker in May and December, forty-six horses were cast and transferred to the Commissariat, sixty-five being received from the remount depôt at Oossoor. During April the regiment moved into camp on account of an epidemic disease which broke out among the horses, but was enabled to return to barracks on the 6th of May.

During 1835 sixty-nine men joined from the depôt in England, fourteen invalids were sent home. One hundred and fifteen remount horses were received, of which seven were Australian horses. "Walers" are here mentioned for the first time. Twenty of the horses came from Oossoor, and eighty-eight from the Bengal stud. Thirty-eight horses were cast and transferred to the Commissariat, and one hundred and seven transferred to native cavalry regiments. The term "recruits" occurs this year for the first time. The usual inspections by Major-General Hawker took place in May, and from November 26th to December 7th.

On July 23rd Major Sir J. Gordon, Bart., 13th Light Dragoons, died at Madras.

The events of 1836 were as follows: Thirty recruits landed at Madras for the regiment; thirteen invalids were sent to England, and two men were embarked on "gratuity" to be discharged in England. Forty-three remount horses joined, and twenty-four were cast and transferred to the Commissariat. This year the regiment was inspected and reviewed by Brigadier-General Vigoureux, C.B., in May and December.

During 1837, that the time of the regiment in India was drawing to a close is now apparent. Only one man joined the regiment— a volunteer from the 63rd Foot. Sixteen invalids were embarked for England, seven men were discharged to reside in India. Seventy-two horses were received from the remount depôt at Oossoor, and fifty-two were cast and delivered to the Commissariat. Brigadier-General Vigoureux, C.B., inspected the regiment in May, and Major-General Sir H. Gough, K.C.B., in December.

For 1838 the events are scanty. One man joined the regiment, being transferred from the 39th Foot. Eight men were discharged, mostly to reside in India and draw pension there. One was discharged by purchase, and another as he had been sentenced to seven years' transportation. Eighteen invalids were embarked for England. Forty-nine remount horses were received from Oossoor and forty-five were cast, six being shot for vice, and forty-one transferred to the Commissariat.

The usual inspections and review by Major-General Sir H. Gough, K.C.B., took place in May and December.

The first two months of 1839 were uneventful. In January and February twenty-six invalids were embarked for England, and fifty-one horses were cast and delivered to the Commissariat.

On April 1st twelve men were discharged on pension to reside in India.

Meanwhile complications with one of the native rulers had arisen, and trouble was brewing. On March 7, therefore, two squadrons of the regiment under Lieut.-Colonel Allan T. Maclean were ordered to Bellary. These troops were commanded by Captains G. Weston, W. Digby Hamilton, Robert Ellis, and William Penn.

The Affairs at Kurnool and Zorapoor.

The 13th Light Dragoons, however, were not destined to leave India without employment on active service in the field. The story of the brief campaign of 1839 is as follows.

A fanatical spirit was abroad among the Mussulman chiefs and the

THE AFFAIRS AT KURNOOL AND ZORAPOOR. 301

people of India which appears to have originated in Scinde, whence emissaries were sent to induce the chiefs to engage in a holy war against the British raj.

Among the chiefs implicated was the Nawab of Kurnool — a potentate of some power and not a little wealth. By treaty he was precluded from storing and collecting war *matériel*, but nevertheless he had amassed a huge quantity of guns, muskets, shot, shell, bullets, swords, matchlocks, English double-barrelled guns and pistols, saltpetre, sulphur, copper, lead, reams of cartridge paper, and about 600,000 lbs. of gunpowder. These warlike stores were cunningly concealed, some being built up in storehouses within the zenana at Kurnool, and hundreds of cannon were ranged in the courtyards hidden by grass which had been allowed to grow over them. The Nawab was called upon for an explanation and refused to offer one.

The Government therefore moved up a force towards Kurnool, a force accompanied by two Commissioners.

On August 13th Captain Pears of the Madras Engineers left Bangalore with the 34th Madras Light Infantry.

The main force was thus composed: F troop Native Horse Artillery, 2 squadrons of the 13th Light Dragoons, Sappers and Miners, and the 34th Madras Light Infantry from Bangalore; the 39th British Foot, one company Foot Artillery, the 39th Native Infantry, and 7th Native Cavalry with heavy guns from Bellary; one company of European artillery, and the 3rd and 51st Native Infantry, with mortars, from Hyderabad, were ordered to assemble at Adoui. This force amounted to about 6000 men.

On August 25th the Sappers and 34th reached Anautapur, on the 29th Gooty, and on September 2nd Adoui, the force from Bellary being two marches in the rear. Arrangements for the crossing of the Toomboodra river at Madaneram were made with some difficulty by the Sappers, and occupied from September 4th to September 21st. On September 24th the force reached Kopatoal, thirty or forty miles from Kurnool. Here the Sappers were left to prepare materials for a siege, as it was anticipated that strong resistance would be offered by the Nawab. A company of the 29th Native Infantry, and one of the 16th, also remained, while the main force encamped about six miles to the front. So matters rested for a fortnight, when the Sappers were ordered to the front and encamped two miles in advance of the main force. The main camp was on the right bank of the river, while the artillery, engineers, and ordnance stores were on the left.

On October 10, the Sappers with the 34th Native Infantry, two companies of the 39th British (80 strong only), two six-pounders, half a troop of Horse Artillery, two howitzers, a company of artillery, a squadron of the 13th Light Dragoons, one of native cavalry, and the Sappers moved off under the command of Colonel Dyce.

Meanwhile Colonel James with the 51st Native Infantry, two companies of the 39th Native Infantry, and a small body of Sappers had taken possession of the fort of Kurnool without resistance a few days before.

The force above-named under Colonel Dyce reached Kurnool on October 12, encamping about two miles off, and the whole was now placed under the command of Colonel James.

For six days the troops were employed in searching for the Nawab's concealed guns and stores—only seven or eight being found mounted on the walls. The details of this search are most amusing, though too lengthy to quote here. But among the guns was found forty or fifty light field-pieces with carriages complete and ready for the field—mostly two- or six-pounders. A "Malabar" gun, ten feet long, mounted on a carriage with 10-ft. wheels, and a 24-foot trail, was discovered behind a wall, but commanding the main street from the gate. It had a 12-inch bore and carried a shot weighing two hundred and forty pounds. Three or four hundred guns were found in the grass in the courtyard, and in another place guns, mortars, and howitzers in large numbers. One howitzer which had been cast by the Nawab, found in a garden, was 9 feet long, and had a bore of 27 inches—the thickness of metal at the muzzle being 9 inches. Between eight and ten lacs of treasure was also seized. Most of the shells were made of pewter, and some were of most fanciful design. The fact was that the British force had arrived six months too soon, and the Nawab's force did not amount to more than 1000 men. While his stores were being disclosed the Nawab remained in an enclosure near the tomb of his father to which he had retired. The fort technically was still his own, and he was permitted to send things in and out—and some treasure was no doubt removed.

On October 17th Colonel Dyce received instructions how to act.

THE AFFAIRS AT KURNOOL AND ZORAPOOR.

Two days previously a party of six or seven officers had penetrated into the enclosure unarmed, and had had an interview with the Nawab. It was a risky thing to do, as his followers crowded the place, and all were fine tall men and armed to the teeth.

It is recorded that this party of officers, save one who belonged to the 13th Light Dragoons, were all small men. The interview, however, though by no means friendly, passed off without violence, and the party withdrew, — having, however, refused the proffered presents of fruit—presents, though, which their syces took possession of and carried away on their heads.

On October 18th arrangements were made to surround the Nawab and his following, and to arrest him.

The troops took up a position between the Nawab's enclosure and the village of Zorapore. Captain Pears and Lieutenant Ouchterlony of the Sappers galloped over to Zorapore, where they found Colonel Dyce holding a parley with some of the leaders of the Nawab's following. The terms offered them were to hand over the Nawab, receiving all arrears of pay and a safe-conduct with their arms to their own country.

The British force was thus disposed: small bodies of the 13th Light Dragoons and the native cavalry were placed on the right. On some high and open ground on the left the artillery were stationed, and within three hundred yards of the Nawab's palace, thus rendering that place untenable. To the left of the guns, and right in front of the burial-ground, the 34th Native Infantry extended across a field as far as the road, and across the road stood the 80 men of the 39th British.

Some time was occupied in pretended discussion, pretended at least on the native side, in which a Persian Munshi took considerable part. But Wullee Khan, the Vizier, would not come to terms, nay, more, was insolent. He came out clad in armour and bristling with weapons, a huge broadsword being specially noticeable. Wullee Khan was a huge fellow, beside whom Colonel Dyce, a man of six foot six in height, did not look tall. Meanwhile the Pathans, of which there were not a few among the troops of the Nawab, disliking the appearance of the guns, cleared out of the enclosure and threw themselves out in front of the British left.

For four hours the force remained quiet, and Colonel Dyce then ordered the buglers to sound "fire." The Nawab with thirty or forty men took refuge in the Durgah, but the rest moved out of the enclosure in the front of the British, some meaning fight, others flight across the river.

For ten minutes Rohillas and Pathans kept up a hot fire, and worked round on the British flank. Captain Pears was sent to bring up some of the 13th Light Dragoons, but on arrival at the river he found that they were fully occupied in endeavouring to prevent the enemy, here numbering some hundreds, from getting round them by means of the river. The enemy would enter the stream, and being out of reach would endeavour to pass up or down, above or below, where the dragoons were posted, and thus escape. The 13th had therefore to keep on the move to prevent it. A body of the 34th Native Infantry were then despatched there, and they shot down numbers both in the river and on sundry sandbanks. The artillery now ceased to fire, and the 39th British with the 34th Native Infantry advanced. Against them rushed out Wullee Khan, his brother, and three other Rohillas, sword in hand.

These five brave fellows were at once bayonetted. The Durgah was now entered, and there the verandah was found full of the enemy. As the intention was to take the Nawab alive, to effect it Captain Pears rushed in, but Major Armstrong of the 34th Native Infantry was already before him and was dragging his captive out, to whom three natives clung, and a soldier of the 39th British. It seems that the soldier believed the Nawab had killed a Lieutenant White of the 39th a few minutes before, and was vowing vengeance. As a matter of fact it was an Arab, Shaik Said, who killed Lieutenant White. An officer of the 34th, Lieutenant Yates, was killed in the scuffle, and Colonel Wright was stabbed by a desperate man who rushed out at him. Lieutenant Ouchterlony was thrice wounded when helping a sepoy against a Rohilla, one cut being a very severe one in the left elbow-joint. He did not, however, quit the field, and even accompanied the 13th half way across the river when they forded it in pursuit of the fugitives. About 25,000 rupees, some jewellery, 85 horses, and 22 elephants, were found in the Durgah.

The British force consisted of 350 to 400 native infantry, 80 of the 39th Regiment, 150 of the 13th Light Dragoons, 150 native cavalry, and the guns. Two British officers were killed, two

THE AFFAIRS AT KURNOOL AND ZORAPOOR.

wounded; five or six men of the 39th fell, and a few were wounded; one of the native infantry killed, and twelve or fourteen wounded.

The enemy numbered 900 men, but had no artillery. Two hundred prisoners were taken, and fully one hundred and fifty killed. The party of the 13th Light Dragoons which forded the river in pursuit of the fugitives was commanded by Lieutenant Cameron. One private of the 13th was drowned while crossing the river, but there were no other casualties in the action. The two squadrons of the 13th returned to Bangalore on November 28, but not without serious loss, for cholera on the march claimed no less than thirty-two men. Of the horses, six were lost. The thanks of the Government for the services of the regiment on this service appeared in general orders.

The following officers of the 13th Light Dragoons were present at the affairs at Kurnool and Zorapore:—

Lieut.-Colonel Allan Thomas Maclean, commanding cavalry brigade.
Captain William Digby Hamilton.
    „   George Weston, commanding a squadron.
Lieutenant William Penn.
    „   John Cameron Campbell.
Lieutenant John Macartney.
    „   James Allan Cameron.
Cornet Charles Cameron Shute, acting adjutant.
Assistant-Surgeon Patrick Nicholson, M.D.

The 13th Light Dragoons had now been serving in India for upwards of twenty years. It was now under orders for England. Early in 1840 the regiment marched from Bangalore for Madras, and on the way lost by cholera forty men as well as many women and children. On arrival in Madras the 13th was received by Major-General Sir R. Dick, K.C.B., K.C.H., and on the next day transferred its horses to the 15th Hussars,—such non-commissioned officers and privates as volunteered to remain in India being permitted to transfer their services to other corps.

Major-General Sir R. Dick on the morning of January 29, 1840, after the review, wrote in the highest possible terms of the regiment. He expressed his high appreciation of everything he had that day witnessed.

He praised the appearance and steadiness of the men and the condition of the horses.

The movements executed were performed with precision and celerity, "notwithstanding the heavy sandy ground," and the horses were well in hand. He greatly regretted that the services of so efficient a regiment would be so soon lost to the Indian Army. Finally, he trusted that Lieut.-Colonel Brunton, the officers, and men, would have a safe passage to England.

The general order issued by Major-General Sir Hugh Gough, K.C.B., and signed R. B. Fearon, D.A.G., was even more highly complimentary. Beginning in more general terms, he concludes as follows:—

> From having been in the Division under his own immediate Command, during a period of more than two years, the Major-General is enabled to bear testimony [as well as from the Reports of his Predecessors] to the uniform correctness of its conduct, and throughout the course of its lengthened Service in Mysore, he believes it may safely be asserted that not an instance has occurred of a complaint or appeal being preferred against an Officer, Non-Commissioned Officer, or Private of this Distinguished Corps, to the Civil Authorities.
>
> In taking leave therefore [for a time he hopes only] of the 13th Light Dragoons, the Major-General begs Lt.-Colonel Brunton will accept himself, and convey to the Officers and Soldiers under his Orders the assurance of the Esteem the Major-General feels for, and the warm interest he shall ever take in the prospects and fair fame of the Regiment, and it will constitute a pleasing part of his Duty to make the General Commanding-in-Chief of His Majesty's Army, acquainted with the sentiments he has thus felt to be due to the Corps, to Express of its character and merits, neither of which are unknown to Lord Hill already, and one in no wise diminished by a Twenty Years' absence from its Native Land.

The 13th Light Dragoons embarked at Madras in February 1840, and landed at Gravesend in the following June.

The regiment had been absent from England for a space of twenty-one years and three months.

During its service in India, of the officers fifteen died, of the non-commissioned officers and men one thousand and fifty-one.

Of the officers of the regiment only five remained of those who had sailed from England more than twenty years before. Lieut.-Colonel Allan T. Maclean, then a captain; Major Henry Stones, then a lieutenant; Captain Thomas Rosser, then the adjutant; Captain William Digby Hamilton, then a cornet; and Captain Robert Ellis, then a cornet. The Colonel of the regiment, the Hon. Sir H. George Grey, was still alive. Lieut.-Colonel Maclean and Captain Rosser it will be remembered fought at Waterloo.

CHAPTER XXVII.

Home Service, 1840-1854.

AFTER disembarking at Gravesend the regiment marched to Canterbury.

The establishment of the regiment was now reduced to six troops, and these six must have been extremely weak numerically.

Not only had the losses in men from cholera during the last few months of its stay in India been very heavy, but not a few non-commissioned officers and privates had been permitted to volunteer into cavalry regiments in India.

Strenuous efforts were required to be made by Lieut.-Colonel Brunton to recruit the regiment to its full strength. Also it was needful to purchase and train young horses upon which to mount the men. The purchase of horses, and the recruiting of men, and the training of both horses and men, fully occupied Lieut.-Colonel Brunton and his officers for some months.

During February 1841 there was an election at Canterbury, and the 13th was for that period quartered at Sandwich, Deal, and Walmer.

On May 11th the regiment was inspected by H.R.H. The Duke of Cambridge, when the success of the efforts of Lieut.-Colonel Brunton and his officers became apparent, and a highly complimentary report was made of the "appearance and forward state of training both of men and horses." It should be noted that more than half of the men inspected on that day had joined the 13th Light Dragoons as recruits since its return from India, and the mounts of the entire regiment were young horses bought and trained during that time.

When the General Election was held in June 1841, the regiment was ordered to occupy Whitstable, Herne Bay, and Margate. On returning to Canterbury after the elections were over, the 13th received a vote of thanks from the inhabitants of Margate, acknowledging the orderly and exemplary conduct of the men during its stay.

The 14th Light Dragoons were now under orders for India, and arrived at Canterbury during the time that the 13th were quartered there, to prepare for service.

The meeting of the two cavalry regiments, who in the Peninsula days had formed the "Ragged Brigade," revived old memories and old regimental traditions, even though long years had elapsed.

To perpetuate a kindly remembrance of their old companions in arms, the 14th presented to the 13th their handsome mess table. This mess table had been originally captured by the 13th at Vittoria with the rest of the baggage, &c., of King Joseph, as has been related.

By the month of August 1841 the regiment was at its full strength.

Orders were now received for the regiment to proceed to Ipswich and Norwich, and the 13th marched from Canterbury to Gravesend, where it crossed the Thames.

At Ipswich and Norwich the regiment remained until January 1842, when orders arrived for the 13th to march to Hampton Court, Slough, and Colnbrook.

Here the regiment remained until February. The occasion of this shift of quarters was the visit to England of the King of Prussia, who came over to act as sponsor at the christening of H.R.H. the Prince of Wales. The ceremony took place on January 26. On February 4th the 13th were ordered to march to Woolwich on escort duty during the review of the Royal Artillery there before the King of Prussia. That day the King, who had taken leave of Her Majesty already, embarked for Ostend, and the 13th returned to quarters.

A few days later the regiment marched back to Ipswich and Norwich, where it remained until the early days of May 1843.

While at Hounslow two officers joined the regiment by exchange from the 9th Lancers — Captain John Anstruther-Thomson and Lieutenant John Edward Madocks. The 9th Lancers went to India in 1842.

In 'Eighty Years Reminiscences,' by Colonel Anstruther-Thomson, he narrates in a most amusing manner how he and Lieutenant Madocks

13TH LIGHT DRAGOONS (1845).

BY M. A. HAYES.

(*Lent by* Major-General Sir STANLEY CLARKE, G.C.V.O., C.M.G.)

came to decide on the 13th Light Dragoons as the regiment into which they would effect an exchange. The stature of the officers of the regiment, at any rate the stature of the three troops which Captain Anstruther-Thomson first saw at Hampton Court, appears to have impressed him. "They are the tallest lot of officers I ever saw. In our three troops there is no one under six feet." Lieutenant Madocks became the lieutenant of the troop commanded by Captain Anstruther-Thomson, and his cornet was Cornet John Morgan Gwynne-Hughes, who had exchanged into the regiment from the 14th Light Dragoons. This officer Captain Anstruther-Thomson tells us was six feet three inches in height.

Permission has kindly been given to avail ourselves of these two volumes of Reminiscences, and from them some details as regards the regiment between the years 1842 and 1847, when he retired, are to be obtained. Later, too, are certain letters written at the time of the Crimean War, which are full of interest. But it is as a sportsman that Colonel Anstruther-Thomson has achieved the greatest renown, and were it not for the record which he kept of regimental sports it would not be easy to obtain any information of the period in question.

The three other troops were then at Watford, but on January 24, 1842, two of them marched to Slough, while the other, that commanded by Captain Anstruther-Thomson, remained at Watford. He records that with his lieutenant he used to dine nightly at Slough, returning to Watford to sleep. Between this date and February 18th Captain Anstruther-Thomson's troop appears to have proceeded from Watford to Colnbrook, for on that day it marched back to Watford, and the regiment then went to its old quarters at Ipswich and Norwich.

On March 22nd an urgent message reached Norwich from Lynn, asking for military assistance to aid the civil power. The troop commanded by Captain Anstruther-Thomson was ordered to mount and proceed thither forthwith. Now it chanced that Captain Anstruther-Thomson was out hunting—the meet that morning was at Hockham, some twenty-five miles away. At 5.15 P.M. the captain found himself at Swaffham Heath, about the same distance from Norwich. His horse was tired, his man with another had gone back to barracks according to his master's instructions, and as a result Captain

Anstruther-Thomson did not get back till 10 P.M.—wet through, tired, and hungry. There he found the whole place lighted up, and his troop about to start for Lynn. Major Wathen, in his absence, was to go in his place. Cornet Gwynne-Hughes, too, happened to be dining out, but returned very shortly. Captain Anstruther-Thomson fed, changed into uniform, and marched for Lynn with his troop. He thus narrates the adventures of that night—

"I had forty horses with me, all five-year-olds. Eight of them tumbled down during the night. It rained part of the time, and froze in the morning and was very slippery. Luckily I had been in the habit of driving the Lynn mail, so knew the road, or we never should have got there. It was so dark that we had to feel the figures on the mile-stones. The mail coach met us on the way, and Tom Raynham, the coachman, said, "You'll find they are ready for you at Dereham" (a town on the road to Lynn). We got the horses put into stables for twenty minutes, and had some coffee and off again. We arrived at Lynn at 10.30. On the way Colonel Oakes, the chief-constable (formerly of the Life Guards), overtook us in a waggonette with some policemen. We formed up in front of the Mayor's house. We had not been there ten minutes when the rioters appeared, eight abreast, arm-in-arm, right across the street. They came to a corner, saw the troop, all stopped, then marched on, turned down a street, and we never saw them again. Our men were sent to their billets, and ordered not to unsaddle their horses. They fed them and lay down on the straw beside them. I got some breakfast, lay down on the hearthrug with a sofa cushion under my head, and fell fast asleep. I had been out twenty-six hours and ridden over 126 miles.

The riots were caused by the dock-porters, who had struck, and had threatened to burn the house of the mayor.

The ringleaders were arrested by the police, and there the matter ended.

Captain Anstruther-Thomson and his troop remained at Lynn for about a month, and then returned to Norwich, their services being dispensed with by the civil power.

On August 10, 1842, extensive manœuvres were held in Germany. Captain Anstruther-Thomson and another officer of the 13th, Lieutenant Samuel Auchmuty Dickson, applied for leave to attend them. Thirty thousand men were under canvas at Eiskirchen, about twelve miles from Bonn. Nearly sixty British officers were present, among them being "The Duke of Cambridge, Lord de Ros, Charles Ibbetson, 11th Hussars; R. Wood, 10th Hussars; Rodolf de Salés, 8th Hussars; Henry de Bathe, Guards; Sir Henry Bethune, Commander-in-Chief of the Persian Army, &c. Lots of Dutchmen, capital fellows. Some of the old ones had been quartered in England in the Brunswick Brigade; no Frenchmen."

While on the subject of foreign reviews, it may here be mentioned that on June 26, 1834, three months' leave from July 1st was granted to Lieut.-Colonel William Persse of the 13th Light Dragoons, to enable him to be present at the reviews of foreign troops on the Continent. These two notices are the only cases of visits abroad for professional purposes recorded down to 1842. Lieut.-Colonel Persse joined the regiment on December 6, 1833, and left it, being appointed to the 16th Lancers, on July 11, 1834. He was never with the regiment in India.

Early in May 1843, being relieved by the Scots Greys, the 13th Light Dragoons received orders to march from Ipswich and Norwich to Hounslow and Hampton Court, sending detachments to Kensington and Sandhurst. At these quarters the regiment remained until May 7, 1844, being mainly occupied in furnishing escorts for Her Majesty.

On May 7, 1844, orders were received to march to Exeter, which was the headquarters; one troop being sent to each of the following places, Brecon, Carmarthen, Cardiff, Trowbridge, and Dorchester (Dorset).

It is indeed difficult to see how the efficiency of a regiment as a whole was to be maintained while scattered about in this haphazard fashion. Captain Anstruther-Thomson's troop was first at Trowbridge, but shifted to Exeter on July 1.

On May 4, 1845, the regiment marched for Exeter and Wales— a somewhat vague address this—*en route* for Liverpool.

Captain Anstruther-Thomson relates that he crossed in the *Duchess of Kent*, and that the other squadrons joined at Dublin. The major seems to have been in command. Captain Anstruther-Thomson's troop went to Naas—the headquarter troop with the major and Lieutenant Madocks went to Cellbridge. A very sad event now took place: the attempted suicide of the major, who had for a little time evinced symptoms of insanity. Through the prompt attention of the surgeons, the life of this unfortunate officer was saved. But of course his military career was ended—he left the regiment and died shortly afterwards.

Captain Anstruther-Thomson's troop went to Limerick, the rest of the regiment being stationed at Cahir, where later his detachment joined. The only duty which he records as being performed at this place was that of escorting meal-carts from Cahir to Clonmel. "There was perhaps a mile and a half of carts with wretched ponies, and a mounted dragoon every 200 yards. It was fourteen miles, and these wretched ponies tired, and occasionally tumbled down and halted the whole line. If any cottages were near, the women used to run out, hold up their petticoats, stick a knife into the sack, get a petticoat full of meal and run away, and of course the men could do nothing. It took a whole day to go the distance. The meal was ground Indian corn.

"In the prison the prisoners were employed breaking stones. The inspector saw one breaking his into powder. On asking the reason, he said, 'Sure it's to mix with the yellow meal.'"

During this year detachments of the regiment also were stationed at Clonmel, Gort, Galway, Kilkenny, and Carrick-on-Suir. One troop which was detached from Galway to Castlebar was employed in protecting voters proceeding to the election for the County Mayo. For the temperate discharge of this duty the men employed received the thanks of the Lord Lieutenant of Ireland.

The year 1845 witnessed the death of General the Hon. Sir H. G. Grey, who had been Colonel of the 13th since the year 1811. He had succeeded Colonel Craig in that year. The new Colonel of the 13th Light Dragoons was Lieut.-General the Hon. E. P. Lygon.

The veteran Lieut.-Colonel Robert Brunton, who had been in the regiment since April 9, 1819, also died on June 27. To him by purchase succeeded Lieut.-Colonel Lawrenson.

In May 1846 the regiment marched to Newbridge, where it remained until June 15, when it was ordered to Dublin to form part of the garrison of that city. Captain Anstruther-Thomson's troop was quartered in Islandbridge Barracks. Sir Edward Blakeney was the General-in-Command, and Colonel Clarke of the Scots Greys commanded the cavalry brigade, which consisted of the Scots Greys, the Queen's Bays, and the 4th Light Dragoons, besides the 13th.

On July 27, 1847, one squadron of the regiment was ordered to march from Dublin to Drogheda, and thence to Trim. Elections were on at these towns, and the aid of the military forces had been invoked by the civil powers in order to prevent disturbances and outrages. The squadron returned to Dublin on August 14.

On March 19, 1847, Captain Anstruther-Thomson retired from the regiment. He had taken over the Mastership of the Atherstone Hounds.

In September of this year the regiment received orders to march from Dublin. A detachment went to Sligo on the 23rd.

A squadron composed of the troops of Captain Doherty and Captain Stewart marched to Ballinrobe on the 27th September and 5th October.

Captain Dickson's troop went to Castlebar on October 4. The headquarters and the three troops commanded by Captain Gore, Captain Madocks, and Captain Holden, went to Longford on October 6th and October 7th.

On November 6, 1847, the regiment was inspected in marching order by Major-General Sir Guy Campbell, Bart., commanding the Athlone District. The report and an extract from a regimental order are here given—not because a good report was a novelty, but because the documents quoted are couched in such terms that they cannot fail to be a source of pride to the 13th.

Extracts from reports have been but sparingly given in these pages. Nine received after the inspections between May 1841 and April 1847 might have been inserted, it is true—suffice it to say, however, that all were complimentary, and specially with regard to interior economy, discipline, and efficiency.

The passages here quoted with regard to the inspection of November 6, 1847, are as follows:—

Regimental Orders.—Major Knox has great pleasure in publishing for general information the following letter, so highly complimentary to the Regiment, and trusts it will be an additional inducement to all Ranks to presevere in good conduct, and by a zealous discharge of all duties, continue to merit the praise so flatteringly bestowed by the highest authorities for Good Conduct and Efficiency.

Extract from a letter from the Adjutant-General of the Forces, addressed to Lieut.-General Sir E. Blakeney, K.C.B., dated, Horse Guards, 22nd November 1847—

The Reports of Major-General His Royal Highness Prince George of Cambridge, on the Regiments of Cavalry stationed in and near Dublin, are extremely satisfactory, more particularly as regards the 13th Light Dragoons and 17th Lancers, the perfect Order and Efficiency which these Corps are represented to be in by His Royal Highness are, I am directed to observe, in the highest degree creditable to Lieut.-Colonel Lawrenson and Colonel St Quentin, their Commanding Officers.

On December 8, 1847, a detachment of the 13th, under the command of Lieutenant Goad, was ordered to Strokestown for the protection of that place and the country adjacent.

On January 7, 1848, one troop under the command of Captain Stewart was detached from Ballinrobe to Dunmore.

The Sligo election came on in April, and in consequence the detachment then at Strokestown was ordered thither to aid in keeping the peace. Its services were dispensed with by the civil authorities in a few days, and it returned to Strokestown on April 12.

On May 24th the regiment was inspected by Major-General Sir Guy Campbell, Bart., commanding the Western District.

The services of the detachment at Strokestown being no longer required, it rejoined headquarters at Longford on June 10. From July 6th to July 18th a detachment was ordered to Sligo in aid of the civil power.

The troop at Dunmore, being no longer required at that station, marched and joined the detachment at Ballinrobe on July 31.

On October 9th the regiment was again inspected by Sir Guy Campbell, and immediately after the inspection a troop marched from Longford for Belfast, to be stationed there.

Three days later one troop left Castlebar for Dundalk. On October 13th the young horses, recruits, &c., marched to the same place; the next day a detachment marched thither from Sligo and one troop (headquarters) from Longford.

On October 16th one troop marched from Longford to Belturbet, to be stationed there.

The troops collected at Dundalk were to compose the garrison of that place.

During the whole of the year 1849 the regiment was off and on employed in detachments giving aid to the civil power,—in the course of this service visiting Downpatrick, Newry, Ballinahinch, Armagh, Banbridge, Castlewellan, and Rathfriland. To some of these places troops went on two and even on three occasions. To soldiers this work is never pleasant, though it has to be performed. On most of these occasions nothing occurred, but while Captain Stewart's troop was at Castlewellan, on July 12, a most serious conflict took place.

The Act of Parliament which made party processions illegal had expired, and the Orangemen had determined to celebrate the anniversary of the Battle of the Boyne on July 12. This date happened also to be the birthday of the Earl of Roden, the Grand Master of the Orangemen. Lord Roden lived at Tollymore Park, near Castlewellan, and thither in procession the Orangemen determined to go—also they determined to go armed. To reach Tollymore you had to pass a steep ridge called Dolly's Brae, across which is a strong pass, and this pass had always been occupied by the Ribbonmen on similar occasions. There was another road skirting the base of the hill, which had been made with a view to avoiding the steepness of the old one, and also in order to give less opportunity for collisions between the rival factions.

The heights were occupied by the Ribbonmen as usual. Accompanied by military and police came the Orangemen, some fifteen hundred strong, with flags, bands, and some four hundred armed with guns and pistols. The rest carried pikes or any weapon they could get hold of. The military force consisted of Captain Stewart's troop of the 13th Light Dragoons, a troop of the Inniskillings, and a company of the 9th Foot (Norfolk Regiment).

This force, to which the police were added, was amply sufficient to overawe the Ribbonmen, moreover it is to be recorded that the priests used every possible endeavour to persuade their people to abstain from any acts of violence. It was agreed that the Ribbonmen would not attack the Orangemen unless they were themselves first attacked. The procession, therefore, passed safely along and reached Tollymore Park. Here they were received by Lord Roden, who made a speech— a not very wise speech; food and drink, and plenty of them, were supplied to the processionists in a tent, erected for that purpose. An adjournment was made to a field in the Park, where a regular drill was gone through, guns were fired, and then full of ale and boasting the Orangemen started back for Castlewellan. Near the hill something exploded—it might have been a gun or a pistol, though it was stated to have been a squib discharged by a boy. It was not surely ascertained to which side the offending individual belonged. Anyhow, the Ribbonmen opened fire on the processionists, the military, and the police alike. The Orangemen, delighted, returned it with interest, and a desultory action was kept up between the contending factions, with the military and police between them, and a target for both.

The soldiers then charged the Ribbonmen and put them to flight: they might with equal justice have charged the Orangemen, only it was to protect them that they were where they were. Several rioters were wounded by musketry. The Orangemen joined in the charge and wreaked their vengeance on all and sundry they got within reach of. Four Ribbonmen were killed, and between thirty and forty wounded. A considerable number of prisoners were taken by the military and police.

It was stated that the Orangemen wantonly shot a poor boy of ten, murdered an aged woman, and beat in the skull of an idiot named Sweeny with the butt-ends of their muskets. An inoffensive old man was also dragged by them into his garden, and bayonetted in sight of his horrified family. Sundry houses were sacked and burnt. The Orangemen escaped with only a few of their party wounded.

An inquiry into this disgraceful outrage was held, despite the attempts made to burke it. In Parliament the matter was taken up strongly. Lord Roden was called to account, and removed from the Commission of the Peace. Several other magistrates suffered the same fate. The shooting of the contending factions was luckily not good, and the troops of the 13th escaped without any casualties.

On August 6, 1849, the troop stationed at Belturbet marched for Belfast, followed on the next day by a squadron from Dundalk,—the duty of the 13th at Belfast being to act as escort during the visit of Her Majesty Queen Victoria. The squadron and the troop returned from Belfast on August 13, a troop which had been for some time stationed at Belfast and Belturbet being relieved. Captain Borrowes' troop relieved that of Captain Gore at Belfast, and Captain Harvey's troop relieved that of Captain Holden at Belfast. Inspections of the regiment were held on September 3, and again on October 11, on the first date by Lieut.-General Sir E. Blakeney, K.C.B., and Commanding in Ireland, and on the second occasion by Major-General Bainbrigge, C.B., Commanding the Belfast District.

On the 13th and 14th of March 1850 three troops marched from Dundalk for Ballinahinch, Downpatrick, and Castlewellan, one troop to each place, in aid of the civil power. Their services being no longer required by the magistrates, the three troops returned to headquarters, Dundalk, on the 19th, 20th, and 21st of March.

Orders were now received for the regiment to proceed to Scotland.

In consequence one troop marched from Belturbet for Charlemount on March 21. Two troops marched from Dundalk for Belfast on the 30th. On April 2nd one troop marched from Dundalk for Belfast, and the troop from Charlemount also moved in to Belfast.

On the 4th and 6th of April five troops (two and a half troops on each date) embarked at Belfast for Scotland, disembarking at Glasgow on the 5th and 6th.

Two troops were stationed in the barracks at Glasgow, one in the barracks at Hamilton, two in Piershill Barracks near Edinburgh—these last to form a part of the garrison of the capital.

On April 9, the headquarters and one troop left Dundalk, arriving at Glasgow on the 10th, whence they marched to Piershill Barracks.

On May 21st the regiment was inspected by Major-General Riddell K.H., Commanding in North Britain.

A troop of the 13th (Captain Holden's) was on June 24th requisitioned by the magistrates of Dunfermline to aid the civil power. Captain Holden's troop rejoined headquarters on June 27.

On August 28, Captain Stewart's troop from the Hamilton Barracks marched to Glasgow, and the troops of Captain Gore and Captain Oldham marched from Glasgow to Edinburgh to reinforce the garrison there during the visit of H.M. Queen Victoria.

On September 6th these three troops returned to their former quarters, arriving next day.

During the remainder of 1850 and for the first three months of 1851 there is nothing whatever to chronicle beyond the customary shiftings of troops from one barrack to another. But on April 1st Captain Goad's and Captain Oldham's troops marched from Piershill Barracks for Newcastle-on-Tyne. On the 16th Captain Jenyns' troop marched from Hamilton Barracks for York, followed on the next day by Captain Gore's troop for the same station. On the 24th Captain Holden's troop marched from Piershill for Leeds, the headquarters and "unformed" horses following for York on the 26th. For the first time mention is made of any journey by railway train in the Regimental Records, and on this occasion it is noted that the dismounted men proceeded by train from Edinburgh to York.

It may be remarked that one hundred and two years had elapsed since the regiment had been in Scotland. For some reason unstated, the troop commanded by Captain Tremayne remained at Piershill Barracks until the 22nd of July, when it marched for York, arriving there a few days prior to the inspection of the regiment on August 15th by Major-General Brotherton, Inspector-General of Cavalry. No other event is recorded in the Regimental Records for this year.

In April 1852 orders were received for the 13th to proceed to Hounslow and Kensington.

The troops commanded by Captain Oldham and Captain Goad, therefore, marched from Newcastle-on-Tyne on April 21. A detachment marched from York for Kensington on the 23rd, and another for Sandhurst on the same date, but received an order to change the route for Hounslow. On the 26th Captain Gore's and Captain Jenyns' troops marched from York for Hounslow, the headquarters of the regiment following on the next day, and with them marched the detachment from Newcastle-on-Tyne. The dismounted men and sick remained at York and Newcastle till May 2, when they were despatched by rail and partly by steamer to Hounslow. Captain Holden's troop remained at Leeds until the 21st of May, when it also marched and joined the regiment at Hounslow.

On July 1, a detachment of the regiment consisting of one sergeant, twelve rank and file, and twenty troop horses, marched to the Military College, Sandhurst.

The inspection of the regiment by H.R.H the Duke of Cambridge, Inspector-General of Cavalry, took place on July 6th at Hounslow. Meanwhile two troops, those commanded by Captain Gore and Captain Jenyns, had been moved to Hampton Court, but were relieved there on September 9th by the troops commanded by Captain Goad and Captain Tremayne, the troops thus relieved rejoined the headquarters at Hounslow.

The detachment then stationed at the Military College, Sandhurst, returned to regimental headquarters at Hounslow on November 6, it being the vacation of the cadets. On the 16th the whole of the effective men and horses from Hounslow Barracks and Hampton Court marched into billets in Upper Westminster, Kensington, and Hammersmith, for the purpose of forming part of the funeral procession of their old leader, Field-Marshal the late Duke of Wellington, and were employed on that duty on November 18. The regiment returned to quarters at Hounslow and Hampton Court on the following day.

On January 11, 1853, a detachment of the same strength as before proceeded from Hounslow to Sandhurst Royal Military College.

The next day the squadron (Captain Goad's troop and Captain Tremayne's troop) was relieved at Hampton Court by the troops commanded by Captain Holden and Captain Oldham, and returned to regimental headquarters at Hounslow.

On the 14th and 19th of May the squadron at Hampton Court and the detachment at the Royal Military College, Sandhurst, also rejoined the regimental headquarters, it being the vacation of the cadets.

The scheme proposed by the late Field-Marshal the Duke of Wellington, but which he did not live to see carried out, of holding a camp of exercise at Chobham, in Surrey, was now about to be put into execution. To the outside public this was a novel spectacle. The ground chosen was an open space on the sandy heath-covered common near the village, and some four miles from Chertsey. As a camping-ground this spot had been occupied during the old war. The tract of country around was well adapted for military operations in several ways, but not so suited for cavalry owing to the marshes, pools, and small streams—in fact, it was rough. Hills there were and hollows and woods in plenty around the camp.

The force was commanded in chief by Lieut.-General Lord Seaton, G.C.B.; the brigade of Guards by Colonel Bentinck; the brigades of Infantry by Major-General Sir de Lacy Evans and Major-General Fane; the cavalry by Major-General the Duke of Cambridge; and the artillery by Lieut.-Colonel Bloomfield and Colonel Vickers.

The forces employed consisted of three battalions of Grenadier, Coldstream, and Scots Fusilier Guards. The 1st Infantry Brigade of the 38th, 93rd, and 2nd battalion of the Rifle Brigade. The 2nd Infantry Brigade of the 42nd, 50th, and 95th.

The 1st Life Guards, the 6th Dragoon Guards, the 13th Light

Dragoons, and the 17th Lancers, composed the Cavalry Brigade. A troop of Royal Horse Artillery, three batteries of Field Artillery, a company of Sappers, and a pontoon train completed the force.

With commendable precision this force, numbering some eight or ten thousand men, arrived in camp, appearing in sight from different points of the compass almost simultaneously, and occupied their allotted stations within half-an-hour of the first arrival.

All the men were under canvas, but straw-thatched stables were furnished for the cavalry and sheds for the guns. The camp extended over a line two miles in length. The 13th marched from Hounslow on June 14, under the command of Lieut.-Colonel Doherty. Operations in the field began on June 21st in the presence of Her Majesty, who, mounted on a black charger, viewed the proceedings. Prince Albert, the King and Queen of Hanover, and other personages of rank were there as spectators. A sham fight—military manœuvres as they would now be called—took place on that and on the succeeding days. Everything went off well with the exception of an accident on a pontoon bridge thrown across the Thames at Runnymede. A body of troops was intended to be thrown across under cover of a heavy fire of artillery posted on Coopers Hill.

Several regiments of cavalry and infantry had made the passage, and one gun had safely followed, but the horses of the second became restive and terrified. One of them plunged into the water dragging with him the other five, the gun, the drivers, and two sappers. The men were saved, but the wheelers were drowned. The rest of the guns were unharnessed and dragged over by the men.

Her Majesty was to have exploded a mine beneath a redoubt by electricity, but the galvanic battery declined to act, and resort had to be had to the common fuse.

The regiment remained under canvas for a month. The health of the troops was very good, there being a large percentage less of men in hospital than usual when in barracks. From the Lieut.-General in command the regiment received thanks for its good conduct and efficiency.

This being the first of the camps of exercise held in modern times, and the progenitor of the large manœuvres of the present day, it has been thought right to thus enter into rather full details thereon.

On July 14th the 13th Light Dragoons marched as follows to the undermentioned places:—

Headquarters with the troops of Captain Holden and Captain Oldham to Birmingham. The troops of Captain Goad and Captain Jenyns to Coventry. Captain Tremayne's troop marched to Nottingham, and Captain White's troop to Newport, Monmouthshire. The dismounted men marched to Hounslow, where they were joined by the non-effectives, left there, and proceeded to Birmingham by rail. Later, Captain Tremayne's troop proceeded from Nottingham to Coventry, where it remained till January 3, 1854.

England was now on the verge of war with Russia. Diplomacy failed to avert it, and hostilities shortly commenced.

Early in 1854 an order was received from the Horse Guards to hold the regiment in immediate readiness for service in the field abroad. To carry out this order Captain Hutchinson's troop was called in to headquarters from Newport, and the regiment was then formed into four service troops—two at Birmingham, and two at Coventry, commanded by Captains Oldham, Goad, Jenyns, and Tremayne respectively; two depôt troops were under the command of Captain Holden and Captain Hutchinson.

The headquarters squadron marched from Birmingham for Coventry under the command of Lieut.-Colonel Doherty on April 10, the squadron at Coventry proceeding the same day to Rugby, *en route* for Canterbury, under command of Major Gore. The intention of the Government had been to send the regiment through France and embark it at Marseilles, but this plan for certain reasons was not carried out.

On arrival of the headquarters at Northampton, a route was received directing the regiment to march to Hounslow. On arrival there the troop commanded by Captain Oldham proceeded to Hampton Court, where it occupied barracks.

The next order was one for immediate embarkation at Portsmouth, the following vessels being named as transports: *Harbinger, Monarchy, Negociator, Calliope, Culloden,* and *Mary Anne.*

On May 1st Captains Goad and Tremayne's troops marched to Chichester, headquarters and Captain Oldham's troop went into billets at Havant, Fareham, and Cosham.

On May 8th Captain Oldham's troop marched into Portsmouth,

and embarked in the sailing transport *Mary Anne*, sailing the same night. Captain Jenyns' troop also arrived in Portsmouth, embarked in the transport *Negociator*, and sailed.

On May 10th Major Gore with detachments of the regiment marched into Portsmouth and embarked in the transport *Culloden*, and sailed.

On May 11th Captain Goad's troop marched into Portsmouth and embarked in the transport *Calliope*, and sailed.

On May 12th the headquarters embarked in the *Harbinger*, and sailed; and Captain Tremayne's troop embarked in the *Monarchy*, and sailed.

This completed the embarkation of the regiment, and it was effected without any casualties.

The strength of these troops is given in the following table :—

Troop.	Officers.	Sergeants.	Trumpeters.	Farriers.	Rank and File.	Horses. Officers.	Horses. Troop.	Women.
Capt. Oldham	3	2	1	...	49	7	46	3
Capt. Jenyns	2	3	1	1	45	5	44	1
Major Gore	3	2	...	...	44	8	38	2
Capt. Goad	3	2	1	1	47	7	47	2
Headquarters	5	4	...	...	46	12	39	1
Capt. Tremayne	4	3	1	1	38	9	36	2
Total	20	16	4	3	269	48	250	11

CHAPTER XXVIII.

The Eastern Campaign, June 1854 to October 24, 1854.

THE history of the services of the 13th Light Dragoons in this campaign is compiled from several sources. Obviously it would not be possible to quote all *in extenso*. The account here given is derived from (1) the MS. Regimental Record; (2) the notes by Captain Percy Smith; (3) the notes by Colonel Tremayne; (4) the letters from the Crimea addressed to Colonel Anstruther-Thomson mostly, and contained in his 'Eighty Years' Reminiscences,' vol. i.; (5) the 'Recollections of a Young Soldier'; and lastly (6) the 'Recollections of One of the Light Brigade.' Kinglake has also been consulted, and various newspapers. Occasional reference has been made also to other publications.

The first two troops to reach the Bosphorus were the B troop, Captain Jenyns, and the E troop, Captain Tremayne. The voyage from Portsmouth to Varna occupied about six weeks. These two troops disembarked at Coolalie on the Bosphorus, about five miles from Constantinople, on June 9. On the 13th Captain Tremayne's troop re-embarked in the same vessel, and accompanied by Captain Jenyns' troop in the transport *Negociator* both vessels sailed for Varna, a Turkish port on the Black Sea, and the place appointed for the rendezvous of the allied armies. Here they arrived on June 15. The experience of barrack accommodation at Coolalie was decidedly unpleasant, though luckily it was brief. Situated on the Asiatic side of the Bosphorus, this Turkish barrack is described as "vast," "dirty," and "full of vermin."

At Varna the two troops of the 13th encamped on the sandy beach, where they remained until the 17th, when they marched to the general encampment at a place about a mile inland from Varna.

The remainder of the regiment arrived at Varna as follows: Captain Oldham's troop on the *Mary Anne* on the 19th, when they disembarked and marched on the 21st. The *Harbinger* with headquarters under Colonel Doherty arrived on the 20th, disembarked the next day, and on the 22nd marched to the general encampment. The *Calliope* with Captain Goad's troop arrived on the 21st, disembarked on the 22nd, and marched the next day. The *Culloden* with Major Gore and detachments of the 1st squadron arrived and disembarked on July 2. The voyage appears on the whole to have been a pleasant one, though lengthy. Captain Goad in one letter reports from Malta that "the men and horses have all been well, and except a few big legs ['Sphinx' among them from a kick] there is nothing much the matter." Captain Jenyns also writes cheerfully about the condition of the men and horses, "very lucky in not losing a horse and landing them all fit to go." He adds, "that it was a fair ship, only too small for the purpose, being the smallest out [570 tons]." "We got," he writes, "a deal of *kudos* about our nags, all others having so many sick or dead. Tremayne only lost one." The *Mary Anne* transport had a decidedly exciting passage. "The first Sunday at sea we were going along with a good breeze, and all sails set, when Captain Oldham, towards night, thought it was too fast for the horses. The captain of the ship altered sail: the ship gave a lurch on the starboard side; the ballast placed in the middle of the ship broke the boards nailed to the outside instead of the in; the ballast rolled under the horses, threw them on their beam ends, and the women began to cry." However, the men got to work and the ship righted. "Entering the Dardanelles the main and foretop masts were broken as one would break a lucifer match." At Gallipoli the *Mary Anne* anchored, and carpenters from the man-of-war, the *Montebello*, came on board and repaired the damage. Private Powell, from whose book of Reminiscences this extract is taken, mentions that at Varna, after landing, he swam half the horses of the troop: which after their 42 days at sea gave them a good washing and did them good. Sergeant Mitchell in his Recollections gives a very graphic account of the voyage out in the transport *Culloden*. At Malta they had to shift all the horses in order to get at the water-casks which were "under the flooring where the horses stood." First the horses had to be moved, then the flooring taken up, and lastly, ballast to the depth of nearly a yard removed to get at the bung-holes of the casks. A water lighter then came alongside, and a party of the 13th was set to work to pump the casks full. Then the ballast was returned above the casks, the flooring again laid down, and the horses tied up in their places. He mentions that the stores were of a most antique character. The beef had made several voyages to and fro from India and then been returned into store. Some barrels of peas even bore the date 1828 plainly painted thereon. It was impossible to boil them—also the pork (salt) was as aged as the salt beef, and as bad.

While the *Culloden* was being towed when abreast of Gallipoli in company with the *Arabia* and *Tyrone* by a steamship called *The City of London*, a dust-storm and squall came suddenly on. The hawser snapped, and the *Culloden* had to drop two anchors to prevent being stranded. The steamship spun round and smashed a paddle-wheel.

Sergeant Mitchell's description of the landing of the men and horses is well told. With three others he was sent ashore with the camp equipage, having orders to put down the picket-pegs and ropes, &c., so that there might be no delay when the horses were brought ashore. The horses were placed in large horse-boats, towed by a couple of man-of-war boats. The horses were placed across the boats, which were just wide enough to admit of it. They stood quite close together, so that they had no room to kick, and each dragoon stood to his horse's head fully accoutred. The sacks containing the saddles were placed in a separate boat, and came ashore at the same time. The last boat-load of horses, however, stuck on a rock and had to remain there until morning. It was by no means a pleasant position this, as there was no room for horse or man to move. Had the wind arisen in the night, they must have had a very rough time of it. Going with six men to a town about three miles distant to get rations, Sergeant Mitchell found himself in the midst of a most cosmopolitan crowd, but the strange appearance of a vivandière seems to have greatly impressed him. She rode astride, "a smart looking lady," and dressed in "dark tunic, red trousers, boots and spurs, with hat and feather worn on the side of the head."

The next day he had experience of a ship-load of ponies that had been bought upon the coast of Syria as remounts for the cavalry, baggage animals, &c. There was a remount question even as far back as 1854. The brutes were absolutely useless, and so savage that "they actually gnawed each other," like Duncan's horses, only the steeds of the Scottish king were "beauteous and swift," while the Syrian ponies were not. The horses of the 13th, however, were in anything but good condition for marching after their long voyage—nor is this to be wondered at. Colonel Tremayne in his Notes confirms this: "We were put on the beach, and after a day or two marched to Devna. I only mention these facts to show how utterly unfit our horses must have been to start on the patrol to the Danube."

Captain Jenyns, in a letter to Colonel Anstruther-Thomson, holds a different opinion as to the native ponies, which he mentions as "clippers, about the size and cut of your grey pony of Cross's."

After being at Devna, to which place the two troops marched from Varna, for a short time, the patrol to the Danube into the Dobrudscha started.

The force consisted of two troops of the 8th Hussars, who together with the 17th Lancers were then at Devna, and two troops of the 13th Light Dragoons, viz.: B troop with Captain Jenyns and Lieutenant Jervis, and E troop with Captain Tremayne, Lieutenant Percy Smith, and Assistant-Surgeon Armstrong; there were also a few Turkish lancers. Lord Cardigan was in command.

The object of this patrol was to get as near as possible to Silistria, and to find out whether the Russians, who were then besieging that place, had any detached parties about the country.

The force marched through Bazargik, a large village, which was deserted, having been plundered both by Bashi Bazouks and Cossacks. Here a halt was made, and another at Karasi. The weather was very hot, the marches long, from sunrise to sunset, and the soil sandy and heavy. Day by day the condition of the unfortunate horses altered. "The fitting of saddles to meet the decreasing girth was of necessity a very perfunctory business," writes Colonel Tremayne. The unwieldy supply of forage and rations carried by each man in bulky heavy nets was an additional burden, and gave a grotesque appearance to the force. But not for long, for the first evening there was a false alarm of Cossacks, and "every man threw his bulky hay-nets away." The quarters at Bazargik were in an empty house, which was infested by starving cats. So great a nuisance did they become during the night that one of the party made use of his drawn sword to repel the feline invasion. On the next night, at Karasi [Kavarna ?], the arrival of some commissariat mules stampeded the horses, and nearly every one in the patrol broke loose from the picket ropes and scattered over the country. At daybreak trumpeters were sent out, and some men on the few horses left, and by degrees all the runaways except a few were regained. Lord Burghersh, the A.D.C. to Lord Raglan, who was with them, lost his horse, and so did the sergeant-major of Captain Tremayne's troop. Here Captain Tremayne was detached with 50 Turks and sent into the Dobrudscha, over the old course of the Danube, on patrol. He was away for twenty hours, but saw no Russians, meeting only a few wandering Bashi Bazouks.

It was expected that Cossacks from the force which had been besieging Silistria might have crossed the river. Rassova was the next place of halting. There the Danube is a broad, yellow, sluggish stream, five or six hundred yards across. Here Cossacks were seen for the first time on the other side of the river. At Rassova Lord Cardigan had 200 Turks under his command.

Food was not very plentiful with the force, and at Rassova it chanced that sundry very tempting looking young pigs were wandering about loose and with owners unknown. Endeavours were made to catch these, or some of them, but without success. The use of revolvers, however, furnished provisions from the herd of swine. Lord Cardigan appears to have been exceedingly wroth at what he considered a disgraceful scene, "cavalry officers shooting pigs with pistols." But all the same he was reported, on the authority of Lord Burghersh, to have enjoyed pork for supper that same night. The assistant-surgeon, however, did not share in the repast, and Lieutenant Percy Smith tells the story: "Like the others, I saw the pigs killed, and then after helping to collect wood for a fire I was so tired that I fell asleep. I was awakened by a very savoury smell, and found that Armstrong had run a long skewer through a slice of the pig's liver, and was grilling it over the fire. I said, 'Oh, you good chap, to get our dinner ready for us!' To which he answered, with the gravest of faces, 'I'm sorry to say this liver isn't fit for you to eat; it's covered with anchylosed cysts.' I promptly waked Jenyns, who was asleep close to us, and we decided the doctor mustn't risk his valuable life by eating food he knew to be unwholesome, so we took it away from him and eat it ourselves." From Rassova a long heavy march, mostly close to the river, brought the little force to Silistria, the siege of which had been abandoned by the Russians three days before. It appears that the patrol of these two squadrons of cavalry had been magnified by rumour into an advance by the Allies to the relief of the place. Silistria was found to be a good deal knocked about. The town was riddled with shot and shell, and up at Arab Tabia things were just as they had been left by the enemy. The Russian battery was within thirty feet of the Turkish one. To such an extent had Arab Tabia been pounded that Lieutenant Percy Smith absolutely passed over some of the defences without knowing it. It was then not much more than a shallow ditch. As Captain Tremayne justly remarks, "the Turks must have fought like demons."

Lieutenant Percy Smith tells us that missing this part of the defences can easily be accounted for. The force arrived at Silistria in the middle of one of the heaviest thunderstorms he had ever encountered; and it was only possible to see a few horses' lengths in front of you. He mentions that every officer and man in the force was wet through, except himself. It appears that he had undergone much chaff in the past, because, prior to leaving England, he had had his cloak waterproofed. Here it was tested, and from his point of view most successfully. After this experience, he adds, "the chaff died away."

From Silistria, the patrol had a full view of the Russian camp on the other side, "in such a jolly country, all grass, and a lovely view." There were between 40,000 and 50,000 of the enemy encamped about two miles the other side of the Danube, and entrenched. There was a battery just opposite on the other bank, and not more than 700 yards distant. In the camp was a large park of artillery, but the strength of cavalry was not great. Ophthalmia now attacked Captain Jenyns, owing to the extreme heat of the sun and the bare exposed country. The horses, too, got bad eyes, and suffered from fever in the feet. Several are said to have died from this last cause. The absurd amount loaded upon each horse was probably largely responsible for this. On home service the weight of an average dragoon in complete marching order would be about twenty stone. Here, on foreign service and in a hot climate too, the unfortunate horses had each to carry in addition, two blankets folded, one on top of the valise and one under the saddle; barley for three days, thirty-six pounds; two hay-nets filled with hay, about twenty pounds; three pounds of biscuits, and three pounds of beef or pork; a small keg holding three pints, and extra ammunition. The patrol then returned to Shumla, where Omar Pacha had a camp pitched for them.

During this reconnaissance through the Dobrudscha, when within a day's march of the Danube, Lord Cardigan decided to go on with only his staff, Lord Burghersh, and an escort of twenty men. Lieutenant Percy Smith volunteered to accompany the party, which was found by the 13th Light Dragoons. It was a long and hard day's work, and on the road back, when within about six or eight miles from the spot where the main body had been left, some of the horses gave out, being completely knocked up. Lieutenant Smith reported this, and got leave to pass the night in a deserted village close by. It was arranged that such horses as were fit should proceed, and the rest put up, rejoining the main body the following morning. Ten of the weakest horses were kept back and were established in an empty khan, which seemed the most defensible place for so small a party. The gates were shut, the fire was lighted, and such forage as could be procured was given to the horses. A sentry was just posted at the gate when a solitary horseman appeared. This turned out to be Lord Burghersh, whose horse had also failed, and he had got leave to come back and pass the night at the khan with Lieutenant Smith and his ten men. It was getting dark and they were thinking of lying down by their horses, when suddenly Turkish music was heard in the distance. The fire was at once put out and strict silence enjoined. The music came nearer and nearer, and presently it was evident that a considerable body of cavalry with a band was approaching. Some dismounted men from this force came to the gate of the khan and attempted to break it down. The sentry thereupon challenged, though he had been ordered not to do so without permission. Lieutenant Smith had thought it possible that the visitors might go elsewhere if they imagined the place locked up. More Turks formed in front of the gate, and two climbed a small minaret near which commanded the courtyard. Evidently the little body of Englishmen were mistaken for Russians. Some fifty or sixty more

Turks now arrived, and declining to believe that the occupants of the khan were English, began to make preparations to set fire to the place and burn them out. Lord Burghersh volunteered to go out and endeavour to explain to the Turkish commanding officer who the party were. Lieutenant Percy Smith, however, refused to let him do so alone, considering it would be too risky. Eventually the two went out together, instructions how to act having been given by Lieutenant Percy Smith to the corporal—the only non-commissioned officer with the party—and what course to pursue in case the two officers should be made prisoners and did not return in a couple of hours. Immediately Lieutenant Smith and Lord Burghersh emerged from the gateway of the khan they were seized and led off to a large fire just outside the village, around which were seated some twenty Turkish officers. Fortunately the staff uniform which Lord Burghersh was wearing was recognised as British, though evidently the Turks considered it very suspicious that he should be in company with one whom they persisted in believing to be a Russian. He was, however, unmolested, though no attention was at first paid to what he said or endeavoured to say in Turkish. Lieutenant Smith was, however, forced down on to the ground, and a black private mounted guard over him with a drawn sword. The fellow evidently desired to use his weapon on Lieutenant Smith as soon as opportunity served, and from his excitement and frequent repetition of the word "Russ! Russ!" it was quite clear what idea he had in his head. The amount of knowledge of the Turkish language possessed by Lord Burghersh was but limited, and he found himself at a loss for the Turkish equivalent for "lieutenant." As a substitute he made use of the word "yuzbashi," which signifies "head of a hundred," and would in English be translated "captain." Unfortunately some of the Turks had managed to look into the courtyard of the khan and had counted the horses, twelve in number. They declined, therefore, to believe in the rank of their suspect. "Yuzbashi? Yok, yok, on-ikki!" they exclaimed; Head of 100? No, no, only 12! However, presently matters began to straighten themselves out. Lord Burghersh was offered coffee and bread, and this he tried to share with Lieutenant Smith. Then the trouble became worse than ever. The black soldier felt his chance would be gone if his captive were allowed to eat and drink with the officers. At length food was sent to Lieutenant Smith by the Turkish colonel, and in high dudgeon the would-be executioner sheathed his sword. The fact was that the shako worn by Lieutenant Smith was precisely the same shape as that worn by some of the Russian cavalry, and the Turks had seen them at Silistria.

On the next day Lord Cardigan picked up the detachment and marched to Rossova. It turned out that the Turks who had seized Lieutenant Smith and Lord Burghersh were a regiment of Bashi Bazouks, about 600 strong; only three of their officers belonged to the Turkish regular army, and of their discipline but little could be said.

From Shumla, the force with Lord Cardigan marched back to Yeni Bazar and Devna, arriving there after travelling all night through a tremendous thunderstorm.

Here for the first time since leaving Portsmouth the regiment was together, and the remainder of the Light Brigade was also there.

The remainder of the 13th Light Dragoons, it will be remembered, had not landed when the squadron was detached under Lord Cardigan. The reconnaissance lasted from June 25 until July 11.

Up to this time there is nothing particular to record with reference to the headquarters and remainder of the regiment.

The morning after the last troop disembarked a parade was ordered by Lord Lucan, and the regiment turned out and was inspected. Lord Lucan appears to have complimented the major on the appearance of the men and horses. It would seem that the horses of the 13th and those of the Royal Dragoons were landed, in the opinion of his lordship, in better condition than any others in the cavalry division. But truth to tell they were not in a fit condition to undertake long marches. The first day's march was to the encampment of the Guards and Highland regiments.

Passing close to Varna, when beneath the walls of the town the march was deflected to the left, then along by the edge of a lake for some distance. Here, with the idea of shortening the road, a bridle-path on the right which led through a wood was taken. This path, however, gradually narrowed till it stopped. Search revealed another path, and the march was resumed. This was hardly more satisfactory, and eventually after wandering for several hours a British Guardsman was sighted on top of a hill far away on the left front. The 13th marched towards him and found that he was a sentry on outlying picket.

The Guardsman directed them down a road in his rear, and the picket was soon met with, snugly lying in a large hut built of boughs.

Passing on, the 13th reached the camp of the 1st Division, the men of which turned out and cheered them as they rode by.

When the regiment reached its appointed ground, which was a small meadow, they halted and dismounted, linking horses, as the ponies with picket-ropes, pegs, and tents had not yet come up. The ponies should have arrived, as they had continued on the right road and had not turned off through the wood. Two hours later one pony turned up. The fact was that the other wretched, unbroken ponies, unaccustomed as they were to carrying packs, had bolted into the lake, kicked off their loads into the water, where they had to be left. Some time after dark the runaways were brought into camp—but minus their packs and saddles.

On the morrow the regiment went into camp with the 8th Hussars, 11th Hussars, and 17th Lancers. The heavy dragoons were encamped a short distance away, and the light division of infantry on the other side of the river.

While the brigade was encamped here it was reviewed by Omar Pacha, the Turkish Commander-in-Chief, who was much impressed by a charge of cavalry. He was reported to have expressed an opinion that no Russian cavalry would ever stand up against a British charge. Events proved that he was not far wrong. Thus were matters with the headquarters when Lord Cardigan returned from his reconnaissance, and the squadron of the 13th rejoined the regiment after its seventeen days of marching and bivouacking. From private letters to Colonel Anstruther-Thomson we learn that the detachment from the 13th received much praise from Lord Cardigan for its services while on the patrol, the writer adding, "who is a capital fellow to be under at this work." But the stress of the campaign had already begun to tell both on men and horses. "The soldiers look such oddities, all rags and filth." "There is a great deal of bad diarrhœa among the men and officers." Particularly as regards the two squadrons of British cavalry which accompanied Lord Cardigan, another extract may be here given. On their return "they were in poor condition, indeed, both men and horses. They had started in robust health, but returned mere shadows of their former selves. They had been gone seventeen days, during which they had made some very long marches, and the whole time were without tents day or night. Their rations consisted of a handful of biscuit and a pound of salt pork per diem; no tea, coffee, or rum, and as it is difficult to procure water at many places in Bulgaria, they were badly enough off." So much for the condition of the men. Of the horses we read, "some of the horses were completely knocked up, and had to be shot."

As July wore on, grass became scarce in the neighbourhood, and the Commissariat officers were perforce compelled to go into the villages some distance away to procure forage by purchase—purchase almost compulsory. A fair price was paid for standing wheat, oats, and barley, and then parties were sent out with led horses, hay-nets, and reaping-hooks, to gather in the corn. Those who could reap managed well enough, but many could not. The ignorant cut themselves often in their endeavours to reap, while those who had the requisite knowledge soon found that they had to do the entire work for all. But it was bad food for the horses, and grass would have been much preferable. Cholera, that dread scourge of armies in the field, now broke out. Several men of the light division died in one night. The light division was then shifted from its camp, a part was sent to Monastir, and the Light Brigade despatched along the road to Schumla and encamped near Yeni Bazar. The first healthy place was Yasi Tepe. All along the road lay the unburied bodies of horses, bullocks, goats, sheep, or dogs, sometimes singly, sometimes in twos or threes. In Bulgaria nobody troubles to bury the dead carcases of animals. Among this offal wild dogs, horrid curs and savage withal, wandered feasting. Cowardly by day, but when in a pack at night, as is their wont, most dangerous to a solitary man. The Bulgarian inhabitants do not interfere with them, but wild-dog hunting by the British officers, mounted on ponies and armed with lances, soon became a frequent and very necessary amusement. At Yeni Bazar the Light Brigade arrived on July 28, and remained in camp until August 26, when it was set in motion for active service; the report being that its destination was the Crimea. That evening the brigade reached

Yesitappe, where it remained till August 28. On August 28th the brigade marched to Derna, and on the 29th to Varna.

Two days later the entire Light Brigade was inspected by Lord Lucan in watering order, and all men considered unfit for active service in the field were weeded out.

One or two facts which occurred at this period before the return to Varna may be mentioned as of interest. At Devna, Lord Lucan ordered that the trumpeters were not to be mounted on grey horses, remarking, it is said, that "a trumpeter was of as much consequence as an officer." Undoubtedly the grey horses were conspicuous and furnished an excellent target—and trumpeters were not too plenty.

On the march to Nani Bazar the wild ponies used for transport proved unmanageable, and several of the troop had to dismount, place the tent poles, &c., on their horses, and walking lead them to Nani Bazar. There they found an abundant supply of water, after their long and dusty march. Troughs had been made at the place by Lord Cardigan, but for fear of cholera the thirsty men were not permitted to drink. The order seemed no doubt cruel—but it was kind. In one week five of the 13th died, and a trumpeter of the regiment was absolutely borrowed by the 17th Lancers to sound the last post over one of that regiment.

Shortly after this the doctor of the 11th Hussars succeeded in obtaining an order forbidding funeral music.

Drill and manœuvring was very regularly performed under Lord Cardigan. It is recorded that the wives of two of the officers, one of the 8th and the other of the 11th, were with the brigade during all the hardships of this trying time, and escaped unscathed.

The food supply was at this time regular—usually one pound of fresh beef per man per day. But vegetables, except onions sometimes, were not to be procured. Rice was served out in lieu, but unfortunately neither pepper nor salt was to be had. These condiments had been forgotten.

By August the weather was very hot, the men's appetites failed, they could not eat the meat, and much was thrown away. Presently the daily ration of meat was increased to a pound and a half, and in consequence nearly a double quantity was wasted. No ration of rum was served out, and except some which was given as a reward to the men by Omar Pacha after the review they had tasted none. But the fear induced by the ravages of cholera caused the authorities to amend this, and for the rest of the campaign a ration of half a gill per day was ordered. This rum, mixed with water, formed the main drink of the British Army in the Crimea.

Later the amount of the issue was doubled. This was the official spirit ration, but of course an illicit traffic with the troops was frequently attempted and often for a time was successfully carried on. The Colonel of the 13th detected one scamp in the canteen tent who was selling the most vile stuff to the men. One visit he paid to the tent but failed to bring the matter home. A few days later, however, having received further information, the colonel ordered a farrier to accompany him there and to bring a sledge-hammer. The cask, a large one, was tested, and being found to be as was suspected rank poison, was immediately stove in and poured out on the ground. The man himself was at once turned out of the camp.

An account is given of the usual manœuvres in which the men were exercised by Lord Cardigan daily. One was "advancing and retiring the front line, the second coming up. Another was to advance a squadron to the front, and at a given signal for every man to disperse and go where he pleased. The "rally" was then sounded to see how speedily the men could get into their formation again. This, together with skirmishing drill, charging in line and by squadrons, outpost drill, &c., rendered the men as efficient as it was possible for them to be. But on the horses the work pressed very hardly, and their condition did not improve.

On the march down the man who had been expelled from the camp turned up again more than once, and on the second occasion was regularly mobbed on account of some swindling transaction in which he had wronged one of the men. The fellow offered violence, throwing a sword snatched from a Turk at the crowd, but luckily did no damage. These native hucksters were the curse of every camp, and were a constant source of trouble to the officers and ruin to the men.

Varna had, at the time that the 13th arrived there for embarkation, recently suffered much from a great fire. The ground selected for the encampment was covered with a thick black dust. During the night a heavy storm of wind arose, and blew down nearly all the tents, as the pegs could not get a hold. The unfortunate men were covered with this black dust for some hours, and until the wind moderated it was impossible to get clean.

At Varna the 13th remained for three days.

On September 1st the regiment, with the exception of Captain Goad and twenty-one men for whom there was no room on board, embarked in the steam transport *Jason*. These were, however, embarked the same day in the *Simla*.

On September 3rd the two transports joined the fleet at Baltschik Bay, about seven miles from Varna, and on the 7th the whole allied fleets and armies sailed for the Crimea. It was an enormous armament, some six hundred sail of all kinds. English, French, and Turkish three-deckers, gunboats, steam transports, and sailing-vessels, large and small.

Progress was extremely slow, and considering the crowd it is not to be wondered at that some accidents took place. One large ship fouled the *Jason*, snapping the main yard, but luckily the fragments did not fall on the deck, which was thronged with men.

On the voyage sickness increased—three men were buried from the *Jason* in a few days at sea.

By the 14th of September the fleet anchored off the Crimean coast at Eupatoria—a low, flat shore. Towards evening a few boat-loads landed, among them being twenty men and horses of the 13th.

On the next day the remainder of the regiment was landed. The horses were put into long flat-bottomed boats, which, however, could not be brought quite to the shore.

The men were fully accoutred with a full amount of ammunition, water, and three days' cooked provisions. The horses, when as close to the land as practicable, were pushed overboard. During the disembarkation one man was nearly drowned.

Captain Tremayne landed in the afternoon of the 16th, and with Lieutenant Percy Smith and some others of the officers was ordered to collect the men and horses already landed and go with Lord Cardigan on patrol. About 100 men and horses of the 13th were thus employed with Lieut.-Colonel Doherty. There was also some other cavalry, two guns of the I Troop of Royal Horse Artillery, and about 150 Rifles. Captain Tremayne's charger had not been landed, and he had to go on a trooper without his own kit. The patrol penetrated as far as a village called "Sak," where a few carts and beasts were

CAVALRY CAMP, CRIMEA (1854).

(*From Simpson's 'Seat of War in the East', 1855-6.*)

taken. On the next day Captain Tremayne was sent with a troop to escort the Assistant Quartermaster-General of the light division. The orders were to go as far south as possible without getting into touch with the enemy.

About three miles from Eupatoria, near Simpheropol, they found from 80 to 100 Cossacks, who endeavoured to get round their left flank. Thereupon the squadron retired slowly, and a company of the Rifle Brigade coming up soon sent the Cossacks away.

Mention has been made of the sickness on board; how this affected the 13th may be judged from the following information culled from Colonel Tremayne's Notes. "The Major, Ormsby Gore [later Lord Harlech], Jenyns, King, and Purcell, were struck by fever on board ship and couldn't land; all went home except Jenyns, a rare plucked one, who reappeared shortly after we reached Balaclava, still very ill. Purcell sank into wretched health."

On September 19th the army moved from its bivouac at the Old Fort, Eupatoria, and marched in the direction of Sebastopol.

On arriving at the river Bulganak, the enemy was found in position.

The Affair at Bulganak, September 19, 1854.

The force of the enemy at Bulganak amounted to about four thousand men: infantry, artillery, and Cossacks. The action began by the Russians sending out cavalry skirmishers.

Under the command of Lord Cardigan the 13th Light Dragoons with a troop of horse artillery were pushed forward to try the strength of the enemy. The right troop of the regiment, with Lieutenant and Adjutant Irwin and Cornet Montgomery, was sent out to skirmish with the Cossacks.

This is the account given in the Regimental Records, but from the Notes of Captain Percy Smith we gather that apparently Lieutenant and Adjutant Irwin was not with Cornet Montgomery, and that the Adjutant sent him to Cornet Montgomery.

After about a quarter of an hour's sharp firing, in which very little damage was done by either side, the troop was retired. This it did steadily, but under artillery fire, as the enemy had brought up some guns. Four horses were killed and four men wounded during the retirement, one of them being Sergeant Priestley of the 13th, who lost a foot, which was taken off by a shell. As this man was a paymaster-sergeant he had no right to be under fire.

Captain Percy Smith tells of this incident thus: "In consequence of Captain Jenyns' illness I had the troop, and was of course covering Sergeant Priestley when the squadron retired. So the shell that killed his horse must have missed me by a few inches. It hit the horse just under the dock, and burst at the same moment, and the first thing I saw was the horse falling on his head, with the belly so completely emptied that I could see the joints of the spine.

Sergeant Priestley is believed to have been the first man wounded in the war who belonged to the British Army.

The other casualties were Private Kay, Private Shaw, and Private Badger.

Other parts of the Light Brigade now came up and the artillery. The latter getting into action, the enemy hastily withdrew, though not without suffering considerable loss.

The army bivouacked close to the river Bulganak that evening.

On the 20th of September the whole of the allied armies, British, French, and Turkish, were reviewed by Lord Raglan the British Commander-in-Chief, and Marshal St Arnaud the Commander-in-Chief of the French Army. The review being concluded, the allied armies marched on the Alma, and they arrived at about 1.30 P.M.

The Battle of the Alma, September 20, 1854.

The advance of the allied armies passed over the line of retreat of the enemy on the previous day, and everywhere evidences were in view of the excellent practice made by the British artillery during the short time in which it was in action. Sixteen dead horses were counted and several men; the latter the enemy had neither stayed to bury nor to carry off. They had evidently retired in great haste, for every few yards something or other that had either been dropped or thrown away was to be seen, — here a small hatchet, there a Cossack's whip, picket-pegs, ropes, &c. Beyond the village of Alma, and the river Alma, a range of heights appeared, and these heights were fully occupied by large bodies of troops. It looked like a very

THE BATTLE OF THE ALMA, SEPTEMBER 20, 1854.

strong position. Up to this time, though the existence of the river Alma was known it was not yet visible, but when seen the enemy's position appeared naturally to be very much stronger, since the forcing of the passage of a river in the face of a powerful enemy is seldom a light task.

As the allied armies approached the village, which also was held by the enemy, the sight according to every account was most grand. It was a bright sunny day, and the flash of steel and the brilliant scarlet uniforms of the majority of the British force mingled with the darker clothing of the Allies was a spectacle to be remembered. On this subject in these days of kharki a remark made by Colonel Tremayne in his Notes is worth quoting. He writes: "What struck me very forcibly was, that seeing as I could the whole force probably four miles to the sea, the black or dark coats of our Rifles, the French and Turks, were more easily discernible than the red of our Guards and line." Almost immediately on the arrival of the allied armies in close proximity to the village of Alma, the battle began. The Russian rifles opened fire, and the village was by them set ablaze simultaneously in several places. The intention of this was probably that the smoke arising from the burning buildings should conceal from the Allies the position of the Russian guns. The Rifles and skirmishers of the 1st Divison, however, soon cleared the village of the enemy, and then proceeded to do the same in the vineyards which lay between the place and the river. All the Russian skirmishers were driven in, and the action then became general.

The position allotted to the 13th Light Dragoons was on the left front of the army and a little in advance. For some time the cavalry were dismounted, halting in a field of melons awaiting orders. Why the Russian cavalry, of which there was plenty, did not make even a feint attack on the British left flank, has never been explained.

The light division of infantry was posted on the right of the light cavalry.

By this time the rear of the allied armies had closed up, and there in view of the 13th were the plumed bonnets of the Highlanders and the bearskins of the Guards, head-dresses which, perhaps, by a trick of eyesight, seemed to give the men an apparently enormous height.

Ahead were the Rifles, lying down in skirmishing order, and ready to spring up the instant the order to advance was given. The order came, and from the right the battle began. Then a gun was fired from a Russian battery opposite the right front of the 13th. The range was, however, too great, but later several round-shot came very close, one horse was wounded in Captain Tremayne's troop, and Lord Lucan also, who was a little way in front of the regiment, had a narrow escape from a shot which pitched close to his horse's fore-feet.

When the riflemen had cleared the village and vineyards, despite the clouds of smoke which blew directly in their faces, the general advance began, as has been said. But no opportunity for action had yet been given to the Light Brigade. There, perforce, they had to remain in the melon-field, watching a strong body of Russian cavalry which was posted just opposite to them on the other side of the river. As this body consisted of several strong regiments, any one of which was numerically superior to the entire light cavalry brigade, their inaction is, as has been mentioned, inexplicable. Moreover, too, the Russian cavalry had some guns with them, and even these were not used. The general advance was now in progress. The passage of the river was forced, and through the smoke of the burning village, when rifts in it permitted a view, the Light Brigade could now see the British red lines forming on the opposite bank of the river. And now the shipping which had been brought into the river joined in the fight. Far away to the right, as far as the eye could reach, the vessels were seen shelling the heights on which the extreme left of the enemy rested. But for the Light Brigade there were yet no orders to advance. Then by degrees to their view was disclosed the infantry, working their way upward and onward in the struggle to gain the heights. And on to those heights the enemy continued to bring up masses of troops. Could the attackers prevail against such numbers? could they be hoped to do so? They could, and they did. Still the Light Brigade remained to watch this terrible struggle; and still the Russian cavalry remained to watch them. Not even an attempt was make to attack the flank of the infantry while toiling up the hillside by this strong body of horse. It may have been that the ground did not permit such an attack, but of this there is no proof, and maps do not point to any special difficulties. Still the red line pressed onward, to be met by fresh troops—troops brought up to replace others that had been retired.

Meanwhile, what of the allied artillery?

For the passage of guns the river was unfordable; and a bridge at the village had been partially destroyed by the enemy. To the repair of this bridge the energies of the Sappers were devoted, and it was rendered practicable for the crossing of artillery. Over went the guns, and coming into action on the other side speedily silenced the Russian batteries one after the other. From their positions on the hillside the enemy was gradually forced upwards, and at too great a speed to enable them to recover any ground which they lost. Nor could the fresh troops do more. Then far away on the left, where the fire of the shipping had produced its effect, the French attack was in full force. Then our allies turned the left flank of the enemy. That done, the end came soon. Resistance slackened, then ceased, and soon the whole Russian army was in full retreat.

And now at length the Light Brigade received the order to advance. Crossing the river by a ford, though not without some difficulty, the opposite bank was reached.

That there was not a serious loss of life was owing to the carelessness of the enemy.

The approach to this ford was through a narrow lane with stone walls on either side, and was not to be traversed at great speed.

The Russians had still one field-battery in position on the extreme right, and its guns, moreover, were still being fought.

These guns were opened on the advancing British cavalry in an endeavour to annihilate them while in this lane.

Trees which should have been cut down, however, had not been so cut down here, though in the lower portion of the river the banks had been cleared. Some shot fell very close amid the trees, but no casualties occurred. The river bank was reached, and at a gallop the passage was made. Even then the Russian cavalry made no attempt, but finding the British had crossed the ford, retired to protect the Russian battery which had already limbered up and had left the field.

Up the hill went the 13th at a gallop in column of troops, passing over the ground that had been so gallantly carried by the British infantry. It was a terrible scene of slaughter. At the top of the hill the British were holding the crest in line, and below and away over the plain could be seen the broken enemy in full retreat. The bodies of the Russian troops in the distance were in some semblance of formation, but the intervening ground was dotted over with small straggling bodies of men and single fugitives. To round these up and drive them in as prisoners the 13th were sent. The artillery of the enemy, which might have opposed this move, still attempted nothing more than getting some guns into position without opening fire. In the distance the Russian rear-guard showed a front till dark, and the 13th remained on the crest of the hill watching them. The regiment was then ordered back down the hill, being presently halted to take up ground for the night. To give some idea of the severity of the struggle, it may be worth while mentioning that to clear space enough for one troop of the 13th no less than seventeen dead bodies had to be moved, besides a dead horse. The regiment bivouacked by the side of a ravine or dell, up which a Russian column had retreated. The slaughter here was occasioned by Captain Maude's troop of Royal Horse Artillery, which, as Colonel Tremayne writes, "had got the range of them high, and I never saw a more ghastly sight than the rows of men with their skulls blown off. To water the horses that night was a task of great difficulty, owing to the huge crowds of men all bent on the same object—the procuring of water for themselves and their mounts; and as it was by that time quite dark, the confusion was not a little."

That night about twenty of the 13th were told off on patrol duty under the command of Lieutenant Jervis. They ascended the hill again, and descending the other side advanced some distance over the plain. They then patrolled right and left across the whole front to watch if any of the enemy were in the neighbourhood.

While taking the muster-roll of the regiment on the evening after the battle, the Adjutant, Lieutenant Thomas Irwin, was suddenly taken ill. He had been seized with cholera. He was at once sent to the coast in an araba, but died on board ship a few days afterwards. Lieutenant Irwin was succeeded as Adjutant by Regimental Sergeant-Major George Gardner, whose commission as Cornet bears date September 27, 1854. A letter from Cornet and Adjutant Gardner to his former Captain (Colonel Anstruther-Thomson), and dated

February 12, 1855, announces the fact that he has received a commission in the 13th, and thanks the old commanding officer of his troop for his "very great kindness in first pointing out to me the proper path to such promotion."

Under date September 22, Captain Tremayne writes:—

Two days after the battle we, the Light Cavalry, were sent on a most extraordinary errand. Guns and all, we were taken by Lord Lucan down a deep sandy lane some three or four miles to the east of the army to the fine broad road leading from Sebastopol to Simpheropol. There we passed the night. On each side of the road was vegetation, trees giving good cover, and I am sure fifty infantry soldiers in this cover could have wrought havoc with impunity in half an hour. At daybreak we rejoined the army. We also advanced under Lord Cardigan to the right front, and found ourselves close to the forts on the north side of Sebastopol, from which we retired at once.

On the 23rd of September the Light Brigade reached the Katche river, and passing across proceeded to Donaukoi. The army bivouacked close to the Katche, but the cavalry, finding no secure place at Donaukoi, returned to within three miles of the army, and remained standing to their horses' heads all night, throwing out a line of vedettes in front of the whole army, no fire or light of any description being permitted.

On the next day, soon after daylight, four Russians, six horses, and a van loaded with camp equipage were taken by the outlying picket of the regiment. On this day one man (Private Murphy) died of cholera. Colonel Tremayne's account of this time is as follows:—

On the 24th we reached the Katche river. We saw from belts, arms, &c., lying on the ground, that about here the Russians had greatly accelerated their retreat. The Greys had landed about now, and the 57th. Next came the "flank march," bringing us from the north to the south of Sebastopol. We marched by narrow tracks through waterless scrub, and sometimes in file only. On the edge of the scrub we found ourselves in an open space close to Mackenzie's Farm. The Greys and some guns had preceded us, and came upon the rear-guard of the Russian army which was retiring from Sebastopol. We galloped a short way to the eastward, and were halted on a brow looking over a fine rich-looking plain, and saw the enemy far away on their road to Simpheropol. Their rear-guard made no stand. We then marched down a broad dusty hillside across a plain, and encamped for the night on the banks of the Tchernaya. The water was welcome. The next day we assisted at the capture of Balaclava, which only made a weak resistance.

From the Regimental Records under date September 24, we gather that on that day the regiment crossed the river Belbec about 2 P.M., and proceeded to the north side of Sebastopol, but on arriving within range of the fort the garrison turned their heavy guns upon the regiment and compelled the whole to retire close to the Belbec, where they bivouacked for the night. At this bivouac the 2nd Dragoons, or Scots Greys, joined, having disembarked at the Katcha river and marched to the Belbec. This account supplements that contained in the Notes of Colonel Tremayne.

The Regimental Record continues as follows:—

25th. Marched about 8 A.M. in front of the army through a thick wood, arriving about 12 noon at a place called Kula Mackenzie, or Mackenzie's Farm, where we came suddenly upon a Russian Force of about 10,000 men under the command of Prince Menzikchoff, and in full retreat upon Backshira. As soon as the Cavalry made their appearance the Russians were panic-stricken and fled in all directions, leaving the whole of their Commissariat Wagons, Ammunition Wagons, and private carriages, horses, &c., &c. The rout of the Russians was complete, and as soon as Lord Raglan saw they would not turn or give battle, he gave up the pursuit, being anxious to get to the north side of Sebastopol. The army remained for about an hour on the heights of Mackenzie's Farm, and then proceeded to the river Tchernaya, after effecting several valuable captures, where they bivouacked for the night.

The Regimental Record states that it was on this day that Lieutenant and Adjutant Irwin was taken ill, and that news of his death reached the regiment on September 29, or four days later. Most probably the account given by Colonel Tremayne, and corroborated both by Sergeant Mitchell and Private Powell, is correct.

About 8 A.M. on the morning of the 26th the bivouac was broken up. A party of Cossacks were observed on the plains of Balaclava, to whom chase was given.

The enemy, however, retreated into Sebastopol, and the pursuit was then abandoned and the cavalry returned to the army which was then in full march on Balaclava. Here it arrived at about noon and captured the place after, as has been said, but little resistance. Near Balaclava the cavalry went into bivouac, and remained there until October 7. During this interval the site of the bivouac was occasionally shifted.

On October 7th the enemy appeared in some force, and the whole brigade turned out, with a troop of horse artillery. After exchanging a few shots the enemy retired and the troops returned to their former ground. From this date until October 24 (the eve of Balaclava) there is nothing to record of any importance—patrolling the country and furnishing vedettes daily appears to have been the employment of the regiment. On many occasions, however, the enemy felt the position, appearing to select the time for so doing when the men were just about to take a meal. These constant calls to "turn out immediately" and the sounding of "boot and saddle" were very vexatious, as it implied packing up everything in readiness to move off at once, and none could tell where the next bivouac would be. Nothing would happen. The vedettes on the hill would be observed "circling," which was a sign that the enemy was approaching. Maybe a strong body of Cossacks would be the cause, but they never came to close quarters. Returned to bivouac, everything was of course packed, the kettles emptied, and the only resource was to pick up the best of the food from the ground and make the most of it.

Sergeant Mitchell gives an account of one affair which may be quoted here, happening as it did at this time.

> The next day a strong reconnoitring party was sent out, and went some distance beyond the village where the Cossacks had shown themselves the day before, and followed a road which led away to the right between two hills. On our left was a steep hill thickly covered with brushwood, and on our right a deep ravine, in some places almost choked with brushwood. At certain places on the right where the bank was most abrupt a stone wall had been built. It was a very crooked road. At one place a large rock overhung the road which looked as if it might fall at any moment. We went some three miles up this road and dismounted, and as the officer in charge did not appear in a hurry we made a few small fires by the roadside, and there being a nice spring of water near we soon had a drop of coffee. We had quite time to get it comfortably, and had strapped our mess tins on our saddles again. We had just received the order "Prepare to mount," when bang goes a carbine from what appeared to us to be the other side of the ravine, but which in reality was on our own side. The road being so crooked it at first had that appearance. The shot was followed by several more, during which time we were all in our saddles, and on looking towards the place from whence the firing came we saw about a dozen Russian hussars and some infantry standing under cover of some rather high trees. Our party, which was composed of men of the 13th and 17th, was under the charge of an officer of that corps, who, thinking there might be a larger number of the enemy in the neighbourhood, ordered us to retire down the road at a trot, until we could reach the open plain. We had to form the rear-guard. Luckily for us, they had not

taken good aim, for the whole of their shots went wide of the mark, some going over our heads and others striking the stone wall at our side. As soon as they saw us retiring a large number came from under the cover and half-a-dozen or so came on at a gallop.

The road being crooked, favoured us, but whenever they came in sight of us rounding a curve they would fire, but always at random. We now passed the overhanging rock I spoke of, and as it jutted out some distance it afforded good cover. The two rear men here made a stand for a moment and gave them a shot each. The two shots struck the leading files, either men or horses, and they all pulled up, thus giving us a chance of placing a good distance between them and us.

Our officer was anxious to get past a certain point, for there was a small beaten track which led down the hill-side, through the brushwood, where probably a party of infantry might be for the purpose of cutting us off. We were just in time, for we were not above three hundred yards below this path when we saw a party of infantry come down it, but they were too late. We returned quietly to camp, and were not disturbed that night.

From the same source an account of the duties of the outlying picket is derived. It is as follows:—

About a couple of days after this [Sergeant Mitchell here refers to his temporary and brief duty as officer's servant to the colonel] we furnished the outlying picket, and my comrade and myself formed part of it. . . . We were glad to find on arriving at the place that the old picket had a good fire, which they handed over to us. Our duty here was to place a mounted vedette on the hillside at our right front, who commanded a view of the road where we had been so nearly cut off a few days before. Half-way between him and the picket a dismounted sentry was placed, whose duty it was to give notice to the picket if he saw the vedette signalling. About a mile to the left another mounted vedette was posted. He commanded a view of a large tract of open country, as well as two or three roads, and a small river which we called the Black river, but which was afterwards known as the river Tchernaya. In like manner, a dismounted man was posted as before. A mounted man was also posted in a village to our right for the double purpose of seeing if any Russian troops made their appearance, as well as to watch a fountain of water and prevent the villagers from tampering with it. . . . After dark we were withdrawn from the top of the hill down into the plain to our rear, it being easier at night to discern any one approaching if you are at the bottom of a hill, as, unless it is very dark indeed you see them the moment they are at the top. . . . Just before daybreak we were marched to our original ground, and had our vedettes posted before daylight, not, however, until a party consisting of about half the picket had advanced some distance to the front and patrolled from right to left to make sure there was no enemy near.

Meanwhile working parties were engaged in trenching in front of Sebastopol, and were nightly fired on by the Russians.

It was now decided to construct some redoubts, beginning on the hill near a village by name Kamara, and stretching away along the ridge where the outlying picket had previously been placed and which separated two plains. They were soon finished, being placed, first, one on a small hill near Kamara; the second on a larger hill two or three hundred yards to the left; and the third and fourth on two mounds on the ridge some considerable distance farther round to the left. Each redoubt contained guns from the ships, one or two only. The redoubts were manned by Turkish troops under the charge of an English artilleryman.

The enemy was now evidently concentrating a force in the rear of the position of the Allies. They daily became bolder, and showed themselves in greater numbers.

One afternoon a party of the 13th were sent into Balaclava for forage which had been landed there. They had just loaded up, and were starting on the return journey, when an officer of a Highland regiment informed them that the enemy was advancing over the hill by Kamara. He had been sent to collect any of the men of his regiment that might be in the town. The party of the 13th hastened back and found the brigade had already turned out and were some distance out on the plain. The loads of hay were speedily thrown down, and off the party started to join them, and took their places in the ranks. It turned out that quite a strong force had advanced on Kamara, but receiving a few shots from the guns in the redoubts, and seeing the British turn out, they retired again. On one occasion a sergeant of the 13th was cut off by the enemy and taken prisoner. The outlying picket had been ordered to proceed to the river Tchernaya, and ascertain if there were any Russians in the village beyond it. Strict injunctions were laid on the officer in command that he was to discover all he could without permitting a man to cross the river. The party consisted of fifteen men and a sergeant and an officer.

The sergeant and four men were ordered to advance to the front and extend their files to about three hundred yards apart from each other and lead on in the direction of the river. The remaining eleven men with the captain followed slowly along the plain.

In the distance, according to the orders they had received, when the advanced party reached the river they closed in on the bridge.

The captain now galloped to the party at the bridge, halting the remainder of his men, and gave some order, after which he returned to the men who were halted. Meanwhile, to their surprise, they saw the sergeant cross the bridge and ascend a hill on the opposite side of the river. Out from the bottom of the hill rode four Russian hussars in pursuit, and over the top, to make matters worse, came three more, who came down to meet him. The sergeant turned to his left and rode along the side of the hill towards the Russian camp, his pursuers riding parallel at first and then gradually drawing in. Eventually he was taken prisoner. The men in the rear then, without orders, moved off in the direction of the river in the hope of effecting a diversion in favour of the sergeant, showing a bold front and enabling him to escape across the river lower down. *En route* they met the officer, who was wroth with them for moving without orders. The situation was explained to him as well and as quickly as possible, but though possessed of a field-glass he could not see the pursuers. The men averred that the sergeant must be taken prisoner. The remark of the officer was characteristic: "And serve him right, too. Why did he not ride at them and bowl them over."

But the matter did not end there. Lord Lucan, by whose personal orders the party had gone out, made a searching investigation into the reason why his explicit orders had been disobeyed. In the result it is stated that the officer (Captain Oldham) was relieved soon after the picket returned and placed under arrest. Whether this arrest was taken off before Balaclava is not stated, but Captain Oldham, as senior captain, commanded the 13th at the battle of Balaclava, and lost his life in the charge of the Light Brigade.

CHAPTER XXIX.

Balaclava, October 25, 1854.

THE battle of Balaclava may be most conveniently divided into four phases—

1. The attack and capture by the Russians of the redoubts which had been erected on Canrobert's Hill and the Causeway Heights. These were garrisoned by Turks, and armed with ship's guns from H.M.S. *Diamond*, to each of which guns a British artilleryman was attached.
2. The defeat of the attack made by the Russian cavalry upon the 93rd Highlanders and a few men of the brigade of Guards, Sir Colin Campbell being in command.
3. The charge made upon the Russian cavalry by the Heavy Brigade, under the command of General Scarlett, by which the Russians were routed and forced to take refuge behind the guns of the Don Cossacks at the eastern extremity of the northern valley.
4. The charge of the Light Brigade, under Lord Cardigan, during which support was given by the 4th Chasseurs D'Afrique, who drove off a battery of Russian artillery posted on the Fedioukine Heights. The 4th Chasseurs D'Afrique were under the command of General D'Allonville.

Here it will be convenient to give a general description of the battle-ground, and to mention in brief the disposition of the forces engaged. About one mile almost due north of Balaclava lay the village of Kadikoi. Three miles due east of Kadikoi lay Kamara. West-north-west of Kamara was a hill known as Canrobert's Hill, on which No. 1 redoubt was erected. To the north of Canrobert's Hill lay the range of heights known as the Causeway Heights, along which ran the Woronzoff Road. On these heights, and along this road, stood redoubts No. 2, No. 3, and No. 4. There were three detached hills at the western extremity of this ridge, and on the 1st and 3rd of these stood redoubts No. 5 and No. 6. At a point between redoubt No. 2 and redoubt No. 3 another spur projected from the Causeway Heights, which took an easterly direction bearing somewhat northwards. South of the two detached hills, at the other extremity of the heights, lay the camps of the Heavy and the Light Brigades. On a small ridge to the north of Kadikoi, and rather to its right, were stationed the 93rd Highlanders. Between this ridge and the Causeway Heights was what is known as the south valley. This valley was the scene of the attack by the Russian cavalry on the Highlanders and some men of the Guards brigade, and also of their repulse. Here also the Heavy Cavalry Brigade charged the main body of the Russian cavalry and routed it. To the north of the Causeway Heights lay another valley, bounded upon the north by the Fedioukine Hills, a long bow-shaped range, in the centre of which there was a kind of horse-shoe shaped indentation due north and south. The eastern end of this valley was almost closed by hills, except at the north where an aqueduct took a somewhat irregular course. Beyond this was the river Tchernaya, bridged at the north by the Tractir Bridge. The aqueduct could be passed in three places.

Beyond the Tchernaya stood Tchorgoum, a town about $4\frac{1}{2}$ miles north-east of Kadikoi. To Tchorgoum a road went which cut the Woronzoff Road at right angles.

The northern valley, which has just been described, was the scene of the charge of the Light Brigade.

This valley was approximately three-quarters of a mile wide at its western extremity, and gradually narrowed at its eastern to half a mile. Its total length was one mile and a half.

An hour before daybreak the cavalry brigades turned out as usual. The Highlanders upon the ridge mentioned were acting in support of the Turks posted in the redoubts.

Not far from the Highlanders the Heavy Brigade of British cavalry was then drawn up, mounted, but not in such a position as to be able to afford the maximum support. As the event turned out, no support was required.

The Light Brigade was drawn up almost due north and south, north of Kadikoi, and south of redoubt No. 5, and facing towards No. 1 redoubt which lay due east, perhaps nearly a mile and a half away.

Now during the night of October 24, or very early in the morning of October 25, the Russians had begun to advance. Kamara was seized, by which means they could with ease bring ten guns to bear on the Turks on Canrobert's Hill. A second force, which proceeded from Tchorgoum, established itself on the Causeway Heights, north and north-east of redoubt No. 1, and to the right of this force another appeared prepared to attack the 2nd redoubt. A fourth force which advanced *viâ* the Tractir Bridge was destined to storm redoubt No. 3. All these columns had guns, and in support of them the powerful main body of Russian cavalry passed obliquely down the northern valley, and accompanied by horse artillery awaited events.

When daylight came the agreed upon signal from the redoubts—two flags—showed that the enemy had advanced in force.

Moreover, too, the cavalry vedettes were circling right and left. Then an overwhelming attack on No. 1 redoubt on Canrobert's Hill began, and simultaneously No. 2 redoubt was assailed. Against these weakly armed, and it must be added none too well-traced works, the Russians were able to bring more than ten thousand men and nearly forty guns. The redoubt on Canrobert's Hill fell, and almost immediately the Nos. 2, 3, and 4 followed in succession. A stream of fugitives from these works tore off towards Balaclava. When the struggle began a troop of British Horse Artillery under Captain Maude, and supported by the Light Brigade, moved out and took up a position between the 2nd and 3rd redoubts, where it commanded the Woronzoff Road and the sloping ground beyond. Captain Maude opened fire on the advancing enemy. The Russians replied, both Captain Maude's guns and the Light Brigade coming in for their attention. A shell bursting near Captain Maude blew off his arm and he was carried to the rear. After exhausting the whole of their supply of ammunition, the Horse Artillery was retired to obtain a fresh supply. Captain Shakespeare of the artillery, who took the guns out of action in passing, was asked by Lord Cardigan by whose orders he had retired. Lord Cardigan, by the way, always slept on board his yacht, and had only just arrived on the field. Captain Shakespeare replied, "We are going for more ammunition, my lord," and added, "Our guns are of no use over 1000 yards, and the enemy's guns are a mile away." There is no doubt that the Russian artillery was good and well served in the main throughout the campaign. Captain Jenyns of the 13th, writing to Colonel Anstruther-Thomson, remarks in one letter: "Their artillery is very good indeed,—I think as good as ours."

When the redoubts were captured none of the guns were spiked except in one instance, that of the last redoubt. The artilleryman in charge of this one, who had been actually left alone in the entrenchment by the Turks when they bolted, complained most bitterly of their behaviour. He said he had hardly been able to persuade them to fight the guns at all, and that after firing a few rounds and seeing the enemy drawing near they had bolted, but he added, "They won't fire the guns at you from this redoubt, for I spiked them before I left." The fact was that the captured guns in the other redoubts not having been spiked, had been unpleasantly used by the enemy at very close range, not only against the redoubts in succession, but also against the cavalry brigades in the plain below. To add to the discomfiture of the Turks, some of the Cossacks got among the fugitives, and not a few were speared. While in this position Cornet Goad of the 13th had his horse killed by a shell, and in the fall that officer's back was so much damaged as to compel him to leave the field. Lord Raglan, on the Sapoune Ridge, in front of the French Corps of Observation, seeing what was happening, gave orders for the advance of two British divisions of infantry, those of the Duke of Cambridge and of General Cathcart. These were to move down from the high ground to check the Russian advance, which now seriously threatened Balaclava; and which was apparently placing the 93rd Highlanders, the sole infantry protection for Balaclava now remaining, in a position of great jeopardy.

But time would be required to move these troops, and had the Russians pressed on at once matters might have gone very seriously for the Allies. The day was one, however, when more than one opportunity was missed.

Lord Raglan's next order was that the cavalry should wait till these infantry divisions arrived, before seriously engaging the enemy.

In consequence of this, the cavalry brigades were withdrawn northwards to ground beneath the heights on which the French

Corps of Observation was posted. The Light Brigade was then drawn up facing eastward down the northern valley, and on the west side of the Woronzoff Road, immediately north of the 6th redoubt.

The Heavy Brigade was posted on their right rear, a little to the north of the vineyard on the south and east of which lay the cavalry camping-ground. Then it was that after missing his opportunity the Russian General Liprandi began the great movement of his cavalry which should have taken place immediately on the fall of No. 4 redoubt. This cavalry was under the command of General Ryjoff, and was accompanied by thirty-two guns, and the force amounted to about 3000 men. After proceeding some distance along the northern valley the Russian force divided, one portion—the smaller—taking the direction of Balaclava, where two battalions were posted, one on the ridge due south-east of Kadikoi and overlooking the road from Kamara to Balaclava, the other, manned by bluejackets, on a hill above the village of Kadikoi, and commanding a part of the southern plain or valley. Against the 93rd, and some men of the Guards brigade that had been collected in Balaclava and sent up, the smaller body of Russian cavalry advanced boldly. And it was, in truth, a very slender force which crowned the ridge and had the task of repelling the attack. Well might Sir Colin Campbell have remarked, as he is stated to have done: "Remember there is no retreat from here; you must die where you stand." But on the part of the gallant 93rd there was no doubt as to the course which should be pursued. Reserving their fire till the advancing Russian squadrons were quite close, they then poured in a volley with great effect. A second delivered at even closer range was sufficient for the enemy. Wheeling to the right, they retreated in disorder and troubled the British infantry no more.

Maps are deceptive, and in all the recognised maps of the battle of Balaclava the approach of the main body of Russian cavalry would appear to have taken place in full view of the Light Brigade. This was not, however, the case. Unseen by either the Heavy or the Light Brigade, this mass of cavalry in close column of squadrons proceeded down the northern valley, westwards. By this time Lord Raglan had perceived the situation of the 93rd, and had ordered the Heavy Brigade to be hurried up again to their support.

From the high grounds, too, on the edge of the Sapoune Heights, the advance of the Russian main body of cavalry had been observed, and some guns in a battery there opened fire on them. This had the effect of causing Ryjoff to turn to the south-west, crossing the Causeway Heights and the Woronzoff Road. Meanwhile the Heavy Brigade had left its position, and was proceeding through the camping-grounds of the brigades by squadrons independently. The tents had been struck, but the path was much encumbered with ropes, &c. The intention of General Scarlett, who was in command, was to re-form the brigade on the flank of the 93rd. Rapidity of action amid the tents and picket-ropes was, however, impossible; nor could the formation, such as it was, be very perfectly maintained. The Scots Greys and the Inniskillings were the most advanced. Following them came the 5th Dragoon Guards, the Royals, and the 4th Dragoon Guards. Suddenly over the crest of the Causeway Heights, and somewhat to the left, appeared this powerful body of Russian cavalry, and distant but a few hundred yards from the Scots Greys and the Inniskillings. It looked as if a serious attack on the flank of the Heavy Brigade was imminent. General Scarlett grasped the situation. His three leading squadrons were wheeled into line, and with an order to those in the rear to support, he prepared to instantly attack the oncoming enemy. And with what force was he about to do so? Two squadrons of the Scots Greys and the second squadron of the Inniskillings were all that were available for the first onset. And there to meet him, descending the slope of the heights, was a solid mass of nearly 3000 of the enemy's cavalry.

For some unexplained reason the Russians then halted, and then into their stationary squadrons dashed Scarlett and his meagre force. There was no delay in the British attack.

The "charge" alone was sounded, and headed by General Scarlett, his A.D.C., his trumpeter, and his orderly, the Greys and Inniskillings made straight for the enemy. Nor were the rest of the Heavy Brigade far behind. To the left rear, on came the 5th Dragoon Guards and the Royals, while on the right rear rode the first squadron of the Inniskillings. This brilliant movement was as unexpected by, as it was unwelcome to, the enemy. General Scarlett and his front line dashed well into the centre of the Russian column. This had the effect of enclosing the three British squadrons, as it were, between two walls of the enemy, and the Russian flank squadrons endeavoured to profit thereby by wheeling inwards in the hope of completely surrounding the Scots Greys and the Inniskillings. But just as this manœuvre was being attempted, right into the Russian left flank charged the other squadron of the Inniskillings, while the Russian right flank was similarly dealt with by a squadron of the Royals. The two squadrons of the 4th Dragoon Guards, who were farther removed to the British left, directed their attack—and most successfully, too—on the right flank of the Russian column at a point about two-thirds of its length down. The squadron of the 5th Dragoon Guards cut into the *mêlée* in close sequence to the attack of the first line and on its left. This series of attacks, brilliantly delivered and completed within the brief space of eight minutes, entirely demoralised the Russian force. Onlookers relate that the first onset made the enemy as it were reel back, and that then by degrees—very rapid degrees it must be observed—the powerful column seemed to become disintegrated. Regular formation, or even the semblance of regular formation, was lost, and in less than ten minutes what had been a strong and compact body of cavalry in column of squadrons was a mob of fugitives, which first scattered and then spread itself over the plain, only to rally far down the northern valley behind the guns of the Don Cossacks.

This stirring piece of cavalry work was performed in full view of the Light Brigade, who for a while sat expecting momentarily to be sent in pursuit, but no order came. Lord Cardigan declared that his orders were to remain in his position; but it was an opportunity lost, this time by the British. Had the pursuit been ordered, without doubt many of the fugitives would have been cut up and more driven in as prisoners. Also it is most improbable that, under the circumstances, the brilliant but sanguinary charge of the Light Brigade would ever then have taken place.

Hitherto there had been little for the Light Brigade to do except to furnish a target for the enemy, save that one troop had been ordered to drive off the Cossacks who were pursuing the flying Turks. A pursuit of the defeated Russian cavalry by Lord Cardigan's brigade would, one cannot but imagine, have produced on the Causeway Heights quite as great an effect as the charge of the 4th Chasseurs D'Afrique later in the day did on the enemy massed on the Fedioukine

Hills. It is but guesswork, still the moral effect on the entire Russian force would have been enormous, and the evening of October 25th would have closed on far more successful and wide-spreading results than it did.

In the charge itself the Heavy Brigade had less than fifty casualties, and the Russian loss closely approached four hundred.

The Light Brigade was now moved by "threes from the right" down to the bottom of the vineyard in the rear of the camp, and through an opening to the left which brought them through the camp. Then bearing up towards the ridge, they crossed it, and were formed up facing eastwards down the northern valley. As they crossed the ridge some fugitive Russian hussars, wounded and dismounted in the fight with the Heavy Brigade, were taken prisoners and sent to the rear. On the ridge, from the spot on which the brigade was now posted, evidences of the capture of the 4th redoubt were visible, and here the enemy had suffered some little loss owing to a battery of French artillery which had got into action from some high ground in the rear.

The Light Brigade was now dismounted, and from the point where they were stationed could contemplate the preparations of the enemy and the disposition of his guns along both sides and at the eastern end of the valley.

With regard to the inaction of the Light Brigade during the charge of the Heavies, Colonel Tremayne writes as follows:—

> We were on the left, under the crown of the ridge, and some few Cossacks came on to the ridge close to us, and were stopped by some grape from Shakespeare's guns. From that place we ought, I think, to have gone at the right flank of the Russians as they advanced against the Heavies, and certainly to have attacked them in their retreat. Intuitively some of the squadrons on the right changed front half right, but Lord Cardigan stopped them. He had orders from Lord Lucan not to move, he said.

At this time some attempts were being made, or appeared to be about to be made, by the Russians to remove the captured guns from the redoubts, and this was visible to Lord Raglan but was not visible to either Lord Lucan or Lord Cardigan. But the Russian guns at the extreme east end of the northern valley were fully in view of all three. This fact is established, and an important one it is.

Undoubtedly Lord Raglan wished to prevent the removal of the captured guns from the redoubts.

For this purpose he sent a written message to Lord Lucan as follows :—

> Cavalry to advance and take advantage of any opportunity to recover the heights. They will be supported by the infantry, which have been ordered to advance on two fronts.

Obviously this referred to the recapture of the Causeway Heights. Thereupon Lord Lucan moved the Heavy Brigade towards the end of the Causeway Heights and awaited the arrival of the infantry. This placed the Heavy Brigade on the right rear flank of the Light Brigade.

A second written message was then sent by Lord Raglan to Lord Lucan in these terms :—

> Lord Raglan wishes the cavalry to advance rapidly to the front, and to try to prevent the enemy carrying away the guns. Troop of horse artillery may accompany. French cavalry is on your left.
> Immediate.
> (Signed) R. AIREY, Quartermaster-General.

It now remains to describe as far as may be the charge of the Light Brigade.

Previously, however, it will be convenient to mention the strength of the regiment on the morning of October 25, 1854, and to give the names of those officers who were actually engaged in the field on that day.

With regard to both these points there is in the case of the state a considerable amount of variation, and in the case of the names of the officers there is some confusion.

STATE OF THE REGIMENT ON OCTOBER 25, 1854.

Lieutenant Percy Smith, who was acting adjutant, in a letter, writes, "the number of horses on parade was 108, exclusive of officers."

The Regimental Record gives the strength of the regiment, including officers, as 128.

The 'History of the 11th Hussars' gives the parade state of the 13th on that day as 130.

Trumpeter Powell, on the authority of Corporal Nagle (both of the 13th), places the strength as low as 103.

From a letter to Colonel Anstruther-Thomson, written by Captain Jenyns, we get yet another figure: "We had 110 horses and eight officers when we went into action (young Goad's horse, the one he jumped the timber on, was knocked over by a round-shot early in the day, and the young 'un hurt in the fall)."

The total strength of the Light Brigade when it started on the charge is usually accepted as 673.

Of the officers of the 13th, the following were present at Balaclava:—

Captains Oldham, Goad, Jenyns, and Tremayne; Lieutenants Jervis and Smith; Cornets Montgomery and Chamberlayne.

Lieut.-Colonel Charles Edmund Doherty was not present. Major Richard Ormsby Gore (afterwards Lord Harlech) was invalided, as also were Lieutenants Purcell and King. Cornet G. Maxwell Goad was injured early in the battle. Of Cornet Maclean there is no information, but he belonged to B Troop. It is, however, certain that he was not in the charge.

Hart's Army List states that Captain Jenyns commanded the regiment in the battle of Balaclava. But he was junior both to Captain Oldham and Captain Goad.

The 'History of the 11th Hussars' states that the 13th Light Dragoons were commanded at Balaclava by "Colonel" Oldham, which is obviously incorrect. The fact is that Captain Jenyns succeeded to the command after the deaths of Captains Oldham and Goad. From the Regimental Records of the 13th no information on this point is to be obtained, nor even is an accurate or any list indeed of the officers at Balaclava given. It is only by sifting evidence that the above names have been arrived at. Lieutenant Percy Smith happened to be acting adjutant because no successor had yet been appointed to the late adjutant, Lieutenant Irwin. Eventually, the Regimental Sergeant-Major George Gardner was gazetted cornet and adjutant.

The officers with the depôt troops in England were Captains Holden and the Hon. John Hely Hutchinson; Lieutenants Clayton and Davis; and Cornets Dearden and Fielden.

These troops were lettered C and F. Consequently at Balaclava the A, B, D, and E troops were engaged, and were officered as follows:—

A Troop—Captain Oldham and Cornet Montgomery.
B Troop—Captain Jenyns and Lieutenant Jervis.
D Troop—Captain Goad and (for a time) Cornet Goad.
E Troop—Captain Tremayne, Lieutenant Percy Smith, and Cornet Chamberlayne.

The A and B troops formed one squadron, the A troop being on the extreme right of the line.

The D and E troops formed the other, E troop being on the left of the other squadron.

From the above it will be understood that any attempt to fix with accuracy the exact number of officers and men of the 13th who were actually engaged in the charge of the Light Brigade is not likely to succeed. We know that there were eight officers, but no amount of consideration will enable us to reconcile the other numbers.

When the second written message was delivered to Lord Lucan by Captain Lewis Edward Nolan of the 15th Hussars and Aide-de-Camp to the Quartermaster-General, his lordship entertained some doubt as to its interpretation. He inquired of Captain Nolan, and it is stated received a verbal communication coupled with a gesture to the effect that the Russian battery at the end of the valley was the desired object of attack. Lord Cardigan was then summoned, and the order was communicated to him. Lord Lucan always averred that he considered Captain Nolan's manner of speech to be somewhat disrespectful. On receipt of the order from Lord Lucan the reply of Lord Cardigan was, "Very good, sir." To the Light Brigade he then gave the word of command, "The Brigade will advance." The balance of evidence goes to show that no trumpet call was used. The men were dismounted when the order came, and were immediately in the saddle when the command was given.

The first line consisted of the 13th Light Dragoons on the right and the 17th Lancers on the left. Lord Cardigan placed himself alone in front of the line, a little on the left of the centre.

The 13th and 17th then moved off, and when they had covered

rather more than 100 yards the 11th Hussars, who were in the second line, moved off also. In due course, and at about the same interval, came the 4th and the 8th. During the day the 11th had been on the left of the first line, but the narrowing of the valley and the width of front occupied by the Cossack battery at the east end necessitated a contraction in the first line.

As it was, the 17th Lancers overlapped the right of the battery, and the 11th Hussars, in support, just brushed the guns with their right flank. The 11th, it will thus be seen, did not actually cover the 17th, but charged down the valley nearer to the Fedioukine Hills. The 11th, the 4th, and the 8th were in echelon. Consequently the 4th came into the battery full front, while the course of the 8th was as against the Russian left. Captain Nolan started to ride with the charge, and it is believed took up a position in the interval between the two squadrons of the 17th. At any rate, it would appear that thence he darted out when he rode obliquely across the front of the advancing line.

It was not long before the 13th and 17th came under the guns of the enemy; but before a shot was fired Captain Nolan, as has been mentioned, darted out. He was seen to be wildly waving his sword, and, as it were, endeavouring to make some communication to Lord Cardigan. It is certain that he was pointing in the direction of the Causeway Heights, as if to indicate the true intention of the order which he had conveyed. Whether he would have succeeded in this, if such was his intention, can never be known, for at this moment the first gun from the Russian battery was fired. Nolan was struck by a fragment of a shell which killed him instantly. His sword fell from his hand, but his arm remained erect, and the grip of his knees kept him in the saddle. It chanced that he was mounted on a troop horse of the 13th. The horse with its dead burden wheeled round and passed through the interval between the squadrons. Nolan's body fell in the rear. By this time the Russian battery on the Fedioukine Hills had opened fire, and the masses of infantry on either side the valley poured in a heavy discharge of musketry. Now, too, the Cossack battery in the front joined in, but yet, with men and horses dropping singly, or by twos or threes, on swept the Light Brigade. On and on they rode, each instant finding gap after gap in the ranks. Riderless horses, as the

THE CHARGE OF THE LIGHT BRIGADE, BALACLAVA.
(Inserted to show the ground.)

(*From Simpson's 'Seat of War in the East*,' 1855-6.)

men dropped, still kept their places in the line; but there was neither pause nor hesitation. "Close in," "close in," was the word as death and destruction was dealt among them. At about 80 yards from the Cossack guns a discharge wrought fearful havoc, but after that those guns spoke no more. Ahead of his men Lord Cardigan dashed into the battery, crushing his knee and receiving a slight wound. Nor were the 13th and 17th far behind. The two squadrons of the former and the right squadron of the latter were speedily among the guns, and were cutting down the artillerymen that remained at their posts. Through the guns they went, and were soon engaged in a hand-to-hand encounter with the enemy that was endeavouring to surround them by closing in on either flank.

Meanwhile, thanks to the dashing attack on the battery and infantry posted on the Fedioukine Hills, which was so gallantly executed by the 4th Chasseurs D'Afrique under General D'Allonville, the line of retirement—one cannot call it retreat—was cleared on one flank for the survivors of the charge. Nothing, however, was attempted by Lord Lucan against the enemy which thronged the Causeway Heights. He advanced down the valley far ahead of his brigade, and penetrated for a distance of more than half a mile on the side of the Woronzoff Road. His brigade came under fire, was halted, and then retired after sustaining some little loss. Lord Lucan considered that the Light Brigade had been wantonly sacrificed, and determined that the Heavy Brigade should not so be destroyed if he could help it.

It will be remembered that the left squadron of the 17th brushed the right flank of the battery, and continuing its course it dashed against the Russian cavalry in the rear.

The 11th in its progress having passed the guns, found a strong body of Russian lancers in its front. Charging these, the enemy did not await the attack, but wheeled round and retreated in confusion far along the valley into the gorge near the aqueduct. The 11th followed in pursuit, and chased them till they halted on the side of a hill with their backs to their pursuers, at whom they looked over their shoulders. Finding the 11th were but few in numbers, an attempt was made by the Russian officers to get their men to attack, but without avail. Matters remained thus for a short time, perhaps not more than a few moments, while pursuers and pursued were in close juxtaposition. Then Cossacks were observed working round in the rear of the 11th, and there was nothing for it but to cut their way back along the valley and past the guns which the Russians were now attempting to remove.

On the road the 11th were pursued by Russian hussars, and nearly cut off by some of Jeropkine's lancers that issued from the horse-shoe. Meanwhile, the fragments of the 13th and 17th having passed through and over the guns found themselves without orders.

What to do next nobody could tell them. Lord Cardigan had already returned along the valley for some distance alone, and had then galloped back towards the Russians, only to retire again.

On his first return he spoke to Sergeant Mitchell, from whose Reminiscences extracts have already been made. After that he met Sir John Ewart and Sir George Cathcart, to whom he said, "I have lost my brigade." They did not understand him, knowing nothing of the charge, and stared without speaking. Lord Cardigan then turned his horse, and, as has been said, galloped back towards the Russians. And so it came about that the "wretched remnant," as Captain Jenyns calls it, when they had got to the guns, "went with such a *right* good cheer, bang through their cavalry, which cut right and left like sheep; on rallying back there were the guns, four hundred yards in the rear, all clear, and no one, worse luck, to carry them off,—the worst part of all, as a very strong regiment of lancers came on our rear, and we had to *cut* our way through them. Lord Lucan never supported us; the Scots Greys, the nearest, at least a mile in our rear." And so, over the ground strewn with dead and wounded men and horses who were not half an hour previously in full vigour, passed the "wretched remnant," and even then not permitted to escape unscathed.

Parties of the enemy's cavalry, regular or Cossack, were ready to beset any stragglers, and there is no doubt that the death-roll of the Balaclava charge was greatly increased by the butchery of wounded men on the field itself, and the spearing of armed or unarmed dismounted officers and privates of the Light Brigade.

Eventually what was left of the five light cavalry regiments arrived in the rear of the Heavy Brigade and were re-formed.

Lieutenant Percy Smith, who, by the way, was the only officer who

THE BALACLAVA GROUP.

(From a Photograph taken the day after the Battle.)

rode through the charge and came back on his original horse, states that when he formed up the remains of the regiment, after the charge, he " could only get hold of fourteen mounted men; and one of them was on a Russian horse which he caught after losing his own. Possibly a few horses had got back before me, and had attached themselves to other regiments, but for the moment the effective [?] strength of the 13th was one officer [myself] and fourteen rank and file."

KEY TO BALACLAVA GROUP.

1. Cornet F. L. Michael.
2. Cornet & Adjt. G. Gardener.
3. Capt. P. S. Smith.
4. Regt. Sergt.-Maj. Johnson.
5. Lieut.-Col. C. E. Doherty.
6. Cornet D. T. Chamberlayne.
7. Pte. Morrisey.
8. Pte. Dearlove.
9. Sergt. J. Malone (V.C.).
10. Tpr. Sergt.-Maj. Hunt.
11. Sergt. Mulcahy.
12. Capt. S. G. Jenyns.
13. Pte. Long.
14. Tpr. Sergt.-Maj. Linkon (died 1910).
15. Pte. Gardner.
16. Unknown.

The total loss of the regiment was three officers killed—Captains Oldham and Goad and Cornet Montgomery; Troop Sergeant-Major Weston, and ten rank and file were also killed. Thirty rank and file were wounded, and two Troop Sergeant-Majors, while ten rank and file were taken prisoners.

Captain Percy Smith was also wounded by a lance-thrust.

These numbers are elsewhere stated thus: killed and missing, 69; roll call, 61.

From Sir Fitzroy Donald Maclean some interesting particulars regarding Captain Oldham's death have been obtained and are here given.

Captain Oldham at the time of the Balaclava charge was second captain in the regiment. How he came to lead the regiment in the charge is as follows:—

Colonel C. E. Doherty was sick; Major Ormsby Gore was in Bulgaria, or had been invalided home; and Captain Holden, the senior captain, was in command of the depôt at home.

On the day of the battle Captain Oldham rode his second charger

—a white mare, his first charger being unfit for work. This white mare was notoriously a brute, and on the occasion of the charge bolted—luckily, straight at the Russian guns. Captain Oldham fell, and was last seen wounded and bleeding with his sword in one hand and his pistol in the other. As a matter of fact, he was the first man to get among the guns. His dead body was never found, and his grave is therefore unknown.

Shortly after the battle a Russian officer came in under a flag of truce to arrange about the burial of the dead. In the presence of Sir Fitzroy Maclean, who was standing close by, he asked, "Who was the officer who rode a white horse and led the charge of Balaclava?" He was told that the officer was Captain Oldham, and at once replied, "a brave man." It may be mentioned that the brother of Captain Oldham fell in New Zealand in an attack on one of the "pahs"; he was wounded, but persisted in pressing on in spite of all suggestions that his wound should be attended to; a few minutes later a second shot killed him.

Lieutenant Chamberlayne, whose horse "Pimento" was shot in the charge, escaped the fate of so many on the return journey in what is stated to be a curious way. Lieutenant Percy Smith on his way back passed him seated by the side of his dead horse—a very favourite horse. Lieutenant Chamberlayne asked what he should better do, and was advised to take off the saddle and bridle and make the best of his way back, for, said Lieutenant Smith, "another horse you can get, but you will not get another saddle and bridle so easily." Lieutenant Chamberlayne took his advice, and placing the saddle on his head returned along the valley, threading his way among the Cossacks who were busily engaged in pillage and killing dismounted and wounded men. He was probably taken for a pillager, and to this, no doubt, owed his life.

From letters home, written by officers of the regiment, it is to be gathered that the death of Captain Goad was a great grief to all.

> I cannot tell you how we do miss him, or what a blow it is to us all [writes Captain Jenyns]. The last I saw of poor Goad was about 150 yards from the guns, when the smoke was so thick we could see no one [at the guns]. Some men saw him lying on the ground wounded, but, of course, having to fight our way back, could not help him. Oldham I saw killed by a shell which burst under his horse and knocked over two or three others. It blew his mare's

Captain J. A. OLDHAM.
Killed at Balaclava.

(*From a Picture lent by* Col. Sir Fitzroy Maclean, Bart., K.C.B.)

hind-legs *off*, and he jumped up himself not hit, when next moment he threw up his hands and fell dead on his face. Montgomery was my right troop leader [first squadron], and I saw him safe *into* the guns; after that on returning, he was seen dead on his face, poor fellow.

Captain Jenyns writes further—

Seventy-six troopers' and seven officers' horses killed on the spot, ten shot afterwards, and eight wounded still alive. I only brought nine mounted men back! Poor old "Moses" [his charger] was shot through his shoulder and through the hip into his guts, but *just* got me back. I had some narrow shaves, as indeed we all had. My cloak rolled in front had three canister-shot through it, besides a piece of shell knocking off the end of it, and catching me on the knee, but only a severe bruise. Percy Smith's horse was the only one not killed. Although so cut up you [Colonel Anstruther-Thomson] will be glad to hear the old corps got tremendous *kudos* from all. It was a fine sight to see the fellows sit down and put their heads straight at the guns.

In his 'Crimean Notes' Colonel Tremayne writes—

The men behaved splendidly. The last thing I heard before I went down [his horse was shot] was one man saying to his neighbour, "Come on; don't let those —— [the 17th Lancers] get ahead of us." Neither did they. Nolan was struck by a shot from the battery on our left, immediately we began to advance. This battery was driven off by some Chasseurs D'Afrique.

Elsewhere it is stated that this battery was on the right.

Oldham's death was not witnessed [a mistake apparently], nor was Goad's. Montgomery was cut in two by a round-shot. Jenyns went right through the guns, and he told me he shot two wheel horses with his revolver in retiring, feeling sure we should be supported. If we had been French, *nous sommes trahis* would have been the cry; as it was, the men seemed to be glad they had not let the Heavies have all the day to themselves.

Captain Percy Smith writes—

You have, of course, seen all the accounts of our charge in the papers, so I will not try to tell you anything more about it, except that "Jenks" [Jenyns] was worth his weight in gold. He was everywhere, and kept his head as well as if he had been at a common field-day. He was on "Moses." The good old horse got shot in four places, and was only just able to get back to the Heavies, behind whom we formed up.

Another reference to the death of Captain Goad is as follows—

The last I saw of poor Goad was just going into the guns on my left. He was killed dead, as the Russians sent back a bill of exchange found on his body.

Cornet C. W. Goad, the younger brother of Captain Goad, who was wounded early in the battle, made most anxious inquiries into the fate of his brother before he left the Crimea. He states—

> I left on the 13th of November. As soon as I heard that my poor brother was missing, I made every inquiry there. The only thing certain is that a man of the 13th, of the name of Farringdon [of Captain Goad's own troop], who, from some cause, was one of the last in the retreat, saw him at the Russian end of the valley half sitting up, with his revolver in his hand. He was then wounded in the lower part of his face or neck, but might also have been elsewhere; even then it is certain that he was either then or afterwards wounded in the chest, for the paper which he had in his breast pocket, and which the Russians sent back, was covered with blood. There are other stories about other men having seen him, but I could not make out that there was any truth in them.

Colonel Tremayne pays a high tribute to the soldierly qualities of Lieutenant Percy Smith, who, he says, "gave us all an example of steadiness." Lieutenant Smith "lost a part of his right hand from a gun accident before the war, and could not draw his sword. He had an iron guard made to slip over his wrist. In the dark that morning he could not find it in the tent, and turned out without it. He went to the end of the charge, and was the only officer who came out on the same horse he went in on; he was not wounded [note—this is wrong; he got a lance prod in the ribs, but would not report it]. He was a good, cool-headed soldier, and when he left was a great loss to the regiment."

As a matter of fact, Lieutenant Smith, unarmed as he was, found himself separated from his men and brought to a standstill by three Russian lancers, one on each side and one in front. He was defenceless, and apparently in a pretty warm corner. The lancer on his right hesitated for a moment and left him with only two to look after. The man on his left attacked first, but he contrived to turn his point off with the upper part of his bridle arm at the cost of a mere scratch from the side of his lance-blade. At the same moment almost, the man in front gave point at his chest. Lieutenant Smith saw he couldn't guard himself without dropping his reins, so instead of that, as he was mounted on a good hunter, he jumped right on to his assailant. The lance-point luckily hit on a bone and came out as the Russian went down, and before the other two could

Captain JOSEPH MALONE, V.C.
(Uniform that of the 6th Dragoons.)

BALACLAVA. SERGT. JOSEPH MALONE GAINS THE V.C.

renew the attack a party of the 11th Hussars came to the rescue, and the lancers had something else to occupy their attention.

The honour of the Victoria Cross came to the 13th Light Dragoons, being awarded to Lance-Sergeant Joseph Malone of the E Troop, commanded by Captain Tremayne.

During the charge, and before reaching the guns, Captain Webb of the 17th Lancers was mortally wounded. To his assistance came Troop Sergeant-Major Berryman of his regiment. He, finding that Captain Webb could no longer keep in the saddle, endeavoured to lift him out,—Lieutenant Percy Smith of the 13th holding the horse in the meantime, and then riding off for a stretcher. Berryman remained with Captain Webb, although that officer besought him to save himself.

Presently Sergeant Farrell, also of the 17th, came to them, and the two remained by Captain Webb till they were joined by Lance-Sergeant Malone of the 13th Light Dragoons. The three remained by the wounded officer under a heavy fire for a considerable time, and finally between them endeavoured to carry him off.

Troop Sergeant-Major Berryman, Sergeant Farrell, and Lance-Sergeant Malone were all subsequently decorated with the Victoria Cross.

About a month before Balaclava Sergeant Malone had done a smart bit of work. At daybreak on September 24, when marching on Balaclava, he volunteered with three others (privates of the 13th Light Dragoons), and captured an escort of the enemy's cavalry and also the baggage which they were taking to Sebastopol.

Lance-Sergeant Malone received a commission in the 6th Dragoons (Inniskillings) on September 7, 1858. A brief notice of his career may be added.

He enlisted on the 31st March 1851, and was later promoted to lance-sergeant without being corporal previously. In the Crimea he was present at the Alma, Balaclava, Inkerman, Tchernaya, and the Siege of Sebastopol. He was also engaged on the expedition to Eupatoria under General D'Allonville. He wore the Crimean Medal with clasps for Alma, Balaclava, Sebastopol, and Inkerman, the Turkish Medal, and the Victoria Cross.

On receiving his commission, as the 6th were in India, Riding-Master Malone proceeded thither, and remained there till April 1867.

He obtained his promotion as Captain on July 1, 1881, and served in South Africa from November 1882 till his death at Pinetown in June 1883.

From Kinglake's 'Invasion of the Crimea' but little information as to the 13th at Balaclava is to be gathered. That historian mentions that 195 was the number of the first muster after the charge, and that the total casualties amounted to 247, out of which 113 were killed and 134 wounded. Of the horses, 475 were killed and 42 wounded, and 43 shot later, as unserviceable through wounds. How many horses were lost in the battle by the 13th Light Dragoons is nowhere stated in the Regimental Records. Sergeant Mitchell, however, gives the following information :—

On that morning the brigade had mounted, I believe, six hundred and seven sabres and lances, our regiment numbering one hundred and ten, or thereabouts, and by noon ours alone had lost eighty-six horses and upwards of fifty men in killed, wounded, and missing.

Of course for 607 we must read 673, and noon should be afternoon, as the charge did not take place till after 2 P.M.

One or two extracts from Sergeant Mitchell's account of the charge may well be quoted—

In a few minutes several casualties occurred, for by this time the guns on our front were playing on us with round-shot and shell, so the number of men and horses falling increased every moment. I rode near the right of the line. A corporal who rode on the right was struck by a shot or shell full in the face, completely smashing it, his blood and brains bespattering us who rode near.[1] His horse still went on with us. By this time the ranks being continually broken it caused some confusion. Oaths and imprecations might be heard between the report of the guns and the bursting of the shells as the men crowded and jostled each other in their endeavour to close to the centre. This was unavoidable at times, especially when a shell burst in the ranks, sometimes bringing down three or four men and horses, which made it difficult to avoid an unpleasant crush in the ranks.

We were now fully exposed to the fire from all three batteries, front, right, and left, as also from the infantry on our right, who were now able to reach us. As we drew nearer, the guns in the front plied us liberally with grape and cannister, which brought down men and horses in heaps. . . . I missed my left hand man from my side. . . . We were now very close to the guns, for we were entering the smoke which hung in clouds in front. I could see some of the

---

[1] The name of the corporal mentioned as being killed at Balaclava has just been ascertained. It was E. W. Aubrey Smith. He was the son of a Major Smith. To his memory quite recently a tablet, grille, and mural paintings have been erected in a church at Hammersmith (May 11, 1911).

gunners running from the guns to the rear, when just at that moment a shell from the battery on the right struck my horse, carrying away the shoulder and part of the chest, and exploding a few yards off. Fortunately I was on the ground when it exploded, or some of the fragments would most likely have reached me. On my recovery from the shock, I found my horse was lying on his near side, my left leg was beneath him, and my right above him. I tried to move, but just at that moment I heard the second line come galloping on to where I lay, and fully expecting to be trampled on I looked up and saw it was the 4th Light Dragoons quite close. I called out, "For God's sake, don't ride over me." Whether they heard me or not I shall never know. . . . After they had passed I tried to extricate my leg, which after a short time I succeeded in doing and stood upright, finding myself unhurt, except my leg, which was a little painful from the crush. I still had my sword in my hand, and soon found there were numberless bullets flying around me, which came from the infantry on the flank of their battery, who fired at any of us who were dismounted. Just at this moment a man of my troop named Pollard [Captain Oldham's troop] came to me, and throwing himself down beside the carcase of my horse for shelter from the bullets, called to me saying: "Come here, Mitchell, this is good cover." I said: "No, we had better make our way back as quick as possible, or we shall soon be taken prisoners, if not killed, if we remain here." Upon this he jumped up, and we both started to get back, but had not gone many yards when a poor fellow called to us to help him. He was in a similar position to mine, and he belonged to our regiment. I took him beneath the arms, and Pollard raised the horse's forepart a little, so that I managed to draw his leg from under the horse; but his thigh was broken, and besides, he had a severe wound on his head which covered him with blood. On seeing his injuries we laid him gently down. He said: "You can do no more for me; I thought my thigh was broken before you pulled me out. Look out for yourselves!" Now this incident had only been the work of a very short time, during which our brigade had passed beyond the guns. The smoke had cleared away, for the guns were silent enough now—that is, the guns we had charged—so that we could see a number of men making their way back the same as ourselves. The number of horses lying about was something fearful. As we went along we somehow got separated, and I got mixed up with some of the 8th and 11th Hussars, and then in another minute found myself alone. Just then Lord Cardigan came galloping up from the direction of the guns, passing me at a short distance, when he turned about again, and meeting me, pulled up and said: "Where is your horse?" I answered: "Killed, my lord." He then said, in his usually stern hoarse voice: "You had better make the best of your way back as fast as you can, or you will be taken prisoner." I needed no telling, for I was doing so as fast as I was able. He then rode a little farther down, and in a few minutes returned past me at a gallop. By this time the mounted were making their way back as fast as they could, some singly, and some in parties of two or three, but whenever the battery on our left could see anything like a party together they would be sure to send a shell at them. In this way many men were killed on their return. There were several riderless horses galloping about the plain. I tried very hard to get one, but could not. I saw two officers' horses belonging to my own regiment. I could tell them by the binding of the sheepskins on the saddles. They appeared almost mad. I would have given a trifle just then to have had my legs across one of them, for I was getting tired, for we had been out since 4 A.M. and had nothing to eat since the day before, and to make it still worse there was a piece of ground that lay in my way which had been cultivated and was very loose, which made it heavy travelling. I looked up to try to measure the distance, when to my dismay I saw the Scotch [Scots] Greys, who had come part of the way down the valley to our support, where they were halted, and were now about five hundred yards from me, in the act of retiring at a trot. I thought there was no chance now, when our support was retiring at a trot at that distance ahead of us. Presently a captain of ours came past me, and shortly after he got up behind a mounted man of ours, and they both rode back together on one horse. I could now see some Cossacks showing themselves in swarms on our right, thinking to cut some of us dismounted men off. As soon as I saw them approaching, I bore more away to my left front, and a party of Chasseurs D'Afrique (who, I had almost forgotten to state, had charged the battery on our left going down), and who had lost many men and horses. These having showed themselves menacingly, it had the desired effect of turning the Cossacks from their purpose.

Sergeant Mitchell now fell in with a man of the Scots Greys who was standing, but blinded by a shell wound, whom he tried to lead into safety, binding up his head with a handkerchief. He now found the man who had ridden on his left lying at the point of death, but a good bit lower down the valley than where he first missed him. Probably the man's horse was shot, and he had tried to make his way back dismounted.

Arriving near No. 4 redoubt, then held by the 68th Light Infantry, who had seized it, Mitchell and his blind companion approached and asked for water. An officer to whom they applied gave them some rum, and they started off again. Very shortly after the pair arrived at the ambulances. The Scots Grey's wound was dressed. He was afterwards discharged from the army with a pension, being temporarily blind, but Sergeant Mitchell, who never saw the man again, understood that eventually his sight was restored.

After this I went down to our camp which was close by, and finding my own tent soon dived into the biscuit bag, and putting two or three handfuls into my havresack, began to make up for lost time, for I was hungry indeed, so, eating as I went, made my way over the ridge again to the ground from whence we had started, and joined the remnant of the brigade, who had by this time nearly all straggled back. I counted thirteen mounted men of my own regiment, but I think there was very little difference, each regiment's losses then appearing to be about equal. I don't mean to say that thirteen was all that came back, but that was all that were mounted and fit for duty. Some had got back as I had done, and in the course of the day and evening several horses found their way back. . . . During the action several batteries of Field Artillery and two divisions of infantry, the 1st and 4th, were marched down from the front to take part in the affair, but the enemy did not attempt another advance, so both parties remained watching each other till night.

This account as given by Sergeant Mitchell is by far the clearest and most level-headed narrative of the retirement given by any member of the 13th Light Dragoons that the writer has been able to discover. He has quoted from it freely, but desires to most fully acknowledge its source.

The Manuscript Regimental Record is as follows:—

The Regiment turned out as usual with the remainder of the Brigade about an hour before daybreak. As daylight appeared the Russians were seen advancing steadily towards the Village of Kamara, and shortly after opened a brisk fire on the entrenchments thrown up and defended by about 2000 Turks. These earthworks were intended to form a check to the enemy in the event of an attack upon Balaclava, or on the rear of the Allied Armies who were now besieging Sebastopol, and they were mounted with six of the "Diamond's" guns. The enemy came on with such force (30,000) that the Turks gave way and the enemy got possession of the entrenchments. The 2000 Turks, British Cavalry, and one Regiment of Highlanders was all the Force at the disposal of Sir Colin Campbell for the defence of Balaclava, which was quite unequal for the defence of the entrenchments against the overwhelming forces of the Enemy, and the Cavalry being so few could only act to cover the retreat of the Turks. The Russians had been in possession of the entrenchments about an hour when the whole Cavalry force was brought into the plain between the Earthworks, and made for the Regiment of Highlanders at full speed. But the Highlanders brought them so fast from their saddles that the whole body turned about and fled. Shortly after the whole force of the enemy's Cavalry re-formed, and then to the number of about 3000 came down upon the Heavy Brigade of British Cavalry, who numbered no more than 700. The Heavy Brigade met them in gallant style and cut through the whole force, then turned about and cut their way back. The Russians would not again turn about, as they got sight of the Light Brigade coming to the assistance of the Heavy Brigade, but fled in great disorder and never pulled up until they got well behind their own guns and infantry.

About 2 P.M. on the same day Lord Cardigan received an order to charge with the Light Brigade, which was at this time formed in Line across the second plain from Balaclava. Lord Cardigan formed the Brigade into two Lines as follows:—

> 1st *Line*.—13th Light Dragoons on the Right, 17th Lancers in the Centre, and 11th Hussars on the Left.
>
> 2nd *Line or Support*.—8th Hussars on the Right, and 4th Light Dragoons on the Left.

The first Line advanced at a trot, closely followed by the 2nd Line.

The first Line had not advanced many hundred yards before a Russian Battery of guns placed on a hill on the Right opened fire, immediately followed by another Russian Battery on a hill on the Left. The first Line broke into a gallop, and immediately after a Battery, extending right across the plain (which had become so narrow by this time that Lord Cardigan doubled back the 11th Hussars for the purpose of forming a second line), opened fire, thus exposing the whole Brigade to a sharp fire in front and from the right and left, all at the same time. But on went the Brigade, cutting their way through the Battery in front and through the whole force of the Russian Cavalry and Infantry, who were formed up in rear of the guns.

Independently of the Batteries mentioned above the whole line of Russian Infantry opened fire upon the Brigade, by which means a great number of men of the Regiment were killed or wounded, and many were dismounted, their Horses having been shot from under them. But few as they were they completely routed the Russians, whose number was estimated at between 25,000 and 30,000. By the time that the Brigade had arrived at the Centre Battery there could not have been more than 200 of them left mounted.

The distance the Regiment had to go on this Charge was more than a mile, the whole way under a severe fire from the enemy. The Regiment numbered when it advanced 128 of all Ranks, and in re-forming after the charge it could only number (mounted) nine of all ranks, exclusive of officers. The loss of the Regiment in the Charge was 3 officers killed—viz., Captains Oldham and Goad and Cornet Montgomery; Troop Sergeant-Major Weston and 10 Rank and File Killed, and 30 Rank and File Wounded; and 2 Troop Sergeant-Majors and 10 Rank and File taken prisoners.

It may be treading on dangerous ground to touch even lightly upon the Lucan-Cardigan-Nolan controversy.

Kinglake (vol. iv., chap. v., pp. 228-230) sums up the military character and ambitions of the gallant but unfortunate Captain Nolan. The historian bases his conclusions on the diary of the deceased officer, which, written up to October 12, 1854, had been placed at his disposal.

But on the private writings of a man—and writings, too, which were meant probably for no other eye than his own—can a just estimate be formed of the public execution by that man of a public duty? This would be a dangerous doctrine indeed. Now where Kinglake's pages seem to the writer to be hard on Captain Nolan is this,—he gives no clue to the antecedents of the officer in question. His military training and experience are unmentioned.

It is a strange fact, but apparently no life of Nolan exists except that which is to be found in the pages of the 'Dictionary of National Biography.' It will be but fair to put it briefly here.

Lewis Edward Nolan was born about 1820. He was the son of

Major Babington Nolan, sometime of the 70th Foot and afterwards Vice-Consul at Milan. Major Nolan had three sons, and all died in battle. Through the influence of one of the Austrian archdukes who was a friend of his father, Lewis Nolan obtained a commission in the Austrian cavalry. He served in the Hungarian Hussars, both in Hungary and on the Polish Frontier. Colonel Haas, the instructor of the Austrian Imperial Cavalry, was his military tutor.

Nolan must have entered the Austrian service at an early age, as he left it in 1839 for the British.

His first commission was that of ensign (by purchase), and is dated March 15, the regiment to which he was gazetted being the 4th King's Own.

On April 23rd of the same year he exchanged into the 15th Light Dragoons (King's Hussars), paying the difference between the price of an ensigncy and a cornetcy.

His new regiment was under orders for India at the time, and he embarked on July 11, 1839. Nolan became lieutenant (by purchase) on June 19, 1841, and captain (also by purchase) on March 8, 1850.

In India, where he mastered several native languages (he was also proficient in French, German, Italian, and Hungarian), Nolan acted for some time as aide-de-camp to Lieut.-General Sir G. F. Berkeley, who commanded the troops in Madras. He was afterwards extra aide-de-camp to Sir Henry Pottinger, the Governor of Madras.

When the 15th was ordered home in 1853, Nolan obtained leave to precede it to Europe. He then went to Russia, where he visited all the chief military stations and studied the Russian military system.

He was sent to Turkey on the outbreak of the Crimean War in advance of the British army, and charged with the double duty of making arrangements there for the reception of the British cavalry, and also with that of purchasing cavalry horses.

Nolan was a noted horseman and swordsman. He was also the author of a book on ' Breaking Cavalry Horses,' and another entitled ' Organization, Drill, and Manœuvres of Cavalry Corps.'

In the Crimea he was aide-de-camp to Brigadier General Airey, commanding an infantry brigade. Now, was this the kind of man who would be mad enough to garble verbally the intention of an order of a superior officer, knowing full well that if he did it merely meant the annihilation of the force employed and his own ruin if he survived.

Here was no tyro, no ignoramus in matters pertaining to his profession, but a most accomplished soldier of at least fifteen years' service in the British army, besides a preliminary training in a foreign land, the cavalry of which ever was, and still is, most highly esteemed. Yet that opinion, certainly among some of the surviving officers of the 13th, tended to blame Nolan is clear.

Captain Jenyns writes from Balaclava on November 18, 1854: "Never was such a mad order given. Nolan is the man to blame."

Colonel Tremayne in his Notes writes: "Nolan gave his message a few yards in front of where I was standing talking to poor old Goad. We were dismounted. There can be no doubt that Nolan gave the order to go where we did go. Cardigan told me this repeatedly afterwards. But I have no doubt Lord Raglan meant us to go along the southern valley and wheel to the left, to prevent the guns being taken out of the Turk's redoubts."

Assuredly the two written orders made this clear, or ought to have so done, to the recipient, Lord Lucan. Colonel Tremayne, however, it will be noticed, gives his opinion second-hand. Hideous the blunder was in its effects. Bitter indeed must have been the feelings of the survivors; but half a century and more has elapsed since the fatal ride, and, looking at the evidence now with calmness, the writer cannot but think that that gallant cavalry soldier, Lewis Edward Nolan, may be acquitted of either mad folly or wilful perversion of the tenour of an order of the import of which he was fully aware.[1]

---

[1] Since these lines were penned, the writer has obtained a number of hitherto unpublished details with regard to the life of Captain Nolan. Those interested are referred to his article on Nolan, appearing in the 'Cavalry Journal,' No. 21, January 1911.

CHAPTER XXX.

The Eastern Campaign—*continued*.

AFTER the wounded had been sent to Balaclava, the base of the allied army, as night came on the camp of the Light Brigade, was moved nearer to Sebastopol. The redoubts being occupied by the enemy rendered this step advisable. The tents were left standing in order to deceive the enemy, and the men slept in the open air. Among the survivors of the charge there was considerable suffering in this way. Cloaks and blankets had been lost with the horses, and the nights were cold. In many cases it was nearly four months before a pea-jacket to supply the place of the lost cloak was served out.

On October 26th the tents were brought in from the old camp. Seventeen wounded horses were inspected, and of these sixteen were shot. The seventeenth recovered and lived in the regiment for some years. The following day the camp was again shifted for about half a mile, to a spot still nearer to Sebastopol. During this day a party was sent out with a flag of truce to ascertain whether the British dead had been buried, and returned to camp on finding that the enemy had performed this duty. The Russians did not object to burying those of the British or French who had fallen, but drew the line at burying the Turks. On the night of October 28th there were two false alarms and the brigade turned out. The second alarm was raised about 5 A.M., and was caused by a stampede of the horses of a Russian picket, some fifty in number. They were grey horses and careered wildly through the camp, running foul of tents and picket-ropes and many falling. There was in consequence a good deal of disorder for a moment or two, but it was soon found that the horses had no riders. The entire crowd of runaways was eventually captured and divided amongst the several regiments of the Light Brigade. Later these horses were turned over to the artillery.

The origin of the stampede was this. During the night a French battery heard some noise from the hill on which it was posted. A fire-ball or flare was fired in the direction, and by the light the Russian picket was plainly seen. At it the French fired a few shells, and this caused the stampede. Owing to the distance and want of light, the riderless horses were supposed to be a body of cavalry galloping up the plain. The French therefore continued to shell them till they were almost in the camp of the brigade.

That afternoon the camp was again moved, this time to the high ground above the Turkish barrier. The valises which had been left behind on board ship now came up. Their contents, or what they ought to have contained, would have been welcome. Unfortunately many had been ransacked by the crews of the transports presumably, and the necessaries of which the men stood so much in need were gone.

By this time the strength of the regiment was not more than half what it had been on leaving England. Sickness was rife and was increasing. Daily, men were sent down sick, and put on board ship for Scutari.

On October 30th the camp was again shifted to the high ground at Inkerman, and pitched close to the camp of the Brigade of Guards. The horses captured from the Russians were a welcome addition to the mounts of the regiment, though many suffered from sore backs. It was surmised that they had marched a very great distance to join Liprandi's army when he concentrated at Balaclava.

The new camp was situated near a windmill which was used as a magazine, and great precautions were taken to avoid any accident. The camp was just in rear of the Guard's camp, and theirs was in the rear of the 2nd Division, which lay close to the ridge overlooking the valley of Inkerman. It was distant four miles from the old camp.

All was quiet here until Sunday, November 5, when just before daybreak the camps were aroused by the fire of musketry just over the ridge in front of the 2nd Division. The brigade at once turned out, and when daylight came the Russians were seen advancing in immense columns. They began an attack on the outlying pickets of the Guards and the 57th Regiment. The Light Brigade was marched towards the front, but the ground was covered with brushwood, and near the camp of the 2nd Division they were halted.

Inkerman, November 5, 1854.

The battle now became general. The artillery of the enemy posted on the opposite side of the valley opened fire, for with daylight it became possible to obtain the range.

The British artillery now came up and got into action, but it soon became apparent that both in weight and numbers the Russian guns were superior. Men now began to fall rapidly among the infantry engaged, and the artillery losses both in men and horses were very heavy. The Russian shot and shell, however, did not do much damage to the Light Brigade, as it came over the ridge and over their heads, plunging into the camps in the rear. Meanwhile, as the men sat in their saddles they could hear the shouts and cheering of the infantry in the fighting line. Soon the British artillery had exhausted their ammunition, and the waggons went forward at a gallop to bring up further supplies.

And now the guns from the Russian shipping in the harbour joined in, making the windmill, which it would seem they knew to be a magazine, their special mark. However, they did not succeed in landing a shell into it, or the results would have been more serious.

Presently the brigade became the object of their attentions, and some large shells came across their front. One burst in or near the ranks of the 17th Lancers, killing or wounding an officer and two men. About the same time the 4th Light Dragoons suffered a few casualties, but on the whole the brigade escaped lightly despite the fact that it was fired into both by the field-batteries and the guns from the ships.

The 13th was on this day commanded by Lieut.-Colonel Doherty, who was present in the field. At this period in the battle the horse of the Duke of Cambridge was shot under him. The Duke mounted his orderly's horse immediately. On the farther side of the ridge, and out of sight of the 13th, the struggle was continuing with terrific slaughter. Then the division of French under General Bosquet came up at a double from their camp, which was at a considerable distance off. They advanced straight towards the ridge and plunged into the fray, losing a good many men before they came to close quarters with the enemy. The Russians, who had been bringing up huge masses of men in succession, now fairly filled the valley beneath the crest of the ridge which had been the main object of their attack. But the crest of that ridge they never could gain, though more than once they approached perilously near to so doing. Then the British heavy artillery was brought up and got into action, playing upon the crowded masses of the enemy in the lower ground. The unfortunate men were absolutely unable to help themselves beneath the fire then turned on them. Panic seized them, and in the result they fled incontinently into Sebastopol. The casualties on both sides in this most sanguinary battle were immense.

On the British side General Sir G. Cathcart and General Strangeways fell, with many other officers and a great number of men. The British loss in wounded, too, was most serious. Of the Russian army it was said that the casualties amounted to nearly 15,000 men. Owing to the heavy loss in horses sustained by the British artillery, about two days after Inkerman the Light Brigade were ordered to proceed across the plateau to Lord Raglan's headquarters and to hand over the Russian horses which had been captured a few days previously. Thus the efficiency of the remains of the Light Brigade as cavalry was again nullified.

Captain Percy Smith gives an interesting description of the Chasseurs D'Afrique at Inkerman. It is well worth quoting—

Not long after this we received an order to place ourselves on the flank of the Chasseurs D'Afrique and support the advance of the French troops. Soon after we had got into our place, the Colonel of the Chasseurs saw a column of Russian infantry which he thought was within the range of the men's carbines, their carbines being nearly as long in the barrel as an infantry rifle. To our astonishment, as soon as the order was given the squadron that was named dismounted. There was no linking horses, but every man left his horse where he was, merely throwing their reins over his head and letting them fall on the ground. The horses stood as steadily as if they were picketed, in spite of some musketry fire, which I think hit one or two of them. I can't be sure about the actual hitting, but I saw the ground cut up under their feet several times, quite often enough to test their steadiness. Meantime the Chasseurs had formed in single rank at about a yard interval from each other. They then lay down on their backs with their feet to the enemy, put one foot over the other, rested the barrel of their carbine on the toe of the upper foot, and so fired. I don't know if they did any harm to the Russians, but they escaped all harm themselves.

Captain Jenyns writes of Inkerman thus—

They put us under a very heavy fire at Inkerman, but luckily for us—no thanks to any General—we had a slight rise on our flank, which ricochetted the balls just over our heads. Some ship shells bowled over some few men and horses, though. It was useless exposure, as we could not act. Lord Cardigan is plucky, but no head or temper. As for Lord Raglan, he has not *once*, literally, been in the cavalry lines or seen our wretched state, and, whatever may be said, was not on the field at Inkerman till two hours after it began. The Duke behaved most pluckily. Nearly all our nags are *dead*. They stand up to their bellies in *mud*, have to fetch their own grub four miles, besides carrying provisions all day six miles to the front, all from want of conveyance in that infernal commissary. It rains all day, and freezes at night, but no cold to hurt any one yet. We are all *capitally* fed, and I have no patience with grumblers on that score, but no care of horses taken. Here are the huts, clothing, &c., all at Balaclava—all very proper and pretty on paper, but not an animal or cart in the commissary to carry it up; the guns the same. The infantry actually carry up the *shot* in long strings, eight good miles from Balaclava to the trenches, up to your knees in mud.

On November 14, in the morning, a terrific storm arose, and about 10 A.M. all the tents were blown down, and the whole of the officers and men, sick included, remained all day without any tents until the hurricane abated at 8 P.M.

A tent was then pitched for the sick with great difficulty, and later a few other tents that were not torn to shreds were erected, and therein officers and men alike huddled till the next morning. The storm was so severe that no man could stand up against it, and officers, men, and horses went the whole day without rations. During the tempest sixteen horses broke loose and were never seen again, others died in the lines from the dire effects of the weather.

Lieutenant Percy Smith writes of this as follows:—

Our next "grief" was the hurricane on the 14th. It was bad enough for *us*, but still worse for the horses. We lost thirteen in five days, from the effects of that one day's cold and wet.

Sergeant Mitchell thus describes the scene—

About seven o'clock our tent was blown clean away from over us and fell in the mud some distance off. The first thing I saw after getting on my feet was a number of Foot Guardsmen's bearskin caps flying through the air, much the same as a flock of birds. They flew away, and were never seen again. A guard had been posted a short distance from us, and their arms being piled in front of the guard-tent, the bearskins had been placed on the bayonets, from whence the wind took them. On looking around we saw we were no worse off than our neighbours, for there was scarcely a tent standing, and to make matters worse the wind had carried away everything else that was lying about, such as blankets, linen, or anything that was movable. . . . Unfortunately for me, on the day before I had taken off my only shirt, and had been to a pond and washed it, and had hung it outside the tent to dry during the night. Of course, that went along with everything else, and I never saw it again; and from that day until 23rd December I was without a shirt. . . . The hospital tent was blown down with the rest, and several men were there who were hardly expected to live from day to day. They were stripped at the time and rolled in their blankets. When the tent went from over them, those that could stand were seen nearly up to their naked knees in the mud, until the wind blew them down, where they lay until some of us went and laid them on the tent, which lay on the ground a little way off. We then got another tent and covered them with it. I need hardly say this day was the death of a good many men of all regiments. . . . I found a tent lying on the ground, and, rolling myself in it, was soon asleep, where I remained until the afternoon. . . . We agreed to try and raise our tent again, but could only find a few pegs, and as the mud was now quite deep our small tent pegs were of little service; so we each took our sword scabbards and drove in as far as we could. . . . We had lots of company. Each tent was constructed to hold fourteen men close packed, but on this occasion we crowded in twenty. We had no room to turn after once lying down. Some were obliged to sit all night.

At this time Captain Tremayne had been attacked by Cholera and was away from the Regiment on board ship. He writes that he "mercifully could not be landed the day before the great storm, when so many of the ships went on to the rocks outside Balaclava, but was taken to Boreugas Bay, where we shipped the French 4th Dragoons, and on our return to Kamiesch heard of the battle of Inkerman."

Between November 14th and December 2nd nothing occurred, save that the sufferings of the horses were intensified by want of food. The storm of the 14th had left the transport animals and the roads in such a condition as to leave it utterly impossible for forage to be conveyed to the camp in sufficient quantity to satisfy the wants of the horses, and as a last resource they gnawed each other's manes and tails. On the 2nd of December the regiment marched from the heights above Inkerman to Kadikoi, there to encamp for the winter.

Captain Tremayne was in temporary command of the regiment on this occasion. He relates that "the horses were so weak that we led them six or seven miles."

Sergeant Mitchell most graphically describes the sufferings of the horses; they would not only gnaw the manes and tails of living horses, but devoured the hair off the skin of those that died in the lines—saddlery, blankets, ropes, and picket-pegs were attacked, and it was not safe for a man to approach a horse carelessly. Lord Raglan stated that it was the fault of the officers for not looking after things if forage were lacking, and that the men had been selling their forage to the French. Lord Lucan told the brigade, and one is tempted to admit that their rage on hearing this most unjustifiable slander was intense.

Between November 14th and December 2nd the horses got no hay, and about three pounds of oats a-day each. So bad was the transport that no more was to be obtained, and on two occasions not even biscuit for the men was served out.

The French cavalry were, however, extremely well taken care of, as regards forage, and it must be supposed that seeing the difference of condition so marked between the horses of the British and their Allies, Lord Raglan formed an unjust and cruel estimate of the cavalry under his command. At Kadikoi the 13th were nearer forage and things got better, though on the march down several horses were too weak to proceed farther, and lay down to die. Available for duty, there were now only thirty-eight horses in the regiment, including "letter parties" on command at the Duke of Cambridge's and Captain Lushington's. From December 2 until February 19, 1855, the regiment was employed with the cavalry division in conveying biscuits, &c., to the divisions in front of Sebastopol, and in carrying the sick thence to Balaclava.

Pickets were furnished by the brigades alternately, to prevent persons crossing the valley towards the Woronzoff Road, where the Russians were established. Sickness abounded everywhere, and was mostly caused by the terrible winter, want of food, and want of clothing.

Horse clothing had been issued, but it soon rotted owing to the horses lying down in the mud and snow.

On February 19, 1855, the regiment was ordered to turn out as strongly as possible, to go on reconnaissance duty under the command of Sir Colin Campbell.

The effective strength of the regiment was five mounted men, one sergeant, one trumpeter, and three privates. To this had the 13th come since December, when the regiment had mustered seventy men and twenty-eight horses.

Under the command, however, of Lieut.-Colonel Doherty, the five men accompanied Sir Colin Campbell's force, returning at 9 A.M. the following day. Many men of the force on this occasion suffered from the effects of frost-bite.

Writing of this time at Kadikoi, Colonel Tremayne tells us of the difficulties attending on the furnishing of patrols and pickets.

> . . . It was a dreary time. We had the pickets still and patrols. As the pickets were composed of men of different regiments, they were sometimes a bit difficult for the officer; as the poor, ill-fed, ill-clad men, in spite of bitter cold, frost, snow, and mud, would sleep, though the Cossack picket was very near us. We had one expedition towards Tchernavoda under Sir Colin. We started at midnight, when it was mild and drizzling. At 2 A.M. I sent in a sergeant (M'Innes) with both ears frost-bitten. The wind had veered to the north, and sweeping over the miles of snow made the change at once.

On May 21, 1855, a draft arrived from England. Considering the state of the regiment and its losses by war and sickness, this draft was sorely required. It consisted of Captain the Hon. J. W. Hely Hutchinson, Lieutenant Dearden, 1 sergeant, 24 privates, and 41 horses. Other drafts were shortly to follow.

On June 18th the regiment turned out under the command of Brevet Major Jenyns, and in conjunction with the division proceeded to take up ground in front of Sebastopol, to prevent civilians or any persons from approaching too near the army, which was about to attack the Redan that day. Field-Marshal Lord Raglan, G.C.B., died on June 28, 1855, being succeeded in the chief command by Lieut.-General James Simpson. On July 7th the second draft arrived, consisting of 1 sergeant, 32 privates, and 56 horses, and on the 31st the third draft, which was under the command of Captain Clayton, and consisted of 2 sergeants, 3 corporals, and 107 rank and file.

A fourth and last draft arrived on August 14, and consisted of 1 sergeant and 23 rank and file, under the command of Lieutenant Vivian.

The cavalry division had now been redistributed. There was a Heavy Brigade or 1st Brigade, a Light Brigade or 2nd, and a Hussar Brigade or 3rd. On the 16th of August the whole division advanced towards the position occupied by the French and Sardinian armies on the Tchernaya.

The 13th turned out at 3 A.M. at a strength of about 200 of all ranks, Lieut.-Colonel Doherty being in command on this occasion. The regiment formed a portion of the second line of the light brigade. Advancing towards the Tractir Bridge, and having halted a short distance from the river, they observed the enemy in full retreat towards the heights of Mackenzie's Farm. The French and Sardinians were in full pursuit, having defeated the Russians after a severe and decisive battle which lasted for six hours.

Colonel Tremayne writes of this as follows:—

> At the Tchernaya we were drawn up just where we lost our men on the 25th of the preceding year. We were again in the 1st line, and I had a grand view of the repulse of the Russians (twice) by the Zouaves of the Guard. Hardly a shot came to us.

The light brigade consisted of the 13th Light Dragoons, the 4th Light Dragoons, the 12th Lancers, and the Carabiniers.

Russell's 'Great War with Russia,' p. 299, makes the French jeering at the British for inaction on this occasion. On this occasion the 13th were lent to General Della Marmora, the Sardinian general, for the day.

> When the Russians began to draw off, he sent an order for us to advance. That advance up to where a Russian Battery still remained in action would have been over two narrow bridges: one over the canal, and another over the Tchernaya.
> A horse shot on either would have caused delay and brought havoc again on us. We could neither ford nor jump the canal. Pelissier (Marshal) who commanded in chief came down at this juncture and sent an A.D.C. to stop us, saying "Why should they go to useless slaughter on the same ground again?" or words to that effect. I had already moved in column of troops to the left when his order came, so that the inaction was the effect of an order given by the French general, whose troops Russell paints as "Jeering us."

So writes Colonel Tremayne in his Notes; and it seems only fitting that the facts of the case should be duly recorded here.

The loss on both sides was very heavy, though the Russian army suffered by far the most. Of Russian dead there were buried 3 generals, 60 officers, and 2300 men. The Russian wounded amounted to 160 officers and 4000 men. The French had 1500 casualties, and the Sardinians 250. As has been already narrated, the light brigade was not brought into action, but was held in reserve to act as circumstances might require, and returned to its encampment at the conclusion of the battle about noon.

Immediately after the battle of Tchernaya the Russian Commander, Prince Gortschakoff, determined to evacuate the city of Sebastopol and the defences on the south side of the harbour. He therefore made preparations for destroying the forts.

On September 8th the Malakoff was stormed by the French. The British attack on the Great Redan failed, for though a lodgment was effected, the supports being insufficient a retirement became inevitable.

That night Sebastopol was set on fire by the Russians, mines exploded, and powder-magazines were blown up. The Russians evacuated the place during the night by means of the bridge which had been established between the two sides of the roadstead. The last of the Black Sea fleet was sunk in the harbour, with the exception of the *Vladimir*, and the ruins of Sebastopol were in the possession of the allied armies. Many wounded Russians were left behind, and the *Vladimir* crossed the harbour on the 10th under a flag of truce to remove them. In one hospital but 500 survived out of 2000. In one room alone no less than 700 lay dead.

The Russian casualties since the battle of Tchernaya by September 7th amounted to more than 17,000 men. On September 8th they lost 7 generals and 13,000 men.

By Christmas 1855 the British losses on the whole campaign amounted to about 22,000 men.

It is open to question whether any struggle, for its perseverance, long endurance of hardships and privations, and a succession of deeds of honour and devotion, has ever equalled the siege of Sebastopol.

Conclusion of the Eastern Campaign.

On September 27th a draft consisting of 50 rank and file, without horses, under the command of Lieutenant Macneill, arrived from England.

Instructions were now received by the regiment to embark on

CONCLUSION OF THE EASTERN CAMPAIGN.

the steam transport *Medway* on October 9, under the command of Lieut.-Colonel Doherty, the strength of the regiment then being 1 lieutenant-colonel, 4 captains, 3 subalterns, 5 staff, 22 sergeants, 5 trumpeters, and 243 rank and file, with 220 horses.

The intention was for the regiment with the other regiments of the light cavalry brigade and some British horse artillery to proceed to Eupatoria, it having been decided to send an expeditionary force thither.

The whole was under the command of Brigadier-General Lord George Paget.

The regiment disembarked at Eupatoria on October 15, and encamped within a few yards of the sea upon the sands. At Eupatoria there was a large force of Turks and a division of French cavalry, both with artillery, under General D'Allonville.

The expeditionary force remained there about six weeks, and were out every week for three days, two of which they were without water.

On October 22nd the light cavalry brigade, as well as the French and Turkish infantry and cavalry, all under the command of General D'Allonville, marched towards Sak, a place at that time in the possession of the enemy. In the evening the Allies encamped at a village called Karazat.

On the morrow the march was continued in the same direction, and during the morning a large force of the enemy's cavalry, estimated as fully eighty squadrons, was observed advancing. The artillery advanced within range of the enemy's skirmishers and opened fire on them. Whereupon the enemy retreated on to their main body, which then also retired, and the Allies marched into Sak. The town was found to be in ruins. Tents were pitched for the night. Great suffering was caused here to the horses owing to the scanty supply of water — of this necessary of life there was hardly enough for the men.

On October 24 the expedition returned to Eupatoria. Precisely the same occurred on October 27.

The expedition marched to Sak and encamped there, the Russians retreating upon their appearance.

On November 2nd two squadrons of the 12th Lancers and the remainder of the light cavalry brigade turned out under Lieut.-

Colonel Tottenham to endeavour to cut off a convoy of supplies destined for the enemy. This expedition was most successful, the troops returning to camp in the afternoon having captured some thousands of sheep and a number of bullocks. These furnished a welcome supply of fresh meat for a considerable time.

Colonel Tremayne writes of this expedition as follows:—

> D'Allonville was a pleasure to work under, very quick and very considerate. He did all he knew to bring a large force of Russian Cavalry into action several times, but they tried to draw us into an entrenched position and never waited for us. D'Allonville spoke and reported highly of us. We succeeded in getting off some supplies and convoys. The Brigade was under Lord George Paget, who succeeded to it on Lord Cardigan going home. The patrols and expeditions were interesting. The lines were on the beach, and the sea was so little salt that before December I saw ice on the beach.

Sergeant Mitchell adds a few details as to the patrols and expeditions from Eupatoria. It appears that when the British horse artillery opened fire on the Russians the enemy's guns promptly replied, and as the light brigade were covering the guns the Russian shot and shell were flying over their heads very speedily. But as they were formed up in a depression they escaped any casualties. Presently the enemy limbered up and took ground to their right, where they came into action again, and opened fire on the Turks who were on the left of the light brigade. The Turkish artillery replied promptly. The 13th were now ordered to dismount, and then a party was remounted and sent to get water from a well. A covering party was sent out from another regiment to protect them while so engaged. Cossacks then appeared near, but did not attack the watering party. On the next day they expected an attack by the enemy, but found that during the night the Russians had retreated; but as the Allies advanced a few shells were fired at them, without, however, causing any casualties.

While at Eupatoria mange broke out among the horses of the brigade. This complaint was owing to the sudden change of the weather from heat to cold, added to the constant exposure.

On November 29th the regiment embarked at Eupatoria to proceed to Scutari where it was proposed to winter.

With the remainder of the brigade it received the thanks of General

CONCLUSION OF THE EASTERN CAMPAIGN.

D'Allonville, which was expressed in a letter to General Simpson commanding the British forces. This letter was communicated through Marshal Pelissier and acknowledged

> the good conduct and soldierlike bearing of the Troops employed upon the expedition, and the strict discipline, zeal, and good feeling which existed in that fine Brigade of Cavalry.

On the 4th of December the regiment disembarked at Coolalie and marched into Scutari the same day, having lost eight horses during the expedition from general debility, occasioned by extreme exposure to the inclemency of the weather.

On arrival at Scutari the regiment was joined by a draft from England consisting of Major Holden, Lieutenants Maclean and Munn, one sergeant, and thirty-two privates, also nine prisoners of war.

A few days later a depôt of the regiment which had been left at Balaclava under the command of Lieutenant Vivian also joined.

The total strength of the regiment was now amounting to 398 men and 264 horses. Colonel Tremayne writes—

> We were sent down to Scutari for the rest of the winter. Peace was already in the wind. From Scutari I went home on leave, and was not allowed to go out again, being ordered to the depôt, which I took command of at Dorchester. The drafts (I forgot to say which we first received) were mostly young men from the depôt and imperfectly drilled. They soon went into hospital, and many died. We later on had some men from a Militia Regiment (Warwick, I think). They were older, and though not the beau ideal of Light Dragoons, were good and serviceable men. All through the campaign the men behaved very well. They were at one time half starved, badly dressed, and hard worked. Cholera, too, and fever, very often among them. But one hardly, if ever, heard more than the average grumble of the British soldier. They were right good fellows.

At Scutari the regiment was quartered in the Haidar Pasha, a Turkish palace. About 2 A.M. on the morning of the 2nd February, 1856, the sentry posted inside the building gave the alarm of "fire," and before the men could be aroused and the engine brought into play the roof began to fall in and the whole palace was enveloped in flames. In spite of the strenuous endeavours of the whole division, who were soon at the scene of the outbreak, in a very short time the building was gutted. Nearly the whole of the men's necessaries, clothing, arms, and appointments were destroyed.

Captain Percy Smith's account of this period is interesting. It relates both to the drafts which joined the regiment in 1855, and to the fire at the Haidar Pasha palace in 1856.

The Regiment had received strong drafts of men and horses early in 1855, and we had our hands full trying to work them up to our old standard. It required a little tact, for there was a very natural feeling among the old soldiers, who had been through the whole campaign, that they knew their drill, and that it was hard lines to give them 3 Field Days a week, because a lot of recruits had everything to learn. Besides this, there were one or two injudicious young subalterns who came out fresh from England, hardly dismissed their own drill, and who had never seen a shot fired in their lives, who spoke to old soldiers as if the latter had only just joined. However, we were getting over all our difficulties, and it was beginning to be a pleasure to see the Regiment on parade, when an unlucky accident put a temporary stop to all our attempts at smartness.

The Regiment was quartered in a Turkish Palace known as Haidar Pasha, from the name of its original owner, the officers being in a detached building some twenty yards away. The palace was built of wood, and the authorities had given us a fire-engine, in charge of an English fireman. This was always kept in the central hall of the building, the fireman having accommodation close to it. At the same time very strict orders were given about fires in the rooms, and about throwing down half-burnt matches, &c. But in spite of this a fire took place. About midnight (I don't remember the date) I heard someone outside our building asking for me. I jumped up at once and ran out to find that Haidar Pasha was on fire. I was dressed (after a fashion), and therefore ran straight to the building. I met my Troop Sergeant-Major near the entrance, who told me all our men were out, and he thought all the rest of the Regiment, but to make sure I ran upstairs to the men's rooms and looked into all those that were not already alight. Coming down again, I met my cornet (Field-Marshal Sir Evelyn Wood, V.C., G.C.B., &c.), who had lately joined us from the Navy, and who was very much put out that I should, as he called it, "have gone up there into the fire alone," without waking him and taking him with me. We went down the last flight of stairs into the central hall together, and there we found the fire-engine and its civilian attendant. I said to him, "Come along, my man, you've no time to waste,—the roof will fall in directly," but to my disgust, though his teeth were chattering with fright, he refused to leave his engine. Wood and I tried persuasive (?) language, and when that failed we tried to drag him away by main force, but he got one of his arms round one of the wheels and we could not move him. Meantime the fire had gone on fast; the ceiling over our heads was blazing, and small pieces of burning wood were beginning to fall on us—in fact, staying there seemed such certain death that I said to Wood, "I can't leave this d——d fool to die by himself, but it's no good your losing your life too, so get away as quick as you can." Wood,

Evelyn Wood
13th Light Dragoons, 1855

(*By permission of 'The Cavalry Journal.'*)

however, was too good a fellow to think of leaving a comrade in such a mess, and I could get nothing out of him but an incessant touching his cap like a sailor and "I'm very sorry, sir, but I can't do that!" When all hope seemed gone, an old soldier of my troop ("Ginger" White) came rushing in through the smoke with "Come away, my Captain; what are you doing?" I explained matters. White ran outside, and in a few seconds appeared with some twenty or thirty more men, who laid hold of the engine and ran it out, fireman and all. Half a minute more and down came the roof. The fire had spread so quickly, what with wooden walls and pouches full of ammunition hanging all around them, that the men had to bolt for their lives. Some saved a pair of overalls, some few a jacket as well, but the majority were in their shirts and drawers. Naturally all parades had to be stopped for a time, and we had the greatest difficulty in providing the men even with sufficient underclothing to go on with. If telegrams and steamships had not existed, we should have had to have come home in our shirt sleeves when Peace was declared.

Sergeant Mitchell states that this disastrous fire was caused by a man and his wife who occupied an upper room. They had both gone to bed drunk, and in a quarrel knocked the stove over which stood in the centre of the room.

While this book was in preparation, a chance glance at 'The Daily Chronicle' for June 1, 1910, revealed a paragraph of no little interest to the regiment. Therein was recorded the death at Portsmouth, on May 31, of "Troop Sergeant-Major Lincoln, one of the few survivors of the famous charge of the Light Brigade at Balaclava." The notice continues, "Lincoln, a fine old man, standing over six feet, was born at Cambridge ninety-five years ago" [*i.e.* in 1805], and "served through the Crimean campaign in the 13th Light Dragoons [now the 13th Hussars]," but which he called the "Bangalore Gallopers." "He led his troop in the famous charge. His horse was shot under him, but he captured a riderless one, that of Captain Nolan, who brought the fatal order, and was shot down early in the charge. Lincoln soon lost his second horse, which was shot under him, and without a scratch he fell sprawling among the wounded and dying. Before he could get on his feet he was gripped by some Russians, frog-marched to Var, and questioned about the English forces, but refused to give any information, though threatened with the knout. Lincoln spent a year in Russia, and used to declare that he had been in every Russian prison. Once he was closely watched by the Tzar Nicholas. He afterwards reached England through an exchange of prisoners." On leaving the army in 1869, Lincoln "had a chequered career as a drill-instructor and insurance-agent, and finally, being unable to take care of himself, agreed to enter the workhouse, where he was one of the honoured veterans."

It appears that an ex-inspector of the Portsmouth police discovered his whereabouts, and gave him a home till his death. His health was good to the last, though he became mentally feeble. John Linkon (not Lincoln) enlisted on October 2, 1835, was promoted corporal, 31st January 1844; sergeant, 15th May 1850; sergeant-major, 25th May 1853. He sailed for the Crimea with the regiment as Troop Sergeant-Major of Captain Goad's troop, and against his name in the Regimental Record is "returned home." The date when he left the regiment is not given, but probably was in 1869, on the return from Canada.

The stories of the frog-march to Var, and the ill-treatment by the Russians, are not borne out by the narratives of other men of the regiment. How Linkon "found his way to England" is not clear. The released prisoners of war were returned to Scutari. Linkon's name is not among those at the depôt at home, and if he had reached England he must have reported himself there. Balaclava was fought October 25, 1854, and the regiment reached Scutari on December 4, 1855, sailing for England on May 4, 1856. A careful search in all available maps fails to locate "Var." There is a Varnutka a few miles from Balaclava, but in the wrong direction; and if Varna is meant by Var, it is some few hundred miles away in Bulgaria. It is just as well to clear up misapprehensions upon such matters; and the frog-march story may be dismissed as apocryphal.

In March 1911 the death was reported of another Balaclava veteran of the 13th Light Dragoons. His name was John Brooks, and he died at Penge, aged 88. He was a private in the "E" Troop, commanded by Captain Tremayne. There was another Brooks (Simon) who enlisted 22nd October, 1827; corporal, 18th June 1834; sergeant, 7th September 1837; died, 23rd April 1839. Possibly this man was a relative of Private John Brooks.

April 7, 1856. On this day the cavalry division composed of the heavy and light brigades was reviewed by His Imperial Majesty the Sultan. The 13th Light Dragoons, owing to the losses of arms and

CONCLUSION OF THE EASTERN CAMPAIGN.

appointments, &c., caused by the calamitous fire at the Haidar Pasha palace, were unable to participate in the review. They were, however, allowed to form the Guard of Honour on the occasion, with the proviso that a sufficient number were able to appear in review order. By strenuous exertions, and great perseverance, the required strength was obtained, and the Guard of Honour was duly furnished by the regiment.

On May 1, orders were received by the 13th Light Dragoons to hold themselves in readiness to embark for England.

In consequence, all the horses which were deemed by the commanding officer to be unfit for embarkation were disposed of by sale to the Turkish Government.

Three days later the regiment embarked on Her Majesty's steam transport *Assistance* for England. The *Assistance* sailed from the harbour of Constantinople on May 5, 1856, and arrived at Portsmouth on the 27th of the same month, after a voyage of twenty-three days.

The 13th Light Dragoons disembarked at Gosport on May 29, and were reviewed by Her Majesty Queen Victoria in the Clarence Dockyard, on which occasion Her Majesty expressed herself in the most glowing terms on the admirable appearance and efficient state of the regiment.

During the eastern campaign eleven non-commissioned officers and men were killed in action and thirty were wounded.

Of the 1st draft two men died of disease and two were invalided to England in one year.

Of the 2nd draft four men died of disease and three were invalided to England in ten months.

Of the 3rd draft fifteen men died of disease and eleven were invalided to England in nine months.

Of the 4th draft one man died of disease and two were invalided to England in eight months.

Of the 5th draft seven men died of disease and four men were invalided to England in eight months.

Of the officers, three were killed in action, Captains Oldham and Goad, and Cornet Montgomery.

Cornet Goad was wounded, as also was Lieutenant Percy Smith

(though unreported). Major Ormsby Gore, Captain Tremayne, Lieutenant Purcell, Cornet Maclean, Lieutenant King, and Lieutenant Dearden, were invalided to England; while Captain the Hon. J. W. Hely Hutchinson died of disease. Three men died prisoners of war.

Three men were guilty of desertion, and these it should be noted were men who came out in drafts and did not originally sail with the regiment.

Two hundred and seventy-three non-commissioned officers and men sailed from England in 1854.

Two hundred and forty-five non-commissioned officers and men joined the regiment during 1855, in the five drafts, making a total of five hundred and thirty-eight non-commissioned officers and men who served with the regiment in the course of the campaign.

For the brilliant services of the 13th Light Dragoons during the Crimean campaign, the following rewards and distinctions were conferred on the undermentioned officers, non-commissioned officers, and men—

Captain Jenyns—A Brevet Majority, the Companionship of the Bath, and the 5th Class of the Order of the Medjidie.

Captain Tremayne—A Brevet Majority, the Legion of Honour, and the 5th Class of the Order of the Medjidie.

Lieutenant Percy Smith—The Sardinian Medal, and the 5th Class of the Order of the Medjidie.

Regimental Sergeant-Major T. G. Johnson—The Legion of Honour (5th Class), and the French War Medal.

Sergeant-Major J. Mulcahy—Medal, and Gratuity for Distinguished Service in the Field.

Sergeants J. Allen, M. Long, and R. Rowley, the same.

Sergeant J. Priestley—Annuity for Distinguished Service in the Field.

Sergeant Davies and Privates Fenton and Dearlove—The French War Medal.

Corporal W. Gardiner—The Sardinian War Medal.

Sergeant Joseph Malone—The Victoria Cross.

Lieut.-Col. Doherty received the 5th Class of the Order of the Medjidie, as also did Lieutenant and Adjutant George Gardner.

CONCLUSION OF THE EASTERN CAMPAIGN.

In commemoration of the gallant conduct of the troops engaged in the Crimean campaign, Her Majesty was graciously pleased to command that the regiments therein engaged should bear on their regimental banners and head-dresses the words—

"ALMA," "BALACLAVA," "INKERMAN," and "SEBASTOPOL."

END OF THE FIRST VOLUME.

www.ingramcontent.com/pod-product-compliance
Lightning Source LLC
Chambersburg PA
CBHW080752300426
44114CB00020B/2708